Medical Treatment and the Law: Issues of Consent

The Protection of the Vulnerable: Children and Adults Lacking Capacity

Second Edition

Medical Treatment and the Law: Issues of Consent

The Protection of the Vulnerable: Children and Adults Lacking Capacity

Second Edition

Richard Harper
A District Judge of the High Court of Justice, Family Division,
sitting at the West London Family Court

fj Family Law

Published by Family Law
a publishing imprint of
Jordan Publishing Limited
21 St Thomas Street
Bristol BS1 6JS

Whilst the publishers and the author have taken every care in preparing the material included in this work, any statements made as to the legal or other implications of particular transactions are made in good faith purely for general guidance and cannot be regarded as a substitute for professional advice. Consequently, no liability can be accepted for loss or expense incurred as a result of relying in particular circumstances on statements made in this work.

Crown Copyright material is reproduced with kind permission of the Controller of Her Majesty's Stationery Office.

The law and ethics of male circumcision: guidance for doctors is reproduced with kind permission of the British Medical Association.

British Library Cataloguing-in-Publication Data

A catalogue record for this book is available from the British Library.

ISBN 978 1 84661 995 3

Typeset by Letterpart Ltd, Caterham on the Hill, Surrey CR3 5XL
Printed in Great Britain by Hobbs the Printers Limited, Totton, Hampshire SO40 3WX

FOREWORD

This is a much enlarged and substantially re-written revision of a book by Richard Harper originally published in 1999. Although in its fundamentals the law as described by our author was by then fairly well established, much has happened since, not least, of course, the implementation in 2007 of the much needed and long awaited Mental Capacity Act 2005. Now that the new jurisdiction of the Court of Protection has become an established part of the legal landscape, the publication of this valuable book is timely.

The author modestly describes his book as an introduction, but it is much more than that, as the detailed 'Contents' show. The author's ambition is to provide assistance to all those, not just the lawyers, who work in this field. It is a difficult task to write a book which on such a complex subject is accessible to both lawyers and non-lawyers, but it is a task which he very successfully achieves.

The book deals comprehensively and illuminatingly both with the substantive law and – of equal importance to practitioners – with practice and procedure. The author deals deftly with the case-law, extracting for the reader in helpful detail both the facts of the cases he discusses and the principles to be drawn from them, and including useful extracts from the judgments. His book will be of equal use and prove a friendly guide both to the aspiring tyro and to the seasoned hand.

Sir James Munby
President of the Family Division and President of the Court of Protection
17 September 2014

PREFACE

This book is intended as an introduction to the complex and rapidly developing area of medical treatment and the law in relation to the vulnerable, namely children and those adults who lack capacity.

Many factors have contributed to the developments in the law, including the advanced nature and choice of medical treatments now available, the need to listen to the wishes and feelings of children with increasing autonomy as young persons, the number of elderly persons fortunately now living longer, the need to the extent possible for independence and self-determination for vulnerable adults, whether lacking capacity or not, the increasing and welcome desire among patients generally to question medical decisions, as well the vexed issues arising from the sanctity of life, autonomy of competent decision-making and end of life care.

The issues arising, often involving principles of law, ethics and medical practice, may impact not only primarily of course on the patient but also upon a range of those concerned with the protection of the vulnerable, including the carer or carers of the adult or child concerned, social workers, the medical profession in its widest sense, the legal profession and the judiciary.

All of the above, including the courts, are having to navigate their way through the minefield of issues often arising in medical treatment cases, particularly in relation to questions of capacity, lack of capacity and consent. What is intended in this book is to provide practical guidance and assistance as to the approach taken by the courts on all of the varying material issues raised in relation to medical treatment and the law, the thread of which throughout is the question of 'consent'.

The substance of this book is intended, accordingly, to be of assistance not only to the legal profession and judiciary but also to those working within the field of medicine or other areas concerned with the welfare and protection of the vulnerable, whether adults or children.

The Mental Capacity Act 2005 is now bedding down, and there have recently been published on 13 March 2014 the House of Lords Select Committee report of post-legislative scrutiny of the Act and on 11 June 2014 the Government response to that report. Much assistance has now been provided by the Supreme Court in its judgment of the 30 October 2013 in the case of *Aintree*

University Hospitals NHS Foundation Trust v James [2013] UKSC 67, the first case to come before that court in relation to the Act.

Care needs to be taken not to infringe the rights of that group of persons who, though vulnerable, are capable of making their own decisions. Many who suffer from mental illness are well able to make decisions about their medical treatment, and it is important not to make unjustified assumptions to the contrary. The Mental Capacity Act 2005 (s 1(6)) provides that, even where a person lacks capacity, any interference with their rights and freedom of action must be the least restrictive possible: this acknowledges that people who lack capacity still have rights and that their freedom of action is as important to them as it is to anyone else.

As was stated by Lady Hale at paragraph 45 of the further Supreme Court judgment in *P and Q v Surrey County Council, Cheshire West and Chester Council v P* [2014] UKSC 19:

> 'In my view, it is axiomatic that people with disabilities, both mental and physical, have the same human rights as the rest of the human race. It may be that those rights have sometimes to be limited or restricted because of their disabilities, but the starting point should be the same as that for everyone else. This flows inexorably from the universal character of human rights, founded on the inherent dignity of all human beings, and is confirmed in the United Nations Convention on the Rights of Persons with Disabilities. Far from disability entitling the state to deny such people human rights: rather it places upon the state (and upon others) the duty to make reasonable accommodation to cater for the special needs of those with disabilities.'

The Supreme Court's judgment in the cases of Tony Nicklinson, Paul Lamb and AM described as Martin (reported at [2014] UKSC 38) encompasses the issues concerning assisted suicide, mercy killing and voluntary euthanasia.

The ability of the court to intervene if necessary in medical treatment cases for the protection and welfare of children remains founded in both the Children Act 1989 as amended by the Children and Families Act 2014 and, where appropriate, the parens patriae inherent jurisdiction of the High Court.

The general principles set out in Part I are elucidated upon in more detail in the remaining Parts II, III and IV of the book.

It is to be noted for readers of this book that the details of leading cases such as that of *Aintree*, which interlink a number of important issues, are referred to at several points in the book. This will enable practitioners to consider those details in the context of the particular subject or chapter they wish to investigate.

I am most grateful to Sir James Munby for writing the Foreword, with thanks too to Gregory Woodgate and his colleagues at Jordan Publishing for their patience, encouragement and advice, and to my family for all their unfailing support and assistance.

RICHARD HARPER

September 2014

CONTENTS

Foreword   v
Preface   vii
Table of Cases   xxi
Table of Statutes   xxix
Table of Statutory Instruments   xxxiii
Table of International Material   xxxv
Abbreviations   xxxvii

PART I
GENERAL PRINCIPLES IN RELATION TO MEDICAL
TREATMENT AND THE LAW

Chapter 1
Medical Treatment and Consent   3
1.1   The meaning of 'consent'   3
1.2   The purpose of consent to treatment   3
1.3   Adults with capacity, adults lacking capacity and children 4
        Adults with capacity   4
            The requirement of consent before medical treatment   4
            The autonomy of the individual and the principle of
                self-determination   4
            Breaching the principles of self-determination and the
                autonomy of the individual   5
            Emergency treatment   8
        Adults who through lack of capacity are unable to consent
                to or refuse medical treatment   8
            The basis of any right to treat in the absence of consent   8
            The previous common law principle of necessity   9
        Children   10
            The parental right to consent to medical treatment for
                and on behalf of a child   10
            The right of a minor to consent to treatment on his or
                her own behalf   11
            The concurrent powers of parent and child to consent to
                treatment   11
            Medical treatment at variance with parental wishes   12
1.4   Next of kin   12

Chapter 2
The 'Best Interests of the Patient' Test   15
2.1   Adults with capacity   15
2.2   Adults who are unable to consent to or refuse medical
             treatment   15
2.3   Children   16
2.4   The principle of the sanctity of life   17
2.5   Prolongation of life may not be in the best interests of the
             patient   17
2.6   End of life care: whether to give life-sustaining treatment and
             the best interests of the patient   19
2.7   The test of 'best interests' under MCA 2005, s 4   21

Chapter 3
The Doctor and the Courts   23
3.1   The interface between the doctor and the courts   23
3.2   The objectives of medical treatment and care   23
3.3   The duty of the doctor   24
             The standard of care by a doctor in relation to medical
                 treatment   25
             A doctor cannot be required to treat a patient (whether
                 adult or child) in a particular way and against his or
                 her clinical judgment   26
3.4   Allocation of resources and the choice of medication   28
Appendix to Chapter 3   33
Medical Innovation Bill   35

Chapter 4
The Mental Capacity Act 2005   39
4.1   The general principles of the Act   39
4.2   The statutory test of incapacity   40
4.3   The test of incapacity   41
4.4   The statutory provisions as to best interests   42
4.5   The test as to best interests   43
4.6   The wishes and feelings of P   45
4.7   Mental Capacity Act 2005, s 5   47
4.8   Deputies   48
4.9   Attorneys   48

PART II
THE RIGHT TO LIFE
THE 'RIGHT TO DIE'

Chapter 5
The Right to Life: Adults: End-of-life Care; Whether to Give
Life-sustaining Medical Treatment   53
5.1   The right to life   53
5.2   The Code of Practice   54

5.3   Guidance   55
5.4   Declarations under section 16 of the MCA 2005   55
5.5   Prohibition on motivation by any desire to bring about death   55
5.6   Attorneys and Deputies: life-sustaining treatment   56
5.7   Whether to give life-sustaining treatment in PVS cases   56
        The meaning and definition of PVS   56
        The case of *Airedale NHS Trust v Bland* [1993] AC 789   57
            The significance of the case   57
            The facts   58
            The relief sought   58
            The reasoning for the decision by the House of Lords   58
        The sanctity of life: the duty to prolong life   61
        Opposition by family to not instigating or continuing with
            life-sustaining treatment   62
        PVS cases where a clinical feature of the condition is absent   64
5.8   Whether to give life-sustaining treatment in cases other than
        PVS   65
        Cardio-Pulmonary Resuscitation (CPR): Do Not Activate
            CPR (DNACPR)   67
        Consulting the patient in relation to DNACPR   70
        Best interests test in relation to whether to give
            life-sustaining treatment   71
        Analysis of the case of *Aintree v James* in relation to best
            interests   75

Chapter 6
The Right to Life: Children: End-of-life Care; Whether to Give
Life-sustaining Treatment   79
6.1   A framework for practice   79
6.2   Parental consent   80
6.3   Due process; emergency applications   81
6.4   A doctor cannot be required to treat a patient against his or
        her clinical judgment   81
6.5   Irreversible brain damage   83
6.6   Discontinuing ventilation immediately and offering palliative
        care   84
6.7   Authorising future discontinuance and/or non-re-instigation of
        artificial ventilation in the event of certain medical
        occurrences   87
6.8   Advanced Care Plans   91
6.9   Conjoined twins: the doctrine of double effect   92

Chapter 7
The 'Right to Die': Suicide; Assisted Suicide; Voluntary
Euthanasia/Mercy Killing   97
7.1   The 'right to die'   97
7.2   Suicide   99
7.3   Assisted suicide   99

7.4   Voluntary euthanasia: mercy killing   115
Appendix to Chapter 7   **123**
Assisted Dying Bill   **125**

PART III
JURISDICTION AND PROCEDURE IN MEDICAL TREATMENT
CASES CONCERNING INCAPACITATED ADULTS AND
CHILDREN

Chapter 8
Jurisdiction: Procedure in Medical Treatment Cases   **137**
8.1   Jurisdiction: procedure in relation to incapacitated adults 137
            Definitions under the COP Rules   137
            Declarations   138
            Starting proceedings, and urgent/interim applications   139
            The legal status of P   140
            The Official Solicitor   141
            Vulnerable persons falling outside the scope of the MCA
               2005   141
            Transparency: hearings in private or in public   142
8.2   Jurisdiction: procedure in relation to children   143
            The twofold jurisdiction: Children Act 1989; inherent
               jurisdiction of the High Court   143
               Children Act 1989   143
               Inherent Jurisdiction of the High Court   144
            Practice and procedure under the Family Procedure
               Rules 2010   146
            Expert evidence; medical examination of children   147
            The legal status of the child who is the subject of any
               medical treatment issue/s   147
            Children's guardian   148
            The representation of parents lacking capacity   149
            Transparency: hearings in private   149
8.3   The transfer of proceedings between the Court of Protection
               and a court having jurisdiction under Children Act 1989 151

Appendices to Chapter 8   **153**
Practice Direction E – Applications relating to serious medical
   treatment (PD9E)   155
Ministry of Justice Court of Protection – healthcare and welfare cases 159
Practice Note March 2013 The Official Solicitor to the Senior Courts:
   Appointment in Family Proceedings and Proceedings under the
   Inherent Jurisdiction in Relation to Adults   160
Practice Direction 12D – Inherent Jurisdiction (including Wardship)
   Proceedings   168
Mental Capacity Act 2005 (Transfer of Proceedings) Order 2007   173
Transparency in the Court of Protection Publication of Judgments
   Practice guidance issued on 16 January 2014 by Sir James Munby,
   President of the Court of Protection   175

PART IV
OTHER SPECIFIC AREAS IN RELATION TO MEDICAL TREATMENT AND THE LAW

Chapter 9
Adult Refusal of Medical Treatment: Non-consensual Treatment 183
9.1 The presumption of capacity to decide 183
    Advance decisions, deputies and lasting powers of attorney 185
9.2 Adults lacking the capacity to decide 186
9.3 Adjudging whether or not an adult patient has the capacity to decide 186
    Re C and the common law three-stage decision-making test as to capacity to decide 188
    The statutory test 189
9.4 Whether to override a refusal of consent to treatment through lack of capacity 189
    Non-competence 189
    Undue influence 190
    Changed circumstances 190
    Specific circumstances 191
        Induced delivery: Caesarean section operation 191
        Fear of needles 197
        Blood transfusions 198
        Amputation 199
        Dialysis treatment 201
        Hunger strikes 202
        Anorexia and force-feeding 203
9.5 The use of reasonable force as a necessary incidence of treatment 205

Chapter 10
Medical Treatment and MHA 1983; Restriction on Deprivation of Liberty under the MCA 2005; The Interface Between MHA 1983 and MCA 2005 209
10.1 Self-determination and the mentally ill 209
    The common law test as to capacity to consent 210
    A person suffering from mental disorder is not necessarily incapable of giving or refusing consent to treatment 210
    Caesarean section operations and MHA 1983 212
10.2 MHA 1983 213
    The meaning of medical treatment 214
    Part IV of MHA 1983: 'consent to treatment' 215
    A positive decision to impose non-consensual medical treatment pursuant to MHA 1983, s 63 218
    A positive decision not to impose treatment under MHA 1983, s 3 218

10.3   Patients lacking the capacity to give or refuse consent to
            medical treatment   220
        Lasting Powers of Attorney   221
        The appointment of a deputy   221
10.4   Informality of decision making in relation to adults lacking
            capacity   222
10.5   Informal admissions to hospital under MHA 1983   222
10.6   Restriction on deprivation of liberty under MCA 2005   224
        The distinction between restriction of liberty and
            deprivation of liberty   225
        Challenging a deprivation of liberty authorised by Sch A1 to
            MCA 2005   229
        Section 4B of MCA 2005   231
10.7   The interface between MHA 1983 and MCA 2005   231

Appendices to Chapter 10   233
**Deprivation of liberty – guidance for providers of children's homes and
residential special schools**   235
**Department of Health (28 March 2014) Deprivation of Liberty
Safeguards (DoLS)**   239
Practice Direction AA – Deprivation of Liberty Applications (PD10AA) 243

Chapter 11
Children: Consent or Refusal of Consent to Medical Treatment   251
11.1   Definition of a child   251
11.2   Parental consent to medical treatment for and on behalf of the
            immature child   251
        The general requirement of consent before treatment   251
        Emergencies   252
        Parental responsibility   252
        Disagreement between parents   253
11.3   Parental refusal of medical treatment for and on behalf of the
            immature child: overriding such refusal if in the best
            interests of the child   254
        The test for the court   255
        The views of the parents and the court's balancing exercise   255
            Liver transplant operation   256
            Downs syndrome   257
            Blood transfusions: Jehovah's Witnesses   258
            Bone marrow transplant   258
            MMR vaccine   259
            Radiotherapy and chemotherapy   261
11.4   A child's rights to consent to medical treatment   261
        A child's common law right to consent   261
            The facts of the *Gillick* case   262
            The *Gillick* competency test   262
            The right of a *Gillick*-competent minor to consent to
                treatment can be overridden by the court   264
        A child's statutory right to consent   264

	Donation of organs or blood	264
11.5	A child's rights to refuse consent to medical treatment	265
	No absolute right of any minor to refuse medical treatment	265
	The parental right to consent to treatment on behalf of a child who is refusing treatment	265
11.6	The power of the court to overrule a child's refusal of consent to treatment	266
	The wide powers of the court to overrule a child's refusal	266
	The child's views	267
	Whether or not the child lacks capacity	267
	Serious medical treatment cases where child near to the age of majority is refusing treatment for a life-threatening condition	268
	The 'best interests of the child' test	269
	Power of the court to order the detention of a child for treatment and the use of reasonable force incidental to treatment	269
	Abortion and young persons	270
	The power of the court to override a child's refusal to submit to medical examination under CA 1989, s 38(6) and to direct the child to be medically examined, assessed and treated	272
11.7	The unborn child	273
	Applications by a father to prevent a mother having an abortion	273
	Applications toward an unborn child	273
	The interests of the unborn child where the mother refuses medical intervention	273
11.8	Medical examinations and interviews of children	275
	Medical examinations prior to or in the absence of legal proceedings	275
	Medical examinations during the currency of family proceedings	275
	Medical examinations and interviews of children in respect of allegations of sexual or other abuse	277

Chapter 12
Advance Decisions or 'Living Wills' — 281
12.1	Advance decisions to refuse treatment	281
12.2	The statutory provisions	281
12.3	Advance decisions generally	283
12.4	Advance decisions to refuse life-sustaining treatment	284
12.5	The jurisdiction of the court	285

Appendices to Chapter 12 — 291
Advance Decisions Precedents — 293
1 Standard advance decision	293
2 Advance decision which the maker defines an intolerable condition	294
3 Advance decision: any supervening illness is not to be actively treated	295

4 Advance statement: maximum treatment   296
5 Advance decision: treatment preferences   297
6 People to be consulted before a treatment decision is made   299
7 Letter registering an advance decision with a client's GP/Consultant   300
Miscellaneous clauses   301

Chapter 13
Medical Treatment other than for Purely Medical Reasons   307
13.1   Sterilisation   307
        Prior sanction of the High Court required   307
        The special features of a sterilisation operation   307
        Children and sterilisation   308
        Adults and sterilisation   310
        Recent cases on sterilisation   312
        Practice and procedure   317
13.2   Human Tissue Act 2004   318
        Code of Practice 1: Consent   321
            Appropriate consent   322
            Valid consent   322
            Scope of consent   323
            Withdrawal of consent   323
        Code of Practice 2: Donation of organs for transplantation   323
            Living organ donation   324
            Adults – special considerations   325
            Children – special considerations   326
            Deceased organ donation   326
        Bone marrow transplant   330
13.3   The Human Fertilisation and Embryology Act 1990   333
        Meaning of 'embryo' and 'gamete'   333
            Section 3: prohibitions in connection with embryos   333
        Consent to use or storage of gametes, embryos and human
            admixed embryos etc.   334
            Formalities of consent   334
            Physical incapacity   334
            Purpose of consent   335
            The collection and storage of embryos and gametes   335
        Withdrawal of consent to the storage/usage of gametes   336
        Parenthood in cases involving assisted reproduction   339
        Parenthood and the use of sperm, or transfer of embryo,
            after death of man providing sperm   340
        Lesbian co-parenting   343
        The role (if any) of the sperm donor in lesbian co-parenting   345
        Schedule 7 Part 2 to the Same Sex (Married Couples Act)
            2013   347
13.4   Surrogacy: parental orders   347
13.5   Scientific testing: paternity testing   349
        Power of court to direct the use of scientific tests   349
        Consents required for taking of bodily sample   351

TABLE OF CASES

References are to paragraph numbers.

A (Children) (Conjoined Twins: Surgical Separation), Re [2001] Fam 147, [2001] 2 WLR
480; *sub nom* Re A (Conjoined Twins: Medical Treatment) [2001] 1 FLR 1; *sub nom*
A (Conjoined Twins: Surgical Operation), Re [2000] 4 All ER 961, CA   6.9
A (Mental Patient: Sterilisation), Re [2000] 1 FLR 549, [2000] 1 FCR 193, [2000] Lloyd's
Rep Med 87, (2000) 53 BMLR 66, [2000] Fam Law 242, (2000) 97(2) LSG 30   4.5,
13.1.4
A Local Authority v A [2010] EWHC 1549 (Fam), [2011] Fam 61, [2011] 2 WLR 878,
[2011] 1 FLR 26, [2011] 3 All ER 706, [2011] PTSR 435, [2011] 2 FCR 553, (2010)
13 CCL Rep 536, [2010] Fam Law 928   13.1.5
A Local Authority v K [2013] EWHC 242 (COP), [2014] 1 FCR 209, (2013) 130 BMLR
195   4.5, 13.1.5
A Local Authority v K, D and L [2005] EWHC 144 (Fam), [2005] 1 FLR 851, [2005]
Fam Law 450   4.5
A Metropolitan Borough Council v DB [1997] 1 FLR 767, [1997] 1 FCR 618, (1997) 37
BMLR 172, [1997] Fam Law 400, (1997) 161 JPN 413   11.6.3, 11.6.6
A-H (Children), Re [2013] EWCA Civ 282, (2013) 157(5) SJLB 31   11.8.3
Aintree University Hospitals NHS Foundation Trust v James [2013] UKSC 67, [2014] AC
591, [2013] 3 WLR 1299, [2014] 1 All ER 573, [2014] 1 FCR 153, (2013) 16 CCL
Rep 554, [2014] Med LR 1, (2014) 135 BMLR 1, (2013) 163(7583) NLJ 16, (2013)
157(43) SJLB 53   2.5, 2.7, 3.3.2, 4.1, 4.5, 4.6, 5.1, 5.8.1, 5.8.4, 6.4, 8.1
Airedale NHS Trust v Bland [1993] AC 789, [1993] 2 WLR 316, [1993] 1 FLR 1026,
[1993] 1 All ER 821, HL   1.3.1, 2.1, 2.4, 2.5, 2.6, 3.1, 3.3, 5.1, 5.7.2, 5.7.3, 7.4
An NHS Foundation Trust v R (Child) [2013] EWHC 2340 (Fam), [2014] Fam Law 294   6.6
An NHS Trust v A [2013] EWHC 2442 (COP), [2014] 2 WLR 607, [2013] Med LR 561,
(2014) 136 BMLR 115   9.4.4, 10.2.2
An NHS Trust v D [2012] EWHC 885 (COP)   12.4
An NHS Trust v DE [2013] EWHC 2562 (Fam), [2013] 3 FCR 343, [2013] Med LR 446,
(2013) 133 BMLR 123   13.1.5
An NHS Trust v KH [2013] 1 FLR 1471, [2013] Med LR 70, [2013] Fam Law 34   8.1.2,
8.2.6
An NHS Trust v L [2013] EWHC 4313 (Fam)   5.8.1
An NHS Trust v MB (A Child Represented By CAFCASS As Guardian Ad Litem) [2006]
EWHC 507 (Fam), [2006] 2 FLR 319, (2006) 9 CCL Rep 568, [2006] Lloyd's Rep
Med 323, [2006] Fam Law 445   5.8.3, 6.6, 6.7, 8.1.2, 8.2.7
An NHS Trust v SR [2012] EWHC 3842 (Fam), [2013] 1 FLR 1297, [2013] 1 FCR 356,
(2013) 130 BMLR 119, [2013] Fam Law 395   11.3.2
Auckland Area Health Board v The Attorney-General [1993] 1 NZLR 235   5.7.3

B (A Minor) (Wardship: Medical Treatment), Re [1981] 1 WLR 1421, (1982) 3 FLR 117,
[1990] 3 All ER 927, FD and CA   11.3.2
B (A Minor) (Wardship: Sterilisation), Re [1988] AC 199, [1987] 2 WLR 1213, [1987] 2
All ER 206, [1987] 2 FLR 314, 86 LGR 417, [1987] Fam Law 419, (1987) 151 LG
Rev 650, (1987) 84 LSG 1410, (1987) 137 NLJ 432, (1987) 131 SJ 625   13.1.1,
13.1.3

B v An NHS Hospital Trust; *sub nom* B (Adult: Refusal of Medical Treatment), Re; B
    (Consent to Treatment: Capacity), Re [2002] EWHC 429 (Fam), [2002] 1 FLR 1090,
    [2002] 2 All ER 449, [2002] Fam Law 423, FD   1.3.1, 2.1
B v Croydon Health Authority [1995] Fam 133, [1995] 2 WLR 294, [1995] 1 FLR 470,
    [1995] 1 All ER 683, [1995] 1 FCR 662, [1995] PIQR P145, [1995] Fam Law 244,
    (1994) 144 NLJ 1696   9.4.4, 10.2.2
Bellinger v Bellinger [2003] UKHL 21, [2003] 2 AC 467, [2003] 2 WLR 1174, [2003] 1
    FLR 1043, [2003] UKHRR 679, [2003] 2 All ER 593, HL   13.8
Bolam v Friern Hospital Management Committee [1957] 1 WLR 582, [1957] 2 All ER
    118, 101 SJ 357, QBD   2.2, 3.3.1, 5.7.2, 10.3

C (A Minor) (Medical Treatment), Re [1998] 1 FLR 384, [1998] 1 FCR 1, [1998] Lloyd's
    Rep Med 1, (1998) 40 BMLR 31, [1998] Fam Law 135   3.3.2, 6.4, 6.7
C (A Minor) (Wardship: Medical Treatment) (No 2), Re [1990] Fam 39, [1989] 3 WLR
    252, [1990] 1 FLR 263, [1989] 2 All ER 791, CA   8.2.1
C (A Minor) (Wardship: Medical Treatment), Re [1990] Fam 26, [1989] 3 WLR 240,
    [1990] 1 FLR 252, [1989] 2 All ER 782, CA   6.5
C (Adult: Refusal of Medical Treatment), Re [1994] 1 WLR 290, [1994] 1 FLR 31, [1994]
    1 All ER 819, [1994] 2 FCR 151   9.3.1, 9.4.4, 10.1.1, 10.1.2, 11.6.3
C (Detention: Medical Treatment), Re [1997] 2 FLR 180, [1997] 3 FCR 49, [1997] Fam
    Law 474, (1997) 94(13) LSG 29, (1997) 141 SJLB 72   11.6.6, 11.6.7
C v S [1988] QB 135, [1987] 2 WLR 1108, [1987] 1 All ER 1230, [1987] 2 FLR 505,
    [1987] Fam Law 269, (1987) 84 LSG 1410, (1987) 131 SJ 624   11.7.1
Centre for Reproductive Medicine v U [2002] EWCA Civ 565, [2002] Lloyd's Rep Med
    259   13.3.6
Cheshire West and Chester Council v P [2014] UKSC 19, [2014] 2 WLR 642, [2014] 2 All
    ER 585, [2014] PTSR 460, [2014] 2 FCR 71, [2014] COPLR 313, [2014] HRLR 13,
    (2014) 17 CCL Rep 5, (2014) 158(13) SJLB 37   10.6.1

D (A Minor) (Wardship: Sterilisation), Re [1976] Fam 185, [1976] 2 WLR 279, [1976] 1
    All ER 326, FD   13.1.3
D (Adult: Medical Treatment), Re [1998] 1 FLR 411, [1998] 1 FCR 498, (1997) 38
    BMLR 1, [1997] Fam Law 787   5.7.5
D (Medical Treatment: Mentally Disabled Patient), Re [1998] 2 FLR 22, [1998] 2 FCR
    178, (1998) 41 BMLR 81, [1998] Fam Law 324, (1997) 94(48) LSG 30, (1998) 142
    SJLB 30   9.4.4
D (Minors) (Child Abuse: Interviews), Re [1998] 2 FLR 10, [1998] 2 FCR 419, (1998)
    162 JPN 702   11.8.3

E (A Minor), Re (1990) 9 BMLR 1   11.3.2
E (Assisted Reproduction: Parent), Re [2013] EWHC 1418 (Fam), [2013] 2 FLR 1357,
    [2013] 3 FCR 532, [2013] Fam Law 962, (2013) 163(7563) NLJ 19   13.3.6
E (Medical Treatment Anorexia), Re [2012] EWHC 1639 (COP), [2012] 2 FCR 523,
    [2012] HRLR 29, (2012) 15 CCL Rep 511, [2012] Med LR 472, (2012) 127 BMLR
    133   2.4, 5.8, 5.8.3, 12.5
Evans v Amicus Healthcare Ltd [2003] EWHC 2161 (Fam), [2004] 2 WLR 713, [2003] 4
    All ER 903, [2004] 1 FLR 67, [2003] 3 FCR 577, (2004) 75 BMLR 115, [2003] Fam
    Law 879, (2003) 100(39) LSG 38, (2003) 153 NLJ 1519, (2003) 147 SJLB
    1150   11.7.3, 13.3.3

F (In Utero) (Wardship), Re [1988] Fam 122, [1988] 2 WLR 1288, [1988] 2 FLR 307,
    [1988] 2 All ER 193, [1988] FCR 529, [1988] Fam Law 337, (1988) 152 JPN 538,
    (1988) 138 NLJ Rep 37, (1988) 132 SJ 820, (1989) 133 SJ 1088   11.7.2
F (Mental Patient: Sterilisation), Re [1990] 2 AC 1, [1989] 2 WLR 1025, [1989] 2 FLR
    376, [1989] 2 All ER 545, (1989) 139 NLJ 789, (1989) 133 SJ 785; *sub nom* F
    (Sterilisation: Mental Patient), Re [1989] 2 FLR 376, CA & HL   1.3.2, 2.6, 10.3,
                                                                                     13.2.3
F v F (MMR Vaccine) [2013] EWHC 2683 (Fam), [2014] 1 FLR 1328, (2014) 136 BMLR
    105, [2014] Fam Law 29   11.3.2

F v West Berkshire Health Authority [1990] 2 AC 1, [1989] 2 WLR 1025, [1989] 2 FLR
    376, [1989] 2 All ER 545, (1989) 139 NLJ 789, (1989) 133 SJ 785, *sub nom* F
    (Sterilisation: Mental Patient), Re [1990] 2 AC 1, [1989] 2 WLR 1025, [1989] 2 FLR
    376, [1989] 2 All ER 545, (1989) 139 NLJ 789, (1989) 133 SJ 785   1.3.1, 1.3.2, 2.2,
                                                                5.7.2, 10.3, 13.1.2, 13.1.4
F, Re [1990] 2 AC 1, [1989] 2 WLR 1025, [1989] 2 All ER 545, [1989] 2 FLR 376,
    (1989) 139 NLJ 789, (1989) 133 SJ 785   13.1.4

G (Persistent Vegetative State), Re [1995] 2 FCR 46   5.7.4
G, Z (Children) (Children: Sperm Donors: Leave to Apply for Children Act Orders), Re
    [2013] EWHC 134 (Fam), [2013] 1 FLR 1334, [2013] HRLR 16, [2013] Fam Law
    530   13.3.7
Gillick v West Norfolk and Wisbech Area Health Authority and Another [1986] AC 112,
    [1986] 1 FLR 224, [1985] 3 All ER 402, [1985] 3 WLR 830, HL; [1985] FLR 736,
    [1985] 1 All ER 533, [1985] 2 WLR 413, CA   11.3, 11.4.1
Glass v United Kingdom (App 61827/00) [2004] 1 FLR 1019, [2004] 1 FCR 553, (2004)
    39 EHRR 15, (2005) 8 CCL Rep 16, (2004) 77 BMLR 120, [2004] Fam Law 410   6.2,
                                                                            11.2.1
Goodwin v United Kingdom and I v United Kingdom (App (28957/95) [2002] IRLR 664,
    [2002] 2 FLR 487, [2002] 2 FCR 577, (2002) 35 EHRR 18, 13 BHRC 120, (2002)
    67 BMLR 199, [2002] Fam Law 738, (2002) 152 NLJ 1171   13.8
Gross v Switzerland (App 67810/10) [2013] 3 FCR 608, (2014) 58 EHRR 7, 35 BHRC
    187, (2013) 134 BMLR 37   7.3
Guzzardi v Italy (A/39) (1981) EHRR 333   10.6.1

H (A Minor) (Blood Tests: Parental Rights), Re [1997] Fam 89, [1996] 3 WLR 506,
    [1996] 4 All ER 28; *sub nom* H (Paternity: Blood Test), Re [1996] 2 FLR 65,
    CA   13.5.3, 13.5.4
H (A Patient), Re [1998] 2 FLR 36, [1998] 3 FCR 174, (1997) 38 BMLR 11, [1998] Fam
    Law 460   5.7.5, 6.7
Haas v Switzerland (App 31322/07) (2011) 53 EHRR 33   7.1, 7.3
Harbin v Masterman [1896] 1 Ch 351, [1896] 65 LJ Ch 195, [1896] 73 LT 591, [1896]
    12 TLR 105, [1895–1899] All ER Rep 695, CA   8.3
Heart of England NHS Foundation Trust v JB (by her litigation friend, the Official
    Solicitor) [2014] EWHC 342 (COP)   1.3.1, 2.1, 9.4.4
HL v UK (App 45508/99) (2005) 40 EHRR 32, 17 BHRC 418, (2004) 7 CCL Rep 498,
    [2005] Lloyd's Rep Med 169, (2005) 81 BMLR 131, [2004] MHLR 236   1.3.2, 10.6

J (A Minor) (Child in Care: Medical Treatment), Re [1993] Fam 15, [1992] 3 WLR 507,
    [1992] 4 All ER 614, [1992] 2 FLR 165, [1992] 2 FCR 753, [1993] 4 Med LR 21,
    [1992] Fam Law 541, (1992) 136 SJLB 207   3.3, 3.3.2, 6.4
J (A Minor) (Wardship: Medical Treatment), Re [1991] Fam 33, [1991] 2 WLR 140,
    [1991] 1 FLR 366, [1990] 3 All ER 930, [1991] FCR 370, [1990] 2 Med LR 67,
    (1990) 140 NLJ 1533   2.3, 2.5, 2.6, 3.3.2, 3.4, 5.7.4, 6.4, 6.7, 11.3.1
JT (Adult: Refusal of Medical Treatment), Re [1998] 1 FLR 48, [1998] 2 FCR 662, [1998]
    Fam Law 23   9.4.4, 10.1.2

K, W and H (Minors) (Medical Treatment), Re [1993] 1 FLR 854, [1993] Fam Law 280,
    (1993) 157 LG Rev 267   11.4.1, 11.5.2, 11.6.3
KH (A Child) [2012] EWHC B18 (Fam)   6.8

L (An Infant), Re [1968] P 119, [1967] 3 WLR 1645, [1968] 1 All ER 20, (1967) 111 SJ
    908   8.2.1
L (Medical Treatment: Gillick Competence), Re [1998] 2 FLR 810, [1999] 2 FCR 524,
    (2000) 51 BMLR 137, [1998] Fam Law 591   11.3.2, 11.4.1, 11.6.3
L (Patient: Non-Consensual Treatment), Re [1997] 2 FLR 837, [1997] 1 FCR 609, (1997)
    35 BMLR 44, [1997] Fam Law 325   9.4.4
LC (Medical Treatment: Sterilisation) [1997] 2 FLR 258, [1997] Fam Law 604   13.1.4

M (A Child) (Refusal of Medical Treatment) [1999] 2 FLR 1097, [1999] 2 FCR 577,
    (2000) 52 BMLR 124, [1999] Fam Law 753   11.6.4
M (Best Interests: Deprivation of Liberty), Re [2013] EWHC 3456, [2014] COPLR 35,
    (2014) 135 BMLR 189   10.6.2
M (Statutory Will), Re, ITW v Z [2009] EWHC 2525 (Fam), [2011] 1 WLR 344, [2010]
    3 All ER 682, (2009) 12 CCL Rep 635, [2010] MHLR 304, [2009] WTLR 1791   4.5,
                                                                                      4.6
M and N (Minors) (Wardship: Publication of Information), Re [1990] Fam 211, [1989] 3
    WLR 1136, [1990] 1 All ER 205, [1990] 1 FLR 149, [1990] FCR 395, [1990] Fam
    Law 22, (1990) 154 JPN 345, (1990) 87(1) LSG 32, (1989) 139 NLJ 1154, (1990)
    164 SJ 165   8.2.1
Malette v Shulman [1990] 67 DLR (4d) 321   1.3.1
MB (Medical Treatment), Re [1997] 2 FLR 426, [1997] 2 FCR 541, [1997] 8 Med LR
    217, (1997) 38 BMLR 175, [1997] Fam Law 542, (1997) 147 NLJ 600   9.4.1, 9.4.4,
                                                                              9.5, 11.7.3, 13.1.5
MM (An Adult) [2007] EWHC 2003 (Fam), [2009] 1 FLR 443, [2008] 3 FCR 788,
    (2008) 11 CCL Rep 119, [2008] Fam Law 213   4.3, 4.6
Ms B v An NHS Hospital Trust [2002] EWHC 429, [2002] 1 FLR 1090, [2002] 2 All ER
    449, [2002] 2 FCR 1, [2002] Lloyd's Rep Med 265, (2002) 65 BMLR 149, [2002]
    Fam Law 423, (2002) 99(17) LSG 37, (2002) 152 NLJ 470, (2002) 146 SJLB
    83   1.3.1, 9.1

Nancy B v Hotel-Dieu De Quebec [1992] 86 DLR (4d) 385   3.3
NHS Trust v A (A Child) [2007] EWHC 1696 (Fam), [2008] 1 FLR 70, [2008] 1 FCR 34,
    (2007) 10 CCL Rep 677, (2007) 98 BMLR 141   8.2.7, 11.3.2
NHS Trust v L [2012] EWHC 2741 (COP)   9.4.4
Norfolk and Norwich Healthcare NHS Trust v W [1996] 2 FLR 613, [1997] 1 FCR 269,
    (1997) 34 BMLR 16, [1997] Fam Law 17   9.4.4, 9.5
Nottinghamshire Healthcare NHS Trust v RC [2014] EWHC 1317 (COP), [2014] Med
    LR 260   9.4.4, 10.2.2, 12.5

OT, Re [2009] EWHC 633 (Fam)   1.3.3, 2.6, 6.3, 6.5, 6.6, 8.2.7

P (A Minor), Re [2003] EWHC 2327 (Fam), [2004] 2 FLR 1117, [2004] Fam Law
    716   11.6.4
P and Q v Surrey County Council [2011] EWCA Civ 190, [2012] Fam 170, [2012] 2
    WLR 1056, [2012] PTSR 727, [2011] 2 FLR 583, [2011] 1 FCR 559, [2011] HRLR
    19, [2011] UKHRR 584, (2011) 14 CCL Rep 209, [2011] MHLR 125, [2011] Fam
    Law 475   10.6.1
Paton v The British Pregnancy Advisory Service Trustees [1979] QB 276, [1978] 3 WLR
    687, [1978] 2 All ER 987, (1978) 122 SJ 744   11.7.1
Portsmouth NHS Trust v Wyatt [2005] EWCA Civ 1181, [2005] 1 WLR 3995, [2006] 1
    FLR 554, [2005] 3 FCR 263, (2006) 9 CCL Rep 131, [2005] Lloyd's Rep Med 474,
    (2005) 86 BMLR 173, [2006] Fam Law 13   2.3, 6.2, 6.5, 6.7, 6.8, 8.1.2, 11.3, 11.3.1
Portsmouth NHS Trust v Wyatt [2005] EWHC 693 (Fam), [2005] 2 FLR 480, [2005] Fam
    Law 614   8.2.7
PS (Incapacitated or Vulnerable Adult), Re [2007] EWHC 623 (Fam), [2007] 2 FLR 1083,
    (2007) 10 CCL Rep 295, [2007] LS Law Medical 507, [2007] Fam Law 695   11.6.7

R (A Minor) (Blood Tests: Constraint), Re [1998] Fam 66, [1998] 2 WLR 796, [1998] 1
    FLR 745, [1998] 1 FCR 41, [1998] Fam Law 256   13.5.4
R (A Minor) (Blood Transfusion), Re [1993] 2 FLR 757, [1993] 2 FCR 544, 91 LGR 623,
    [1993] Fam Law 577, (1994) 158 LG Rev 341, (1993) 137 SJLB 151   11.3.2
R (A Minor) (Wardship: Medical Treatment), Re [1992] Fam 11, [1991] 3 WLR 592,
    [1992] 1 FLR 190, [1991] 4 All ER 177, [1992] 2 FCR 229, [1992] 3 Med LR 342,
    [1992] Fam Law 67   1.3.3, 3.3.2, 6.4, 11.2.1, 11.2.4, 11.4.1, 11.6.3, 11.6.5
R (Adult: Medical Treatment), Re [1996] 2 FLR 99, [1996] 3 FCR 473, [1996] 7 Med LR
    401, (1996) 31 BMLR 127, [1996] Fam Law 535   2.5, 6.7

R (on the application of B) v Haddock (Responsible Medical Officer) [2006] EWCA Civ
961, [2006] HRLR 40, [2006] Lloyd's Rep Med 433, (2007) 93 BMLR 52, [2006]
MHLR 306   10.2.2

R (on the application of Burke) v General Medical Council [2005] EWCA Civ 1003,
[2006] QB 273, [2005] 3 WLR 1132, [2005] 2 FLR 1223, [2005] 3 FCR 169, [2005]
HRLR 35, [2006] UKHRR 509, (2005) 8 CCL Rep 463, [2005] Lloyd's Rep Med
403, (2005) 85 BMLR 1, [2006] ACD 27, [2005] Fam Law 776, (2005) 155 NLJ
1457   3.3.2, 6.3, 6.4, 6.8

R (on the application of C) v A Local Authority [2011] EWHC 1539 (Admin), (2011) 14
CCL Rep 471, [2011] Med LR 415, [2011] ACD 105   10.7

R (on the application of Muhammad) v Secretary of State for the Home Department
[2013] EWHC 3157 (Admin)   8.1.6

R (on the application of Nicklinson and AM) v Ministry of Justice [2012] EWHC 2381
(Admin), [2012] 3 FCR 233, [2012] HRLR 32, [2012] Med LR 544, (2012) 127
BMLR 197, [2012] ACD 118, (2012) 109(32) LSG 18   7.1, 7.4

R (on the application of Nicklinson) v Ministry of Justice; R (on the application of AM) v
DPP [2014] UKSC 38, [2014] 3 WLR 200   7.3

R (on the application of Pretty) v DPP [2001] UKHL 61, [2002] 1 AC 800, [2001] 3 WLR
1598, [2002] 1 FLR 268, [2002] 1 All ER 1, [2002] 2 Cr App R 1, [2002] 1 FCR 1,
[2002] HRLR 10, [2002] UKHRR 97, 11 BHRC 589, (2002) 63 BMLR 1, [2002]
ACD 41, [2002] Fam Law 170, (2001) 151 NLJ 1819   7.1, 7.3

R (on the application of Purdy) v DPP [2009] UKHL 45, [2010] 1 AC 345, [2009] 3 WLR
403, [2009] 4 All ER 1147, [2010] 1 Cr App R 1, [2009] HRLR 32, [2009] UKHRR
1104, 27 BHRC 126, (2009) 12 CCL Rep 498, [2009] LS Law Medical 479, (2009)
109 BMLR 153, (2009) 179 NLJ 1175, (2009) 153(31) SJLB 28   7.3

R (on the application of Tracey) v Cambridge University Hospitals NHS Foundation Trust
[2014] EWCA Civ 822   3.3, 5.8.1, 5.8.2

R v Bournewood Community and Mental Health NHS Trust ex parte L [1999] 1 AC 458,
[1998] 3 WLR 107, [1998] 2 FLR 550, [1998] 3 All ER 289, [1998] 2 FCR 501,
(1997-98) 1 CCL Rep 390, (1998) 44 BMLR 1, [1998] COD 312, [1998] Fam Law
592, (1998) 95(29) LSG 27, (1998) 148 NLJ 1014, (1998) 142 SJLB 195   1.3.2, 10.3,
10.5

R v Brown (Anthony); R v Laskey (Colin); R v Jaggard; R v Lucas (Saxon); R v Carter; R
v Cadman [1994] 1 AC 212, [1993] 2 WLR 556, [1993] 2 All ER 75, HL   13.7

R v Cambridge District Health Authority, ex p B [1995] 1 WLR 898, [1995] 1 FLR 1056,
[1995] 2 All ER 129, [1995] 2 FCR 485, [1995] 6 Med LR 250, [1995] COD 407,
[1995] Fam Law 480, (1995) 145 NLJ 415   3.3.2, 3.4, 6.4

R v Inglis (Frances) [2010] EWCA Crim 2637, [2011] 1 WLR 1110, [2011] 2 Cr App R
(S) 13, (2011) 117 BMLR 65, [2011] Crim LR 243, (2010) 154(44) SJLB 30   7.4

R v North West Lancashire Health Authority ex parte A, D and G (unreported) 21
December 1998 (High Court)   3.4

R-B v Official Solicitor: Re A (Medical Sterilisation) (1999) 53 BMLR 66   13.1.5

RB (A Patient) v Brighton and Hove Council [2014] EWCA Civ 561   4.3

RB (Adult) (No 4), Re [2011] EWHC 3017 (Fam), [2012] 1 FLR 466, [2012] Fam Law
142   8.3

Rochdale Healthcare (NHS) Trust v C [1997] 1 FCR 274, FD   9.4.4

S (A Minor) (Consent to Medical Treatment), Re [1994] 2 FLR 1065   11.3.2

S (A Minor) (Medical Treatment), Re [1993] 1 FLR 376, [1993] Fam Law 215   11.3.2

S (Adult: Surgical Treatment), Re [1993] Fam 123, [1992] 3 WLR 806, [1992] 4 All ER
671, [1993] 1 FLR 26, [1992] 2 FCR 893, [1993] 4 Med LR 28, [1993] Fam Law
221, (1992) 142 NLJ 1450, (1992) 136 SJLB 299   9.4.4

S (An Infant, by her Guardian ad Litem the Official Solicitor to the Supreme Court) v S;
W v Official Solicitor (Acting as Guardian ad Litem for a Male Infant Named PHW)
[1972] AC 24, [1970] 3 WLR 366, (1970) FLR Rep 619, [1970] 3 All ER 107,
HL   13.5.3

S (Hospital Patient: Court's Jurisdiction), Re [1996] Fam. 1; [1995] 3 WLR 78, [1995] 1
FLR 1075, [1995] 3 All ER 290, [1995] 3 FCR 496, [1995] Fam Law 412, (1995)
92(15) LSG 40, (1995) 139 SJLB 87   1.3

S (Medical Treatment: Adult Sterilisation), Re [1998] 1 FLR 944, [1999] 1 FCR 277,
    [1998] Fam Law 325   13.1.1, 13.1.4
SA (Vulnerable Adult with Capacity: Marriage), Re [2005] EWHC 2942 (Fam), [2006] 1
    FLR 867, [2007] 2 FCR 563, (2007) 10 CCL Rep 193, [2006] Fam Law 268   8.1.6
Secretary of State for the Home Department v Robb [1995] Fam 127, [1995] 2 WLR 722,
    [1995] 1 All ER 677, [1995] 1 FLR 412, [1995] 1 FCR 557, [1995] Fam Law 185,
    (1994) 144 NLJ 1695   9.1, 9.4.4, 10.1.2
SK (An Adult) (Forced Marriage: Appropriate Relief), Re [2004] EWHC 3202 (Fam),
    [2006] 1 WLR 81, [2005] 3 All ER 421, [2005] 2 FLR 230, [2005] 2 FCR 459,
    [2005] Fam Law 460   8.1.6
South Glamorgan County Council v W and B [1993] 1 FCR 626, [1993] Fam Law
    398   11.6.7
St George's Healthcare NHS Trust v S [1999] Fam 26, [1998] 3 WLR 936, [1998] 3 All
    ER 673, [1998] 2 FLR 728, [1998] 2 FCR 685, (1997-98) 1 CCL Rep 410, (1998)
    44 BMLR 160, [1998] COD 396, [1998] Fam Law 526, (1998) 95(22) LSG 29,
    (1998) 148 NLJ 693, (1998) 142 SJLB 164   1.3.1, 9.1, 9.4.4, 9.5, 10.1.2, 10.1.3,
                                                                           10.2.2, 11.7.3
Storck v Germany (App 61603/00) (2005) 43 EHRR 6, [2005] MHLR 211   10.6.1
Superintendent of Family and Child Service and Dawson, Re [1983] 145 DLR (3d) 610   2.6,
                                                                               6.7
Swindon and Marlborough NHS Trust v S [1995] Med LR 84   5.7.5

T (A Minor) (Wardship: Medical Treatment), Re [1997] 1 WLR 242, [1997] 1 FLR 502,
    [1997] 1 All ER 906, [1997] 2 FCR 363, [1997] 8 Med LR 166, (1997) 35 BMLR
    63, (1996) 93(42) LSG 28, (1996) 146 NLJ 1577, (1996) 140 SJLB 237   2.5, 11.3.2
T (Adult: Refusal of Medical Treatment), Re [1993] Fam 95, [1992] 3 WLR 782, [1992] 2
    FLR 458, [1992] 4 All ER 649, [1992] 2 FCR 861, [1992] 3 Med LR 306, [1993]
    Fam Law 27, (1992) 142 NLJ 1125   1.3.1, 1.4, 5.7.4, 9.3, 9.4.2, 9.4.3, 9.4.4
Tameside and Glossop Acute Services NHS Trust v CH (A Patient) [1996] 1 FLR 762,
    [1996] 1 FCR 753, (1996) 31 BMLR 93, [1996] Fam Law 353   9.4.4, 9.5, 10.2.2
The Mental Health Trust, The Acute Trust and The Council v DD [2014] EWHC 11
    (COP)   1.3.1, 9.4.4, 9.5
Trust A and Trust B v H (An Adult Patient) [2006] EWHC 1230 (Fam), [2006] 2 FLR
    958, (2006) 9 CCL Rep 474, [2006] Fam Law 842   4.5

W (A Minor) (Consent to Medical Treatment), Re [1993] 1 FLR 1   1.2, 1.3.3
W (A Minor) (Medical Treatment: Court's Jurisdiction), Re [1993] Fam 64, [1992] 3 WLR
    758; *sub nom* W (A Minor) (Consent to Medical Treatment), Re [1993] 1 FLR 1; *sub
    nom* W (A Minor) (Medical Treatment), Re [1992] 4 All ER 627, CA   8.2.1, 11.3,
                                       11.4.1, 11.4.3, 11.5.2, 11.6.1, 11.6.2, 11.6.3, 11.6.5
W v M [2011] EWHC 2443 (Fam), [2012] 1 WLR 1653, [2012] 1 FLR 495, [2012] 1 All
    ER 1313, [2012] PTSR 1040, [2012] 1 FCR 1, (2011) 14 CCL Rep 689, [2011] Med
    LR 584, (2011) 122 BMLR 67, [2011] Fam Law 1330, (2011) 108(39) LSG 18,
    (2011) 156 NLJ 1368   2.4, 2.6, 5.8, 5.8.1, 5.8.3, 12.5
Warren v Care Fertility (Northampton) Ltd [2014] EWHC 602 (Fam), [2014] 2 FCR 311,
    [2014] Med LR 217, [2014] Fam Law 803, (2014) 158(12) SJLB 41   13.3.5
Westminster City Council v IC, KC and NNC [2007] EWHC 3096 (Fam)   8.1.6

X (A Child), Re [2014] EWHC 1871 (Fam)   11.6.7
X (Adult Patient: Sterilisation), Re [1998] 2 FLR 1124, [1999] 3 FCR 426, [1998] Fam
    Law 737   13.1.4
X NHS Trust v T (Adult Patient: Refusal of Medical Treatment) [2004] EWHC 1279
    (Fam), [2005] 1 All ER 387, [2004] 3 FCR 297, (2005) 8 CCL Rep 38, [2004]
    Lloyd's Rep Med 433, (2004) 80 BMLR 184   11.3.2
X Primary Care Trust v XB [2012] EWHC 1390 (Fam)   12.5

Y (Mental Incapacity: Bone Marrow Transplant), Re [1997] Fam 110, [1997] 2 WLR 556,
    [1996] 2 FLR 787, [1997] 2 FCR 172, (1997) 35 BMLR 111, [1997] Fam Law
    91   4.5, 13.2.3
YLA v PM and MZ [2013] EWHC 4020 (COP), [2014] COPLR 114   8.1.2

Z (A Minor) (Identification: Restrictions on Publication), Re [1997] Fam 1, [1996] 2 WLR
88, [1995] 4 All ER 961; *sub nom* Z (A Minor) (Freedom of Publication), Re [1996]
1 FLR 191, CA   8.2.1, 11.3.2

TABLE OF STATUTES

References are to paragraph numbers.

Abortion Act 1967   13.6
  s 1   11.6.7, 13.6
Administration of Justice Act 1960
  s 12   8.2.7
Anatomy Act 1984   13.2

Care Standards Act 2000   10.7
  s 3   10.7
Children Act 1989   2.3, 8.2.1, 8.2.2,
       8.2.3, 8.2.4, 8.2.5, 8.3, 11.1,
       11.5.2, 13.2.2, 13.3.7, 13.4
  s 1   2.3, 8.2.1, 8.2.4
  s 1(3)   11.3.2
  s 2   11.2.4
  s 2(9)   11.2.3
  s 3   11.2.3
  s 3(5)   11.2.3
  s 4   11.2.4
  s 8   2.3, 8.2.1, 11.5.2, 13.3.7
  s 10(9)   13.3.7
  s 12   11.2.3
  s 25   11.6.6
  s 31   11.8.3
  s 33(3)(a)   11.2.3
  s 38   11.8.2
  s 38(6)   2.3, 8.2.1, 11.6.7, 11.8.2
  s 38(7)   11.8.2
  s 38(7A)   11.8.2
  s 38(7B)   11.8.2
  s 41(6)   8.2.4
  s 44(6)(b)   11.8.2
  s 44(7)   11.8.2
  s 44(8)   11.8.2
  s 92(7)–(10)   13.4
  s 100(3)   8.2.1, 11.3.2, 11.6.7
  s 100(4)   8.2.1
  s 100(5)   8.2.1, 11.6.7
  s 105   11.1
  s 105(1)   8.2.1
  Sch 11
    Pt 1   13.4
Children and Families Act 2014   8.2.1
  s 13(1)   8.2.3, 11.8.2
  s 13(3)   8.2.3, 11.8.2
  s 13(6)   8.2.3, 11.8.2
  s 13(11)   11.8.2
Coroners and Justice Act 2009
  s 59   7.3

Education Act 1996   10.7

Family Law Act 1986
  s 55A   13.3.6, 13.5.1
  s 56   13.5.1
Family Law Reform Act 1969   11.1,
       13.5.3, 13.5.4
  s 1(1)   11.1
  s 8   1.3.3, 11.4.2, 11.4.3
  s 20   13.5.1, 13.5.2, 13.5.3, 13.5.4
  s 21   13.5.2
  s 21(3)   13.5.4
  s 22   13.5.1
  s 23   13.5.2, 13.5.3
  s 23(1)   13.5.3
Female Genital Mutilation Act 2003   13.9

Gender Recognition Act 2004   13.8,
       13.8.1
  ss 1–8   13.8.1
  s 1(1)(a)   13.8.1
  ss 9–21   13.8.1
  ss 22–29   13.8.1
  Schs 1–6   13.8.1

Human Fertilisation and Embryology
  Act 1990   13.2, 13.3, 13.3.1, 13.6
  s 1   13.3.1
  s 1(1)   13.3.1
  s 1(1)(a)   13.3.1
  s 1(4)   13.3.1
  s 1(6)   13.3.1
  s 3   13.3.1
  s 3(2)   13.3.1
  s 3ZA(5)   13.3.1
  s 4A   13.3.1
  s 12   13.3.3
  s 13(5)   13.3.6
  s 26   13.3.1
  s 27   13.3.4
  s 28   13.3.2
  s 30   13.4
  s 35A   13.3.1
  Sch 3   13.3.2
    para 1(1)   13.3.3
    para 1(2)   13.3.2
    para 2(1)   13.3.2
    para 4   13.3.3
    para 4A   13.3.3
    para 4A(3)   13.3.3

Human Fertilisation and Embryology
  Act 2008
s 1	13.3.1
s 3	13.3.1
s 4	13.3.1
s 13	13.3.2
s 14(3)	13.3.4
s 33	13.3.4
s 35	13.3.4, 13.3.5, 13.3.8, 13.4
s 36	13.3.4, 13.3.5, 13.4
s 37	13.3.4
s 38	13.3.4
s 38(1)	13.3.4
s 38(2)	13.3.5
s 39	13.3.5
s 40	13.3.8
s 42	13.3.5, 13.3.6, 13.3.8, 13.4
s 42(1)	13.3.7
s 43	13.3.5, 13.3.6, 13.4
s 44	13.3.6
s 45(1)	13.3.7
s 46	13.3.8
s 48(2)	13.3.7
s 54	13.4
s 58(2)	13.3.4
Sch 3	13.3.2
para 7	13.3.3

Human Fertilisation and Embryology
  (Deceased Fathers) Act
2003	13.3.2
Human Organ Transplants Act 1989	13.2

Human Reproductive Cloning Act
2001	13.3.1
Human Rights Act 1998	13.3.3, 13.3.5, 13.8
s 3	13.3.5
s 4(6)	7.3
s 6(1)	7.4
s 10)	7.3
Human Tissue Act 1961	13.2
Human Tissue Act 2004	13.2, 13.2.2, 13.2.3
s 2	13.2
s 3	13.2
s 4	13.2
s 27(4)	13.2
s 43	13.2
s 44	13.2
s 45	13.2
s 47	13.2
s 54(9)	13.2

Infant Life (Preservation) Act 1929
s 1	11.7.2, 13.6

Matrimonial Causes Act 1973
s 11(c)	13.8
Medical Act 1983	
s 35	5.3
s 45A	3.4
Mental Capacity Act 2005	1.3.2, 1.4,
	4.1, 4.5, 5.1, 5.8.4, 7.3, 7.4, 8.1,

Mental Capacity Act 2005—*continued*
	8.1.3, 8.1.4, 8.1.6, 8.2.6, 9.1,
	9.4.4, 10.1.2, 10.3, 10.4, 10.6,
	12.2, 12.3, 12.5, 13.1.6, 13.2.1,
	13.2.2
s 1	4.1
s 1(2)	9.1
s 1(3)	4.1, 9.1
s 1(3)(c)	4.3
s 1(4)	9.1
s 1(5)	1.3.1, 1.3.2, 2.2, 3.3.1, 4.4, 9.2,
	9.3, 10.1.2, 10.7, 13.1.5
s 1(6)	4.1, 10.1, 13.1.5
s 2	4.2, 13.1.5
s 2(1)	4.2, 9.2
s 2(2)	9.2
s 3	4.2, 9.3.2, 13.1.5
s 3(1)	9.3.2
s 3(2)	9.3.2
s 3(3)	9.3.2
s 3(4)	9.3.2
s 4	2.7, 4.4, 4.5, 4.6, 4.8, 4.9, 5.8.3,
	10.6.2, 13.1.5
s 4(2)	4.6, 13.1.5
s 4(3)	4.1
s 4(4)	4.1
s 4(5)	5.5, 5.7.3
s 4(6)	1.4, 2.7, 5.7.4, 5.8.3, 12.5
s 4(6)(c)	13.1.5
s 4(7)	1.4, 5.7.4, 5.8.3, 12.5, 13.1.5
s 4(10)	12.4
s 4A	10.6
s 4A(1)	1.3.2, 10.6
s 4A(3)	1.3.2, 10.6
s 4A(5)	1.3.2, 10.6
s 4B	10.6, 10.6.3
s 5	1.3.1, 1.3.2, 4.7, 9.2, 9.3, 9.5,
	10.1.2, 10.4, 12.4
s 6	4.7, 9.5, 10.4
s 9	4.9
ss 9–14	10.3.1
s 9(1)	10.3.1
s 10	1.3.1, 1.4, 9.1.1
s 11(8)	1.3.1, 1.4, 5.6, 9.1.1
s 15	8.1.2, 9.5, 10.3
s 15(1)	8.1.2
s 15(1)(c)	9.5
s 15(2)	8.1.2
s 16	1.3.1, 1.4, 4.8, 5.4, 9.1.1, 10.3.2
s 16(2)(a)	10.6
s 16(4)	10.3.2
s 20(5)	1.3.1, 1.4, 5.6, 9.1.1
s 21	8.3
s 21A	10.6.2
s 24	1.3.1, 9.1.1, 9.4.4
ss 24–26	10.2.2
s 25	1.3.1, 9.1.1, 9.4.4
s 25(3)	12.5
s 25(5)	12.2
s 25(5)(a)	12.5
s 26	1.3.1, 9.1.1, 9.4.4
s 26(4)	12.5
s 28(1)	10.7
s 42	5.2, 8.1

Mental Capacity Act 2005—*continued*
s 42(4)	5.2, 8.1
s 42(5)	8.1
s 46	8.1.1
s 46(2)(a)	13.1.6
s 64(5)	10.6.1
Sch A1	1.3.2, 10.6
Mental Health Act 1983	1.3.1, 9.4.4,
	10.1, 10.1.2, 10.2, 10.3, 10.4,
	10.5, 10.6, 13.5.2
s 1(2)	10.2
s 1(2A)	10.2
s 1(2B)	10.2
s 2	1.3.1, 9.1, 10.1.3, 10.2
s 2(2)	10.1.3
s 2(2)(a)	10.1.3
s 2(2)(b)	10.1.3
s 3	9.4.4, 10.2, 10.2.2
s 3(4)	10.2.1
s 7	10.2
s 17A	10.2
s 20	10.2
s 20A	10.2
ss 35–38	10.2
s 45A	10.2
s 47	10.2
s 48	9.4.4, 10.2
s 51	10.2
s 56(1)	10.7
s 57	10.2.2
s 58	10.2.2
s 58A	10.2.2
s 62	10.2.2
s 63	9.4.4, 10.1.3, 10.2.2

Mental Health Act 1983—*continued*
s 72(1)(b)	10.2
s 72(1)(c)	10.2
s 72(4)	10.2
s 131	10.5
s 131(1)	1.3.2
s 135	9.4.4
s 145	3.2
s 145(1)	10.2.1, 10.2.2
s 145(4)	10.2.1, 10.2.2
Mental Health Act 2007	10.2
National Health Service Act 1977	3.2
s 1(1)	3.2, 3.4
s 3(1)	3.2, 3.4
s 13	3.2
Offences Against the Person Act 1861	
s 20	13.7.2
s 47	13.7.2
Same Sex (Married Couples Act) 2013	
Sch 7	
Pt 2	13.3.8
Sexual Offences Act 1956	13.7.2
Suicide Act 1961	
s 1	7.2
s 2	7.3, 7.4
s 2(1)	7.3
s 2A(1)	7.3
Tattooing of Minors Act 1969	13.7.1

TABLE OF STATUTORY INSTRUMENTS

References are to paragraph numbers.

Civil Procedure Rules 1998,
  SI 1998/3132
  Pt 21   8.1.6
Court of Protection (Amendment)
  Rules 2011, SI 2011/2753   8.1
Court of Protection Rules 2007,
  SI 2007/1744   8.1, 10.6.2
  Pt 3
    r 9   8.1.6
  Pt 7
    r 40   8.1.4
  Pt 8   8.1.3, 8.1.6
  Pt 9   8.1.3
    r 73(2)   8.1.4
    r 73(4)   8.1.4
  Pt 10   8.1.3
  Pt 13
    r 90   8.1.7
    r 91   8.1.7
    r 92   8.1.7, 13.1.6
    r 93   8.1.7
  Pt 17
    r 140(1)   8.1.4
    r 141(1)   8.1.4

Family Procedure Rules 2010,
  SI 2010/2955
  r 2.3   8.2.6
  Pt 12   8.2.1, 8.2.2
  r 12.1   8.2.2
  r 12.36(1)   8.2.2
  r 12.37   8.2.4
  r 15.2   8.2.6

Family Procedure Rules 2010,
  SI 2010/2955—continued
  r 16.2   8.2.4, 8.2.5
  r 16.4   8.2.5
  r 16.6   8.2.5
  r 16.24   8.2.5
  r 27.10   8.2.7
  r 27.11   8.2.7
  r 27.11(1)   8.2.7
  r 27.11(2)   8.2.7
  r 27.11(3)   8.2.7

Human Fertilisation and Embryology
  (Statutory Storage Period for
  Embryos and Gametes)
  Regulations 2009,
  SI 2009/2581   13.3.5
  reg 4(3)   13.3.5
  reg 4(3)(a)   13.3.5
  reg 4(3)(b)   13.3.5
  reg 7(3)   13.3.5
  reg 7(3)(a)   13.3.5
  reg 7(3)(b)   13.3.5
Human Tissue Act 2004 (Persons who
  Lack Capacity to Consent and
  Transplants) Regulations 2006,
  SI 2006/1659   13.2.2, 13.2.3

Mental Capacity Act 2005 (Transfer of
  Proceedings) Order 2007,
  SI 2007/1899   8.3
  art 3(3)(c)   8.3

TABLE OF INTERNATIONAL MATERIAL

References are to paragraph numbers.

European Convention for the Protection of Human Rights and Fundamental Freedoms 1950

art 2   2.4, 5.1, 5.8, 6.3, 9.4.4, 10.2.2, 11.7.2, 11.7.3, 13.3.3

art 3   5.8, 6.1, 6.3, 9.4.4

art 5   9.4.4, 10.6

art 8   5.8, 5.8.2, 6.3, 7.1, 7.3, 7.4, 8.1.2, 9.4.4, 11.2.1, 11.7.3, 13.1.5, 13.3.3, 13.3.5

art 8(2)   7.3

art 12   13.1.5, 13.3.3

art 14   13.3.3

International Covenant on Civil and Political Rights 1966

art 6   2.4

ABBREVIATIONS

ABE	achieving best evidence
ANH	artificial nutrition and hydration
BMA	British Medical Association
CA 1989	Children Act 1989
COP	Court of Protection
CPR	cardio-pulmonary resuscitation
DNACPR	do not activate CPR
ECHR	European Convention for the Protection of Human Rights and Fundamental Freedoms (1953)
ECtHR	European Court of Human Rights
FPR 2010	Family Procedure Rules 2010
GID	Gender Identity Dysphoria
GMC	General Medical Council
HTA	Human Tissue Authority
HT Act 2004	Human Tissue Act 2004
LPA	Lasting Power of Attorney
MCA 2005	Mental Capacity Act 2005
MCS	minimally conscious state
MHA 1983	Mental Health Act 1983
NHS	National Health Service
NHSBT	NHS Blood and Transplant
NIV	non-invasive ventilation
PD	Practice Direction
PVS	permanent vegetative state

PART I

GENERAL PRINCIPLES IN RELATION TO MEDICAL TREATMENT AND THE LAW

CHAPTER 1

MEDICAL TREATMENT AND CONSENT

1.1 THE MEANING OF 'CONSENT'

'Consent' is the voluntary and continuing permission of a patient to receive a particular medical treatment, based on an adequate knowledge of the purpose, nature, likely effects and risks of that treatment including the likelihood of its success and any alternatives to it. Permission given under any unfair or undue pressure is not a true 'consent'.

1.2 THE PURPOSE OF CONSENT TO TREATMENT

There are two purposes of seeking consent from a patient, whether that patient is an adult or a child, or from someone with authority to give that consent on behalf of the patient. One purpose is legal and the other is clinical.

The legal purpose of consent is to provide those concerned in the treatment with a defence to a criminal charge of assault or battery or a civil claim for damages for trespass to the person. It does not, however, provide them with any defence to a claim that they negligently advised a particular treatment or negligently carried it out.

The clinical purpose of consent is that the co-operation and confidence of the patient in the efficiency of the treatment is often a major factor in the success of the treatment. Failure to obtain consent can not only disadvantage the patient and the medical staff, but can also make it more difficult to administer the treatment. This can be the case if consent is given on behalf of, rather than by, the patient himself. However, in the case of young children, knowledge of the fact that the parent has consented may help.

This dual purpose of consent to medical treatment is set out in the case of *Re W (A Minor) (Consent to Medical Treatment)* [1993] 1 FLR 1.

1.3   ADULTS WITH CAPACITY, ADULTS LACKING CAPACITY AND CHILDREN

The law respects the right of adults with capacity to physical autonomy. Generally speaking, no one is entitled to touch, examine or operate upon such persons without their consent, express or implied. It is up to such persons to give or withhold consent as they wish, for reasons good or bad.

This simple rule cannot be applied in cases of children and those lacking capacity, because they may be unable to form or express any, or any reliable, judgment of where their best interests lie: *Re S (Hospital Patient: Court's Jurisdiction)* [1995] 1 FLR 1075, CA at 1087.

1.3.1   Adults with capacity

The requirement of consent before medical treatment

At common law, a doctor cannot lawfully operate on adult patients of sound mind, or give them any other treatment involving the application of physical force, however slight, without their consent: in *Re F (Sterilisation: Mental Patient)* [1990] 2 AC 1, HL at 55.

Generally it is the patient's consent which makes invasive medical treatment lawful. It is not lawful to treat a patient who has capacity and refuses that treatment. Nor is it lawful to treat a patient who lacks capacity if he has made a valid and applicable advance decision to refuse it: see the Mental Capacity Act 2005 (MCA 2005), ss 24 to 26. Nor is it lawful to treat such a patient if he has granted a lasting power of attorney (under s 10) or the court has appointed a deputy (under s 16) with the power to give or withhold consent to that treatment and that consent is withheld; but an attorney only has power to give or withhold consent to the carrying out or continuation of life-sustaining treatment if the instrument expressly so provides (s 11(8)) and a deputy cannot refuse consent to such treatment (s 20(5)).

If a doctor does operate on such patients or give them other treatment without their consent, that doctor is liable to be subject to a criminal charge of assault or an action in tort of trespass to the person.

The autonomy of the individual and the principle of self-determination

If an adult of sound mind refuses consent to medical treatment, the doctor must abide by his patient's decision. This is called the 'principle of autonomy of the patient'. It is described by Lord Goff in his article entitled 'A Matter of Life and Death' (1995) 3 *Medical Law Review* Spring.

The extent of the principle of autonomy and self-determination is such that every adult has the right and capacity to decide whether or not he will accept medical treatment, even if a refusal may risk permanent injury to his health or even lead to premature death. Furthermore, it does not matter whether the reasons for the refusal are rational or irrational, unknown or even non-existent: *Re T (An Adult) (Consent to Medical Treatment)* [1992] 2 FLR 458, CA at 473.

The right of self-determination was considered in *Airedale NHS Trust v Bland* [1993] AC 789, per Lord Goff at 864:

> '... it is established that the principle of self-determination requires that respect must be given to the wishes of the patient, so that if an adult patient of sound mind refuses, however unreasonably, to consent to treatment or care by which his life would or might be prolonged, the doctors responsible for his care must give effect to his wishes, even though they do not consider it to be in his best interests to do so ... To this extent, the principle of the sanctity of human life must yield to the principle of self-determination ... and, for present purposes perhaps more important, the doctor's duty to act in the best interests of his patient must likewise be qualified.'

The leading cases of *B v An NHS Hospital Trust* [2002] EWHC 429 (Fam) and *Heart of England NHS Foundation Trust v JB (by her litigation friend, the Official Solicitor)* [2014] EWHC 342 clearly enunciate the above principle too.

It is necessary to emphasise that there are occasions when an individual lacks the capacity to make decisions about whether or not to consent to treatment. The presumption of capacity to decide is rebuttable, yet often it may be difficult for medical practitioners to adjudge whether an adult has or has not the requisite capacity to decide.

Breaching the principles of self-determination and the autonomy of the individual

The principles of self-determination and the autonomy of the individual and the effects of breaching them were reinforced in the case of *St George's Healthcare NHS Trust v S; R v Collins and Others ex parte S* [1998] 2 FLR 728, CA. On seeking to register as a new patient at a local NHS practice, S, who was 36 weeks pregnant, was found to be suffering from pre-eclampsia and was advised by the doctor that she needed urgent attention and admission to hospital for an induced delivery and that without such treatment her health and life and the life of her baby were in danger. S fully understood the potential risks but rejected the advice as she wanted her baby to be born naturally. She was seen by a social worker approved under the Mental Health Act 1983 (MHA 1983) and two doctors. They repeated the advice but she again refused to accept it. On the social worker's application, S was admitted to a mental hospital against her will for assessment under s 2 of the 1983 Act. A few hours later, again against her will, she was transferred to another hospital where she adamantly refused to consent to treatment and recorded her refusal in writing. She also then consulted solicitors. In view of her continuing refusal to consent to treatment, an ex parte application was made to the court without the issue of a summons and without the judge being informed either that S had instructed solicitors or that she and her solicitors were ignorant of the proceedings. The judge granted a declaration dispensing with S's consent to treatment and later the same evening her baby was born by Caesarean section. A few days later, S was returned to the mental hospital. Two days after that, her detention under s 2 of the 1983 Act was terminated and she immediately discharged herself from the hospital. She appealed the grant of the declaration dispensing with her consent to treatment and applied for a judicial review of her admission and detention in the mental hospital, her transfer, detention and treatment in the second hospital and her return to the mental hospital.

In relation to the autonomy of the patient involved and breaching such autonomy, the findings of the Court of Appeal in S's favour amounted to the following:

(1) even when his or her own life depends on receiving medical treatment, an adult of sound mind is entitled to refuse it;

(2) whilst pregnancy increases the personal responsibilities of a woman, it does not diminish her entitlement to decide whether or not to undergo medical treatment;

(3) an unborn child is not a separate person from its mother and its need for medical assistance does not prevail over her rights;

(4) a woman is entitled not to be forced to submit to an invasion of her body against her will, whether her own life or that of her unborn child depends on it;

(5) her right is not reduced or diminished merely because her decision to exercise it may appear morally repugnant;

(6) the declaration in the case granted at first instance involved the removal of the baby from within the body of her mother under physical compulsion. Unless lawfully justified, this constituted an

infringement of the mother's autonomy. Of themselves, the perceived needs of the foetus did not provide the necessary justification;

(7) in relation to her unlawful admission or detention in hospital, the patient's application for a judicial review was granted and appropriate declaratory relief ordered;

(8) more particularly, however, in relation to the patient's refusal of consent to the medical treatment proposed, the Court of Appeal allowed the patient's appeal against the declaration granted by the judge at first instance. The declaration was set aside *ex debito justitiae*.

It was held that the judge had erred in making a declaratory order on an ex parte application, in proceedings which had not been instituted by the issue of the summons, without the patient's knowledge or without any attempt to inform her or her solicitor of the application. Further, the order had been made without any evidence and without any provision for the patient to apply to vary or discharge the order.

The consequence generally of an invasion of a person's autonomy without consent may be a cause of action for damages for trespass to the person. For example, in the Canadian case of *Malette v Shulman* [1990] 67 DLR (4d) 321, the court upheld an award of $20,000 to a patient who had been given a blood transfusion in order to save her life but against her known wishes. She was a card-carrying Jehovah's Witness. In the *St George's Healthcare NHS Trust v S* case, the Caesarean section performed on the patient S (together with the accompanying medical procedure) amounted to trespass. Whilst it might be available to defeat any claim based on aggravated or examplary damages on the particular facts of the case, the Court of Appeal held that the judge's decision at first instance, which was set aside on appeal, would provide no defence to the patient's claim for damages for trespass against the hospital.

There will be examined in detail in Chapter 9 (Adult Refusal of Medical Treatment: Non-consensual treatment) the significant case of *Ms B v An NHS Hospital Trust* [2002] EWHC 429 in which the judge determined, as one of the material issues, that the applicant patient had been treated *unlawfully* for a period by the Hospital Trust.

In contrast and within the remit of the MCA 2005, the High Court 'caesarean section' case of *The Mental Health Trust, The Acute Trust and The Council v DD* [2014] EWCOP 11 determined: that the 36-year-old pregnant mother DD lacked capacity to decide where to give birth to her unborn child and to decide how to give birth to her child;

that it was in the mother's best interests, and therefore lawful, for her to be conveyed to a hospital in order for there to be carried out a planned Caesarean section procedure and all necessary ancillary care; that there was authorisation from the court to take such necessary, reasonable and proportionate measures to give effect to the latter, to include if necessary forced entry into her home, restraint and sedation.

This legal authority is considered again in more detail within Chapter 9.

Emergency treatment

It is lawful for a doctor to treat an adult of sound mind without his or her consent in an emergency where, for example, as a result of an accident or otherwise, he or she is unconscious and an operation or other treatment cannot be safely delayed until he or she recovers consciousness: *Re F* [1990] 2 AC 1, at 55. Sections 1(5) and 5 of MCA 2005 would pertain here.

1.3.2   Adults who through lack of capacity are unable to consent to or refuse medical treatment

The basis of any right to treat in the absence of consent

The principles referred to may encompass a range of adults from those with long-term mental disability to those ordinarily competent adults who are found temporarily to be lacking in capacity.

A doctor is to treat an adult lacking capacity to consent in accordance with MCA 2005, and in particular under s 1(5) any act done or decision made for or on behalf of such a person must be done, or made, in his best interests.

The common law principle was that a doctor may lawfully operate on, or give other treatment to, an adult patient who is incapable, for one reason or another, of consenting to the doctor's doing so, provided that the operation or treatment concerned was in the best interests of the patient. The operation or other treatment was in the patient's best interests if, but only if, it was carried out in order to save his life or to ensure improvement or prevent deterioration in his physical or mental health.

In many cases, it was not only lawful for doctors to operate on or give other medical treatment to adult patients disabled from giving their consent, it was also their common law duty to do so: *Re F* [1990] 2 AC 1 at 55, 56.

The previous common law principle of necessity

The justification in common law for medical intervention and treatment for those patients lacking the capacity to consent used to lie in the common law principle of necessity.

In the case of *Re F* [1990] 2 AC 1, the courts struggled to find the proper basis of jurisdiction for the determination of whether a 36-year-old handicapped woman should have a sterilisation operation. In this regard, the High Court determined that the court was entitled, jurisdictionally, to grant a declaration that such an operation would be lawful as being in her best interests. Lord Goff was of the view that the principle of necessity applied beyond cases of emergency and that the lawfulness of the doctor's action was to be found at least in its origin in the principle of necessity. There was not unanimity in the House of Lords in the case of *Re F* as to the applicability of the principle of necessity, since the emphasis was on the jurisdiction or question referred to above. Lord Bridge, in *Re F*, was concerned to stress that too rigid a criterion of necessity to determine what is and is not lawful in the treatment of the incompetent would be undesirable since then many of those unfortunate enough to be deprived of the capacity to make rational decisions by accident, illness or unsoundness of mind might be deprived of treatment which it would be entirely beneficial for them to receive.

In *R v Bournewood Community and Mental Health NHS Trust ex parte L* [1998] 2 FLR 550, the adult patient, L, was 48 years old and autistic. He was so profoundly mentally incapacitated that he was incapable of consenting to medical treatment. The principal question in the case was whether, as a person incapable of consenting to treatment, he could be admitted to hospital for his mental disorder informally under s 131(1) of the MHA 1983 and thereby without compulsory detention. The House of Lords held that adults who are incapable of consenting may be admitted under s 131(1) for treatment without a compulsory detention.

Since, then, the safeguards provided by the MHA 1983 to those compulsorily detained would not apply, the question arose as to the justification in law for the medical treatment of those informally admitted to hospital.

It was firmly held that the common law principle of necessity justified the medical treatment of L during his admission and there was fortification for the proposition raised in *Re F* that, generally, the justification in common law for medical intervention and treatment for adults who are unable to consent to such treatment lies in the principle of necessity.

The case was taken to the European Court of Human Rights in *HL v UK* (2005) 81 BMLR 131. As stated above, the patient was an informal patient, not compulsorily detained under the MHA 1983, in the intensive behavioural unit of Bournewood Hospital.

The court held that he had been deprived of his liberty in breach of Article 5. The court identified accordingly 'the Bournewood gap' in our legal framework for control over the deprivation of liberty in the case of an incapable person affected otherwise than pursuant to the MHA 1983. Parliament sought to fill the gap by making insertions into the MCA 2005 which, by s 4A(5) and Sch A1, sets up a framework for such control in the case of a person receiving care or treatment in a hospital or a care home and which, by s 4A(1) and (3), renders any other such deprivation lawful only if made pursuant to a court order that is in his or her best interests.

Section 5 of the MCA 2005 replaces in wider terms the common law doctrine of necessity. It provides the basis upon which the vast majority of medical treatment decisions in relation to an incapacitated person can be taken without seeking any court authorisation. The section provides protection from liability for anyone involved in providing care or treatment for a person who lacks capacity to consent to such care or treatment, provided that they are acting in the person's best interests and without negligence. In this way, the Act clarifies in the statute the common law principle of necessity, setting out the circumstances in which caring actions and decisions can lawfully be taken on behalf of adults who lack capacity to consent to them.

1.3.3   Children

The parental right to consent to medical treatment for and on behalf of a child

A doctor is not entitled to treat a child without the consent of someone who is authorised to give consent. Generally speaking, treatment which is administered to a child without parental consent is unlawful, constituting a civil trespass and possible criminal assault: *Re OT* [2009] EWHC 633 (Fam).

An immature child is incapable of giving consent to medical treatment, such that a parent or person with parental responsibility will consent on the child's behalf. Until a child achieves the capacity to consent, the right of the parent or the person with parental responsibility to make the decision continues save only in exceptional circumstances. Exceptional circumstances may justify the doctor proceeding to treat the child as a matter of necessity without parental knowledge or consent, such as an emergency, parental neglect, abandonment of the child or the inability to find the parents.

The right of a minor to consent to treatment on his or her own behalf

At common law, a child will be able to consent to medical treatment for and on his own behalf when he achieves a sufficient understanding and intelligence to enable him to understand fully what is proposed. This has become known as meeting the '*Gillick*-competence' test. At the age of 16 years, a minor is provided with a statutory right of consent under s 8 of the Family Law Reform Act 1969.

The concurrent powers of parent and child to consent to treatment

In *Re R (A Minor) (Wardship: Medical Treatment)* [1992] 1 FLR 190 and *Re W (A Minor) (Consent to Medical Treatment)* [1993] 1 FLR 1, the court was concerned with two female minors.

In *Re R* the minor was 15 years old with mental health problems.

In *Re W* the minor had attained the age of 16 years and suffered from anorexia nervosa. Each girl was refusing medical treatment. The issue in each case was the nature and extent of the power of a minor to refuse medical treatment.

The firm view taken by the court was that no minor of whatever age has power, by refusing consent to treatment, to override a consent to treatment on their behalf by a parent or person with parental responsibility for them.

The reasoning is that throughout a child's minority the parental right to consent is retained. It does not determine when the child achieves *Gillick*-competence. Upon the achievement of *Gillick*-competence, the child's power of consent is concurrent with that of the parent or guardian. The consent of either the parent or child may enable treatment to be given lawfully. Only a refusal of consent by all those with the power of consent can create a veto. This means that once a minor is *Gillick*-competent either the minor or parent can give a valid consent to medical treatment of the minor and neither can override the other's consent and exercise a veto.

Medical treatment at variance with parental wishes

The proposition that it is not right or practicable to give or withhold medical treatment against the wishes of parents is incorrect in law. Whilst the requirement to parental consent is prioritised to the extent possible, the best interests decision and thus its consequences in terms of treatment is committed to the judge where parents and professionals cannot agree. That means there must always be a real possibility of an outcome at variance with parental wishes. The views of parents must be accorded profound respect and given weight but they cannot be decisive.

1.4   NEXT OF KIN

An adult of sound mind will be able to consent to or refuse treatment as he or she wishes. An adult lacking capacity for whatever reason will not be able to do so. Such a latter person may have granted a lasting power of attorney under s 10 of the MCA 2005 or the court may have appointed a deputy under s 16 of the Act with the power to give or withhold consent to medical treatment. An attorney only has power to give or withhold consent to the carrying out or continuation of life-sustaining treatment if the instrument expressly so provides (s 11(8)) and a deputy cannot refuse consent to such treatment (s 20(5)).

Next of kin or relatives may be asked to approve a medical decision made, but the decision itself rests with the doctor acting in the best interests of the patient. It is undoubtedly proper and good practice and humane for the next of kin or close relatives to be consulted and listened to. The legal position, however, is as follows, per Lord Donaldson in *Re T (An Adult) (Consent to Medical Treatment)* [1992] 2 FLR 458 at 461:

> 'There seems to be a view in the medical profession that in such emergency circumstances the next of kin should be asked to consent on behalf of the patient and that, if possible, treatment should be postponed until that consent has been obtained. This is a misconception because the next of kin has no legal right either to consent or to refuse consent.'

What may emanate, however, from consultation with the next of kin or close relatives is whether the patient has made an advance statement or 'living will' orally or in writing expressing his specific wishes, if any, in relation to medical treatment including, for example, refusal of any form of medical treatment or otherwise.

Under the MCA 2005 the person determining what is in a person's best interests must include taking into account under s 4(7), if it is practicable and appropriate to consult them, the views of:

(a) anyone named by the person as someone to be consulted on the matter in question or on matters of that kind;

(b) anyone engaged in caring for the person or interested in his welfare;

(c) any donee of a lasting power of attorney granted by the person; and

(d) any deputy appointed for the person by the court.

Such views will also include consideration of the matters set out in s 4(6) as to the subject person's past and present wishes and feelings, as well as the beliefs and values that would be likely to influence his or her decision if he or she had capacity.

CHAPTER 2

THE 'BEST INTERESTS OF THE PATIENT' TEST

2.1 ADULTS WITH CAPACITY

Pursuant to the principle of self-determination, if an adult of sound mind refuses, however unreasonably, to consent to treatment or care, the doctors responsible for his care must give effect to his wishes, even though they do not consider it to be in his best interests to do so: *Airedale NHS Trust v Bland* [1993] AC 789, HL at 864.

The leading cases of *B v An NHS Hospital Trust* [2002] EWHC 429 (Fam) and *Heart of England NHS Foundation Trust and JB (by her litigation friend, the Official Solicitor)* [2014] EWHC 342 clearly enunciate the above principle too.

2.2 ADULTS WHO ARE UNABLE TO CONSENT TO OR REFUSE MEDICAL TREATMENT

A doctor at common law could lawfully operate on or give other treatment to adult patients who are incapable, for one reason or another, of consenting to his doing so, provided that the operation or other treatment concerned was in the best interests of the patient. The operation or other treatment was in the patient's best interests if, but only if, it was carried out in order either to save their lives or to ensure improvement or prevent deterioration in their physical or mental health: *Re F* [1990] 2 AC 1, at 55.

The standard of care of any such medical treatment is be judged by the test laid down in *Bolam v Friern Hospital Management Committee* [1957] 1 WLR 582, per Lord Goff in *Re F (Mental Patient: Sterilisation)* [1990] 2 AC 1, at 78:

> 'I have said that the doctor has to act in the best interests of the assisted person. In the case of routine treatment of mentally disordered persons, there should be little difficulty in applying this principle. In the case of more serious treatment, I recognise that its application may create

problems for the medical profession; however, in making decisions about treatment, the doctor must act in accordance with a responsible and competent body of relevant professional opinion on the principles set out in *Bolam* ...'

By s 1(5) of the Mental Capacity Act 2005 (MCA 2005):

'An act done, or decision made, under this Act for or on behalf of a person who lacks capacity must be done, or made, in his best interests.'

2.3   CHILDREN

There is only one test. The court's prime and paramount consideration is the best interests of the minor: *Re J (A Minor) (Wardship: Medical Treatment)* [1991] 1 FLR 366.

In the decision in *Portsmouth NHS Trust v Wyatt* [2006] 1 FLR 554, the Court of Appeal set out the 'intellectual milestones' for the court to consider. They are:

(1)   the judge must decide what is in the best interests of the child;

(2)   in doing so, the child's welfare is a paramount consideration;

(3)   the judge must look at it from the assumed point of view of the patient;

(4)   there is a strong presumption in favour of the course of action that would prolong life but that presumption is not irrebuttable;

(5)   the term 'best interests' encompasses medical, emotional and all other welfare issues; and

(6)   the court must conduct a balancing exercise in which all relevant factors are weighed.

The court performs accordingly a balancing act bringing all the relevant expert evidence and other evidence before it so as to enable the court to decide whether the proposed treatment is or is not in the minor's best interests.

The parents' view must be weighed and heeded, yet they cannot prevail over the court's view of the ward's best interests.

The decisions by the court as to medical treatment will often be made within the inherent jurisdiction of the High Court in its parens patriae function.

There are circumstances, however, where the Children Act 1989 (CA 1989) will be appropriate for a decision. A parent may seek, for example, a specific issue order under s 8 of the Act. In care proceedings, a decision may have to be made under s 38(6) as to medical examinations or other assessments of the child. In these circumstances, the terms of the Act must apply. These include the paramountcy test and checklist factors under s 1 of the Act.

2.4   THE PRINCIPLE OF THE SANCTITY OF LIFE

The principle of the sanctity of life is a fundamental principle and recognised internationally both in Article 2 of the European Convention for the Protection of Human Rights and Fundamental Freedoms (ECHR) (1953) (Cmd 8969), and in Article 6 of the International Covenant on Civil and Political Rights 1966.

In any case involving medical treatment, the court's high respect for the sanctity of human life imposes a strong presumption in favour of taking all steps capable of preserving it. In due course there will be detailed analysis of two leading cases emphasising the weight placed by the court on the sanctity of life and wish to preserve life if possible: *W v M* [2011] EWHC 2443 (Fam) and *Re E (Medical Treatment Anorexia)* [2012] EWHC 1639 (COP).

The principle, however, is not an absolute one. It does not compel a medical practitioner to treat a patient, who will die if he does not give treatment, contrary to the expressed wishes of the patient. It does not authorise forcible feeding of prisoners who are competent and on hunger strike. It does not compel the temporary keeping alive of patients who are terminally ill where to do so would merely prolong their suffering. On the other hand, it forbids the taking of active measures to cut short the life of a terminally ill patient: *Airedale NHS Trust v Bland* [1993] AC 789, HL at 859. The right to life is not necessarily equated with the right to be kept alive.

2.5   PROLONGATION OF LIFE MAY NOT BE IN THE BEST INTERESTS OF THE PATIENT

It is emphasised in various decisions that the preservation and sanctity of life is presumed to be of the highest importance by the courts. Notwithstanding this presumption, prolongation of life cannot be and is not the sole objective of the courts:

> 'The doctor who is caring for ... a patient cannot, in my opinion, be under an absolute obligation to prolong his life by any means available to him, regardless of the quality of the patient's life. Common humanity requires

otherwise, as do medical ethics and good medical practice ...' *Airedale NHS Trust v Bland* [1993] AC 789, at 867.

The Supreme Court judgment in the case of *Aintree University Hospitals NHS Foundation Trust v James* [2013] UKSC 67 provides significant guidance to the judiciary and legal and medical practitioners generally in relation to this difficult and sensitive legal area. There will be in due course a detailed analysis of the judgment given in this case.

In *Re J (A Minor) (Wardship: Medical Treatment)* [1991] 1 FLR 366, the Court of Appeal considered the case of a child born prematurely with serious brain damage and who originally required resuscitation by means of mechanical ventilation. The child thereafter suffered convulsions, episodes when he stopped breathing and again was placed on a ventilator. The court at first instance approved the recommendation of the consultant neurologist in charge of the case that, in the event of further convulsions requiring resuscitation, the child should not be revived by means of mechanical ventilation unless to do so seemed appropriate to those involved in his care in that situation. The Court of Appeal dismissed an appeal against that decision. It was held that, although there was a strong presumption in favour of the preservation of life, no principle of public policy regarding the sanctity of life displaced the paramountcy of the best interests of the child in question. Lord Taylor LJ said, at 381B:

> 'The plight of baby J is appalling and the problem facing the court in the exercise of its wardship jurisdiction is of the greatest difficulty. When should the court rule against the giving of treatment aimed at prolonging life?'

At 383H, he further said:

> 'I consider the correct approach is for the court to judge the quality of life the child would have to endure if given the treatment, and decide whether in all the circumstances such a life would be so afflicted as to be intolerable to that child.'

The approach of Lord Taylor was echoed by Sir Stephen Brown, the President of the Family Division, in *Re R* [1996] 2 FLR 99, at 107. The test throughout adopted by the court is to determine what is in the best interests of the patient. In *Re R*, the court made clear that the test was the same whether the patient was a child or, as in that case, an adult who was critically handicapped.

The extent of the dilemma for the courts as to what may be in the best interests of a patient is evidenced by the case of *Re T (Wardship:*

Medical Treatment) [1997] 1 FLR 502. The Court of Appeal there emphasised that to prolong life was not the sole objective of the court and to require it at the expense of other considerations might not be in a child's best interests. Butler-Sloss LJ took the view that the mother and baby 'were one for the purpose of this unusual case'. The baby was suffering from a life-threatening liver defect and, without a transplant, would not live beyond the age of two and a half. The medical opinion was that the prospects of success of a transplant were good. The parents did not wish the operation to take place. The issue for the court was whether to give consent for the operation and thereby to overrule the decision of the parents. The mother, knowing that the baby had only a short time to live if no operation was performed, had focused on the present peaceful life of the baby without the pain, stress and upset of intrusive surgery against a future with the operation and treatment taking place. The conclusion of the Court of Appeal was that the baby's best interests required that his future treatment be left in the hands of his parents.

2.6 END OF LIFE CARE: WHETHER TO GIVE LIFE-SUSTAINING TREATMENT AND THE BEST INTERESTS OF THE PATIENT

Any decision whether or not to give life-sustaining treatment in the absence of clear instructions from the patient himself or herself, must be made in the best interests of the patient.

There are broadly two categories in which to consider the patient's best interests.

There are cases in which, having regard to all the circumstances, including in particular the poor quality of life which may be prolonged for the patient if the treatment is successful, it may be judged not to be in the patient's best interests to provide it or to continue to provide it. *Re J (A Minor) (Wardship: Medical Treatment)* [1991] 1 FLR 366, is an example of this type of case. It concerned a child who suffered severe brain damage. The most optimistic view was that he would develop spastic quadriplegia, that he was likely to be blind and deaf and that he would never be able to speak or develop even limited intellectual abilities. He was not dying or on the point of death. He had previously spent periods on a ventilator. The question was what should be done if baby J suffered another collapse. The doctors unanimously recommended that, in that event, there should be no mechanical re-ventilation on the basis that it was an invasive and painful procedure which might itself cause deterioration and at best could only bring about minimal improvement. The Court of Appeal endorsed the decision at first instance, holding that it would not be in the child's best interests to subject him to a mechanical ventilator if he stopped breathing, whilst at the same time leaving the doctors free to take more active measures to preserve the child's life if the situation improved. In this category of case, the court will weigh up all the relevant considerations and reach a decision as to whether the proposed medical treatment is in the best interests of the patient.

In *Re J*, Taylor LJ, at 383H summarised his approach to the weighing exercise:

> 'I consider the correct approach is for the Court to judge the quality of life the child would have to endure if given the treatment, and decide whether in all the circumstances such a life would be so afflicted as to be intolerable to that child. I say "to that child" because the test should not be whether the life would be tolerable to the decider. The test must be whether the child in question, if capable of exercising sound judgment, would consider the life tolerable. This is the approach adopted by McKenzie J in *Re Superintendent of Family and Child Service and Dawson* [1983] 145 DLR (3d) 610 in the passage at page 620 ...'

There are then cases such as that of Anthony Bland where life-sustaining treatment can be of no benefit to the patient because he is totally insensate and there is no prospect of improvement in his condition. As was said in the House of Lords in *Airedale NHS Trust v Bland* [1993] AC 789, in this situation there is in reality no weighing operation to be performed. The justification and lawfulness for the initial life-sustaining treatment in *Bland* was the hope and expectation that there might be some improvement in the patient's condition or hope of recovery, however imperfect. Pursuant to the rationale and reasoning in *Re F (Mental Patient: Sterilisation)* [1990] 2 AC 1, it was lawful and it was the duty of the doctors to treat Anthony Bland accordingly in his best interests by taking all steps to preserve his life. However, once the justification for such medical treatment was gone, because there was no prospect of recovery or improvement, it could no longer be the duty of the doctors, nor perhaps was it lawful for them, to continue such medical treatment as being in his best interest:

> 'If I am right so far in my analysis, the critical decision to be made is whether it is in the best interests of Anthony Bland to continue the invasive medical care involved in artificial feeding. That question is not the same as, "is it in Anthony Bland's best interests that he should die?" The latter question assumes that it is lawful to perpetuate the patient's life: such perpetuation of life can only be achieved if it is lawful to continue to invade the bodily integrity of the patient by invasive medical care. Unless

the doctor has reached the affirmative conclusion that it is in the patient's best interests to continue the invasive care, such care must cease': per Lord Browne-Wilkinson, *Airedale NHS Trust v Bland* [1993] AC 789, HL at 884.

The court has been confronted with very similar issues to those above in cases where the patient has been suffering from minimal consciousness, examples of which include the following: the case of *W v M* [2011] EWHC 2443 concerned an adult patient in a state of minimal consciousness; as can be seen at paragraph 71 of the judgment; the case of *Re OT* [2009] EWHC 633 (Fam) concerned a child patient who was minimally conscious.

2.7   THE TEST OF 'BEST INTERESTS' UNDER MCA 2005, S 4

The statutory test of best interests in relation to adults who lack capacity is set out within the detailed terms of s 4 of MCA 2005. Chapter 4 of this book in relation to MCA 2005 will provide a more detailed analysis of this statutory provision, as well as others within the statute.

The Supreme Court case of *Aintree University Hospitals NHS Foundation Trust v James* [2013] UKSC 67 has provided to the judiciary and legal and medical practitioners generally significant guidance as to the interpretation of the terms of the Act, including as to s 4.

At paragraph 39 of the Supreme Court judgment Lady Hale says:

> 'The most that can be said, therefore, is that in considering the best interests of this particular patient at this particular time, decision-makers must look at his welfare in the widest sense, not just medical but social and psychological; they must consider the nature of the medical treatment in question, what it involves and its prospects of success; they must consider what the outcome of that treatment for the patient is likely to be; they must try and put themselves in the place of the individual patient and ask what his attitude to the treatment is or would be likely to be; and they must consult others who are looking after him or interested in his welfare, in particular for their view of what his attitude would be.'

Section 4(6) specifically requires, in determining best interests, consideration of (a) the subject person's past and present wishes and feelings (and, in particular, any relevant written statements made by him when he had capacity); (b) the beliefs and values that would be likely to influence his decision if he had capacity; and (c) the other factors that he would be likely to consider if he were able to do so.

The Supreme Court in the case of *Aintree* disagreed with the view that the test of the patient's wishes and feelings was an objective one, what the reasonable patient would think.

Lady Hale said at paragraph 45 of the judgment:

> 'Finally, insofar as Sir Alan Ward and Arden LJ were suggesting that the test of the patient's wishes and feelings was an objective one, what the reasonable patient would think, again I respectfully disagree. The purpose of the best interests test is to consider matters from the patient's point of view. That is not to say that his wishes must prevail, any more than those of a fully capable patient must prevail. We cannot always have what we want. Nor will it always be possible to ascertain what an incapable patient's wishes are. Even if it is possible to determine what his views were in the past, they might well have changed in the light of the stresses and strains of his current predicament. In this case, the highest it could be put was, as counsel had agreed, that "It was likely that Mr James would want treatment up to the point where it became hopeless". But insofar as it is possible to ascertain the patient's wishes and feelings, his beliefs and values or the things which were important to him, it is those which should be taken into account because they are a component in making the choice which is right for him as an individual human being.'

CHAPTER 3

THE DOCTOR AND THE COURTS

3.1 THE INTERFACE BETWEEN THE DOCTOR AND THE COURTS

The relationship between and the respective roles of the doctor and the courts is well and succinctly set out by Lord Goff in *Airedale NHS Trust v Bland* [1993] AC 789, HL at 871 as follows:

> 'The truth is that, in the course of their work, doctors frequently have to make decisions which may affect the continued survival of their patients, and are in reality far more experienced in matters of this kind than are the judges. It is nevertheless the function of the judges to state the legal principles upon which the lawfulness of the actions of doctors depend; but in the end the decisions to be made in individual cases must rest with the doctors themselves. In these circumstances, what is required is a sensitive understanding by both the judges and the doctors of each other's respective functions, and in particular a determination by the judges not merely to understand the problems facing the medical profession in cases of this kind, but also to regard their professional standards with respect. Mutual understanding between the doctors and the judges is the best way to ensure the evolution of a sensitive and sensible legal framework for the treatment and care of patients, with a sound ethical base, in the interest of the patients themselves.'

3.2 THE OBJECTIVES OF MEDICAL TREATMENT AND CARE

The objectives of medical treatment and care are to benefit the patient. They include:

(1) preventing the occurrence of injury, deformity or other illness before they occur;

(2) to cure illness when it does occur;

(3) where illness cannot be cured, to prevent or delay deterioration of the patient's condition;

(4) to relieve pain and suffering in body and mind.

Since the advance of medical technology, the question has arisen as to whether and to what extent it is or should be an object of medical treatment to prolong a patient's life by any means available to the doctor, regardless of the quality of the patient's life.

The meaning of medical treatment for the purposes of the Act is set out in s 145 of the Mental Health Act 1983 (MHA 1983).

The statutory duty of the Secretary of State to provide treatment and facilities for the prevention of illness and the cure of persons suffering from that illness are set out under s 1(1) and s 3(1) of the National Health Service Act 1977. Section 13 of the Act provides for directions to be given to health authorities to exercise on the Secretary of State's behalf such functions under the statute relating to the Health Service as he may specify.

3.3   THE DUTY OF THE DOCTOR

A medical practitioner owes a fundamental duty to his or her patient, subject to obtaining any necessary consent, to treat the patient in accordance with his or her own best clinical judgment: *Re J (A Minor) (Medical Treatment)* [1992] 2 FLR 165, at 172, 173.

However, such a duty to act in his or her patient's best interests will be qualified if an adult patient of sound mind refuses, however unreasonably, to consent to treatment or care. Even if the effect of the refusal may be serious damage to the patient's health or, at worst, death, the doctor responsible for his or her care must give effect to his or her wishes, even though he or she does not consider it to be in the patient's best interests to do so. It has been held, for example, in *Nancy B v Hotel-Dieu De Quebec* [1992] 86 DLR (4d) 385, that a patient of sound mind may, if properly informed, require that life support should be discontinued. The basis in law for qualifying the doctor's duty accordingly is that the principle of the sanctity of human life must yield to the principle of self-determination.

The doctor's duty must also be qualified where the patient's refusal to give his consent to treatment has been expressed at an earlier date (before, for example, he became unconscious or otherwise incapable of communicating it); although, in such circumstances, special care may be necessary to ensure that the prior refusal of consent is still properly to be regarded as applicable in the circumstances which have subsequently occurred: *Airedale NHS Trust v Bland* [1993] AC 789, HL at 864.

It is recognised in relation to the duty of a doctor that the function of a doctor per Lord Donaldson in *Re J (A Minor) (Medical Treatment)* [1992] 2 FLR 165, at 173:

'is not a limited technical one of repairing or servicing a body. They are treating people in a real life context'.

A material and helpful document in relation to all of the above is the Guidance produced by the General Medical Council of 2 June 2008 entitled: 'Consent: patients and doctors making decisions together'.

As was stated in the Court of Appeal case of *R (Tracey) v Cambridge University Hospitals NHS Foundation Trust* [2014] EWCA Civ 822 at paragraph 98 of the judgment:

'In the context of this court's decision, it may be helpful to re-consider the oft repeated GMC guidance that was endorsed by Lord Phillips of Worth Matravers MR in *R (Burke) v General Medical Council* [2006] QB 273 at [50] which can be summarised as follows:

i) The doctor, exercising his professional clinical judgment, decides what treatment options are clinically indicated;
ii) The doctor offers those treatment options to the patient, explaining the risks, benefits and side effects of the same;
iii) The patient then decides whether he wishes to accept any of the treatment options and, if so, which one;
iv) If the patient chooses one of the options offered, the doctor will provide it;
v) If the patient refuses all of the options he may do so for reasons which are irrational or for no reason at all or he may inform the doctor that he wishes to have a form of treatment that the doctor has not offered;
vi) If, after discussion with the patient, the doctor decides that the form of treatment requested is not clinically indicated he is not required to provide it although he should offer to arrange a second opinion.'

3.3.1 The standard of care by a doctor in relation to medical treatment

The standard of care required of a doctor and, subject to obtaining any necessary consent, is that laid down in *Bolam v Friern Hospital Management Committee* [1957] 1 WLR 582, namely that a patient should be treated or cared for in accordance with good medical practice recognised as appropriate by a competent body of professional opinion.

Section 1(5) of the MCA 2005 states that: 'An act done or decision made, under this Act for or on behalf of a person who lacks capacity must be done, or made, in his best interests'.

Attached at the end of this Chapter is the Medical Innovation Bill; it is simply worded and self-explanatory but would have significant ramifications if enacted in relation to the scope and remit of medical treatment.

3.3.2 A doctor cannot be required to treat a patient (whether adult or child) in a particular way and against his or her clinical judgment

In *Re C (Medical Treatment)* [1998] 1 FLR 384, Sir Stephen Brown, President of the Family Division, was concerned with a girl aged 16 months who was suffering from a desperately serious disease. It was a 'no chance' situation within the then *Framework of Practice: Withholding or Withdrawing Life-Saving Treatment in Children* published by the Royal College of Paediatrics and Child Health.

Her disease was so severe that life-sustaining treatment would simply delay death without significantly alleviating suffering. The doctors, accordingly, wished to withdraw ventilation and did not believe that reinstating ventilation, even in the highly probable event of the child's further respiratory relapse, would be in her best interests. The parents were prepared for ventilation to be withdrawn to see whether C would survive without it, but wished it to be reinstated in the event of further respiratory relapse. The hospital sought and was granted the court's approval for the withdrawal of ventilation and non-resuscitation in the event of respiratory arrest. The President of the Family Division was unwilling to require the doctors to undertake a course of treatment which they themselves were unwilling to undertake.

In *Re R (A Minor)* [1992] 1 FLR 190, CA at 200, Lord Donaldson said:

> 'No doctor can be required to treat a child, whether by the court in the exercise of its wardship jurisdiction, by the parents, by the child or anyone else. The decision whether to treat is dependent upon an exercise of his own professional judgment, subject only to the threshold requirement that, save in exceptional cases usually of emergency, he has the consent of someone who has authority to give that consent.'

In *Re J (A Minor) (Wardship: Medical Treatment)* [1991] 1 FLR 366, at 370, again Lord Donaldson put the matter as follows:

'No one can *dictate* the treatment to be given to the child – neither court, parents nor doctors. There are checks and balances. The doctors can recommend treatment A in preference to treatment B. They can also refuse to adopt treatment C on the grounds that it is medically contraindicated, or for some other reason is a treatment which they could not conscientiously administer. The court or parents, for their part, can refuse to consent to treatment A or B or both, but cannot insist upon treatment C. The inevitable and desirable result is that choice of treatment is, in some measure, a joint decision of the doctors and the court or parents.'

In *Re J (A Minor) (Medical Treatment)* [1992] 2 FLR 165, the court was concerned with a child aged 16 months who was severely handicapped both mentally and physically. His expectation of life was short. He was with foster parents. His breathing was assisted by oxygen. The consultant paediatrician in charge of his case said that it was not medically appropriate to intervene with intensive therapeutic measures such as artificial ventilation if the child were to suffer a life-threatening event. The local authority, supported by the mother, asked the court to require the health authority to continue to provide all available treatment, including 'intensive resuscitation'. The local authority was granted an interim injunction by a judge requiring the health authority, if the baby suffered a life-threatening collapse, to 'cause such measures (including, if so required to prolong his life, artificial ventilation) to be applied to the child for so long as they are capable of prolonging his life'.

This order was set aside by the Court of Appeal and Lord Justice Balcombe said, at 175:

'... I agree with the Master of the Rolls that I can conceive of no situation where it would be a proper exercise of the jurisdiction to make such an order as was made in the present case: that is to order a doctor, whether directly or indirectly, to treat a child in a manner contrary to his or her clinical judgment. I would go further. I find it difficult to conceive of a situation where it would be a proper exercise of the jurisdiction to make an order positively requiring a doctor to adopt a particular course of treatment in relation to a child, unless the doctor himself or herself was asking the Court to make such an order. Usually all the Court is asked, or needs to do is to authorise a particular course of treatment where the person or body whose consent is requisite is unable or unwilling to do so.'

At paragraph 18 of the judgment of Lady Hale in the case of *Aintree University Hospitals NHS Foundation Trust v James* [2013] UKSC 67, she says:

'The judge began in the right place. He was careful to stress that the case was not about a general power to order how the doctors should treat their patient. This Act is concerned with enabling the court to do for the patient what he could do for himself if of full capacity, but it goes no further. On an application under this Act, therefore, the court has no greater powers than the patient would have if he were of full capacity. The judge said: "A patient cannot order a doctor to give a particular form of treatment, although he may refuse it. The court's position is no different" (para 14). In *Re J (A Minor) (Child in Care: Medical Treatment)* [1991] Fam 33, at 48, Lord Donaldson MR held that the court could not "require the [health] authority to follow a particular course of treatment. What the court can do is to withhold consent to treatment of which it disapproves and it can express its approval of other treatment proposed by the authority and its doctors." He repeated that view in *Re J (A Minor) (Child in Care: Medical Treatment)* [1993] Fam 15, at 26–27, when it was clearly the ratio decidendi of the case. To similar effect is *R v Cambridge District Health Authority, ex p B* [1995] 1 WLR 898, where the court would not interfere with the health authority's decision to refuse to fund further treatment of a child with leukaemia. More recently, in *R (Burke) v General Medical Council* [2005] EWCA Civ 1003, [2006] QB 273, Lord Phillips MR accepted the proposition of the General Medical Council that if a doctor concludes that the treatment which a patient wants is "not clinically indicated he is not required (ie he is under no legal obligation) to provide it" (para 50), and "Ultimately, however, a patient cannot demand that a doctor administer a treatment which the doctor considers is adverse to the patient's clinical needs" (para 55). Of course, there are circumstances in which a doctor's common law duty of care towards his patient requires him to administer a particular treatment, but it is not the role of the Court of Protection to decide that. Nor is that Court concerned with the legality of NHS policy or guidelines for the provision of particular treatments. Its role is to decide whether a particular treatment is in the best interests of a patient who is incapable of making the decision for himself.'

3.4   ALLOCATION OF RESOURCES AND THE CHOICE OF MEDICATION

This aspect in relation to medical treatment was raised in the case of *R v Cambridge District Health Authority ex parte B* [1995] 1 FLR 1055. The facts were as follows. In January of 1995, the child, aged 10 years, suffered a relapse of acute myeloid leukaemia. Since first becoming ill, five years previously, she had been treated with two courses of chemotherapy, total body irradiation and a bone marrow transplant. The doctors who had treated her and other experts consulted by them were of the opinion that the child had a very short time to live and that no further treatment could usefully be administered. Unwilling to accept that view, the father obtained further medical opinion to the effect that a further course of chemotherapy might be undertaken with a chance of success estimated at 10 to 20 per cent at a cost of £15,000, followed, if that was successful, by a second transplant with a similar chance of success, at a cost of £60,000. The respondent district health authority, taking into account that assessment together with the opinion of the child's medical advisers and the Department of Health guidelines on the funding of treatment not of a proven nature, stated that it was unwilling to fund further treatment.

Its decision was based on two grounds. First, that the proposed treatment would cause considerable suffering and not be in the child's best interests. Secondly, that the substantial expenditure on treatment with such a small prospect of success and of an experimental nature would not be an effective use of limited resources, bearing in mind the present and future needs of other patients. The child applied by her father as next friend by way of judicial review for an order of certiorari quashing that decision. The judge at first instance allowed the application and quashed the respondent's decision. The district health authority appealed. The Court of Appeal reversed the judge's decision and allowed the appeal of the district health authority.

The Court of Appeal made quite clear that, in judicial review proceedings, the only function of the court was to rule upon the lawfulness of the decision. The courts could not be arbiters as to the merits of cases of this kind. The powers of the court, it was held, were not such as to enable it to substitute its own decision in a matter of this kind for that of the health authority which was legally charged with making the decision. The Court of Appeal was unable to say that the district health authority, on the particular facts, had acted in a way that exceeded its powers or which was unreasonable in the legal sense.

It is clear, and important to note, that funding was not raised as the issue in itself which lay behind the district health authority's decision. Insofar as it was raised as a factor, and no doubt an important factor, the authority took into account the Department of Health guidelines on the funding of treatment not of a proven nature. The treatment of the child proposed by the father was described by Sir Thomas Bingham MR in the Court of Appeal as being 'at the frontier of medical science', even if the word 'experimental' was not the appropriate word: it was a treatment, he said, unlike many courses of treatment, which did not have a well-tried track record of success.

The decision of the district health authority was based on an amalgam of factors, a clinical assessment by the child's medical advisers and an assessment of the medical treatment proposed by the father, the child's welfare as well as the funding element.

Sir Thomas Bingham MR, in the Court of Appeal, was certainly willing to entertain the consideration that difficulties in financial resources could legitimately be raised as a factor in the decision by the health authority:

> 'I have no doubt that in a perfect world any treatment which a patient, or a patient's family, sought would be provided if doctors were willing to give it, no matter how much it cost, particularly when a life was potentially at stake. It would however, in my view, be shutting one's eyes to the real world if the court were to proceed on the basis that we do live in such a world. It is common knowledge that health authorities of all kinds are constantly pressed to make ends meet. They cannot pay their nurses as much as they would like; they cannot provide all the treatments they would like; they cannot purchase all the extremely expensive medical equipment they would like; they cannot carry out all the research they would like; they cannot build all the hospitals and specialist units they would like. Difficult and agonising judgments have to be made as to how a limited budget is best allocated to the maximum advantage of the maximum number of patients. That is not a judgment which the court can make. In my judgment, it is not something that a health authority such as this authority can be fairly criticised for not advancing before the court.'

It is trite but nevertheless an important point to make that, insofar as the allocation of resources is raised in any case before the courts, the weight to be given to such issue, accordingly, will depend on the particular facts of the case and the reasons for any decisions made.

References in case-law are scant to the question of the allocation of resources and conflicting choices. It is to be noted that, obiter in *Re J (A Minor) (Wardship: Medical Treatment)* [1991] 1 FLR 366, CA at 370G, Lord Donaldson said:

> 'In an imperfect world, resources will always be limited and on occasion agonising choices will have to be made in allocating those resources to particular patients.'

The question of the allocation of limited healthcare resources was, however, central to the case of *R v North West Lancashire Health Authority ex parte A, D and G* (unreported) 21 December 1998 (High Court). The applicants were three transsexuals who were challenging the decision of the health authority in question not to fund gender re-assignment treatment for themselves, including surgery for the removal of the male sex organs. The court was requested to consider policy documents of the authority, including one which listed a number of procedures which would not be purchased 'except in cases of overriding clinical need'. These included gender reassignment, cosmetic plastic surgery and reversal of sterilisation. The applicants' case was that they had, on medical advice, a demonstrable clinical need for the required surgery and treatment and that the health authority's policy (despite the wording 'except in cases of overriding clinical need') was in reality a blanket ban on such treatment. The health authority's case, again on medical advice, was that there was no 'overriding clinical need' which would justify the allocation of its limited resources to the treatment requested.

The judge accepted that, on the authorities, it was not for the court to seek to allocate scarce resources in a tight budget. The court was, however, entitled to consider the lawfulness of the authority's decision and policy in the context of the authority's duty to exercise on behalf of the Secretary of State duties under ss 1(1) and 3(1) of the National Health Service Act 1977. These include the duty to provide treatment and facilities for the prevention of illness and the cure of persons suffering from such illness. Much evidence turned on the nature, medically, of transsexualism or Gender Identity Dysphoria (GID) and the proper treatment for it.

The judge concluded that the health authority had reached its decisions without sufficient consideration of the question of what is proper treatment for what is recognised as an illness. Further, the court determined that the decisions and policy, including the words 'except in cases of overriding clinical need' – unclear and uncertain as they were – unlawfully fettered the authority's exercise of its discretion in discharging its statutory duty (referred to above) to provide medical treatment. Accordingly, the authority was held to have acted unlawfully and irrationally in its decisions and relief was granted in judicial review as sought by the applicants. The application of the authority for leave to appeal to the Court of Appeal was refused by the judge, on the basis that, if any such leave was to be sought, application would have accordingly to be made to the Court of Appeal.

It is made clear within the Supreme Court judgment in the *Aintree* case ([2013] UKSC 67) that the Court of Protection is not concerned with the legality of NHS policy or guidelines for the provision of particular treatments. Its role is to decide whether a particular treatment is in the best interests of a patient who is incapable of making the decision for himself.

APPENDIX TO CHAPTER 3

MEDICAL INNOVATION BILL

A BILL TO Make provision about innovation in medical treatment.

BE IT ENACTED by the Queen's most Excellent Majesty, by and with the advice and consent of the Lords Spiritual and Temporal, and Commons, in this present Parliament assembled, and by the authority of the same, as follows: –

1 Responsible innovation

(1) The purpose of this section is to encourage responsible innovation in medical treatment (and accordingly to deter innovation which is not responsible).

(2) It is not negligent for a doctor to depart from the existing range of accepted medical treatments for a condition, in the circumstances set out in subsection (3), if the decision to do so is taken responsibly.

(3) Those circumstances are where, in the doctor's opinion -

    (a) it is unclear whether the medical treatment that the doctor proposes to carry out has or would have the support of a responsible body of medical opinion, or

    (b) the proposed treatment does not or would not have such support.

(4) A responsible decision for the purposes of subsection (2) is one which is based on –

    (a) the doctor's opinion that there are plausible reasons why the proposed treatment might be effective, and

    (b) consideration by the doctor of –

        (i) all the matters listed in subsection (5), and

        (ii) any other matter that appears to the doctor to be appropriate to take into account in order to reach a clinical judgement.

(5) The matters mentioned in subsection (4)(b)(i) are –

    (a) the relative risks that are, or can reasonably be expected to be, associated with the proposed treatment and other treatments,

    (b) the likely success rates, in the doctor's reasonable judgement, of the proposed treatment and other treatments,

    (c) the likely consequences, in the doctor's reasonable judgement, of carrying out, or failing to carry out, the proposed treatment and other treatments,

    (d) opinions or requests expressed by or in relation to the patient, and

    (e)   opinions expressed by colleagues whose opinions appear to the doctor to be appropriate to take into account.

(6) A responsible decision for the purposes of subsection (2) is one made in accordance with a process which is accountable, transparent and allows full consideration by the doctor of all relevant matters.

(7) The factors that may be taken into account in determining whether a process satisfies the requirements of subsection (6) include, in particular –

    (a)   whether the doctor has discussed the proposed treatment with the patient and given the patient the explanation that the doctor would in the circumstances be expected to give of the doctor's reasons for carrying out the treatment,

    (b)   whether the decision has been made within a multi-disciplinary team, and

    (c)   whether the doctor has given notification in advance to the doctor's responsible officer (if any).

(8) Nothing in this section permits a doctor –

    (a)   to provide treatment without consent that is otherwise required by law, or

    (b)   to carry out treatment for the purposes of research or for any purpose other than the patient's best interests.

2 Interpretation

(1) In this Act –

    (a)   "doctor" means a registered medical practitioner;

    (b)   a reference to treatment of a condition includes a reference to its management (and a reference to treatment includes a reference to inaction).

(2) The reference in section 1(7)(c) to a doctor's responsible officer is to the responsible officer (or one of the responsible officers) nominated or appointed under section 45A of the Medical Act 1983 for a designated body with which the doctor has a prescribed connection for the purposes of section 45A of that Act.

3 Extent, commencement and short title

(1) This Act extends to England and Wales only.

(2) Sections 1 and 2 come into force on such day or days as the Secretary of State may by order made by statutory instrument appoint.

(3) An order under subsection (2) may –

    (a)   appoint different days for different purposes;

    (b)   make transitional or saving provision.

(4) This section comes into force on the day on which this Act is passed.

(5) This Act may be cited as the Medical Innovation Act 2014.

CHAPTER 4

THE MENTAL CAPACITY ACT 2005

4.1 THE GENERAL PRINCIPLES OF THE ACT

The Mental Capacity Act 2005 (MCA 2005) introduced a new legislative framework dealing with loss of mental capacity, following a number of consultation documents and reports of the Law Commission.

The MCA 2005 provides for decisions to be made on behalf of people who are unable to make decisions for themselves. Everyone who makes a decision under the Act must do so in the best interests of the person concerned.

The Act is concerned with enabling the court to do for the patient what he could do for himself or herself if of full capacity; on an application under the Act, the court has no greater powers than the patient would have if he or she were of full capacity.

As was stated by the Supreme Court in the case of *Aintree University Hospitals NHS Foundation Trust v James* [2013] UKSC 67, 'the role of the court is to decide whether a particular treatment is in the best interests of a patient who is incapable of making the decision for himself'.

Section 1 (the principles) provides:

'(1) The following principles apply for the purposes of this Act.

(2) A person must be assumed to have capacity unless it is established that he lacks capacity.

(3) A person is not to be treated as unable to make a decision unless all practicable steps to help him to do so have been taken without success.

(4) A person is not to be treated as unable to make a decision merely because he makes an unwise decision.

(5) An act done, or decision made, under this Act for or on behalf of a person who lacks capacity must be done, or made, in his best interests.

(6) Before the act is done, or the decision is made, regard must be had to whether the purpose for which it is needed can be as effectively achieved in a way that is less restrictive of the person's rights and freedom of action.'

The 2005 Act marked a radical change in the treatment of persons lacking capacity.

First, it brought together under one common statutory framework the powers of the court to make decisions about an incapacitated person's personal welfare and property.

Secondly, it applies not only to decisions that the court might make, but also to decisions that others (carers, doctors, deputies) might make.

Thirdly, there is an assumption that a person has capacity unless it is established that he lacks capacity. As evidenced too for example by ss 1(3), 1(6), 4(3) and 4(4) of the Act, the statute seeks to emphasise throughout the need for individuals to act and to be assisted to act autonomously in their decision making to the best extent possible.

Fourthly, the test of incapacity is finely calibrated, as will be further considered below.

Fifthly, the overarching principle is that any decision under the Act made on behalf of a person lacking capacity must be made in his or her best interests, again as will be further considered below.

4.2 THE STATUTORY TEST OF INCAPACITY

Section 2(1) provides that:

'A person lacks capacity in relation to a matter if at the material time he is unable to make a decision for himself in relation to the matter because of an impairment of, or a disturbance in the functioning of, the mind or brain.'

Section 3 elaborates the meaning of inability to make a decision. It provides, so far as relevant:

'(1) For the purposes of section 2, a person is unable to make a decision for himself if he is unable –
(a) to understand the information relevant to the decision,
(b) to retain that information,

(c)   to use or weigh that information as part of the process of making the decision, or

(d)   to communicate his decision (whether by talking, using sign language or any other means).

...

(4) The information relevant to a decision includes information about the reasonably foreseeable consequences of –

(a)   deciding one way or another, or

(b)   failing to make the decision.'

4.3   THE TEST OF INCAPACITY

The test of incapacity is finely calibrated. The Act recognises that the test of incapacity is issue specific. A person may well have capacity in relation to some matters, while lacking capacity as regards others. A person's capacity may also vary from time to time. One of the ingredients in the test is to ask whether a person is able to 'use or weigh' information in making a decision (s 1(3)(c)). In their report the Law Commission explained the thinking behind this (at paragraph 3.17). They said:

'There are cases where the person concerned can understand information but where the effects of a mental disability prevent him or her from using that information in the decision-making process. We explained in Consultation Paper No 128 that certain compulsive conditions cause people who are quite able to absorb information to arrive, inevitably, at decisions which are unconnected to the information or their understanding of it. An example is the anorexic who decides not to eat ... We originally suggested that such cases could be described as cases where incapacity resulted from the inability to make a "true choice". Common to all these cases is the fact that the person's eventual decision is divorced from his or her ability to understand the relevant information. Emphasising that the person must be able to use the information which he or she has successfully understood in the decision-making process deflects the complications of asking whether a person needs to "appreciate" information as well as understand it. A decision based on a compulsion, the overpowering will of a third party or any other inability to act on relevant information as a result of mental disability is not a decision made by a person with decision-making capacity.'

The case of *MM (An Adult)* [2007] EWHC 2003 (Fam) before Munby J (as he then was) provides a helpful detailed analysis in relation to the issues concerning determining capacity and how questions of capacity are issue specific.

The Court of Appeal case of *RB v Brighton and Hove Council* [2014] EWCA Civ 561 emphasises that the starting point for adjudging capacity has to be the plain words of the Act.

4.4 THE STATUTORY PROVISIONS AS TO BEST INTERESTS

Section 4 of the Act expands on the concept of 'best interests' referred to in s 1(5), namely that any decision made on behalf of a person lacking capacity must be made in his or her best interests.

Section 4 provides (so far as relevant):

'(1) In determining for the purposes of this Act what is in a person's best interests, the person making the determination must not make it merely on the basis of –
(a)   the person's age or appearance, or
(b)   a condition of his, or an aspect of his behaviour, which might lead others to make unjustified assumptions about what might be in his best interests.

(2) The person making the determination must consider all the relevant circumstances and, in particular, take the following steps.

(3) He must consider –
(a)   whether it is likely that the person will at some time have capacity in relation to the matter in question, and
(b)   if it appears likely that he will, when that is likely to be.

(4) He must, so far as reasonably practicable, permit and encourage the person to participate, or to improve his ability to participate, as fully as possible in any act done for him and·any decision affecting him.

(5) Where the determination relates to life-sustaining treatment he must not, in considering whether the treatment is in the best interests of the person concerned, be motivated by a desire to bring about his death.

(6) He must consider, so far as is reasonably ascertainable –
(a)   the person's past and present wishes and feelings (and, in particular, any relevant written statement made by him when he had capacity),
(b)   the beliefs and values that would be likely to influence his decision if he had capacity, and
(c)   the other factors that he would be likely to consider if he were able to do so.

(7) He must take into account, if it is practicable and appropriate to consult them, the views of –

(a) anyone named by the person as someone to be consulted on the matter in question or on matters of that kind,

(b) anyone engaged in caring for the person or interested in his welfare,

(c) any donee of a lasting power of attorney granted by the person, and

(d) any deputy appointed for the person by the court,

as to what would be in the person's best interests and, in particular, as to the matters mentioned in subsection (6).'

4.5 THE TEST AS TO BEST INTERESTS

Every assessment of the best interests of a person under MCA 2005 is by its very nature fact specific. There is no hierarchy in the list of factors in s 4, and the weight to be attached to the various factors will depend upon the individual circumstances: *Re M (Statutory Will), ITW v Z* [2009] EWHC 2525 (Fam), at [32].

The weight to be attached to the various factors will, inevitably, differ depending on the individual circumstances of the particular case. A feature or factor which in one case may carry great, possibly preponderant weight may in another, superficially similar case, carry much less, or even very little, weight: *Re M (Statutory Will), ITW v Z*. There may, in the particular case, be one or more features or factors which, as Thorpe LJ frequently put it, are of 'magnetic importance' in influencing or even determining the outcome of the case: *Re M (Statutory Will), ITW v Z*.

Any benefit of treatment has to be balanced and considered in the light of any additional suffering or detriment the treatment option would entail: *Re A (Male Sterilisation)* [2000] 1 FLR 549, at 560.

The treatment applied for in declaratory relief must be proportionate and the least restrictive step, with risk management being better than invasive treatment: *A Local Authority v K* [2013] EWHC 242 (COP).

The decision must be made in the best interests of the person lacking capacity, not in the interests of others although the interests of others may indirectly be a factor insofar as they relate to that person's best interests: *Re Y (Mental Incapacity: Bone Marrow Transplant)* [2007] 2 FCR 172 and *Re A (Male Sterilisation)* [2000] 1 FLR 549.

The court is not tied to any clinical assessment of what is in the best interests of the person lacking capacity and should reach its own conclusion on the evidence before it: *Trust A and Trust B v H (An Adult Patient)* [2006] EWHC 1230. The decision is for the judge not the expert. Their roles are distinct and it is for the judge to make the final decision: *A Local Authority v K, D and L* [2005] 1 FLR 851. The overarching statutory principle is that any decision made on behalf of a person lacking capacity must be made in his or her best interests.

The structured decision-making process set out under s 4 of the Act applies to all decisions, whether great or small, to be made on behalf of persons lacking capacity. Moreover, it is a decision-making process which must be followed, not only by the court, but by anyone who takes decisions on that person's behalf. This includes carers, doctors, and deputies.

In making his decision, the decision maker must consider 'all relevant circumstances'. The Act expressly directs the decision maker to take a number of steps before reaching a decision. These include encouraging the person lacking capacity to participate in the decision. He must also 'consider' the person's past and present wishes, and his beliefs and values and must 'take into account' the views of third parties as to what would be in that person's best interests.

Having gone through those steps, the decision maker must then form a value judgment of his own giving effect to the paramount statutory instruction that any decision must be made in that person's best interests.

The judgment of the Supreme Court in *Aintree University Hospitals NHS Foundation Trust v James* [2013] UKSC 67 is clear that in weighing the best interests of a particular patient, they must consider his or her welfare in the widest sense.

As is stated at paragraph 39 of the above Supreme Court judgment:

> 'The most that can be said, therefore, is that in considering the best interests of this particular patient at this particular time, decision makers must look at his welfare in the widest sense, not just medical but social and psychological; they must consider the nature of the medical treatment in question, what it involves and its prospects of success; they must consider what the outcome of treatment for the patient is likely to be; they must try and put themselves in the place of the individual patient and ask what his attitude to the treatment is or would be likely to be; and they must consult others who are looking after him or interested in his welfare, in particular for their view of what his attitude would be.'

4.6 THE WISHES AND FEELINGS OF P

There is to be considered further the issue of the wishes and feelings of the person lacking capacity, and the approach to be taken in this regard. Section 4 of the Act requires the decision maker to consider the present wishes and feelings of the person whose best interests are to be determined, and those are necessarily wishes and feelings entertained by a person who lacks mental capacity in relation to the decision being made on his or her behalf. The Act expressly requires them to be considered, and for consideration to be given to the past wishes and feelings expressed by that person, including when he or she had capacity.

The decision maker must consider too the beliefs and values that would be likely to influence the person's decision if he or she had capacity and also the other factors that the person would be likely to consider if he or she were able to do so. This does not necessarily require those to be given effect.

As the Code of Practice for the MCA 2005 explains at paragraph 5.38:

'In setting out the requirements for working out a person's "best interests", section 4 of the Act puts the person who lacks capacity at the centre of the decision to be made. Even if they cannot make the decision, their wishes and feelings, beliefs and values should be taken fully into account – whether expressed in the past or now. But their wishes and feelings, beliefs and values will not necessarily be the deciding factor in working out their best interests. Any such assessment must consider past and current wishes and feelings, beliefs and values alongside all other factors, but the final decision must be based entirely on what is in the person's best interests.'

In *Re M (Statutory Will), ITW v Z* [2009] EWHC 2525 (Fam) Munby J as he then was set out his views (at paragraph 35) on the question of the weight to be afforded to the wishes and feelings of the person lacking capacity:

'I venture, however, to add the following observations:
i) First, P's wishes and feelings will always be a significant factor to which the court must play close regard: see *Re MM; Local Authority X v MM (by the Official Solicitor) and KM* [2007] EWHC 2003 (Fam), 2009 1 FLR 443, at paras [121]–[124].
ii) Secondly, the weight to be attached to P's wishes and feelings will always be case specific and fact specific. In some cases, in some situations, they may carry much, even, on occasions, preponderant, weight. In other cases, in other situations, and even where the

circumstances may have some superficial similarity, they may carry little weight. One cannot, as it were, attribute any particular *a priori* weight or importance to P's wishes and feelings; it all depends, it must depend, on the individual circumstances of the particular case. And even if one is dealing with a particular individual, the weight to be attached to their wishes and feelings must depend upon the particular context; in relation to one topic P's wishes and feelings may carry great weight whilst at the same time carrying much less weight in relation to another topic. Just as the test of incapacity and the 2005 Act is, as under the common law, "issue specific", so in a similar way the weight to be attached to P's wishes and feelings will likewise be issued specific.

iii) Thirdly, in considering the weight and importance to be attached to P's wishes and feelings the court must of course, and as required by section 4(2) of the 2005 Act, have regard to all the relevant circumstances. In this context the relevant circumstances will include, though I emphasise that they are by no means limited to, such matters as:

a) the degree of P's incapacity, for the nearer to the borderline the more weight must in principle be attached to P's wishes and feelings: *Re MM; Local Authority X v MM (by the Official Solicitor)* and KM [2007] EWHC 2003 (Fam), [2009] 1 FLR 443, at para [124];

b) the strength and consistency of the views being expressed by P;

c) the possible impact on P of knowledge that her wishes and feelings are not been given effect to: see again *Re MM; Local Authority X v MM (by the Official Solicitor)* and KM [2007] EWHC 2003 (Fam), [2009] 1 FLR 443 , at para [124];

d) the extent to which P's wishes and feelings are, or are not, rational, sensible, responsible and pragmatically capable of sensible implementation in particular circumstances; and

e) crucially, the extent to which P's wishes and feelings, if given effect to, can properly be accommodated within the court's overall assessment of what is in her best interests.'

At paragraph 45 of the Supreme Court judgment in *Aintree University Hospitals NHS Foundation Trust v James* [2013] UKSC 67, the Supreme Court did not agree that the test of a patient's wishes and feelings was an objective one. The Supreme Court said (at paragraph 45):

'The purpose of the best interests test is to consider matters from the patient's point of view. That is not to say that the patient's wishes must prevail, any more than those of the fully capable patient must prevail. We cannot always have what we want. Nor will it always be possible to ascertain what an incapable patient's wishes are ... But insofar as it is possible to ascertain the patient's wishes and feelings, his beliefs and values or the things which were important to him, it is those which should be taken into account because they are a component in making the choice which is right for him as an individual human being.'

The past and present wishes and feelings of the person lacking capacity are a very significant aspect of that person's best interests and are accordingly to be given much weight but there is no statutory presumption that those wishes and feelings are to be paramount or must be implemented if they can be ascertained. The wishes and feelings of the person lacking capacity are an important part of the balancing act to be carried out under the 'balance sheet' approach, bearing in mind that the overall imperative is that the decision must be made in the person's best interests.

4.7   MENTAL CAPACITY ACT 2005, S 5

Section 5 of the Act provides protection from liability for anyone involved in providing care or treatment for a person who lacks capacity to consent to such care or treatment, providing they are acting in the person's best interests and without negligence.

This statutory provision replaces the common law doctrine of necessity. It provides the basis upon which the vast majority of medical treatment decisions in relation to an incapacitated person can be taken without seeking any court authorisation. Issues arising in serious medical treatment decisions will continue to need to be decided by the court, including whether or not to give life-sustaining treatment, non-therapeutic sterilisations and organ or bone marrow donations by persons lacking capacity to consent.

Section 5 will not protect from negligence. It will allow restraint of the incapacitated person, provided there is a reasonable belief that it is necessary to do the act to prevent harm and the act is a proportionate response. Section 5 will not, however, authorise a deprivation of liberty: MCA 2005, s 6.

The protection from liability under s 5 does not allow acts contrary to a decision made within the scope of their authority of either an attorney under a lasting power of attorney or a deputy. However, the MCA specifically provides that this is not to stop any person providing life-sustaining treatment or doing an act to prevent serious deterioration whilst a decision on any relevant issue is sought from the court.

4.8   DEPUTIES

Section 16 of the Act gives the Court power to appoint a deputy or to make decisions on behalf of a person who lacks mental capacity.

It provides so far as relevant:

'(1) This section applies if a person lacks capacity in relation to a matter for matters concerning –
(a)   P's personal welfare, or
(b)   P's property and affairs.

(2) The court may –
(a)   by making an order, make the decision or decisions on P's behalf of in relation to the matter or matters, or
(b)   appoint a person (a "deputy") to make decisions on P's behalf in relation to the matter or matters.

(3) The powers of the court under this section are subject to the provisions of this Act and, in particular, to sections 1 (the principles) and 4 (best interests).

(4) When deciding whether it is in P's best interests to appoint a deputy, the court must have regard (in addition to the matters mentioned in section 4) to the principles that –
(a)   a decision by the court is to be preferred to the appointment of a deputy to make a decision, and
(b)   the powers conferred on a deputy should be as limited in scope and duration as is reasonably practicable in the circumstances.'

4.9   ATTORNEYS

Section 9 of the MCA 2005 defines a Lasting Power of Attorney (LPA) as 'a power of attorney' under which one party (the donor) confers on another (the donee) authority to make certain decisions. A LPA is therefore at heart 'a power of attorney' so that the principles governing the relationship in law between principal and agent apply to it.

Under a LPA the donor may confer authority on the attorney to make decisions, including decisions in circumstances where the donor no longer has capacity in relation to the donor's personal welfare or specified matters concerning the donor's personal welfare.

In respect of welfare decisions, the LPA only operates where the donor lacks capacity to make decisions, and where the attorney makes decisions on behalf of the donor which the donor lacks capacity to make, the attorney must also act in the donor's best interests, applying the criteria laid down in s 4 of the MCA 2005, as well as the Code of Practice.

PART II

THE RIGHT TO LIFE

THE 'RIGHT TO DIE'

CHAPTER 5

THE RIGHT TO LIFE: ADULTS: END-OF-LIFE CARE; WHETHER TO GIVE LIFE-SUSTAINING MEDICAL TREATMENT

5.1   THE RIGHT TO LIFE

Article 2 of the European Convention on Human Rights (ECHR) provides:

> '1. Everyone's right to life shall be protected by law. No one shall be deprived of his life intentionally save in the execution of a sentence of a court following his conviction of a crime for which the penalty is provided by law.
>
> 2. Deprivation of life shall not be regarded as inflicted in contravention of this article when it results from the use of force which is no more than absolutely necessary:
> (a)   in the defence of any person from unlawful violence;
> (b)   in order to effect a lawful arrest or to prevent the escape of a person lawfully detained;
> (c)   in action lawfully taken for the purpose of quelling a riot or insurrection.'

All human life is of value and our law contains the strong presumption that all steps will be taken to preserve it, unless the circumstances are exceptional. The principle is reflected in Article 2 ECHR, which provides that everyone's life shall be protected by law. It is the most fundamental of the Convention rights.

However, the principle is not absolute and may yield to other considerations in exceptional circumstances: *Airedale NHS Trust v Bland* [1993] AC 789.

The Mental Capacity Act 2005 (MCA 2005) too does not give absolute priority to the preservation of life. The approach taken by the Act is accurately reflected in the MCA Code of Practice at paragraph 5.31:

'All reasonable steps which are in the person's best interests should be taken to prolong their life. *There will be a limited number of cases where treatment is futile, overly burdensome to the patient or where there is no prospect of recovery.*'

The words above were accepted as an accurate statement of the law by the judge at first instance, by the Court of Appeal and by the Supreme Court as set out in the latter's judgment in the case of *Aintree NHS Foundation Trust v James* [2013] UKSC 67. However, the judge at first instance and the Court of Appeal differed as to the meaning of the words in italic within paragraph 5.31. The Supreme Court preferred the approach of the judge at first instance to be the correct one as to the meaning of those words. There will follow within this chapter a detailed analysis of the landmark Supreme Court judgment in the case of *Aintree*.

However in considering end of life care medical treatment cases, it is important to note at this point that the Supreme Court made clear that the fundamental question in these cases is whether it is lawful to give the treatment, not whether it is lawful to withhold it. As it says in paragraph 22 of the judgment, the focus is on whether it is in the patient's best interests to give the treatment, rather than on whether it is in his best interests to withhold or withdraw it.

Accordingly, where such medical treatment is being given, the issue in a case may surround whether such treatment should or should not be continued. Equally where the treatment in prospect is not being given, the issue in the case may surround whether such treatment should or should not be instigated.

5.2   THE CODE OF PRACTICE

Section 42 of the MCA 2005 requires the Lord Chancellor to prepare a code or codes of practice for those making decisions under the Act. Any person acting in a professional capacity or for remuneration is obliged to have regard to the Code (s 42(4)) and a court must take account of any provision in or failure to comply with the Code which is relevant to a question arising in any civil or criminal proceedings. The Code is not a statute and should not be construed as one but it is necessary for it to be considered accordingly.

In the above Supreme Court case of *Aintree*, the Court made clear that were there to be any conflict between what is said in any guidance issued by the medical profession and what is contained within the Code, then the Mental Capacity Act Code must prevail.

5.3   GUIDANCE

There is the guidance given by the General Medical Council (GMC) in 2010 under s 35 of the Medical Act 1983 entitled 'Treatment and care towards the end of life: good practice in decision-making'. There is also produced by the British Medical Association: 'Withholding and Withdrawing Life – Prolonging Medical Treatment: Guidance for Decision-making' (3rd edn, 2007).

The Supreme Court in the *Aintree* case makes clear that there is nothing in its judgment which is inconsistent with the sensible advice given by the GMC in their above guidance on treatment and care towards the end of life.

The GMC makes it quite clear that doctors cannot be required to provide treatment which they believe is not clinically appropriate. They must consult those close to the patient as far as practical. Doctors should seek the views of those close to the family in order to obtain the patient's wishes, feelings and views and the beliefs and values of the patients, but they must not give the family the impression that they are being asked to make a decision.

5.4   DECLARATIONS UNDER SECTION 16 OF THE MCA 2005

Declarations made by the court will be permissive in their effect. If the court determines that it is in the best interests of the patient and lawful to withhold or not to administer forms of treatment, such a decision will have the effect that, in the view of the court, doctors or staff would not need to embark on such forms of treatment. However, the making of such a determination by the court would not prevent or deter a doctor or staff from giving any or all of such forms of treatment if he or they thought fit at the time.

5.5   PROHIBITION ON MOTIVATION BY ANY DESIRE TO BRING ABOUT DEATH

Section 4(5) and (10) of the MCA 2005 was an addition while the Bill was passing through Parliament: in considering whether treatment which is necessary to sustain life is in the patient's best interests, the decision maker must not be motivated by a desire to bring about the patient's death. Like much else in the Act, this reflects in any event the existing law.

5.6   ATTORNEYS AND DEPUTIES: LIFE-SUSTAINING TREATMENT

An Attorney only has power to give or withhold consent to the carrying out or continuation of life-sustaining treatment if the instrument expressly so provides: s 11(8) of MCA 2005.

A Deputy cannot refuse consent to such life-sustaining treatment: s 20(5) of MCA 2005.

5.7   WHETHER TO GIVE LIFE-SUSTAINING TREATMENT IN PVS CASES

5.7.1   The meaning and definition of PVS

Professor Bryan Jennett and Professor Plum coined the term 'PVS' in 1972. It describes the syndrome that was being increasingly encountered as the life-saving and life-sustaining technologies of intensive care were securing the survival of some patients with brain damage of a severity that would previously have proved fatal.

PVS is a recognised medical condition, quite distinct from other conditions sometimes known as 'irreversible coma', 'the Guillain-Barré syndrome', 'the locked-in syndrome' and 'brain death'. In PVS, the cortex, that part of the brain which is the seat of cognitive function and sensory capacity, is destroyed through prolonged deprivation of oxygen. The cortex resolves into a watery mass. The consciousness which is the central feature of individual personality departs forever. However, the brain stem, which controls the reflexive functions of the body, in particular heartbeat, breathing and digestion, continues to operate. In the eyes of the medical world and of the law, a person is not clinically dead so long as the brain stem retains its function, ie the PVS patient continues to breathe unaided and his digestion continues to function. However, although his eyes are open, he cannot see or hear; although capable of reflex movement, particularly in response to painful stimuli, the patient is incapable of voluntary movement and can feel no pain; he cannot taste or smell; he cannot speak or communicate in any way; he has no cognitive function and can thus feel no emotion, whether pleasure or distress. A common feature of the vegetative patient is that, after a variable time in coma, wakefulness returns with long periods of spontaneous eye opening.

A Review by a Working Group convened by the Royal College of Physicians entitled the 'Permanent Vegetative State' is set out in the

Journal of the Royal College of Physicians of London vol 30, no 2, March/April 1996, p 119. The Review states that the condition is to be known as the permanent vegetative state, as opposed to the persistent vegetative state. It covers wide-ranging guidance to the medical profession on the condition, including the definition of PVS and the criteria for diagnosis. The last page of the Review sets out a table, indicating the distinguishing factors between PVS, coma, locked-in syndrome and brain stem death. The Review also specifies the three clinical criteria which must all be fulfilled for the diagnosis to be considered. First, there shall be no evidence of awareness of self or environment at any time. There shall be no volitional response to visual, auditory, tactile or noxious stimuli. There shall be no evidence of language comprehension or expression. Secondly, there shall be the presence of cycles of eye closure and eye opening which may simulate sleep and waking. Thirdly, there shall be sufficiently preserved hypothalamic and brain stem function to ensure the maintenance of respiration and circulation. The view of the Working Group is that a diagnosis of PVS may reasonably be made when a patient has been in a continuing vegetative state following head injury for more than 12 months or following other causes of brain damage for more than six months.

It is also helpful in this regard to read the analysis by Sir Stephen Brown, President of the Family Division, of the medical evidence presented to him at first instance in the *Bland* case, including that of Professor Jennett in relation to the distinguishing factors between PVS and coma, locked-in syndrome and brain stem death.

5.7.2 The case of *Airedale NHS Trust v Bland* [1993] AC 789

The significance of the case

The case raised for the first time in the English courts the following question: in what circumstances, if any, can a doctor lawfully discontinue life-sustaining treatment, including nutrition and hydration, without which a patient will die? At issue in the case was whether, as was advised by the hospital where Anthony Bland was cared for, a declaration should be granted that it was lawful to discontinue the artificial feeding and supply of antibiotics to him, with the result that, inevitably, within about one or two weeks, he would die. Sir Thomas Bingham MR in the Court of Appeal put the matter to be as whether artificial feeding and antibiotic drugs might lawfully be withheld or withdrawn from an insensate patient with no hope of recovery when it was known that, if that was done, the patient would shortly thereafter die. The judgments at first instance, in the Court of Appeal and in the House of Lords, raise and embrace wide-ranging issues involving principles of law, morality, ethics and medical practice.

The facts

Anthony Bland, who was then 17 years old, was present at the football match at Hillsborough in Sheffield where, owing to the failure of crowd control, a number of people in the crowd were crushed. Tragically many were killed. He suffered serious injuries and, as a result of them, the supply of oxygen to his brain was interrupted. He suffered catastrophic and irremediable damage to his brain. His condition was that of PVS; the space which the cortex of his brain should have occupied was filled with watery fluid. He had been a PVS patient for more than two and a half years by the time his case came before the court and the evidence was that he could have continued to live for many years longer. Because he could still breathe, he did not need the assistance of a respirator. He was fed by means of a tube, threaded through his nose and down into his stomach, through which liquefied food was mechanically pumped; his bowels were evacuated by enema; his bladder was drained by catheter. He was subject to repeated bouts of infection affecting his urinary tract and chest. He was, on the evidence, totally insensate. After careful thought, his family agreed that the feeding tubes should be removed.

The relief sought

With the agreement of Mr Bland's family, as well as the consultant in charge of his case, and the support of two independent doctors, the Airedale NHS Trust, as plaintiffs in the action, applied by originating summons to the Family Division of the High Court for declarations that they might lawfully discontinue all life-sustaining treatment and medical support measures designed to keep him alive, including the termination of ventilation, nutrition and hydration by artificial means. A declaration was further sought that they might lawfully discontinue, and thereafter need not furnish, medical treatment to him, except for the sole purpose of enabling him to end his life and die peacefully with the greatest dignity and the least pain, suffering and distress.

The reasoning for the decision by the House of Lords

(a) Omission as opposed to positive act

English criminal law draws a sharp distinction between acts and omissions. If an act resulting in death is done without lawful excuse and with intent to kill, it is murder. However, an omission to act with the same result and with the same intent is, in general, not an offence at all. To the latter general principle there is the exception at common law that a person may be criminally liable for the consequences of an omission if he stands in such a relation to the victim that he is under a duty to act. It was held by the House of Lords in the *Bland* case that the cessation of artificial nutrition and hydration was an omission, not an act. Accordingly, such cessation of treatment amounted to the doctor simply allowing his patient to die of his pre-existing condition (per Lord Goff at 866):

> 'I agree that the doctor's conduct in discontinuing life support can properly be categorised as an omission. It is true that it may be difficult to describe what the doctor actually does as an omission, for example where he takes some positive step to bring the life support to an end. But discontinuation of life support is, for present purposes, no different from not initiating life support in the first place. In each case, the doctor is simply allowing his patient to die in the sense that he is desisting from taking a step which might in certain circumstances prevent his patient from dying as a result of his pre-existing condition: and as a matter of general principle an omission such as this, will not be unlawful unless it constitutes a breach of duty to the patient.'

In drawing a distinction between acts and omissions the law forbids the taking of active measures to cut short the life of a terminally ill patient. Lord Goff, in seeking to describe the difference, in legal consequences, between the doctor discontinuing life support as against him or her ending a patient's life by a lethal injection, went on to say at 866:

> '... But in the end the reason for that difference is that, whereas the law considers that discontinuance of life support may be consistent with the doctor's duty to care for his patient, it does not, for reasons of policy, consider that it forms any part of his duty to give his patient a lethal injection to put him out of his agony.'

(b) The duty or right, if any, of a doctor to treat where treatment is futile and of no benefit

Having reached the view that the withdrawal of treatment would amount to an omission, not an act, the court then had to consider whether, notwithstanding such omission, the doctors were, or were not, still under a continuing duty to treat Anthony Bland. The cessation or withdrawal of treatment would not be a criminal act unless the doctors were under a duty to continue the regime of treatment.

It is appropriate to emphasise that Anthony Bland had never been able to consent to or refuse the treatment given to him. He had left no advance statement or 'living will' as to his wishes and feelings. Accordingly, he could only be treated in the absence of his consent as permitted by the common law. The principles of *Re F (Sterilisation: Mental Patient)* [1990] 2 AC 1, in those circumstances, were viewed to be applicable to Anthony Bland by the House of Lords, namely that a doctor is under a duty to treat a patient who is incapable of consenting, provided that the treatment concerned is in the best interests of such a patient. However, a doctor's decision as to whether invasive care is in the best interests of the patient falls to be assessed by reference to the test laid down in *Bolam v Friern Hospital Management Committee* [1957] 1 WLR 582. The test is whether a decision as to medical treatment is in accordance with a practice accepted at the time by a responsible body of medical opinion.

The doctors into whose charge Anthony Bland originally came made decisions about his care and treatment which he could not make for himself. Those decisions were made in line with the principles of *Re F* in his best interests. Throughout the period when the possibility still existed that he might recover, his best interests justified the application of the necessary life support system without his consent.

The agreed medical evidence was that no benefit at all would be conferred by continuance of the treatment, given that he was totally insensate, with no hope of recovery.

In the light of the test set out in the case of *Re F*, accordingly, it was held by the House of Lords in the *Bland* case that the doctors could be under no duty to continue to treat Anthony Bland when they, the medical practitioners, felt such treatment which could be of no benefit to him, was not in his best interests. Lord Keith of Kinkel, at 858 and 859, said:

> '... a medical practitioner is under no duty to continue to treat such a patient where a large body of informed and responsible medical opinion is to the effect that no benefit at all would be conferred by continuance. Existence in a vegetative state with no prospect of recovery is by that opinion regarded as not being a benefit, and that ... at least forms a proper basis for the decision to discontinue treatment and care: *Bolam v Friern Hospital Management Committee* [1957] 1 WLR 582.'

Lord Browne-Wilkinson went further, in taking the view that there could be no question of the doctors being under a duty to treat him, since their original right to treat had now gone (at 883–884):

'In my judgment it must follow from this that if there comes a stage where the responsible doctor comes to the reasonable conclusion (which accords with the views of a responsible body of medical opinion) that further continuance of an intrusive life support system is not in the best interests of the patient, he can no longer lawfully continue that life support system: to do so would constitute the crime of battery and the tort of trespass to the person. Therefore he cannot be in breach of any duty to maintain the patient's life.'

It is not possible to do justice to the wide variety of issues raised in the *Bland* case, nor to the differing emphases of the varying judges in their judgments from first instance through to the House of Lords. It suffices to note what Lord Goff said at 869:

'But in the end, in a case such as the present, it is the futility of the treatment which justifies its termination. I do not consider that, in circumstances such as these, a doctor is required to initiate or to continue life-prolonging treatment or care in the best interests of his patient. It follows that no such duty rests upon the respondents, or upon Dr H, in the case of Anthony Bland, whose condition is in reality no more than a living death, and for whom such treatment or care would, in medical terms, be futile.'

5.7.3 The sanctity of life: the duty to prolong life

The fundamental principle of the sanctity of life is not absolute and may yield to other factors, in exceptional circumstances. A doctor caring for a patient is not under an absolute obligation to prolong the patient's life by any means available to him or her, regardless of the circumstances and the quality of the patient's life.

A doctor who has under his or her care a patient suffering painfully from terminal cancer cannot be under an absolute obligation to perform upon such a patient major surgery to abate another condition which, if unabated, would, or might, shorten his life still further: *Auckland Area Health Board v The Attorney-General* [1993] 1 NZLR 235 at 253.

The principle of the sanctity of life does not compel a doctor to treat a patient of sound mind who will die if he does not, contrary to the express wishes of the patient. It does not authorise similarly forcible feeding of prisoners of sound mind who are on, for whatever reason, hunger strike. Nor does it compel the temporary keeping alive of patients who are terminally ill, where to do so would merely prolong their suffering. The principle of the sanctity of life would, however, prohibit as unlawful the taking of active measures to cut short the life of a terminally ill patient: see *Airedale NHS Trust v Bland* [1993] AC 789 at 859.

It is to be noted under s 4(5) of the MCA 2005 that: 'Where the determination (as to best interests) relates to life sustaining treatment he must not, in considering whether the treatment is in the best interests of the person concerned, be motivated by a desire to bring about his death.'

5.7.4 Opposition by family to not instigating or continuing with life-sustaining treatment

In the case of *Re G (Persistent Vegetative State)* [1995] 2 FCR 46, a married man, then aged 24, was involved in a serious motorcycle accident. He suffered head injuries that resulted in him becoming unconscious. Subsequently, he suffered a cardiac arrest that interrupted the flow of blood to his brain and he sustained further brain damage. He never regained consciousness, and in December 1992, some 18 months after the accident, he was diagnosed as being in a persistent vegetative state. All the medical evidence supported this view. G received artificial nutrition and hydration through a gastrostomy tube. In June 1993, Mr J, the consultant orthopaedic surgeon who had the care of G, discussed the future care of G with his wife. She indicated that she considered it not to be in his best interests to continue the artificial hydration and nutrition. The doctor agreed. The patient's mother, however, disagreed and wished it to continue. The Hospital Trust where G was cared for sought declarations from the court that would permit the withdrawal of feeding and which would inevitably lead to G's death. The Official Solicitor representing G supported the Hospital Trust's application. The patient's mother was a party to the originating summons, which was issued on 16 February 1994, seeking the declaratory relief referred to. It was submitted on behalf of the mother that her opposition should operate as a veto. This argument was rejected by the court. The approach taken by the court was consistent with the then guidelines of the BMA on treatment decisions for patients in the permanent vegetative state, paragraph 5 of which reads:

> 'It is good practice for doctors to consult the wishes of people close to the patient but their views alone cannot determine the treatment of the PVS patient. People close to the patient may be able to throw light on the wishes of the PVS patient regarding the prolongation of treatment and this is likely to be helpful in decision making. Treatment decisions, however, must be based upon the doctors' assessment of the patients' best interests.'

Whilst it is good practice, accordingly, to consult the wishes and feelings of those close to the patient in relation to treatment, the decision is for the doctor and his or her team who have responsibility for the care of the patient. As a matter of law, the next of kin of the patient has no legal right either to consent or to refuse consent on behalf of the patient: *Re T (An Adult) (Consent to Medical Treatment)* [1992] 2 FLR 458 at 461B, per Lord Donaldson MR. This is reflected at paragraph 2.5 of the then consultation paper 'Withdrawing and Withholding Treatment' from the BMA's Medical Ethics Committee.

Both Lord Donaldson's dicta in *Re T* and paragraph 2.5 of the then consultation paper indicate that the importance of consulting with close family and/or next of kin may lie in revealing or throwing light on the wishes of the PVS patient himself or herself.

Section 4(7) of MCA 2005 requires that there is taken into account, in determining best interests, the views of (a) anyone named by the subject person as someone to be consulted on the matter in question or on matters of that kind, (b) anyone engaged in caring for the person or interested in his welfare, (c) any donee of a lasting power of attorney granted by the person, and (d) any deputy appointed for the person by the court.

As may be seen in Chapter 12 on Advance Statements or 'living wills', those responsible for the patient's care must take account of and respect the patient's own views, when known, whether these are formally recorded in a written document (an advance refusal or advance directive) or not. Such a duty by a doctor to his or her patient is envisaged and reflected at p 121 of the then Review Paper headed 'The Permanent Vegetative State' of the Working Group convened by the Royal College of Physicians: Journal of the Royal College of Physicians of London vol 30, no 2, March/April 1996, p 119. The importance of the view of the patient was also to be seen in paragraph 10 of the Official Solicitor's Practice Note on PVS of 26 July 1996 [1996] 2 FLR 375.

Section 4(6) of MCA 2005 requires there to be consideration, in determining best interests, of (a) the subject person's past and present wishes and feelings (and, in particular, any relevant written statement made by him when he had capacity), (b) the beliefs and values that would be likely to influence his decision if he had capacity, and (c) the other factors that he would be likely to consider if he were able to do so.

In *Re G*, the court held that it would be an appalling burden to place on any relative the responsibility of making a decision in such a grave case. Relief was granted by the court, notwithstanding the patient's mother's objections.

In a case involving a critically ill minor – not a PVS case – *Re J (A Minor) (Wardship: Medical Treatment)* [1991] 1 FLR 366 at 381, Taylor LJ said:

> '... the views of the parents, although they should be heeded and weighed, cannot prevail over the court's view of the ward's best interests.'

5.7.5 PVS cases where a clinical feature of the condition is absent

In two separate cases, namely in *Re D (Medical Treatment)* [1998] 1 FLR 411 and *Re H (A Patient)* [1998] 2 FLR 36, the court considered the guidelines on PVS issued by the Royal College of Physicians.

Whilst, in each case, the mandatory three clinical requirements were met in relation to diagnosis of PVS, other clinical features are referred to in the guidelines including 'there will not be nystagmus in response to ice water caloric testing, the patient will not have visual fixation, be able to track moving objects with the eyes or show a "menace response"'.

In *Re D* at 418H, it was found that the patient was able to track movements with the eyes and show a menace response and there was nystagmus in response to ice water caloric testing. In *Re H*, referred to above, there was evidence again of visual tracking.

In both cases, although the patients did not fit four squarely with one particular guideline, they were each in a state of PVS: neither had any degree of awareness whatsoever; neither was susceptible, on the evidence, to any change; each patient was in a state falling within the description of a 'living death'. In neither case was there any evidence of any meaningful life.

It is perhaps obvious to say that, in any case of suggested PVS, the court will wish to scrutinise the evidence carefully to ensure that the condition of PVS is established: *Swindon and Marlborough NHS Trust v S* [1995] Med LR 84.

5.8 WHETHER TO GIVE LIFE-SUSTAINING TREATMENT IN CASES OTHER THAN PVS

The two legal authorities analysed below emphasise the weight placed by the court on the sanctity of life and only wish to preserve life if possible.

At paragraph 77 of the judgment in *W v M* [2011] EWHC 2443 (Fam), Baker J reviews the cases in which courts have authorised the withholding or withdrawal of life-sustaining treatment from patients not in PVS.

The judge says at that paragraph of his judgment, however, that there was no reported case available to him in which a court had been asked previously to authorise the withdrawal of ANH from the patient diagnosed as being in a minimally conscious state (MCS).

In the above case of *W v M* [2011] EWHC 2443 (Fam), M suffered viral encephalitis which left her with extensive and irreparable brain damage. She fell into a coma and was then diagnosed as being in a vegetative state. In the course of subsequent investigations, however, it was discovered that she was in fact in a minimally conscious state – above the vegetative state – and was aware to some extent of herself and her environment but she did not have full consciousness.

The judge pointed out that: 'there is a spectrum of minimal consciousness extending from patients who are only just above the vegetative state to those who are bordering on the full consciousness'.

The medical evidence indicated that M had a very profound physical and cognitive impairment and was in a minimally conscious state (MCS). Although she made certain limited responses that indicated awareness of her environment, she was unable to communicate effectively to make basic choices even at the lowest level. She had no functional communication.

The applicant family submitted that the overall quality of wakeful and conscience experiences were predominantly negative, referring to the likelihood that she experienced a constant level of background pain without any truly positive experiences but instead only neutral states of contented wakefulness.

The Primary Care Trust invited the court to reach the opposite conclusion, taking into account the importance of preserving life, the agreed fact that she had some environmental awareness, her life was not without some positive elements, and that further steps could be taken to increase the likely positive experiences for her and to reduce her negative experiences.

In her evidence to the court the principal medical expert said that she supported the withdrawal of ANH, given that it was very improbable that M would ever emerge from her condition and that her negative experiences outweighed her positive ones. She said that no one had been able to positively identify things that caused specific pleasure for M.

The judge did not agree with the above view that M's experiences were clearly negative: whilst accepting that her life had a number of negative aspects, he also found that it had positive elements, and he accepted the evidence of the carers of the patient who he said had had far greater experience of living with M in recent years that had members of her family.

He accepted that M had positive experiences and that, although her life was extremely restricted, it was not without pleasures, albeit small ones. He accepted the evidence of the carers that there was a reasonable prospect that her positive experiences and quality of life could be extended by changes to her care plan that carefully exposed her to increased stimulation.

The determination of the judge, Baker J, was that it was not in M's best interests for artificial nutrition and hydration (ANH) to be withdrawn.

The case of *Re E (Medical Treatment Anorexia)* [2012] EWHC 1639 (COP) raised for the first time the real possibility of life-sustaining treatment not being in the best interests of a person who, while lacking capacity, was fully aware of her situation.

The 32-year-old woman E suffered from extremely severe anorexia nervosa, and other chronic health conditions. She was refusing to eat, and was taking only a small amount of water. Her death was imminent. She was being looked after in a community hospital under a palliative care regime whose purpose was to allow her to die in comfort.

The main resulting issue in the case was whether it was in her best interests to receive life-sustaining treatment in the form of forcible feeding with all necessary associated measures.

Peter Jackson J says at paragraph 5 of his judgment:

'E's case has raised for the first time in my experience the real possibility of life-sustaining treatment not being in the best interests of a person who, while lacking capacity, is fully aware of her situation. She is in many ways the opposite of a PVS patient or a person with an inevitably fatal condition. She is described as an intelligent and charming person. Albeit gravely unwell, she is not incurable. She does not seek death, but above all she does not want to eat or to be fed.'

The judge at paragraph 117 of his judgment makes clear that, in contrast to the above case of *W v M* [2011] EWHC 2443 where the patient was in a stable, minimally conscious state, in this case E was in an inextricably deteriorating but highly conscious state.

He determined that he would not have overruled E's wishes if further treatment was futile, but it was not. He determined that although the further treatment would be extremely burdensome to E, there was a possibility that it would succeed.

He determined that it was lawful and in E's best interests for her to be fed, forcibly if necessary. He found that the resulting interference with her rights under Articles 3 and 8 of the ECHR was proportionate and necessary in order to protect her right to life under Article 2.

5.8.1 Cardio-Pulmonary Resuscitation (CPR): Do Not Activate CPR (DNACPR)

Reference should be made to 'Decisions relating to cardiopulmonary resuscitation: A joint statement from the British Medical Association, the Resuscitation Council and the Royal College of Nursing, October 2007'.

Reference equally should also be made to 'End of life care: Cardiopulmonary resuscitation' produced by the General Medical Council in 2010.

In respect of cardio-pulmonary resuscitation (CPR), the GMC Guidance refers to the nature of CPR in that it is invasive and can include chest compression, drugs and electrical shocks. There is a reasonable success rate in some circumstances but generally the success rate of CPR is very low and there is a risk of adverse clinical outcomes such as damage to the ribs, brain injury and increased physical disabilities.

The GMC Guidance confirms that if the use of CPR is not successful, the patient may die in an undignified and traumatic manner and if it is not in the best interests of the patient to undergo resuscitation then a do not attempt resuscitation entry should be recorded in the patient's notes.

The Court of Appeal case of *R (Tracey) v Cambridge University Hospitals NHS Foundation Trust* [2014] EWCA Civ 822 is significant in considering the need to consult the patient in relation to DNACPR. There will be consideration and analysis of this case in due course in this chapter. The effect of the judgment is that the terms of the October 2007 Joint Statement referred to above may need to be revised by the professional bodies involved.

As already indicated previously, in the case of *W v M* [2011] EWHC 2443 (Fam) Baker J concluded that it was not in the patient M's best interests for artificial nutrition and hydration to be withdrawn. However, the court made a declaration that the current 'Do Not Resuscitate' order was to be continued. It was not disputed that, because of her condition, it would not be in M's interests to receive cardiopulmonary resuscitation having regard to all the benefits and burdens of such treatments.

In *An NHS Trust v L,* where judgment was given on 8 October 2012 and reported at [2013] EWHC 4313 (Fam), Moylan J was concerned with a 55-year-old man who had suffered a severe brain injury. There was indicated to be an extremely poor prognosis of any functional or neurological recovery.

Prior to the proceedings being instituted, a 'Do Not Resuscitate' order had been placed on L's medical notes without prior consultation with the family, which was in breach of the Trust's own policy. The Trust accepted it had acted wrongly.

The case of the Hospital Trust was that it was not in L's best interest if there was a significant deterioration in his condition, including cardiac and respiratory arrest, for him to be resuscitated.

The family's position was that all treatment should be given in the event of any deterioration. None of the doctors who gave evidence saw it as appropriate to provide resuscitation. It was contended that, if L suffered a further cardiac arrest, the prospects of successful resuscitation was very low; if he did not die there was a high probability of further brain damage. The judge carried out a balancing act, using a 'balance sheet'. There were no treatment options available to the judge.

The judge determined that the balance came down in favour of granting the Trust's application as the burdens outweighed by far the benefits.

The judge said:

> 'Harsh though it will sound, if CPR was attempted it would amount to prolonging L's death and not to prolong in any meaningful way his life.'

In *Aintree University Hospitals NHS Foundation Trust v James* [2013] EWCA Civ 65, the court was concerned with a patient, DJ, who was suffering from multi-organ failure, with respiratory failure, cardiovascular failure and renal failure.

The judge at first instance refused to make declarations sought by the applicant hospital treating DJ that it would be lawful, being in his best interests, for the following treatment to be withheld in the event of DJ sustaining a clinical deterioration: cardiopulmonary resuscitation; invasive support for a circulatory problem; or renal replacement therapy in the event of deterioration in renal function.

The judge at first instance refused to give permission to the hospital to place a 'Do Not Attempt Resuscitation' instruction on DJ's medical records.

The Court of Appeal allowed the appeal, granted declarations that it was in the best interests of DJ and lawful for the Trust to withhold the three forms of treatment in the event of a clinical deterioration, including in relation to CPR.

The Court of Appeal referred to the burden of CPR being that the resuscitation process involves manually inflating the lungs and that the force of the compression in a significant number of cases causes rib fractures. Such treatment involved a high degree of risk. The court bore in mind the frailty of the malnourished patient, that his medical condition was extreme, and that his ability to stave off death was declining fast.

I shall return further on in detail to the *Aintree* case for its deliberations and considerations as to the meaning of best interests in relation to near-end-of-life cases. It suffices to say here that the Supreme Court dismissed the appeal from the Court of Appeal judgment on the basis that the latter's decision was correct at the time the case came before it, given by then the patient's deteriorating medical condition. That said, the Supreme Court in its judgment significantly takes issue with the approach of the Court of Appeal towards the issues in the case, both as a matter of law and otherwise.

5.8.2   Consulting the patient in relation to DNACPR

The Court of Appeal case already referred to at **5.8.1** of *R (Tracey) v Cambridge University Hospitals NHS Foundation Trust* [2014] EWCA Civ 822 involved a claim for judicial review brought by Mr Tracey against the Cambridge University Hospitals NHS Foundation Trust ('the Trust') and the Secretary of State for Health arising from the placing of DNACPR notices on the notes of Mr Tracey's wife, Janet Tracey, who was admitted to Addenbrookes Hospital ('the Hospital') on 19 February 2011 and died on 7 March 2011. The Trust is responsible for the Hospital.

The claim advanced against the Trust was that it breached Mrs Tracey's rights under Article 8 of the ECHR because in imposing the first notice, it failed (i) adequately to consult Mrs Tracey or members of her family; (ii) to notify her of the decision to impose the notice; (iii) to offer her a second opinion; (iv) to make its DNACPR policy available to her; and (v) to have a policy which was clear and unambiguous. The claim advanced against the Secretary of State was that he breached Mrs Tracey's Article 8 rights by failing to publish national guidance to ensure (i) that the process of making DNACPR decisions is sufficiently clear, accessible and foreseeable and (ii) that persons in the position of Mrs Tracey have the right (a) to be involved in discussions and decisions about DNACPR and (b) to be given information to enable them so to be involved, including the right to seek a second opinion.

The hospital trust did not seriously dispute that Article 8 is engaged by a decision to impose a DNACPPR notice. The contention on behalf of the Secretary of State that Article 8 was not so engaged was rejected by the court. At paragraph 32 of the Court of Appeal judgment it is said:

> 'In my judgment however none of the submissions on behalf of the Secretary of State justifies the conclusion that article 8 is not engaged by the decision to impose a DNACPR notice. A decision as to how to pass the closing days and moments of one's life and how one manages one's death touches in the most immediate and obvious way a patient's personal autonomy, integrity, dignity and quality of life. If there were any doubt as to that, it has been settled by the decision in *Pretty*.'

The court added that the question whether Article 8 is engaged is not to be confused with the separate question of whether it is breached in the circumstances of any particular case.

The Court of Appeal was satisfied that Mrs Tracey did wish to be consulted about any DNACPR notice that the clinicians were contemplating completing and placing in her notes up to the time of the first notice.

The Court of Appeal said at paragraph 53 of its judgment in relation to the need to consult:

'But I think it is right to say that, since a DNACPR decision is one which will potentially deprive the patient of life-saving treatment, there should be a presumption in favour of patient involvement. There need to be convincing reasons not to involve the patient.'

At paragraph 93 of the judgment – and responding to the concerns expressed by the Resuscitation Council – it is said:

'These concerns are entirely understandable and I would hope that the formulation that the clinician has a duty to consult the patient in relation to DNACPR "unless he or she thinks that the patient will be distressed by being consulted and that that distress might cause the patient harm" will go some substantial way to meeting those concerns.'

Accordingly the Court of Appeal has now given clear guidance as to the presumption in favour of patient involvement in relation to DNACPR decisions.

In the particular case it was concerned with, the Court of Appeal granted a declaration against the hospital trust that it violated Mrs Tracey's Article 8 right to respect for private life in failing to involve her in the process which led to the first notice. The other relief claimed against the Trust was refused. The relief claimed against the Secretary of State was refused.

5.8.3 Best interests test in relation to whether to give life-sustaining treatment

The MCA Code of Practice at paragraph 5.31 says in full:

'All reasonable steps which are in the person's best interests should be taken to prolong their life. There will be a limited number of cases where treatment is futile, overly burdensome to the patient or where there is no prospect of recovery. In circumstances such as these, it may be that an assessment of best interests leads to the conclusion that it would be in the best interests of the patient to withdraw or withhold life-sustaining treatment, even though this may result in the person's death. The decision maker must make a decision based on the best interests of the person who lacks capacity. They must not be motivated by a desire to bring about the person's death for whatever reason, even if this is from a sense of compassion. Health care and social care staff should also refer to relevant professional guidance when making decisions regarding any sustaining treatment.'

In the case of *An NHS Trust v MB* [2006] EWHC 507 (Fam), Holman J at paragraph 58 of his judgment says:

'The test is one of best interests, and the task of the court is to balance all the factors. The Court of Appeal have suggested that the best and safest way of reliably doing this is to draw up a list on which are specifically identified, on the one hand, the benefits or advantages and, on the other hand, the burdens or disadvantages of continuing or discontinuing treatment in question.'

The judge in this case asked the advocates to draw up and lodge such lists, and the balancing act of the judge in the above case was to conclude, as already indicated, that it was not in the child's best interests currently to discontinue ventilation with the inevitable result that he would immediately die.

Whilst the NHS Trust and Guardian emphasised in the balancing act the detriments to the child in continuing artificially to keep him alive; the judge gave significant weight to the prolongation of life, accepting the evidence of the parents for example that the child was attentive to TV, DVDs, CDs, stories and speech, as well as the bonded relationship between the child and his parents.

The judge in *W v M* [2011] EWHC 2443 (Fam), Baker J, contrasted and balanced the factors in favour of the withdrawal of ANH against those in favour of the continuation of ANH for M.

It is material to note at this juncture that the judge rejected the contention of the Official Solicitor that the 'balance sheet approach' was inappropriate in respect of the patient in a state of minimal consciousness who was clinically stable.

The advantages of withdrawing ANH, he said, included: the fact that she would be free from pain and discomfort, from the indignities of the current circumstances, from further distress, from further intrusive assessments, and being allowed to die would accord with the number of comments she had made prior to her illness as to her wishes and feelings. Further, by authorising the withdrawal of ANH and thereby allowing her to die with dignity, the court would be acting in accordance with what family members firmly believed M would have wanted.

The advantages of continuing ANH, he said, included: that the preservation of life was a fundamental principle, she would continue to experience life as a sensate being with a degree of awareness of herself and her environment, she would continue to experience life at this level for a number of years, she would be able to continue to gain pleasure from the things that give her pleasure at present, and that her enjoyment of life could be extended.

Baker J said that in his judgment the importance of preserving life was the decisive factor in this case.

He determined that he did not find that M's current life was overwhelmingly negative or 'overly burdensome' in the words of paragraph 5.31 of the Code of Practice, or that there was no prospect of any improvement in the quality and enjoyment of her life.

Within the overall consideration of best interests, s 4(6) of the MCA 2005 requires the court to consider, so far as reasonably ascertainable, the patient's past and present wishes and feelings.

Again with the overall consideration of best interests, s 4(7) of the MCA 2005 requires the court to take into account the views of anyone engaged in caring for the patient or interested in his or her welfare.

The MCA Code of Practice at paragraph 5.38 says:

> 'In setting out the requirements for working out a person's best interests, section 4 of the Act puts the person who lacks capacity at the centre of the decision to be made. Even if they cannot make the decision, their wishes and feelings, beliefs and values should be taken fully into account – whether expressed in the past or now. But their wishes and feelings, beliefs and values will not necessarily be the deciding factor in working out their best interests. Any such assessment must consider past and current wishes and feelings, beliefs and values alongside all other factors, but the final decision must be based entirely on what is in the person's best interests.'

The case put forward on behalf of M's family was based substantially on what they were saying M's wishes and feelings were. The judge recognised that the law rightly required the court to take into account her wishes and feelings when determining the best interests, as well as indeed those of her family.

The judge noted importantly that M had not made any formal advance decision that she wished artificial nutrition and hydration to be withdrawn in the circumstances that existed at the time of the hearing. He said that had she done so, the court would have abided by that advance decision.

The judge said that whilst he accepted entirely the veracity of what family members said had been M's wishes and feelings, nevertheless M's statements then were not specifically directed at the question that now arose, namely whether ANH should be withdrawn from her in a minimally conscious state; nor did he find that he could consider those statements as a clear indication some eight years on from the onset of her illness of what M would now want to happen.

Whilst the judge took into account M's earlier statements, he did not attach significant weight to them.

The judge in *Re E (Medical Treatment Anorexia)* [2012] EWHC 1639 (COP) contrasted and balanced the factors in favour of continued palliative care against those in favour of treatment by forcible feeding.

The factors in favour of palliative care included the following: that it reflected E's wishes; it respected E's personal autonomy; it spared E the risks associated with treatment; it avoided the harrowing aspects of treatment; it allowed E to die with dignity and close to home; the treatment had limited prospects of success; E's parents and clinicians are best sceptical about it.

The factors in favour of treatment by forcible feeding included the following: without treatment, E would die; without treatment, E would lose the chance to recover and lead a relatively normal life; there was medical opinion that E was treatable with some prospect of success; the longer E lived, the greater the opportunity for her to benefit from treatment and to revise her views about the future.

The judge found the competing factors were almost exactly in equilibrium but found that the balance is tipped slowly but unmistakably in the direction of life preserving treatment.

In his decision on best interests in the case of *Re E (Medical Treatment Anorexia)* [2012] EWHC 1639 (COP), Peter Jackson J said:

> '129. In E's, any decision is a heavy one. The balancing exercise is not mechanistic but intuitive and there are weighty factors on each side of the scales.

130 On one side, I have been struck by the fact that the people who know E best do not favour further treatment. They think that she has had enough and believe that her wishes should be respected. They believe that she should be allowed a dignified death ...

137 Against [those weighty factors], I place E's life in the other scale. We only live once – we are born once and we die once – and the difference between life and death is the biggest difference we know. E is a special person, whose life is of value. She does not see it that way now, but she may in future.'

5.8.4 Analysis of the case of *Aintree v James* in relation to best interests

I return to the case of *Aintree University Hospital NHS Foundation Trust v James*. The Court of Appeal judgment is reported at [2013] EWCA Civ 65. The Supreme Court judgment is reported at [2013] UKSC 67.

The Court of Appeal indicated they were considering the situation where, at the time the case was before them, life was ebbing away for DJ, in circumstances where there was no real prospect of recovery, the patient having a less than 1 per cent chance of ever being released from the intensive care unit. He was slowly dying.

The court was unable to uphold the reasoning and conclusion of the judge at first instance that the quality of life of DJ 'was not truly awful or non-existent'. The court concluded that the treatments which were the subject of the application would be unduly burdensome for DJ, and not in his best interests. The court took the view that the judge at first instance had erred in law in adopting too narrow a view of futility.

The court stated that the judge at first instance had applied the wrong test when considering the guidance in the Code of Practice.

As is stated at paragraph 5.30 of the Code of Practice to the MCA 2005:

'It is up to the doctor or health care professional providing treatment to assess whether the treatment is life-sustaining in each particular situation.'

Sir Alan Ward said:

'In other words the focus is on the medical interests of the patient when treatment is being considered to sustain life. This is not to say the doctors determine the outcome for it is the court must decide where there is a dispute about it and the court will always scrutinise the medical evidence with scrupulous care.'

Within the judgment of the Court of Appeal in this case is its consideration of the term 'best interests'.

There is a reiteration that there is no duty to maintain the life of the patient at all costs. There is no duty needlessly to prolong dying. They rejected the view that, regardless of the pain and suffering involved, life prolonging treatment had to be administered on the basis that human life was to be preserved at all costs.

The Court of Appeal agreed with the view that a right question to ask in end-of-life decisions is whether the treatment is worthwhile in the sense that it will bring therapeutic benefit to the patient.

They referred to the definition in the third edition of what started as Kennedy and Grubb's *Principles of Medical Law*, in which it is stated:

'Treatment can properly be categorised as futile if it cannot cure or palliate the disease or illness from which the patient is suffering and thus serves no therapeutic purpose of any kind.'

The Supreme Court in the case ofxpp*Aintree* at paragraphs 43 and 44 of its judgment disagreed with the latter above statement of principle in relation to the meaning of futility. Lady Hale said at paragraph 43:

'It follows that I respectfully disagree with the statements of principle in the Court of Appeal where they differ from those of the judge. Thus it is setting the goal too high to say that treatment is futile unless it has a real prospect of curing or at least palliating the life-threatening disease or illness from which the patient is suffering ... A treatment may bring some benefit to the patient even though it has no effect upon the underlying disease or disability.'

Lady Hale then says at paragraph 44:

'I also respectfully disagree with the statement that "no prospect of recovery" means "no prospect of recovering such a state of good health as will avert the looming prospect of death if the life-sustaining treatment is given". ... But where a patient is suffering from an incurable illness, disease or disability, it is not very helpful to talk of recovering a state of "good health". The patient's life may still be very well worth living. Resuming a quality of life which the patient would regard as worthwhile is more readily applicable, particularly in the case of a patient with permanent disabilities ... it is not for others to say that a life which the patient would regard as worthwhile is not worth living.'

The Supreme Court judgment is important in relation to the issue of a patient's wishes and feelings, and the correlation between the latter and determining what is in the patient's best interests. Lady Hale, at paragraph 45 of the judgment makes clear that, in so far as the Court of Appeal were suggesting that the test of a patient's wishes and feelings was an objective one, what the reasonable patient would think, she disagreed. She said:

'The purpose of the best interests test is to consider matters from the patient's point of view. That is not to say that his wishes must prevail, any more than those of the fully capable patient must prevail. We cannot always have what we want. Nor will it always be possible to ascertain what an incapable patient's wishes are. Even if it is possible to determine what his views were in the past, they might well have changed in the light of the stresses and strains of his current predicament. In this case, the highest good record was ... that it was likely that Mr James would want treatment up to the point where it became hopeless. But in so far as it is possible to ascertain the patient's wishes and feelings, his beliefs and values or the things which were important to him, it is those which should be taken into account because they are a component in making the choice which is right for him as an individual human being.'

It is to be noted indeed that towards the end of paragraph [24] of the Supreme Court judgment there is reference to the preferences of the patient concerned being an important component in deciding where his best interests lie.

As to the width and extent of the meaning of best interests, Lady Hale says at paragraph [39] of the judgment:

'The most that can be said, therefore, is that in considering the best interests of this particular patient at this particular time, decision-makers must look at his welfare in the widest sense, not just medical but social and psychological; they must consider the nature of the medical treatment in question, what it involves and its prospects of success; they must consider what the outcome of that treatment for the patient is likely to be; they must try and put themselves in the place of the individual patient and ask what his attitude to the treatment is or would be likely to be; and they must consult others who are looking after him or interested in his welfare, in particular for their view of what his attitude would be.'

CHAPTER 6

THE RIGHT TO LIFE: CHILDREN: END-OF-LIFE CARE; WHETHER TO GIVE LIFE-SUSTAINING TREATMENT

6.1 A FRAMEWORK FOR PRACTICE

The ethics of withholding or withdrawing life support are set out in a publication by the Royal College of Paediatrics and Child Health routinely used by practitioners and the court. It is entitled 'Withholding or Withdrawing Life Sustaining Treatment in Children: A Framework for Practice' (2nd edn, May 2004). This provides as follows (pp 28 and 29):

> **'3.1.3 Circumstances of withholding or withdrawal of treatment**
>
> *The "No Chance" Situation.* Treatment delays death but neither improves life's quality nor potential. Needlessly prolonging treatment in these circumstances is futile and burdensome and not in the best interests of the patient; hence there is no legal obligation for a doctor to provide it. Indeed, if this is done knowingly (futile treatment) it may constitute an assault or "inhuman and degrading treatment" under Article 3 of the European Convention on Human Rights. Consider for example a child with progressive metastatic malignant disease whose life would not benefit from chemotherapy or other forms of treatment aimed at cure.
>
> *The "No Purpose" Situation.* In these circumstances the child may be able to survive with treatment, but there are reasons to believe that giving treatment may not be in the child's best interest. For example, the child may develop or already have such a degree of irreversible impairment that it would be unreasonable to expect them to bear it. Continuing treatment might leave the child in a worse condition than already exists with the likelihood of further deterioration leading to an "impossibly poor life". The child may not be capable now or in the future of taking part in decision making or other self directed activity.
>
> In all the above circumstances it is appropriate to consider withholding or withdrawing treatment. If it is likely that future life will be "impossibly poor" then treatment might reasonably be withheld. If such a life already exists and there is likelihood of it continuing without foreseeable improvement, treatment might reasonably be withdrawn.

The "Unbearable" Situation. This situation occurs when the child and/or family feel that further treatment is more than can be borne they may wish to have treatment withdrawn or to refuse further treatment irrespective of the medical opinion that it may be of some benefit.'

6.2 PARENTAL CONSENT

Treatment which is administered to a child without parental consent is 'unlawful' constituting a civil trespass and possible criminal assault.

In *Glass v UK* (App 61827/00) ('*Glass No 2*') at paras 48 and 75, the European Court of Human Rights, analysing the English legal position, said that the regulatory framework in the United Kingdom is firmly predicated on the duty to preserve the life of a patient, save in exceptional circumstances, and that that same framework prioritises the requirements of parental consent and, save in exceptional cases, requires doctors to seek the intervention of the courts in the event of parental objection.

Whilst it is lawful for a doctor to obtain the consent of one parent and this may often suffice, where there is clearly a difference of view between the two parents over a concerning issue of medical treatment, the appropriate course must be to seek determination of the issue by the court.

In the *Glass* case the Court held that the decision to impose treatment on a child in defiance of the objections of his mother gave rise to an interference with the child's right to respect for his private life and in particular his right to physical integrity. In the case a 'do not resuscitate' notice had been placed on the notes of a disabled child who was thought to be about to die and diamorphine was administered contrary to his mother's wishes.

In the circumstances where there is a clear difference of opinion over medical treatment concerning a child between the clinicians and parents, the views of parents take precedence until the court is able to make a determination. Thus, in the period between the issue of proceedings and the judgment, the usual situation is that the views of the parents prevail unless the clinicians cannot, consistent with their professional views, follow the parents' instructions. As was stated by the Court of Appeal in *Portsmouth Hospital NHS Trust v Wyatt* [2005] 1 WLR 3995 the court accepted the submission that although clinicians owe no legal duty of care to parents, they have legal obligations to give effect to their wishes unless and until superseded by the court.

6.3 DUE PROCESS; EMERGENCY APPLICATIONS

It is clear from the legal authorities that it is always necessary so far as possible for parents to be in a position to address any application made in relation to medical treatment. Emergency applications, which may have to be made, present the difficulty that they cannot take place with the extensive and detailed medical evidence and argument that would pertain at a more substantive and lengthier hearing.

Often in serious medical treatment cases substantive hearings can be brought forward and expedited to be heard more expeditiously. Depending on the particular case, an emergency application will be quite necessary and justified. As was stated by Parker J in *Re OT* [2009] EWHC 633 (Fam), there was nothing in *Glass No 2* to suggest that emergency applications to the court in themselves are in breach of human rights, and she noted indeed that the European Court referred to the possibility that such applications might be made. What is important is that parents should be permitted time in order to present their case and should be able to be in a position to address the application.

Withdrawal of life-sustaining treatment which is no longer in the patient's best interests (whether an adult or a child) is not a breach of Articles 2, 3 or 8 of the European Convention on Human Rights (ECHR): *R (Burke) v General Medical Council* [2005] EWCA Civ 1003.

6.4 A DOCTOR CANNOT BE REQUIRED TO TREAT A PATIENT AGAINST HIS OR HER CLINICAL JUDGMENT

A doctor cannot be required to treat a child, whether by the court, in the exercise of its wardship jurisdiction, by the parents, by the child or anyone else. The decision whether to treat is dependent upon an exercise of his or her own professional judgment, subject only to the threshold requirement that, save in exceptional circumstances of emergency, he or she has the consent of someone who has authority to give that consent (*Re R (A Minor) (Wardship: Medical Treatment)* [1992] 1 FLR 190, at p 200).

This principle was drawn into sharp focus in *Re J (A Minor) (Medical Treatment)* [1992] 2 FLR 165. The child, aged 16 months, was severely handicapped, both mentally and physically, with a short expectation of life. He was placed with devoted foster carers by the local authority. His breathing had, on occasion, been assisted by the administration of oxygen. The doctor in whose charge the child was, was of the view that it would not be medically appropriate to intervene with intensive therapeutic measures, such as artificial ventilation, if the child were to suffer a life-threatening event.

The local authority applied to invoke the inherent jurisdiction of the High Court to determine whether artificial ventilation and/or other life-saving measures should be given to the child if he suffered a life-threatening event.

At a hearing on 12 May 1992, which was listed for the full hearing, but was treated as an interim hearing, the judge made an interim injunction, requiring the health authority, in the event of a life-threatening condition developing, to take all measures to prolong his life and provide artificial ventilation.

The Court of Appeal set aside the order, leaving the health authority free, subject to consent not being withdrawn, to treat J in accordance with their best clinical judgment. This left entirely to the doctors the decision whether or not to use mechanical ventilation in the light of changing circumstances. What the Court of Appeal firmly rejected was the suggestion that the medical practitioner in question should be required to treat the child in the way suggested and against his wishes or clinical recommendation. Lord Donaldson held that it would be an abuse of judicial power directly or indirectly to require the child to be treated contrary to the doctor's best clinical judgment.

In the case of *Re C (Medical Treatment)* [1998] 1 FLR 384, the court took the same approach, holding that the parents' contention that their child should be medically treated as they sought was tantamount to requiring the doctors to undertake a course of treatment which they were unwilling to do. It was held that the court could not consider making an order which would require the doctors to medically treat the child against their best clinical judgment.

At paragraph 18 of the judgment of Lady Hale in *Aintree NHS Foundation Trust v James* [2013] UKSC 67, she said:

> 'The judge began in the right place. He was careful to stress that the case was not about a general power to order how the doctors should treat their patient. This Act is concerned with enabling the court to do for the patient what he could do for himself if of full capacity, but it goes no further. On an application under this Act, therefore, the court has no greater powers than the patient would have if he were of full capacity. The judge said: "A patient cannot order a doctor to give a particular form of treatment, although he may refuse it. The court's position is no different" (para 14). In *Re J (A Minor) (Child in Care: Medical Treatment)* [1991] Fam 33, at

48, Lord Donaldson MR held that the court could not "require the [health] authority to follow a particular course of treatment. What the court can do is to withhold consent to treatment of which it disapproves and it can express its approval of other treatment proposed by the authority and its doctors". He repeated that view in *Re J (A Minor)(Child in Care: Medical Treatment)* [1993] Fam 15, at 26–27, when it was clearly the ratio decidendi of the case. To similar effect is *R v Cambridge District Health Authority, ex p B* [1995] 1 WLR 898, where the court would not interfere with the health authority's decision to refuse to fund further treatment of a child with leukaemia. More recently, in *R (Burke) v General Medical Council* [2005] EWCA Civ 1003, [2006] QB 273, Lord Phillips MR accepted the proposition of the General Medical Council that if a doctor concludes that the treatment which a patient wants is "not clinically indicated he is not required (ie he is under no legal obligation) to provide it" (para 50), and "Ultimately, however, a patient cannot demand that a doctor administer a treatment which the doctor considers is adverse to the patient's clinical needs" (para 55). Of course, there are circumstances in which a doctor's common law duty of care towards his patient requires him to administer a particular treatment, but it is not the role of the Court of Protection to decide that. Nor is the Court concerned with the legality of NHS policy or guidelines for the provision of particular treatments. Its role is to decide whether a particular treatment is in the best interests of a patient who is incapable of making the decision for himself."

6.5 IRREVERSIBLE BRAIN DAMAGE

In *Re C (A Minor) (Wardship: Medical Treatment)* [1990] Fam 26, a newborn baby suffering from congenital hydrocephalus was made a ward of court. The local authorities sought the court's determination as to the appropriate manner in which she should be treated medically should she contract a serious infection, or her existing feeding regimes become unviable. Baby C was assessed as severely and irreversibly brain-damaged. The prognosis was hopeless. The doctor, in whose charge the baby was, recommended that the objective of any treatment should therefore be to ease suffering rather than prolong her life. Whilst not specifying the instigation or discontinuance of any particular procedures, he further advised consultation with the baby's carers as to the appropriate method of achieving that objective. It was held that the court was entitled to approve, as being in her best interests, recommendations designed to ease the suffering rather than prolong life.

In the case of *Re OT* [2009] EWHC 633 (Fam) the court was concerned with a 9½-month-old baby boy suffering from an extremely rare mitochondrial condition of genetic origin. The brain damage he had suffered was irreversible, and it was highly likely that he would die at any time between the time of the hearing and three years of age. He was minimally conscious. The parents were absolutely devoted to him and wanted to preserve his life for as long as possible. Their view of his condition and his prognosis was profoundly at odds with that of the hospital. The parents disagreed with the hospital and the treating clinicians as well as the experts who had been instructed as to their son's prognosis and with their unanimous view that further intensive medical intervention was not appropriate, save for palliative care, and that the baby's life should come peacefully to an end.

The judge, Parker J, stated that whilst the child had a right to life, in her view he did not have the right to be kept alive in all the circumstances. She stated that the baby's medical circumstances came within the 'No Chance' Situation and the 'No Purpose' Situation within the 2004 Framework for Practice. At paragraph 164 of her judgment she said:

> 'Turning to the discipline of *NHS Trust v Wyatt and Another* [2005] 1 WLR 3995, I am in no doubt that in the baby's present position it is not in his best interests to suffer any more. I do not see any basis upon which his suffering can be alleviated to any meaningful extent. Looking at this from the assumed point of view of the baby himself, bearing in mind all the factors which I considered during the course of this judgment, and bearing in mind his lack of quality of life and the inevitable process of decline, particularly in the very dreadful circumstances in which he now finds himself, I believe that he would not wish to continue suffering in this way. The presumption that life should be prolonged is not irrebutable.'

6.6 DISCONTINUING VENTILATION IMMEDIATELY AND OFFERING PALLIATIVE CARE

Three legal authorities evidence the approach to be taken in relation to such applications for the immediate withdrawal of artificial ventilation, with the consequences if granted of palliative care to the suffering child. The case of an *NHS Trust v MB* [2006] EWHC 507 (Fam) was heard before Holman J. The case of *Re OT* [2009] EWHC 633 (Fam) was heard before Parker J. The case of *An NHS Foundation Trust v R (Child)* [2013] EWHC 2340 (Fam) was heard before Jackson J.

In each of these cases the court carefully analysed and weighed the best interests of the respective children. In each of these cases such process of analysis included the compilation of 'balance sheet lists' weighing the advantages and disadvantages of the options presented to the court. In the first case of *MB*, Holman J was not satisfied the court should authorise the immediate discontinuation of ventilation of the child. In each of the cases of *OT* and *R* the court was satisfied that it should authorise the immediate discontinuation of ventilation.

In *An NHS Trust v MB* [2006] EWHC 507 (Fam), Holman J was concerned with an 18-month-old boy who had been diagnosed with spinal muscular atrophy, a genetic condition that gradually removes the ability to move muscles voluntarily. He had been in hospital throughout since he was 7 weeks old. He was suffering from the most severe form of the condition and by the time of the hearing could not move at all, save for movement of his eyes and possible slight but barely perceptible movement of his eyebrows. He was not able to breathe unaided. He required positive pressure ventilation via a tube. He could not swallow at all and was being fed through a tube.

It was accepted that he may have normal cognitive function and that he could hear and occasionally see. It was accepted that MB was going to die, and that he would probably die within about a year although he might live longer. The judge in paragraph 12 of his judgment said that he was unable to use the description that 'it was almost a living death'.

Holman J said at paragraph 11 of his judgment:

'So far as I am aware, no court has yet been asked to prove that, against the will of the child's parents, life support may be withdrawn or discontinued, with the predictable, inevitable and immediate death of a conscious child with sensory awareness and assumed normal cognition and no reliable evidence of any significant brain damage.'

There were realistically two options, treatment wise.

The first was to continue broadly along the present management plan including ventilation by tube.

The second was that supported by the NHS Trust and Guardian for the child, who considered that the quality of life for MB was so low and the burden of living was so great that it was unethical/cruel to continue artificially to keep him alive, and that his ventilation tube should be withdrawn. By the use of sedatives, he could then have a peaceful pain-free and dignified death.

The judge determined that he was not persuaded that it was currently in the best interests of MB to discontinue ventilation with the inevitable result that he would immediately die.

The circumstances of the child in the case of OT have already been touched upon above. The child's condition was serious, incurable and life limiting. The Hospital Trust applied for orders that ventilation should be withdrawn immediately and the child should be offered appropriate treatment and nursing care. The expert evidence was that the child could not continue to be ventilated at the current pressures without lung damage. The judge accepted that the prospect for the child of painful and distressing interventions was inevitable if she did not make the order. The judge stated that if she did not grant the application to withdraw ventilation the child would decline. The spectrum of presentation would be from death fairly immediately from organ failure and chronic lung damage to a series of crises during which more and more desperate attempts would be made to provide treatment against the background of parental demands to escalate treatment.

At paragraph 163 of her judgment Parker J said:

> 'When this case commenced I hoped there might be a way in which the decision to withdraw life support might be obviated. I note that in *NHS Trust v MB* [2006] EWHC 507 (Fam) where a child was suffering from spinal muscular atrophy, Holman J did not accede to an application to withdraw life support in respect of this child, although he did make a limitation of treatment order very similar to that which I am being asked to endorse. Holman J stressed that in that case the child did have some quality of life. He had normal cognition and the normal likely reactions of a child of his age to his family and his surroundings and no brain damage. I regret that OT is in a very different position.'

In the third case concerning baby R before Jackson J the child was 14 months of age. He had profound developmental delay and had never left hospital. He could not breathe for himself and required continuous artificial ventilation. The judge accepted that he had a level of awareness, some capacity to react to light and sound. His condition was progressive and ultimately fatal. If ventilation was continued, his life expectancy was reduced but uncertain. If ventilation was withdrawn, he would rapidly die. The issue in the case was that the child's parents, along with the whole family, wanted him to move to live at home with a package of care including long-term ventilation. The treating doctors considered that this would be too burdensome for the child and that it would be in his best interests for ventilation to be withdrawn, allowing him to die in comfort. It was the unanimous view of the treating clinicians that it was not in his best interests to continue living by means of long-term ventilation. They considered that such treatment was delaying the child's death without significantly alleviating the suffering.

They concluded that his condition fell into the 'No Chance' category of the 2004 Royal College of Paediatrics and Child Health guidance framework for practice.

In the balancing act the judge took into account that he must inevitably reflect first on the child's most precious possession, his life. With continued ventilation the child might live for some years. A conclusion that it was in his best interests to be allowed to die could only be reached if it was clearly shown to be in his best interests. If there was doubt it must be resolved in favour of continued life, reflecting the unique value that society places on life itself. The judge next took account of the deeply held views of the parents and wider family, and love and care that they were willing to provide to the child. Despite such committed love, the judge commented that it was the child alone, however, who would have to bear the burdens of long-term ventilation while experiencing little if any pleasure. At paragraph 62 of his judgment, in determining that it was in the child's best interests for ventilation to be withdrawn, the judge said:

> 'Continued long-term ventilation would be futile and would progressively cause him more and more suffering, while giving him very little in terms of any positive experience of the life that was being preserved by such intrusive medical intervention.'

Sadly, the child R died on 31 October 2013.

6.7 AUTHORISING FUTURE DISCONTINUANCE AND/OR NON-RE-INSTIGATION OF ARTIFICIAL VENTILATION IN THE EVENT OF CERTAIN MEDICAL OCCURRENCES

In *Re J (A Minor) (Wardship: Medical Treatment)* [1991] 1 FLR 366, the Official Solicitor asked the court for guidance as to the proper approach with regard to children who were severely handicapped but not dying. The submission of the Official Solicitor was that, aside from the case of a child who is already terminally ill, there was an absolute rule that the court was never justified in withholding consent to treatment which would enable a child to survive a life-threatening condition, whatever the pain or the side effects inherent in the treatment and whatever the quality of life which it would experience thereafter.

The child was born in May 1990, prematurely, weighing only two and a half pounds. Due to shortage of oxygen and impaired blood supply, the little boy suffered severe brain damage. There were recurrent convulsions and episodes where he stopped breathing and, as a result, he spent two periods of 6 weeks on a ventilator. The child was not dying or on the point of death. The most optimistic view was that he would develop spastic quadriplegia, that he was likely to be blind and deaf and that he would never be able to speak or develop even limited intellectual abilities.

The child was made a ward of court. The question arose as to whether the court should approve what was proposed by the doctors. The fundamental medical issue was whether, if the child suffered another collapse and stopped breathing, he should be put back on a mechanical ventilator. On the evidence, the doctors were unanimous that, in his present condition, Baby J should not be put back on to such a mechanical ventilator. Three factors stood out. First, the severe lack of capacity of the child in all his faculties, which, even without any further complication, would make his existence barely sentient. Secondly, further mechanical ventilation, if required, would itself involve the risk of a deterioration in the child's condition and of further brain damage. Thirdly, all the doctors drew attention to the invasive and distressing nature of mechanical ventilation and the intensive care required to accompany it.

The Court of Appeal endorsed the judge's decision at first instance, approving the medical recommendations and holding that it would not be in the child's best interests to subject him to a mechanical ventilator if he stopped breathing, whilst at the same time leaving the doctors free to take more active measures to preserve the child's life if the situation improved.

The court rejected the submission of the Official Solicitor referred to above. Taylor LJ at 381B–E said this:

> 'The plight of Baby J is appalling and the problem facing the court in the exercise of its wardship jurisdiction is of the greatest difficulty. When should the court rule against the giving of treatment aimed at prolonging life?
>
> Three preliminary principles are not in dispute. First, it is settled law that the court's prime and paramount consideration must be the best interests of the child. That is easily said but not easily applied. What it does involve is that the views of the parents, although they should be heeded and weighed, cannot prevail over the court's view of the ward's best interests. In the present case the parents, finding themselves in a hideous dilemma have not taken a strong view so that no conflict arises.

Secondly, the court's high respect for the sanctity of human life imposes a strong presumption in favour of taking all steps capable of preserving it, save in exceptional circumstances. The problem is to define those circumstances.

Thirdly, and as a corollary to the second principle, it cannot be too strongly emphasised that the court never sanctions steps to terminate life. That would be unlawful. There is no question of approving, even in a case of the most horrendous disability, a course aimed at terminating life or accelerating death. The court is concerned only with the circumstances in which steps should not be taken to prolong life.'

This passage by Taylor LJ encompasses the three preliminary principles to be applied. Indeed, such approach has been endorsed in cases relating to incapacitated adults, including *Re R (Adult: Medical Treatment)* [1996] 2 FLR 99 at 107 and *Re H (A Patient)* [1998] 2 FLR 36 at 40.

The strong presumption in favour of prolonging life is not irrefutable. The court must balance all the evidence, giving due weight to the sanctity of life and looking at the problem, not from the point of view of the decider but from the assumed point of view of the patient. It is important to emphasise that even a very severely handicapped person may find a quality of life rewarding which to the unhandicapped might seem manifestly intolerable.

Taylor LJ at 383H put the matter in this way:

'I consider the correct approach is for the court to judge the quality of life the child would have to endure if given the treatment, and decide whether in all the circumstances such a life would be so afflicted as to be intolerable to that child. I say, "to that child" because the test should not be whether the life would be tolerable to the decider. The test must be whether the child in question, if capable of exercising sound judgment, would consider the life tolerable. This is the approach adopted by McKenzie J in *Re Superintendent of Family and Child Service and Dawson* [1983] 145 DLR (3d) 610 in the passage at page 620 ...

In *Re C (Medical Treatment)* [1998] 1 FLR 384, a child of 16 months was suffering from the fatal disease spinal muscular atrophy. Her doctors described her as being in a 'no chance' situation, meaning that her disease was so severe that life-sustaining treatment would simply delay death without significantly alleviating suffering and they considered such treatment inappropriate.

The child had been placed on ventilation to support her breathing. The doctor, in whose charge the child was, had come to the conclusion that it was not in the child's best interests for her to continue on indefinite ventilation, which would produce increasing distress and would inevitably involve a tracheotomy operation under anaesthetic, which might itself give rise to epilepsy, but that she should be taken off ventilation. He was further of the view that, if she were then, as was highly probable, to suffer a further respiratory relapse, it would be against her interests to seek to place her back on ventilation or indeed to engage in resuscitative treatment.

The hospital sought, through issuing an originating summons, the court's approval for the withdrawal of ventilation and non-resuscitation in the event of a respiratory arrest. The parents were prepared for ventilation to be withdrawn to see if their child would survive without it, but wished it to be reinstated in the event of further respiratory relapse.

The judge, Sir Stephen Brown, President of the Family Division, approached the course proposed by the hospital trust. The Framework for Practice was referred to the judge and particularly paragraph 2.2.2 on p 10, where it was stated:

> '... withdrawal of treatment in paediatric intensive care units accounts for up to sixty five percent of deaths. Examples might be [and the second example is] the paediatric neurologist might reasonably withhold ventilator care in a child with progressive respiratory failure from anterior-horn cell disease.'

In this case the judge made an order in the following terms:

> 'There be leave to treat the minor C as advised by Doctor H, such treatment to include the withdrawal of artificial ventilation and non-resuscitation in the event of a respiratory arrest and palliative care to ease her suffering and permit her life to end peacefully and with dignity, such treatment being in C's best interest.'

In *Portsmouth NHS Trust v Wyatt* [2005] EWCA Civ 1181, [2005] 1 WLR 3995, a case concerning a two-year-old child born 14 weeks prematurely and suffering from chronic respiratory and kidney problems with profound brain damage, Hedley J at first instance, upheld by the Court of Appeal, made a series of declarations unlimited in time authorising doctors to withhold ventilation in the event that the child suffered an infection that led or might lead to a collapsed lung.

As already indicated previously above, in the case of *An NHS Trust v MB* [2006] EWHC 507 (Fam) Holman J was unwilling to declare that it was in the best interests of the 18-month-old child M to discontinue ventilation with the inevitable result that he would immediately die.

However, the judge stated that there were procedures which went beyond maintaining ventilation, which required the positive infliction of pain and which, if required, would, in his view mean that M had moved naturally towards his death despite the ventilation. He said that if that point were to be reached, it would then be in the child's best interests to withhold those procedures even though he would probably die.

The judge was accordingly willing to make a declaration to the effect that it was in M's best interests and lawful to withhold or not to administer what he described as 'the most invasive and no longer justifiable forms of treatment', comprising cardiopulmonary resuscitation (CPR), ECG monitoring, the administration of intravenous antibiotics, and blood sampling. The judge referred to the fact that the administration of intravenous antibiotics and blood sampling, like CPR, requires the infliction of pain. These would be indicated by some new and serious infection in MB indicating possibly that death was near and it would not be in his best interests or justified to embark upon the infliction of pain.

Holman J stressed that:

> '... a declaration reflecting the above will be permissive in its effect. It will have the effect that, in the view of this court, doctors or staff *need* not embark on the listed treatments; but neither the declaration nor anything in this judgment should deter or would prevent a doctor or staff from giving any of the listed treatments if he or they thought fit at the time.'

6.8   ADVANCED CARE PLANS

In the judgment in the case of *Portsmouth Hospital NHS Trust v Wyatt* [2005] EWCA Civ 1181 at paragraphs 117 and 118 the Court of Appeal said the following:

> '117. We would, however, as a matter of practice, counsel caution in making declarations involving seriously damaged or gravely ill children which are open-ended. In the same way that this court said in *R (Burke) v GMC* that it is not the function of the court to be used as a general advice centre (see paragraph 21 of the court's judgment), it is, in our view, not the function of the court to oversee the treatment plan for a gravely ill child. That function is for doctors in consultation with the child's parents. Judges take decisions on the basis of particular factual substrata. The core function is to make a particular decision on a particular issue.

118. As a general proposition, therefore, we have reservations about judges making open-ended declarations which they may have to revisit if circumstances change. But all that said, we came to the clear conclusion that Hedley J had indeed thought through the implications of what he was doing, and was entitled both to make and renew the declaration.'

In the case of *Re KH (A Child)* [2012] EWHC B18 (Fam) the Trust invited the court to declare that it was lawful and in the child's best interests 'to have medical treatment withheld in the circumstances as described in the Advanced Care Plan'.

The Court made clear that the Trust had rightly brought the matter before the court at a time when the child appeared relatively well, rather than as an urgent application at the time of deterioration. It enabled the issues to be investigated in a way that would be impossible in a crisis.

The trade-off for those advantages, however, was that the medical situation had not crystallised, as it would by definition have done in a crisis. Accordingly the range of issues was the greater and the timescale might be indefinite. Jackson J determined that the declaration sought should only extend to matters where the factual basis was known. He said it would be unwise to endorse aspects of a plan that may change in its details. He said the plan also contained provisions for which legal endorsement was unnecessary, or which were matters of detail only. He determined that the appropriate approach was to identify the treatment issues that needed to be determined and not likely to change over time.

6.9   CONJOINED TWINS: THE DOCTRINE OF DOUBLE EFFECT

The case of *Re A (Children) (Conjoined Twins: Surgical Separation)* [2001] Fam 147 shows that the court is able to fashion means of permitting doctors to act in a way which accords with the demands of humanity. The case concerned two baby girls, Jodie and Mary, who were born joined at the lower abdomen. Jodie was stronger than Mary. If Mary had been born a singleton, she would not have been viable and would have died shortly after birth. She remained alive because a common artery enabled Jodie to circulate sufficient oxygenated blood for Mary to survive for the time being. If the twins were surgically separated, the evidence was that Jodie would have a good prospect of a healthy and normal life, but Mary would die within minutes. If no operation were performed, both twins would die within months because Jodie's heart would not be able to sustain both Mary and herself in the longer term.

The court granted an application by the hospital for a declaration that it could lawfully carry out separation surgery. The judges had no difficulty in concluding that it was better that one twin should have a normal life than that neither should survive the first few months of life. But there was a formidable question whether the operation, carried out in the knowledge that it was sure to result in Mary's immediate death, would amount to murder.

The court considered three possible defences: lack of causation, lack of intent and necessity, overshadowed by a concept of quasi-self-defence. It concluded that the operation would be lawful, but the three members of the court expressed their reasoning in different ways. Ward LJ concluded that where a doctor was faced with conflicting duties towards two patients whose lives were at risk, it was lawful for him to adopt the course which would be the lesser of two evils. He did not use the language of necessity, but his reasoning may be said to fall within the doctrine. Brooke LJ conducted a lengthy and comprehensive analysis of the doctrine of necessity, at 219–238, and he concluded that the principle applied on the unusual facts of the case. He said at 240:

> 'According to Sir James Stephen there are three necessary requirements for the application of the doctrine of necessity: (i) the act is needed to avoid inevitable and irreparable evil; (ii) no more should be done than is reasonably necessary for the purpose to be achieved; (iii) the evil inflicted must not be disproportionate to the evil avoided. Given that the principles of modern family law point irresistibly to the conclusion that the interests of Jodie must be preferred to the conflicting interests of Mary, I consider that all three of these requirements are satisfied in this case.

> Finally, the doctrine of the sanctity of life respects the integrity of the human body. The proposed operation would give these children's bodies the integrity which nature denied them.'

Robert Walker LJ concluded, at 258–259, that whereas it would be unlawful to kill Mary intentionally, that is, to undertake an operation with the primary purpose of killing her, Mary's death would not be the purpose of the operation. Although Mary's death would be foreseen as an inevitable consequence of an operation which was intended, and necessary, to save Jodie's life, Mary's death would not be the intention of the surgery. She would die 'because tragically her body, on its own, is not and never has been viable'. His judgment therefore combined all three strands of necessity, lack of intent and lack of causation.

The analysis that Mary's death would be regarded in the eyes of the law as caused by the fact that her body was not viable on its own comes from case-law which has given rise to the so-called doctrine of double effect.

The origin of the doctrine may be traced to the summing up of Devlin J in the case of *Adams*. Dr Adams was charged with the murder of an elderly patient by overdosing her with morphia and heroin. His defence was that he had prescribed the drugs for the alleviation of pain. The trial was in 1957 and the case was unreported, but Lord Devlin wrote an account of it in 1985 in his book *Easing the Passing*. In his summing up, as he recounted it, he said:

> 'If the first purpose of medicine, the restoration of health, can no longer be achieved, there is still much for a doctor to do, and he is entitled to do all that is proper and necessary to relieve pain and suffering, even if the measures he takes may incidentally shorten life. This is not because there is a special defence for medical men but because no act is murder which does not cause death. We are not dealing here with the philosophical or technical cause, but with the commonsense cause. The cause of death is the illness or the injury, and the proper medical treatment that is administered and that has an incidental effect on determining the exact moment of death is not the cause of death in any sensible use of the term. But ... no doctor, nor any man, no more in the case of the dying than of the healthy, has the right deliberately to cut the thread of life.'

He also directed the jury that if the defendant did 'some act capable, if the necessary intent was present, of being murderous', the prosecution had also to prove the intent to murder.

The summing up therefore left it open to the jury to acquit Dr Adams, if they considered it possible that his purpose was the alleviation of pain, either on the basis that the death should be regarded as the consequence of the patient's infirmity rather than the drugs which were intended to alleviate its consequences, or on the basis that there was a lack of intent. Both strands can be seen in Robert Walker LJ's analysis in *Re A*.

A particular feature of *Re A* was the duty to protect Jodie's life and the recognition that it was imperilled, albeit unintentionally, by the parasitic life of Mary. Ward LJ said at 203:

> 'Mary uses Jodie's heart and lungs to receive and use Jodie's oxygenated blood. This will cause Jodie's heart to fail and cause Jodie's death as surely as a slow drip of poison. How can it be just that Jodie should be required to tolerate that state of affairs? One does not need to label Mary with the American terminology which would paint her to be "an unjust aggressor",

which I feel is wholly inappropriate language for the sad and helpless position in which Mary finds herself. I have no difficulty in agreeing that this unique happening cannot be said to be unlawful. But ... I can see no difference in essence between ... resort to legitimate self-defence and the doctors coming to Jodie's defence and removing the threat of fatal harm to her presented by Mary's draining her life blood. The availability of such a plea of quasi-self-defence, modified to meet the quite exceptional circumstances nature has inflicted on the twins, makes intervention by the doctors lawful.'

Similarly Robert Walker LJ said at 255:

'There is on the facts of this case some element of protecting Jodie against the unnatural invasion of her body through the physical burden imposed by her conjoined twin. That element must not be overstated. It would be absurd to suggest that Mary, a pitiful and innocent baby, is an unjust aggressor ... Nevertheless, the doctors' duty to protect and save Jodie's life if they can is of fundamental importance to the resolution of this appeal.'

CHAPTER 7

THE 'RIGHT TO DIE': SUICIDE; ASSISTED SUICIDE; VOLUNTARY EUTHANASIA/MERCY KILLING

7.1 THE 'RIGHT TO DIE'

The 'right to die' refers to those who seek not to be prevented by the state from being assisted to die or undergoing voluntary euthanasia.

Article 8 of the European Convention on Human Rights (ECHR) provides:

> '1. Everyone has the right to respect for his private and family life, his home and his correspondence.
>
> 2. There shall be no interference by a public authority with the exercise of this right except such as is in accordance with the law and is necessary in a democratic society in the interests of national security, public safety or the economic well-being of the country, for the prevention of disorder or crime, for the protection of health or morals, or for the protection of the rights and freedoms of others.'

Article 8 protects values which are the birth right of every person: a right to personal autonomy, to self-determination and to dignity.

The leading medical treatment cases of *Pretty*, *Purdy*, *Nicklinson*, *AM* and *Lamb* have all included consideration of the interrelationship between the criminal law in this country (in relation to assisted suicide and voluntary euthanasia) and the rights of the applicants in those cases to personal autonomy, self-determination and to dignity under Article 8 of the Convention.

Save by possible self-starvation, none of those persons were capable of ending their own lives unaided.

As is stated in the case of *Haas v Switzerland* (App 31322/07) (2011) 53 EHRR 33 which will be further considered below: 'The vast majority of member states to the Convention appear to place more weight on the protection of an individual's life than the right to end one's life.'

The anxieties and concerns evidenced by the above leading cases pertain
to those individuals who may not necessarily be terminally ill but are
living with constant unbearable suffering and loss of dignity, and have a
clear and settled autonomous wish to bring about their death at a time
and in a manner of their choosing, whether through assisted suicide or
voluntary euthanasia.

The complex legal and ethical issues arising were set out by Lord Steyn
in his judgment in the case of *R (Pretty) v Director of Public
Prosecutions* [2002] 1 AC 800 at paragraph 54:

> 'The subject of euthanasia and assisted suicide has been deeply
> controversial long before the adoption of the Universal Declaration of
> Human Rights in 1948, which was followed two years later by the
> European Convention on Human Rights and Freedoms (1950). The
> arguments and counter arguments have ranged widely. There is a
> conviction that human life is sacred and that the corollary is that
> euthanasia and assisted suicide are always wrong. This view is supported
> by the Roman Catholic Church, Islam and other religions. There is also a
> secular view, shared sometimes by atheists and agnostics that human life is
> sacred. On the other side, there are many millions who do not hold these
> beliefs. For many the personal autonomy of individuals is predominant.
> They would argue that it is the moral right of individuals to have a say
> over the time and manner of their death. On the other hand, there are
> utilitarian arguments to the contrary effect. The terminally ill and those
> suffering great pain from incurable illnesses are often vulnerable. And not
> all families, whose interests are at stake, are wholly unselfish and loving.
> There is a risk that assisted suicide may be abused in the sense that such
> people may be persuaded that they want to die or that they ought to want
> to die. Another strand is that, when one knows the genuine wish of a
> terminally ill patient to die, they should not be forced against their will to
> endure a life they no longer wish to endure. Such views are countered by
> those who say it is a slippery slope or the thin end of the wedge. It is also
> argued that euthanasia and assisted suicide, under medical supervision,
> will undermine the trust between doctors and patients. It is said that
> protective safeguards are unworkable. The countervailing contentions of
> moral philosophers, medical experts and ordinary people are endless. The
> literature is vast: see for a sample of range of views ... It is not for us, in
> this case, to express a view on these arguments. But it is of great
> importance to note that these are ancient questions on which millions in
> the past have taken diametrically opposite views and still do.'

As Mr Justice Royce said at paragraph 151 of the judgment in the first
instance case of *R (on the application of R (Nicklinson and AM) v
Ministry of Justice* [2012] EWHC 2381 (Admin):

'Each case gives rise to the most profound ethical, moral, religious and social issues. Some will say the judges must step in to change the law. Some may be sorely tempted to do so. But the short answer is that to do so here would be to usurp the function of Parliament in this classically sensitive area. Any change would need the most carefully structured safeguards which only Parliament can deliver.'

7.2 SUICIDE

Section 1 of the Suicide Act 1961 provides:

'The rule of law whereby it is a crime for a person to commit suicide is hereby abrogated.'

As Lords Bingham and Hope pointed out in the case of *Pretty*, it is wrong to say there is a right to commit suicide; s 1 of the 1961 Act can more accurately be described as conferring immunity from the criminal process for those who actually commit suicide.

7.3 ASSISTED SUICIDE

Section 2 of the Suicide Act 1961 was amended by s 59 of the Coroners and Justice Act 2009, but the purpose was to clarify, rather than change, the law on assisted suicide.

Section 2 in its amended form provides:

'(1) A person ("D") commits an offence if –
(a) D does an act capable of encouraging or assisting a suicide or attempted suicide of another person, and
(b) D's act was intended to encourage or assist suicide or an attempt at suicide.

(1A) The person referred to in subsection (1)(a) need not be a specific person (or class of person) known to, or identified by, D.

(1B) D may commit an offence under this section whether or not a suicide, or an attempted suicide, occurs.

(1C) An offence under this section is triable on indictment and a person convicted of such an offence is liable to imprisonment for a term not exceeding 14 years.

    ...

(4) No proceedings shall be instituted for an offence under this section except by or with the consent of the Director of Public Prosecutions.'

Section 2A(1) provides:

> 'If D arranges for a person ("D2") to do an act that is capable of encouraging or assisting the suicide or attempted suicide of another person and D2 does that act, D is also to be treated for the purposes of this Act as having done it.'

The terms and effect of the Supreme Court judgment in the appeals concerning Tony Nicklinson, Paul Lamb and AM described as Martin reported at [2014] UKSC 38 is considered and analysed in due course in this chapter. The formal title of the case is *R (on the application of Nicklinson) v Ministry of Justice; R (on the application of AM) v Director of Public Prosecutions* [2014] UKSC 38.

The legal authorities here and in Europe preceding the above Supreme Court judgment are considered first of all.

The case of *R (Pretty) v DPP* as heard by the House of Lords is reported at [2001] UKHL 61, [2002] 1 AC 800.

Mrs Pretty suffered from motor neurone disease. She wanted to be able to enlist her husband's help to commit suicide. He was willing to assist, but only if he could be sure that he would not be prosecuted under s 2. The DPP refused to give such an undertaking. She applied for judicial review of his refusal to do so or alternatively for a declaration that s 2 was incompatible with Article 8.

Lord Bingham at paragraph 9 referred to two principles which he described as 'deeply embedded in English law'. The first was the distinction between the taking of one's own life by one's own act and the taking of life through the intervention or with the help of a third party. The former was permissible; the latter was not. The second distinction was between the cessation of lifesaving or life prolonging treatment on one hand and the taking of action lacking medical, therapeutic or palliative justification but intended solely to terminate life on the other.

He went on to say:

> 'It is not enough for Mrs Pretty to show that the United Kingdom would not be acting inconsistently with the Convention if it were to permit is assisted suicide; she must go further and establish that the United Kingdom is in breach of the Convention by failing to permit it or would be in breach of the Convention if it did not permit it. Such a contention is in my opinion untenable.'

Lord Bingham held, at paragraphs 26 to 30, that Article 8 was not engaged by s 2; but that, if Article 8 was engaged, s 2 was not incompatible with it.

The case was heard by the European Court of Human Rights (ECtHR) in Strasbourg and the judgment is reported at (2002) 35 EHRR 1.

There were two aspects of the decision of the ECtHR. First, as to whether Article 8 was engaged by s 2 of the Suicide Act 1961 as amended. Secondly, in Mrs Pretty's case as to whether there had been a violation of Article 8.

The ECtHR disagreed with the House of Lords opinion that Article 8 was not engaged, but agreed that Article 8 was not breached in her case.

As to the engagement of Article 8, at paragraph 65 of the judgment of the ECtHR it was said:

'The very essence of the Convention is respect for human dignity and human freedom. Without in any way negating the principle of sanctity of life protected under the Convention, the court considers that it is under Article 8 that notions of the quality of life take on significance. In an era of growing medical sophistication combined with longer life expectancies, many people are concerned that they should not be forced to linger on in old age or in states of advanced physical or mental decrepitude which conflict with strongly held ideas of self and personal identity.'

Further on the issue as to the engagement of Article 8, and paragraph 67 of the judgment it was said:

'The applicant in this case is prevented by law from exercising her choice to avoid what she considers will be an undignified and distressing end to her life. The Court is not prepared to exclude that this constitutes an interference with her right to respect for private life as guaranteed under Article 8(1) of the Convention.'

The ECtHR then went on to consider whether in fact there had been a breach of Article 8.

On the question of compliance, the Court said that s 2 of the Suicide Act 1961 as amended was designed to safeguard life by protecting the weak and vulnerable, and that it (the Court) would take into account that 'a margin of appreciation' is left to the national authorities whose decision remains subject to review by the Court for conformity with the requirements of the Convention. 'The margin of appreciation' to be accorded to the competent national authorities will vary in accordance with the nature of the issues and the importance of the interests at stake.

The judgment of the European Court contained three material points. First, a blanket ban on assisted suicide was not disproportionate in the view of the court. Secondly, it was not arbitrary to reflect the importance of life by prohibiting assisted suicide, while providing a system of enforcement which allowed due regard to be given in each particular case to the public interest, the requirements of deterrence and such like. Thirdly, strong objection could be raised against any claim by the executive to exempt in advance any individual or classes of individuals from the operation of the law.

The case of *R (Purdy) v DPP* was heard in the House of Lords and is reported at [2009] UKHL 45; [2010] AC 345.

Mrs Purdy suffered from multiple sclerosis. She expected that a time would come when she would regard her life as unbearable and would want to end it while still physically able to do so. By that stage she would need her husband's assistance to travel to a country where assisted suicide was lawful. He was willing to help her, but she was concerned about his risk of prosecution under s 2. She asked the DPP to set out the factors which he would take into account in deciding whether to bring a prosecution, but he declined to be drawn. She sought judicial review of his refusal on the ground that, without such clarification, the law relating to assisted suicide did not satisfy the Article 8(2) requirements of accessibility and foreseeability.

The House of Lords agreed and made the order which led to the DPP issuing a final policy statement in February 2010. Lord Hope and others in the judgments said that Parliament should be the lawmaker in the area of assisted suicide.

The judgments of the House of Lords contain a narrower and a broader strand of reasoning of a significantly different nature.

The narrower line of reasoning reflected the argument advanced by leading counsel for the applicant. He contended that the scope of the law of assisted suicide was for Parliament to decide, not for the court or the DPP, but in order for the law to comply with the convention requirements of accessibility and foreseeability it was necessary for the DPP to clarify the factors which he would take into account in giving his consent for prosecution. How he chose to do so was a matter for the DPP.

The broader line of reasoning appears in parts of the judgments of Lady Hale and Lord Browne.

On Lady Hale's approach, the problem with the law was not simply one of accessibility, but was more fundamental, namely that s 2 was potentially incompatible with Article 8 because of its blanket nature, and that in order to make it compliant with Article 8 it was necessary for the DPP to produce guidelines which would limit its scope.

In the case before the Divisional Court concerning *Tony Nicklinson and AM* [2012] EWHC 2381 (Admin) to be considered in more detail in due course, the Court accepted and adopted the narrower strand of reasoning in the judgments of the Lords in *Purdy* concerning the interpretation of the Strasbourg judgment in *Pretty*.

The DPP issued his final policy statement ('the Policy')in February 2010 (available at http://www.cps.gov.uk/publications/prosecution/assisted_suicide_policy.html). The policy statement lists 16 factors tending in favour of prosecution and six factors tending against prosecution.

The factors identified as tending in favour of prosecution (paragraph 43) are:

'1.   the victim was under 18 years of age;
2.   the victim did not have the capacity (as defined by the Mental Capacity Act 2005) to reach an informed decision to commit suicide;
3.   the victim had not reached the voluntary, clear, settled and informed decision to commit suicide;
4.   the victim had not clearly and unequivocally communicated his or her decision to commit suicide to the suspect;
5.   The victim did not seek the encouragement or assistance of the suspect personally or on his or her own initiative;
6.   the suspect was not wholly motivated by compassion; for example, the suspect was motivated by the prospect that he or she or a person closely connected to him or her stood to gain in some way from the death of the victim;
7.   the suspect pressured the victim to commit suicide;
8.   the suspect did not take reasonable steps to ensure that any other person had not pressured the victim to commit suicide;
9.   the suspect had a history of violence or abuse against the victim;
10.   the victim was physically able to undertake the act that constituted the assistance to him or herself;
11.   the suspect was unknown to the victim and encouraged or assisted the victim to commit or attempt to commit suicide by providing specific information via, for example, a website or publication;

12. the suspect gave encouragement or assistance to more than one victim who were not known to each other;

13. the suspect was paid by the victim or those close to the victim for his or her encouragement or assistance;

14. the suspect was acting in his or her capacity as a medical doctor, nurse, other healthcare professional, a professional carer (whether for payment or not), or as a person in authority, such as a prison officer, and the victim was in his or her care;

15. the suspect was aware the victim intended to commit suicide in a public place where it was reasonable to think that members of the public may be present;

16. the suspect was acting in his or her capacity as a person involved in the management or as an employee (whether for payment or not) of an organisation or group, a purpose of which is to provide a physical environment (whether for payment or not) in which to allow another to commit suicide.'

The factors identified as tending against prosecution (paragraph 45) are:

'1. the victim had reached a voluntary, clear, settled and informed decision to commit suicide;

2. the suspect was wholly motivated by compassion;

3. the actions of the suspect, although sufficient to come within the definition of the offence, were of only minor encouragement or assistance;

4. the suspect had sought to dissuade the victim from taking the course of action which resulted in his or her suicide;

5. the actions of the suspect may be characterised as reluctant encouragement or assistance in the face of a determined wish on the part of the victim to commit suicide;

6. the suspect reported the victim's suicide to the police and fully assisted them in their enquiries into the circumstances of the suicide or the attempt and his or her part in providing encouragement or assistance.'

The ECtHR case of *Haas v Switzerland* (2011) 53 EHRR 33 is of significance in relation to assisted suicide.

The applicant lived in Switzerland, where assisted suicide is permitted. He had a long history of mental illness and wished to commit suicide. No doctor was willing to help him to do so. He complained about the refusal of the Swiss authorities to permit him to obtain lethal drugs, without a prescription, in a sufficient quantity to enable him to end his life in a dignified manner. He contended that the authorities thereby violated his right under Article 8 to decide when and how to end his life. The court held there was no violation.

The court accepted at paragraph 51 that the right of an individual to decide how and when to end his life, provided that he is in a position to make up his own mind in that respect, is one aspect of the right to respect for private life within the meaning of Article 8. The question whether there has been a violation depends on Article 8(2). As to that, the court said at paragraph 55:

> 'The Convention and the Protocols thereto must be interpreted in the light of the present day conditions ... In Switzerland, under article 115 of the Criminal Code, incitement to commit or assistance with suicide are only punishable where the perpetrator of such acts commits them for selfish motives. By comparison, the Benelux countries in particular have decriminalised the act of assisting suicide, but only in well-defined circumstances. Certain other countries only allow "passive" acts of assistance. The vast majority of member states, however, appear to place more weight on the protection of an individual's life than on the right to end one's life. The court concludes that the states have a wide margin of appreciation in that respect.'

This case is accordingly significant in reiterating the understanding that, within the remit and purpose of the Convention, member states have a wide margin of appreciation as to the nature of their approaches to statutory provisions concerning criminalisation or otherwise of assisted suicide.

The case of *R (on the application of AM) v DPP* at first instance in the Divisional Court is reported at [2012] EWHC 2381 (Admin), and on appeal to the Court of Appeal at [2013] EWCA Civ 961.

The applicant AM, described as Martin (not his real name) through the judgment, suffered from catastrophic physical disabilities but his mental processes were unimpaired in the sense that he was fully conscious of his predicament. He suffered from 'locked in syndrome'. He determined that he wished to die with dignity and without further suffering but his condition made him incapable of ending his own life. He was not terminally ill and he faced the prospect of living for many years.

Martin was capable of physically assisted suicide, but this would involve someone else committing an offence under s 2 of the Suicide Act 1961 as amended. It was possible for him to end his life at a Dignitas clinic in Zurich without an offence being committed under Swiss law; and if Martin's wife was willing to help him to do so, it was unlikely that she would face prosecution in England under the policy published by the DPP following the judgment in *Purdy*. However, Martin's wife, who was herself a nurse and devoted to his care, was understandably not willing to support him for that purpose, with which she did not agree, although she wished to be with him to provide comfort and make her final farewell, if he was to succeed in his purpose by the help of others.

The relief sought by Martin was an order that the DPP should clarify his published policy so that other people, who might on compassionate grounds be willing to assist Martin to commit suicide through the use of Dignitas, would know, one way or the other, whether they would be more likely than not to face prosecution in England. The potential helper or helpers might be a member of the public who had no previous knowledge of Martin, a health professional or a solicitor who might act as an intermediary in making the necessary arrangements.

In the Court of Appeal, leading counsel for Martin accepted that s 2 of the 1961 Act was compatible with the convention law and was not a disproportionate interference with the Article 8 right providing only the DPP exercised his discretion not to initiate a prosecution against someone assisting a person to commit suicide in any case where to do so would involve a disproportionate interference with Article 8 rights. It was submitted that, in the light of Martin's desperate and undignified condition and his settled wish to die, that to prosecute any doctor or other professional who now assisted him to bring about his own death would necessarily infringe Martin's Article 8 rights – it was said that it would be a wholly disproportionate interference, frustrating his choice of how and when he should die.

The judgment of the court in *AM* at first instance in the Divisional Court addresses specifically the issue of whether s 2 of the Suicide Act as amended is incompatible with Article 8. It was noted, in this context, that the amendments to s 2 were made as recently as 2009.

At paragraph 148 of the judgment, Toulson LJ said:

> 'As I see it, the issue of the compatibility of section 2 with article 8 has been determined at the highest level, subject to the argument about further clarification, which I have rejected. However, if it were open to this court to consider the matter afresh, I would reject the claim in any event on the grounds that the law relating to assisted suicide is an area of law where member states have a wide margin of appreciation (Haas) and that in the UK this is a matter for determination by Parliament, as the House of Lords recognised in Purdy.'

In the Court of Appeal in *AM*, it was held that the blanket prohibition on assisted suicide did not constitute a disproportionate interference with the Article 8 rights of Martin. The Master of the Rolls said at paragraph 112 of his judgment:

'In our judgment, it would be inappropriate for the courts to fashion domestic Article 8(1) rights exceeding the protection afforded by the requirements of Strasbourg in direct opposition to the will of Parliament as reflected in section 2 of the 1961 Act. The courts have to concede a very wide margin of judgment to Parliament in a controversial area raising difficult moral and ethical issues such as assisted suicide, and the current law cannot conceivably be said to stray beyond it.'

At paragraph 114 of his judgment, he went on to say:

'In relation to Martin, this means that he has no right to require the DPP to desist from prosecuting a carer or doctor who helps him to die; and the DPP cannot be required as part of his section 2 prosecution policy to identify a category of cases where the prosecution will not be initiated because to do so would infringe Article 8 rights.'

The remaining and different submission advanced on behalf of Martin in the Court of Appeal, upon which his appeal succeeded, focused upon another aspect of the DPP's Policy. The argument turned upon the requirement in Article 8(2) that any interference with the Article 8 right must be 'in accordance with the law'. The law for these purposes means not simply the primary statute but also other subordinate rules of which affects the way in which the law may operate in practice. The phrase 'in accordance with the law' incorporates requirements relating to the clarity of the law in question, and in particular imposes an obligation upon the state to make the law accessible and foreseeable.

The essence of this point made on behalf of Martin was that the DPP Policy was an unjustified interference with his Article 8 rights since the interference constituted by the Policy was too uncertain to be 'in accordance with the law' as required by Article 8(2).

Leading counsel for Martin submitted that the DPP's policy provided the necessary degree of clarity only for what he described as 'class 1 helpers', that is, family members and friends who were willing to provide assistance out of compassion. Debbie Purdy's husband fell within that class, and so would Martin's wife if she was willing to help. However, he contended the policy was defective in that it failed to give adequate clarity as to another group, which he described as 'class 2 helpers', comprising individuals who were willing to act selflessly, with compassion and without suspect motives, but who had no personal connection with the individual who wished to end his or her life. These 'class 2 helpers' might be professionals, carers or others.

Counsel pointed to inconsistencies concerning potential class 2 helpers: on the one hand there were several factors in the policy tending to favour prosecution of health care professionals, where the helper is acting as a healthcare professional life and the victim is in his or her care (paragraph 43(14)); where the helper is paid by the victim (paragraph 43(13)); the helper is motivated in part by the prospect of financial gain (paragraph 43(12)). On the other hand, there were also several factors in the policy tending against prosecution which might well relate to some class 2 helpers. Such a helper might well be highly motivated by compassion (paragraph 45(2)); if he or she might have sought to dissuade the victim from taking the course of action which resulted in suicide (paragraph 45(4)); the actions of such a helper might be characterised as reluctant encouragement or assistance in the face of a determined wish on the part of the victim to commit suicide (paragraph 45(5)). It was said that some class 2 helpers might reasonably expect remuneration to provide their services as carers; some may be professionally qualified, for example a doctor who provides a report in connection with the victim's application to Dignitas.

The overall point being made was that the policy gave no indication of how these various factors were to be weighed by the DPP in a class 2 case.

It was contended that further clarification was required from the DPP in the above regard as to this other group and that, without it, the position of those who might be willing to help Martin, including particularly Health Care professionals and solicitors, was too uncertain to satisfy the requirements of the Convention.

In the Divisional Court at first instance, the leading judgment of Toulson LJ sets out his reasoning rejecting the case for the further clarification sought on behalf of Martin, including stating that it would be impractical, if not impossible, for the DPP to lay down guidelines which could satisfactorily embrace every person in any such class 2, so as to enable that person to be able to tell as a matter of probability whether he or she would be prosecuted in a particular case.

The Court of Appeal, however, by a majority of two to one, with the Lord Chief Justice dissenting, disagreed with the Divisional Court on this point taking the majority view that further clarification was required from the DPP.

The Master of the Rolls stated that the starting point that the Strasbourg legal authorities firmly establish is that any law interfering with Convention rights must reach a certain level of clarity before it can constitute a legitimate interference. In relation to the degree of clarity required by Article 8(2), the basic principle is that it must satisfy a measure of foreseeability.

The report of the Commission on Assisted Dying published in January 2012 indicates that paragraph 43(14) of the DPP's Policy is causing difficulty and confusion amongst healthcare professionals. Amongst other things, it says:

> 'The factors for and against prosecution make a special case of health and social care professionals, making it clear they are more likely to be prosecuted for providing assistance with suicide than other members of the public. This has many consequences, including particular insecurities for doctors and other health or social care professionals whose legal position in relation to various forms of minor assistance (such as providing medical records) remains unclear and may come into conflict with their duties of care and patient confidentiality.'

At paragraph 138 of the judgment, the Master of the Rolls says:

> 'Despite the wording of the order made in Purdy, we consider that it is not sufficient for the policy merely to list the factors that the DPP will take into account in deciding whether to consent to a prosecution under section 2(1). A list of factors which contains no clue as to how the discretion to grant or withhold consent will be exercised is not sufficient to meet the requirements of Article 8(2).'

At paragraph 140, he says:

> 'In our judgment, the policy is in certain respects not sufficiently clear to satisfy the requirements of Article 8(2) in relation to healthcare professionals. It is not surprising that they are reluctant to assist victims to commit suicide. Paragraph 43(14) is particularly problematic. How does it apply in the case of a medical doctor or nurses caring for a patient and out of compassion is willing to assist the patient commit suicide, but is not, as it were, in the business of assisting individuals to commit suicide and perhaps has never done so before? How much weight is given by the DPP to 43(14) alone? ... Suppose that (i) none of the factors set out in 43 are present (apart from 43(14)) and (ii) all the factors set out in 44 are present. What is the likelihood of a prosecution in such a situation? The policy does not say ...'

It was accepted by the Court of Appeal majority that it would be impractical, if not impossible, for the DPP to lay down guidelines which would embrace every class 2 case so as to enable every doctor or other professional to be able to tell as a matter of probability whether he or she would be prosecuted in a particular case. It was not for the court to prescribe how the policy should be worded, but the Policy had to allow a reasonable degree of foreseeability, not only in relation to class 1 cases but also in relation to class 2 cases.

The Master of the Rolls makes express reference (at paragraph 144) to the example provided by leading counsel for Martin which – were it to accord with the DPP's Policy – would suffice to make the consequences of the Policy adequately clear:

> 'At the heart of the consideration of competing factors are three considerations: the public interest in protecting individuals' autonomy, the public interest in the protection of vulnerable individuals from abuse, and individuals' right to respect for the way in which they choose to pass the closing moments of their lives. When factors pull in different directions, these three considerations should be used to determine the relative importance of each factor. The first and third world normally outweigh the second where individuals with capacity have reached autonomous decisions, where they receive only help that they have themselves requested, and where there are no particular concerns about the exploitation or abuse of a vulnerable person.'

The Court of Appeal to some extent were influenced in their decision by the case of *Gross v Switzerland* (App 67810/10) in a judgment delivered on 14 May 2013 (reported at (2014) 58 EHRR 7).

Miss Gross was a citizen of Switzerland. She was not terminally ill. The Chamber divided by four votes to three. She wished to end her own life. Her complaint was that she was deprived of the possibility of obtaining a lethal dose of medication because the doctors from whom she sought the drug were prevented from doing so 'by the medical practitioners' code of conduct or [they] feared lengthy judicial proceedings and, possibly, negative professional consequences'. The case did not address questions of assisting suicide, or its criminalisation. The single question was whether it was permissible to limit the circumstances in which a person intending suicide, wishing to act lawfully to end her life in accordance with the law of Switzerland should be provided with the means to do so. The majority concluded that the absence of 'clear and comprehensive legal guidelines' constituted a violation of a right to respect for Miss Gross's private life, but they did so 'without in any way taking up a stance on the substantive context of such guidelines'.

The joint dissenting opinion underlined that comparative research continued to show that the majority of member states prohibit any form of assisting suicide. Only four states allow medical practitioners to prescribe a legal drug to enable a patient to end his or her life. The minority judgment ended by observing that:

'The court should not oblige the state to adopt some laws or provisions for broader regulation of certain questions that the state has by itself determined in a clear and comprehensive manner.'

The Lord Chief Justice in his dissenting judgment indicated that his conclusion would have been to dismiss Martin's appeal. He said that in his judgment the list of factors already in place tending for and against prosecution together with the general approach evinced in paragraphs 46 and 47 of the Policy provided a comprehensive analysis of the factors which the DPP would take into account in making a decision whether to prosecute an individual who committed the offence of assisting suicide. Paragraph 47 says: 'These lists of public interest factors are not exhaustive and each case must be considered on its own facts and on its own merits.'

He said prosecutorial policy decisions must remain fact specific, and the court should not keep ordering and re-ordering the DPP to issue fresh guidelines to cover each new situation. It was, he said virtually inevitable that, in a case such as Martin's, some of the very many factors identified in the Policy as tending to favour prosecution may arise but others, favourable to a non-prosecution, would also arise. A one-by-one tick box approach to those factors, he said, would not only be inappropriate but unwise. A decision did not depend on whether a larger or lower number of factors fell within the prosecution or non-prosecution compartments – a decision has to be made on the overall facts, balancing all these factors. He said he disagreed that the policy was insufficient for those described as class 2 helpers. He said the crucial question was the extent to which the suspect is motivated by compassion for the victim, and that a non-family member was not at any disadvantage under the policy.

In relation to the issue of payment, he said a common sense approach was required – whilst the policy indicated an understandable concern about the motivation of anyone standing to make a financial gain from assisting suicide, what was anticipated in Martin's case could hardly be described as profiteering.

In relation to the circumstances in which a professional carer assisting in the death might be prosecuted pursuant particularly to paragraph (14) of the factors in favour of a prosecution, the Lord Chief Justice said one particular concern was that of undue influence over the victim, but:

'As I read this paragraph (43(14)) it does not extend to an individual who happens to be a member of a profession, or indeed a professional carer, brought in from outside, without previous influence or authority over the victim, or his family, for the simple purposes of assisting the suicide after the victim has reached his or her own settled decision to end life, when, although emotionally supportive of him, his wife cannot provide the necessary physical assistance.'

Such circumstances as might be likely to unfold in Martin's case, would seem to him to be most unlikely to attract any criminal prosecution, and any decision to prosecute in those circumstances would be open to serious question.

He concluded in his dissenting judgment that he did not believe that the distinction between class 1 and class 2 helpers was helpful, and that the policy was sufficiently clear to enable Martin, or anyone who assists him, to make an informed decision about the likelihood of prosecution.

The Court of Appeal gave the DPP permission to appeal and Martin permission to cross-appeal as he contended that the order of the Court of Appeal in his case did not go far enough.

The Supreme Court unanimously allowed the appeal of the DPP and dismissed the cross appeal of Martin. The judgment is reported at [2014] UKSC 38.

At paragraph 141 of the Supreme Court judgment it is said:

'141. Accordingly, we are here concerned with a very unusual crime which is the subject of a specific policy. However, that does not undermine the force of the constitutional argument that it is one thing for the court to decide that the DPP must publish a policy, and quite another for the court to dictate what should be in that policy. The purpose of the DPP publishing a code or policy is not to enable those who wish to commit a crime to know in advance whether they will get away with it. It is to ensure that, as far as is possible in practice and appropriate in principle, the DPP's policy is publicly available so that everyone knows what it is, and can see whether it is being applied consistently. While many may regret the fact that the DPP's policy is not clearer than it is in relation to assistance given by people who are neither family members nor close friends of the victim, and while many may believe that the policy should be the same for some categories of people who are not family members or close friends as for those who are, it would not be right for a court in effect to dictate to the DPP what her policy should be.'

Following the above judgments referred to in detail above, it would appear to be the case that health care professionals, including doctors and nurses acting out of compassion are unlikely to be prosecuted in assisting someone's suicide even if paid for doing so. However, the victim must not be in the care of the professional assisting (apart from temporarily for the purpose only of assisting the suicide) since the professional in those circumstances would be in a position of trust.

Any professional therefore considered to be caring for a person wishing to be assisted to commit suicide will be at risk of prosecution if they assist in the process.

This appears to mean that a person with a settled and autonomous wish to be assisted to commit suicide is unable to request or use the services of, for example, their own long-standing general practitioner whom they might trust to assist in their suicide, if the doctor was willing to so assist.

It needs to be remembered that, notwithstanding the above judgments, the statutory terms of the criminal law in relation to assisted suicide in this country remain in force and accordingly any act or acts of assistance remain illegal. The issues of concern remain the circumstances in which any prosecution is decided upon and pursued.

Alongside the appeal in the case of Martin, the Supreme Court also heard the appeals from the Court of Appeal concerning the cases of Tony Nicklinson and Paul Lamb. This judgment too is reported at [2014] UKSC 38.

The cases of Tony Nicklinson and Paul Lamb as presented in the Divisional Court and Court of Appeal are considered at 7.4. This is because, as explained at paragraphs 153 and 318 of the Supreme Court judgment, in those courts the focus of their cases was on voluntary euthanasia rather than assisted suicide.

In the Supreme Court, however, the case then advanced was that a machine like that of Dr Nitschke would offer a feasible means of suicide: this machine, after being loaded with a lethal drug, could be set up so as to be digitally activated by the person wishing to commit suicide using a pass phrase, via an eye blink computer.

The cases advanced in the Supreme Court focused accordingly on assisted suicide. The first contention was that the prohibition on assisting suicide in s 2(1) of the Suicide Act 1961, as amended by s 59 of the Coroners and Justice Act 2009, should be read to permit such assistance to be volunteered. Secondly, if the latter was not possible it was contended that the prohibition in s 2(1) of the 1961 Act should be declared incompatible with Article 8 of the ECHR.

Seven of the Supreme Court judges dismissed the appeals of Tony Nicklinson and Paul Lamb. Two of the Supreme Court judges would have allowed the appeals.

Of those seven judges, four took the view that the question whether the current law on assisting suicide was compatible with Article 8 involved a consideration of issues which Parliament was inherently better qualified than the courts to assess, and that under the present circumstances the courts should respect Parliament's assessment.

Of those seven judges, three however took the view that the court had the jurisdiction if it wished to properly hold that s 2(1) of the Suicide Act 1961 infringes Article 8. As set out in paragraph 112 of the judgment, it is explained that the court would have to consider an application to make a declaration of incompatibility on its merits, and that it would be inappropriate to fetter the judiciary's role in this connection in advance. It is said:

> 'More specifically, where the court has jurisdiction on an issue falling within the margin of appreciation, I think it would be wrong in principle to rule out exercising that jurisdiction if Parliament addresses the issue: it could be said with force that such an approach would be an abdication of judicial responsibility … Further, in practical terms, given the potential for rapid changes in moral values and medicine, it seems to me that such an approach may well turn out to be inappropriate in relation to this particular issue.'

However, those three judges concluded that it would not be appropriate to grant a declaration of incompatibility at this time. At paragraph 113 of the judgment it is stated:

> 'In my opinion, before making such a declaration, we should accord Parliament the opportunity of considering whether to amend section 2 so as to enable applicants, and quite possibly others, to be assisted in ending their lives, subject of course to such regulations and other protective features as Parliament thinks appropriate, in the light of what may be said to be the provisional views of this Court, as set out in our judgments in these appeals.'

In relation to Parliament considering the provisional views of the Supreme Court, it needs to be reflected that, as well as the above three judges who were of the view that the court was able to grant a declaration of incompatibility but that it was not the right time to do so, there were also the judgments of the two judges who would have allowed the appeals.

Those two judges who would have allowed the appeals were not only of the view that the court was able to grant a declaration of incompatibility but also took the view that such a declaration should be granted now.

Lady Hale at paragraph 321 of the judgment said:

'Left to myself, therefore, I would have allowed the appeal and made a declaration that section 2(1) of the Suicide Act 1961 is incompatible with Article 8, to the extent that it does not provide for any exception for people who have made a capacious, free and fully informed decision to commit suicide but require help to do so. It seems to me that as a general rule, the prohibition is justified. It is the lack of any exception to meet the particular circumstances of the sorts of case before us that is incompatible.'

Of the nine judges accordingly, five were of the view that the court has the jurisdiction to hold that s 2(1) of the Suicide Act 1961 infringes Article 8 of the ECHR.

It is awaited to be seen whether or not Lord Falconer's Assisted Dying Bill passes into legislation. The Bill applies only to those who are terminally ill and reasonably expected to die within 6 months. The Bill is reproduced at the end of this Chapter.

It must be widely acknowledged that more generally, at some juncture, the matter of assisted suicide will now need to be addressed in any event by Parliament.

If in the future the Supreme Court was to grant a declaration that s 2(1) of the Suicide Act 1961 is incompatible with Article 8, it is constitutionally acceptable for this to occur. At paragraph 191, the Supreme Court judgment includes the following statement:

'The effect (of granting a declaration of incompatibility) is not, of course, to override the sovereign legislative authority of the Queen in Parliament, since if primary legislation is declared to be incompatible the validity of the legislation is unaffected (section 4(6)) and the remedy lies with the appropriate minister (section 10), who is answerable to Parliament. The 1998 Act gives the courts a very specific, wholly democratic, mandate.'

7.4 VOLUNTARY EUTHANASIA: MERCY KILLING

The subject of voluntary euthanasia and mercy killing is profoundly difficult and complex, raising a myriad of moral, medical and practical considerations.

It is not unlawful for a doctor to prescribe medical treatment which will necessarily hasten death where the purpose is to relieve pain and suffering. This is known as the double effect principle. As Lord Mustill pointed out in *Airedale NHS Trust v Bland* [1993] AC 789, this has nowhere been the subject of a specific decision but seems to have been generally assumed to be the law by criminal practitioners.

Nor is it unlawful to withdraw medical assistance from a patient even though the inevitable result of this is to bring about that person's death: that was the principle enunciated by the House of Lords in the *Bland* case itself. The law has drawn the clear and consistent line between withdrawing medical support, with the consequence that the patient will die of his own medical condition, and actually bring about the patient's death by a positive act.

In the case of *Bland*, both Lord Browne-Wilkinson and Lord Mustill expressed unease that the law should distinguish between acts and omissions in this way when ethically there was, in their view, difficulty in identifying any rational point of distinction between the two courses of conduct.

Lord Goff also recognised that the distinction could attract a charge of hypocrisy but nonetheless thought that allowing a doctor to kill a patient, however humanitarian the concerns, would be:

> 'To cross the Rubicon which runs between on the one hand the care of the living patient and the other hand euthanasia—actively causing his death to avoid or to end his suffering.'

R (Nicklinson) v Ministry of Justice is reported at [2012] EWHC 2381 (Admin).The case was heard at first instance before the Divisional Court, together with the case of *AM* (known as Martin).

The case was heard on appeal, reported at [2013] EWCA Civ 961. Tony Nicklinson died before the case was heard before the Court of Appeal, and at the appeal hearing his wife Jane Nicklinson was an appellant in her own right and as administratrix of her deceased husband. The different case of Paul Lamb, whose circumstances were similar to those suffered by Tony Nicklinson when he was alive, was added to the appeal as a further appellant to argue the case as Tony Nicklinson would have been able had he been still alive.

The claimant Tony Nicklinson suffered from catastrophic physical disabilities but his mental processes were unimpaired in the sense that he was fully conscious of his predicament. He was suffering from 'locked in syndrome'. He determined that he wished to die with dignity and without further suffering but his condition made him incapable of ending his own life. He was not terminally ill and he faced the prospect of living for many years.

The only way in which he could end his life other than by self-starvation would be by voluntary euthanasia. With his wife's help he could probably travel to Switzerland, but that would not help him because euthanasia is outside the scope of Dignitas's activities. No country in the world permits the practice of voluntary euthanasia in the case of non-residents.

Tony Nicklinson was not in a condition to be able to commit assisted suicide. He wished, at a time of his choosing, to use the assistance of his general practitioner or another doctor to terminate or assist in the termination of his life.

Paul Lamb's condition was as follows. He was 57 years of age, divorced from his wife and had two grown up children. In 1990 he was involved in a car accident as a result of which he sustained multiple injuries leaving him paralysed. He was completely immobile with the exception only of his right hand which he can move to a limited extent. He required constant care and had carers with him 24 hours a day. He spent the whole of every day in his wheelchair. He experienced a significant amount of pain every day and had done so ever since the accident, with the consequences that he was constantly on morphine. He felt that he was trapped in his body, and that he could not enjoy or endure a life that was so monotonous and painful and lacking in autonomy. His condition was irreversible. He wished that a doctor should end his life.

Voluntary euthanasia involves a person actively bringing about someone's death to avoid or to end his or her suffering. Euthanasia is not lawful at common law. Such voluntary euthanasia usually connotes a medical practitioner being asked to actively cause someone's death at their request to avoid or to end his or her suffering. Mercy killing usually connotes a family member or close friend being asked to cause someone's death at their request to avoid or to end his or her suffering.

The appellants sought a declaration that it would not be unlawful, on the grounds of necessity, for a doctor to terminate or to assist the termination of his life.

The submissions of the appellants were twofold. First, they contended that the common law should give respect to their autonomy and dignity by recognising that voluntary euthanasia can provide a defence to murder through reliance on the principle of necessity. Secondly, they contended that their illnesses had condemned them to living in conditions in which they were deprived of all usual dignity and the law had deprived them of the right to say that enough was enough – autonomy and dignity, humanity and justice required that they should be permitted to end their lives, and it was submitted that Article 8 gave them the right to do so. For them to be prohibited from doing so, it was contended there would be a disproportionate interference with their Article 8 rights.

The Divisional Court indicated that it was not open to it to make a declaration that the current law of murder was incompatible with the Convention insofar as it criminalises voluntary active euthanasia, since murder is not a statutory offence, although there are certain statutory defences. The court's position was that if it were satisfied that Article 8 required that voluntary active euthanasia should in relevant circumstances be a defence to murder, then its proper course in accordance with s 6(1) of the Human Rights Act 1998 would be to recognise that there is such a defence under the doctrine of necessity.

As a further alternative, a declaration was sought from the court that the legislation under which murder carries a mandatory sentence of life imprisonment is incompatible with the European Convention in the case of genuinely compassionate voluntary active euthanasia.

The court proceeded to consider the case that at common law voluntary euthanasia should provide a defence to murder. It rejected such case, taking into account the legal authorities and other material set out below.

Lord Mustill in the case of *Airedale NHS Trust v Bland* [1993] AC 789 said, at 892:

> 'So far as I am aware no satisfactory reason has ever been advanced for suggesting that it makes the least of difference in law, as distinct from morals, if the patient consents to or indeed urges the ending of his life by active means. The reason must be that, as in the other cases of consent to being killed, the interest of the state in preserving life overrides the otherwise all- powerful interests of patient autonomy.'

The Law Commission considered the issue in Part 7 of its report on *Murder, Manslaughter and Infanticide* (2006, Law Com 304). At paragraph 7.4 – under the heading 'All mercy killings are unlawful homicides' – they say the law of England and Wales does not recognise any defence of mercy killing , and that if a defendant intentionally kills a victim in the genuine belief that it is in the victim's best interests to die, then he is guilty of murder. This is so even if the victim wished to die and consented to being killed.

In *R v Inglis (Frances)* [2010] EWCA Crim 2637, [2011] 1 WLR 1110, Lord Judge, giving the judgment of the Court of Appeal Criminal Division, said at paragraph 37:

> 'We must underline that the law of murder does not distinguish between murder committed for malevolent reasons and murder motivated by familial love. Subject to well established partial defences, like provocation or diminished responsibility, mercy killing is murder.'

As to possible changes in the law, Lord Judge said at paragraph 39:

> 'How the problems of mercy killing, euthanasia, and assisting suicide should be addressed must be decided by Parliament, which, for this purpose at any rate, should be reflective of the conscience of the nation. In this appeal we are constrained to apply the law as we find it to be. We cannot amend or ignore it.'

The textbooks too are equally unequivocal as to the position at common law of euthanasia and mercy killing. *Smith and Hogan's Criminal Law* (13th edn, 2011), p 589 states: 'English law admits of no defence of mercy killing or euthanasia'.

Lord Justice Toulson, in the *Nicklinson* case at first instance, said at paragraph 79 of his judgment that, in relation to constitutionality, it was one thing for the courts to adapt and develop the principles of the common law incrementally in order to keep up with the requirements of justice in a changing society, but major changes involving matters of controversial social policy were a matter for Parliament.

At paragraph 84 of his judgment, he said:

> 'A decision by the court to alter the common law so as to create a defence to murder in the case of active voluntary euthanasia would be to introduce a major change in an area where there are strongly held conflicting views, where Parliament has rejected attempts to introduce such a change, and where the result would be to create uncertainty rather than certainty. To do so would be to usurp the role of Parliament.'

It is necessary to recognise in any event that were Parliament to ever legalise any form of euthanasia, it would not be likely do so without a surrounding framework regarding end of life care and without procedural safeguards.

Toulson LJ said that, where on the Strasbourg authorities a matter is within the margin of appreciation left to individual states, it is also up to the state to determine which organ of state should decide what legal regime to adopt.

The court in *Nicklinson* at first instance also rejected his alternative case that Article 8 justified his claim. It reiterated that since it had been held by both the House of Lords and Strasbourg that a blanket ban on assisted suicide was not incompatible with Article 8, the same must apply with added force to the ban on voluntary euthanasia.

At paragraph 122 it was stated:

> 'I conclude that it would be wrong for this court to hold that Article 8 requires voluntary euthanasia to afford a possible defence to murder. To do so would be to go far beyond anything which the Strasbourg Court has said, would be inconsistent with the judgments of the House of Lords and the Strasbourg Court in Pretty, and would be to usurp the proper role of Parliament.'

The court at first instance finally addressed the issue of whether the mandatory sentence of life imprisonment for murder was incompatible with the Convention in cases of genuine voluntary euthanasia. At paragraph 149 of the judgment it is stated:

> 'There is strong evidence (considered by the Law Commission in its review of the law of murder) that the public does not regard the mandatory sentence of life imprisonment as appropriate in cases of genuine voluntary euthanasia, and there have been calls for it to be changed, but whether it is incompatible with the Convention is a matter which the court should decide only in a case in which it is necessary to do so. The question might arise if a person were convicted of murder and sentenced to life imprisonment in a case of genuine voluntary euthanasia carried out from a compassionate motive, but it is not necessary to decide the question in this case because it cannot realistically affect Tony's position whether a doctor, or other person, who carried out an act of voluntary euthanasia would be exposed to such a grave penalty or lesser punishment. On any view, the risk of conviction for homicide is likely to be a strong deterrent for any person, especially a professional person.'

The appeals of both Mrs Nicklinson and Paul Lamb were dismissed by the Court of Appeal. The Court of Appeal rejected the contention that voluntary euthanasia can provide a defence to murder through reliance on the principle of necessity. The appeals failed too on the Article 8 contention advanced by the appellants. The Court of Appeal held that the blanket prohibition on euthanasia did not constitute a disproportionate interference with the Article 8 rights of the appellants.

The Court of Appeal gave to the widow of Mr Nicklinson and to Mr Lamb permission to appeal to the Supreme Court. As already indicated at **7.3**, the focus of their case presented to the Supreme Court changed to concentrate on the issues of assisted suicide and whether the prohibition contained within s 2 of the Assisted Suicide Act 1961 infringes Article 8 of the ECHR.

Notwithstanding the above, the judges of the Supreme Court encompass in the 131 pages of the judgment wide-ranging views and comments on the issues of mercy killing and voluntary euthanasia as well as assisted suicide. It is a significant judgment indeed.

The judgment includes drawing a distinction between euthanasia or mercy killing on the one hand and assisted suicide on the other hand. The terms of paragraphs 94 and 95 of the judgment in this regard are set out below.

'94. To my mind, the difference between administering the fatal drug to a person and setting up a machine so that the person can administer the drug to himself is not merely a legal distinction. Founded as it is on personal autonomy, I consider that the distinction also sounds in morality. Indeed, authorising a third party to switch off a person's life support machine, as in *Bland* or *Re B (Treatment)* seems to me, at least arguably, to be, in some respects, a more drastic interference in that person's life and a more extreme moral step, than authorising a third party to set up a lethal drug delivery system so that a person can, but only if he wishes, activate the system to administer a lethal drug.

95. Indeed, if one is searching for a satisfactory boundary between euthanasia or mercy killing and assisted suicide, which Lord Sumption discusses at para 227 below, I believe that there may be considerable force in the contention that the answer, both in law and in morality, can best be found by reference to personal autonomy. Subject to those cases where the act can be classified as an "omission" (eg, to my mind somewhat uncomfortably in terms of common sense, switching off a life-supporting machine at least if done by an appropriately authorised person, as in *Bland* and *Re B (Treatment)*), it seems to me that if the act which immediately causes the death is that of a third party that may be the wrong side of the line, whereas if the final act is that of the person himself, who carries it out pursuant to a voluntary, clear, settled and informed decision, that is the permissible side of the line. In the latter case, the person concerned has not been "killed" by anyone, but has autonomously exercised his right to end his life. (I should perhaps make it clear that I am

not thereby seeking for a moment to cast doubt on the correctness of the decisions in *Bland* and *Re B (Treatment)*, both of which appear to me to have been plainly rightly decided).'

APPENDIX TO CHAPTER 7

ASSISTED DYING BILL

A BILL TO Enable competent adults who are terminally ill to be provided at their request with specified assistance to end their own life; and for connected purposes.

BE IT ENACTED by the Queen's most Excellent Majesty, by and with the advice and consent of the Lords Spiritual and Temporal, and Commons, in this present Parliament assembled, and by the authority of the same, as follows: –

1 Assisted dying

(1) A person who is terminally ill may request and lawfully be provided with assistance to end his or her own life.

(2) Subsection (1) only applies where the person –

    (a) has a clear and settled intention to end his or her own life;

    (b) has made a declaration to that effect in accordance with section 3; and

    (c) on the day the declaration is made –

        (i) is aged 18 or over; and

        (ii) has been ordinarily resident in England and Wales for not less than one year.

2 Terminal illness

(1) For the purposes of this Act, a person is terminally ill if that person –

    (a) has been diagnosed by a registered medical practitioner as having an inevitably progressive condition which cannot be reversed by treatment ("a terminal illness"); and

    (b) as a consequence of that terminal illness, is reasonably expected to die within six months.

(2) Treatment which only relieves the symptoms of an inevitably progressive condition temporarily is not to be regarded as treatment which can reverse that condition

3 Declaration

(1) For the purposes of this Act, a person has a clear and settled intention to end their own life if –

    (a) the person has made and signed a declaration to that effect in the form in the Schedule in the presence of a witness (who must not be a relative or directly involved in the person's care or treatment) who signed the declaration in the person's presence; and

(b)   that declaration has been countersigned in accordance with
       subsection (3) by –
       (i)   the registered medical practitioner from whom the person
              has requested assistance to end their life ("the attending
              doctor"); and
       (ii)   another registered medical practitioner ("the independent
              doctor") who is not a relative, partner or colleague in the
              same practice or clinical team, of the attending doctor;

neither of whom may also be the witness required under paragraph
(a).

(2) The attending doctor (but not the independent doctor) may, but need
not be, the registered medical practitioner who diagnosed that the
person is terminally ill or first informed the person of that diagnosis.

(3) Before countersigning a person's declaration the attending doctor
and the independent doctor, having separately examined the person and
the person's medical records and each acting independently of the other,
must be satisfied that the person –

(a)   is terminally ill;
(b)   has the capacity to make the decision to end their own life; and
(c)   has a clear and settled intention to end their own life which has
       been reached voluntarily, on an informed basis and without
       coercion or duress.

(4) In deciding whether to countersign a declaration under subsection
(3), the attending doctor and the independent doctor must be satisfied
that the person making it has been fully informed of the palliative,
hospice and other care which is available to that person.

(5) A declaration under this section shall be valid and take effect on the
day that it is countersigned by the independent doctor.

(6) A person who has made a declaration under this section may revoke
it at any time and revocation need not be in writing.

(7) For the purpose of subsection (1)(b)(ii), an independent doctor is
suitably qualified if that doctor holds such qualification or has such
experience in respect of the diagnosis and management of terminal
illness as the Secretary of State may specify in regulations.

4 Assistance in dying

(1) The attending doctor of a person who has made a valid declaration
may prescribe medicines for that person to enable that person to end
their own life.

(2) Any medicines prescribed under subsection (1) shall only be delivered to the person for whom they are prescribed –

   (a) by the attending doctor; or

   (b) by –

      (i)   another registered medical practitioner; or

      (ii) a registered nurse;

who has been authorised to do so by the attending doctor;

   (c) after the assisting health professional has confirmed that the person has not revoked and does not wish to revoke their declaration; and

   (d) after a period of not less than 14 days has elapsed since the day on which the person's declaration took effect.

(3) If the attending doctor and the independent doctor agree that a person's death from terminal illness is reasonably expected to occur within one month of the day on which a declaration takes effect, the period specified in subsection (2)(d) is reduced to six days.

(4) In respect of a medicine which has been prescribed for a person under subsection (1), an assisting health professional may –

   (a) prepare that medicine for self-administration by that person;

   (b) prepare a medical device which will enable that person to self-administer the medicine; and

   (c) assist that person to ingest or otherwise self-administer the medicine;

but the decision to self-administer the medicine and the final act of doing so must be taken by the person for whom the medicine has been prescribed.

(5) Subsection (4) does not authorise an assisting health professional to administer a medicine to another person with the intention of causing that person's death.

(6) The assisting health professional must remain with the person until the person has –

   (a) self-administered the medicine and died; or

   (b) decided not to self-administer the medicine;

and for the purpose of this subsection the assisting health professional is to be regarded as remaining with the person if the assisting health professional is in close proximity to, but not in the same room as, the person.

(7) The Secretary of State may by regulations specify –

   (a) the medicines which may be prescribed under this section;

   (b)   the form and manner in which such prescriptions are to be issued; and

   (c)   the manner and conditions under which such medicines are to be dispensed, stored, transported, used and destroyed.

(8) Regulations under subsection (7)(c) shall provide that an assisting health professional –

   (a)   must only deliver any medicine prescribed under this section to the person for whom they have been prescribed immediately before their intended use; and

   (b)   in the event that the person decides not to self-administer the medicine, must immediately remove it from that person and, as soon as reasonably practicable, return it to the pharmacy from which it was dispensed.

(9) Regulations under subsection (7) may –

   (a)   make different provision for different purposes; and
   (b)   include consequential, incidental, supplementary or transitional provisions.

(10) In this section, "assisting health professional" means the attending doctor or a person authorised by the attending doctor in accordance with subsection (2)(b).

5 Conscientious objection

A person shall not be under any duty (whether by contract or arising from any statutory or other legal requirement) to participate in anything authorised by this Act to which that person has a conscientious objection.

6 Criminal liability

(1) A person who provides any assistance in accordance with this Act shall not be

guilty of an offence.

(2) In the Suicide Act 1961, after section 2B (course of conduct), insert –

"2C Assisted dying

Sections 2, 2A and 2B shall not apply to any person in respect of the provision of assistance to another person in accordance with that Act.".

7 Inquests, death certification etc.

(1) A person is not to be regarded as having died in circumstances to which section 8(1)(a) or (b) of the Coroners Act 1988 (duty to hold

inquest) apply only because the person died as a consequence of the provision of assistance in accordance with this Act.

(2) In the Births and Deaths Registration Act 1953, after section 39A (regulations made by the Minister: further provisions), insert –

"39B Regulations: Assisted Dying

(1) The Secretary of State may make regulations –

    (a) providing for any provision of this Act relating to the registration of deaths to apply in respect of deaths which arise from the provision of assistance in accordance with the Assisted Dying Act 2013 with such modifications as may be prescribed in respect of –
        (i) the information which is to be provided concerning such deaths;
        (ii) the form and manner in which the cause of such deaths is to be certified; and
        (iii) the form and manner in which such deaths are to be registered;

    (b) requiring the Registrar General to prepare at least once each year a report providing a statistical analysis of deaths which have arisen from the provision of assistance in accordance with the Assisted Dying Act 2013;

    (c) containing such incidental, supplemental and transitional provisions as the Secretary of State considers appropriate.

(2) Any regulations made under subsection (1)(a)(ii) shall provide for the cause of death to be recorded as "assisted death".

(3) Any report prepared by the Registrar General in accordance with regulations made under subsection (1)(b) shall be laid before Parliament by the Secretary of State.

(4) The power of the Secretary of State to make regulations under this section is exercisable by statutory instrument.

(5) A statutory instrument containing regulations made under this section by the Secretary of State is subject to annulment in pursuance of a resolution of either House of Parliament.".

8 Codes of practice

(1) The Secretary of State may issue one or more codes of practice in connection with –

    (a) the assessment of whether a person has a clear and settled intention to end their own life, including –

(i)   assessing whether the person has capacity to make such a decision;

(ii)   recognising and taking account of the effects of depression or other psychological disorders that may impair a person's decision-making; and

(iii) the information which is made available on treatment and end of life care options available to them and of the consequences of deciding to end their own life; and

(b)   such other matters relating to the operation of this Act as the Secretary of State thinks fit.

(2) Before issuing a code under this section the Secretary of State shall consult such persons as the Secretary of State thinks appropriate.

9 Monitoring

(1) The relevant Chief Medical Officer shall –

(a)   monitor the operation of the Act, including compliance with its provisions and any regulations or code of practice made under it;

(b)   inspect and report to the relevant national authority on any matter connected with the operation of the Act which the relevant national authority refers to the relevant Chief Medical Officer; and

(c)   submit an annual report to the relevant national authority on the operation of the Act.

(2) The Chief Medical Officers may combine their annual reports for the same year in a single document ("a combined report") in such manner as they consider appropriate.

(3) The relevant national authority must publish each annual report or combined report it receives under this section and –

(a)   the Secretary of State must lay a copy of each report before Parliament; and

(b)   the Welsh Ministers must lay a copy of each report before the National Assembly for Wales.

(4) In this section –

"relevant Chief Medical Officer" means –

(a)   in England, the Chief Medical Officer to the Department of Health; and

(b)   in Wales, the Chief Medical Officer to the Welsh Assembly Government;

"relevant national authority" means –

(a) in England, the Secretary of State; and
(b) in Wales, the Welsh Ministers.

10 Offences

(1) A person commits an offence if the person –

(a) makes or knowingly uses a false instrument which purports to be a declaration made under section 3 by another person; or
(b) wilfully conceals or destroys a declaration made under section 3 by another person.

(2) A person (A) commits an offence if, in relation to another person (B) who is seeking to make or has made a declaration under section 3, A knowingly or recklessly provides a medical or other professional opinion in respect of B which is false or misleading in a material particular.

(3) A person guilty of an offence under subsection (1)(a) which was committed with the intention of causing the death of another person is liable, on conviction on indictment, to imprisonment for life or a fine or both.

(4) Unless subsection (3) applies, a person convicted of an offence under this section is liable –

(a) on summary conviction, to imprisonment for a term not exceeding 6 months or a fine not exceeding the statutory maximum (or both);
(b) on conviction on indictment, to imprisonment for a period not exceeding five years or a fine or both.

11 Regulations

(1) Any power of the Secretary of State under this Act to make regulations is exercisable by statutory instrument.

(2) A statutory instrument containing regulations under this Act is subject to annulment in pursuance of a resolution of either House of Parliament.

12 Interpretation

In this Act –

"attending doctor" has the meaning given in section 3;
"capacity" shall be construed in accordance with the Mental Capacity Act 2005;

"independent doctor" has the meaning given in section 3; "relative", in relation to any person, means –

(a) the spouse or civil partner of that person;
(b) any lineal ancestor, lineal descendant, sibling, aunt, uncle or cousin of that person or the person's spouse or civil partner; or
(c) the spouse or civil partner of any relative mentioned in paragraph (b),

and for the purposes of deducing any such relationship a spouse or civil partner includes a former spouse or civil partner, a partner to whom the person is not married, and a partner of the same sex; and

"terminal illness" has the meaning given in section 2(1)(a).

13 Citation, commencement, repeal and extent

(1) This Act may be cited as the Assisted Dying Act 2013.

(2) The following come into force on the day on which this Act is passed –

(a) sections 4, 7 and 11 so far as they confer a power to make regulations;
(b) section 8 so far as it confers a power to issue codes of practice;
(c) sections 11 and 12; and
(d) this section.

(3) Subject to subsection (2), the provisions of this Act come into force at the end of the period of two years beginning with the day on which this Act is passed.

(4) At any time during the period of 12 months beginning on the day ten years after the provisions in subsection (3) come into force, this Act may be repealed by a resolution of each House of Parliament.

(5) This Act does not extend to Scotland or Northern Ireland.

SCHEDULE

Section 3

FORM OF DECLARATION

Declaration: Assisted Dying Act 2013

Name of declarant: Date of Birth:

Address:

I have [condition], a terminal condition from which I am expected to die within six months of the date of this declaration.

The Attending Doctor and Independent Doctor identified below have each fully informed me about that diagnosis and prognosis and the treatments available to me, including pain control and palliative care.

Having considered all this information, I have a clear and settled intention to end my own life and, in order to assist me to do so, I have asked my attending doctor to prescribe medicines for me for that purpose.

I make this declaration voluntarily and in the full knowledge of its significance.

I understand that I may revoke this declaration at any time.

Signature: Date:

Witness

Name of witness:

Address:

This declaration was signed by [name of declarant] in my presence and signed by me in [his/her] presence.

Signature: Date:

Countersignature: Attending Doctor

Schedule — Form of declaration

I confirm that [name], who at the date of this declaration is [age] years of age and has been ordinarily resident in England and Wales for [time]:

(1) is terminally ill and that the diagnosis and prognosis set above is correct;

(2) has the capacity to make the decision to end their own life; and

(3) has a clear and settled intention to do so, which has been reached on an informed basis, without coercion or duress, and having been informed of the palliative, hospice and other care which is available to [him/her].

Signature: Date:

Name and Address of Attending Doctor:

Countersignature: Independent Doctor

I confirm that [name], who at the date of this declaration is [age] years of age and has been ordinarily resident in England and Wales for [time]:

(1) is terminally ill and that the diagnosis and prognosis set above is correct;

(2) has the capacity to make the decision to end their own life; and

(3) has a clear and settled intention to do so, which has been reached on an informed basis, without coercion or duress, and having been informed of the palliative, hospice and other care which is available to [him/her].

Signature: Date:

Name and Address of Independent Doctor:

PART III

JURISDICTION AND PROCEDURE IN MEDICAL TREATMENT CASES CONCERNING INCAPACITATED ADULTS AND CHILDREN

CHAPTER 8

JURISDICTION: PROCEDURE IN MEDICAL TREATMENT CASES

8.1 JURISDICTION: PROCEDURE IN RELATION TO INCAPACITATED ADULTS

The jurisdiction is governed by the Mental Capacity Act 2005 (MCA 2005). The procedure is governed by the Court of Protection Rules 2007 and the Court of Protection (Amendment) Rules 2011 ('the Rules'). The Rules are supplemented by a raft of Practice Directions. These all establish the procedure to be adopted in welfare and medical treatment cases. There is also the Code of Practice to the Act. Section 42 of the Act requires the Lord Chancellor to prepare a code or codes of practice for those making decisions under the Act. Any person acting in a professional capacity or for remuneration is obliged to have regard to the code (s 42(4)) and a court must take account of any provision in or failure to comply with the code which is relevant to a question arising in any civil or criminal proceedings (s 42(5)). The Code is not a statute and should not be construed as one but requires material consideration. It was accepted in *Aintree University Hospitals NHS Foundation Trust v James* [2013] UKSC 67 in the Supreme Court that if there was any conflict between what is said in the Code and what is said in any Guidance by the General Medical Council or British Medical Association, then the Mental Capacity Act Code must prevail.

8.1.1 Definitions under the COP Rules

- 'P' means any person (other than a protected party) who lacks or, so far as consistent with the context, is alleged to lack capacity to make a decision or decisions in relation to any matter that is the subject of an application to the court and references to a person who lacks capacity to be construed in accordance with the Act.

- 'Protected party' means a party or an intended party (other than P or a child) who lacks capacity to conduct the proceedings.

- 'Child' means a person under 18.

- 'Judge' means a judge nominated to be a judge of the court under the Act.

In this latter regard concerning judicial input, attention is drawn to s 46 of the Act and Practice Direction 12A supplementing Part 12 of the Rules entitled 'the Court's jurisdiction to be exercised by certain judges'.

8.1.2   Declarations

An application may be made for a declaration under s 15 of MCA 2005. Section 15(1) provides that the court may make declarations as to whether a person lacks capacity, either in relation to a specified decision or in relation to specified matters, and as to the 'lawfulness or otherwise of any act done, or yet to be done, in relation to that person'. Section 15(2) expressly provides that 'act' includes an omission and a course of conduct.

In the case of *YLA v PM and MZ* [2013] EWHC 4020 (COP) Parker J embarked on a detailed analysis both as to the discretionary nature of the power to make declarations under s 15 of MCA 2005 and to the factors going to the exercise of that discretion. The purpose of a declaration is to engage the powers of the Court of Protection. The judge drew a distinction between the factors going to declarations in relation to capacity and those going to declarations in relation to best interests. She determined that a declaration that a person lacks capacity in any particular respect is not an invasion of private family life; that wishes and feelings, together with the obligation to respect for private and family life under Article 8 of the European Convention on Human Rights (ECHR) are relevant to the best interests test rather than to capacity. The court's discretion in respect of best interests declarations depends on the assessment of best interests, which is not an unfettered discretion. The court has to apply the statute. However, the question of whether it is in the best interests of P is not a relevant consideration in deciding whether to make a declaration that he or she lacks capacity as to the decision-making in question. The assessment of capacity has to be detached and objective.

In the case of *An NHS Trust v MB* [2006] EWHC 507 (Fam) concerning a child who was going to die, the court made a declaration to the effect that it was in his best interests and lawful to not administer a number of forms of treatment including CPR. At paragraph 99 of his judgment, the judge said: 'I stress that a declaration reflecting the above will be permissive in its effect. It will have the effect that, in the view of this court, doctors or staff *need* not embark on the listed treatments; but neither the declaration nor anything in this judgment should deter or would prevent a doctor or staff from giving any of the listed treatments if he or they thought fit at the time.'

As was stated by the Supreme Court in the *Aintree* case, the role of the court is to decide whether a particular treatment is in the best interests of the patient who is incapable of making the decision for himself. In cases concerning whether to continue or to instigate life-sustaining medical treatment this basic principle underlying the Act will often be manifested by the making of declarations which are *permissive* in their effect. Although the court may actually make decisions concerning medical treatment under the statute, in serious or developing situations a declaration as to thexpp*lawfulness* of medical treatment will often be preferred because this appropriately delegates to the medical profession the decision as to whether treatment is appropriate in the circumstances.

In the case of *An NHS Trust v KH* [2013] 1 FLR 1471, concerning the best interests of a child whose life expectancy was said to be short but who might live for a number of years, the judge Peter Jackson J considered within paragraphs 41 to 47 of his judgment *the scope* of the declarations to be made. The judgment echoes the views of the Court of Appeal in the case of *Portsmouth NHS Trust v Wyatt* [2005] EWCA Civ 1181 at paragraphs 117 and 118 of its judgment expressing caution and reservations about judges making *open-ended declarations* which might have to be revisited if circumstances changed. It was not the function of the court to be used as a general advice centre or to oversee treatment plans for those who are gravely ill. Judges take decisions on the basis of particular factual sub-strata, and the court's function is to make a particular decision on a particular issue. In the above-mentioned case of *KH*, the judge determined that the declarations he was making should only extend to matters where the factual basis was known, that it was unwise to endorse aspects of the plan that might change in their details. The approach he took was to identify the treatment issues that needed to be determined and that were not likely to change over time.

8.1.3 Starting proceedings, and urgent/interim applications

The MCA 2005 provides that, except in circumstances set out in the Act or the Rules, permission will need to be obtained to make an application to the court. Most welfare and health care cases will require permission.

Part 8 of the Rules and the Practice Direction supplementing it (PD8A) set out the procedure to be followed in seeking permission.

Part 9 of the Rules and the Practice Directions supplementing it (PD9A, PD9B, PD9C, PD9D, PD9E, PD9F, PDG and PD9H) set out the procedure to be followed for starting proceedings.

PD9E is specifically concerned with starting 'applications relating to serious medical treatment'. This Practice Direction is reproduced at the end of this chapter and, as can be seen, sets out the procedure to be followed when the application concerns serious medical treatment in relation to the person who lacks capacity (P). The meaning of 'serious medical treatment' and of 'serious consequences' is set out at paragraphs 3 and 4 of the Practice Direction. More particularly, paragraphs 5, 6 and 7 set out the type of medical treatment issues which should be brought before the court. Paragraph 12 sets out the requirement for the proceedings to be heard by a judge of the court who has been suitably nominated.

It is to be noted that PD9B sets out the persons who are to be notified that an application form has been issued. It is also to be noted that Practice Direction B supplementing Part 10 of the rules (PD10B) sets out the procedure to be followed for *urgent and interim applications*.

8.1.4   The legal status of P

Whilst rule 40 of Part 7 of the Rules provides for a general requirement to notify P of 'any matter or document', rule 73(4) is clear that 'Unless the court orders otherwise, P shall not be named as a respondent in any proceedings'.

P accordingly is not automatically a party to proceedings brought under the MCA 2005. By rule 73(2): 'The court may order a person to be joined as a party if it considers that it is desirable to do so for the purpose of dealing with the application.' Accordingly the court will consider whether P is to be joined as a party. Deciding whether or not to make P a party is an important decision. There may be cases where notification to P is sufficient and there is no need for him or her to become a party. Indeed such courts might be distressing to P. On the other hand there will be cases where P is at the centre of the issues before the court and it is only correct that P is made a party. The court will need to consider P's best interests, the overriding objective of the need to do justice, weighing the correct balance of protection that P requires, as well as the issue of proportionality.

By rule 141(1), P, if a party to proceedings, must have a litigation friend. By rule 140(1) a person who may act as a litigation friend must be able to fairly and competently conduct proceedings on behalf of P, and must have no interests adverse to him or her.

8.1.5 The Official Solicitor

The Official Solicitor is a litigation friend of last resort. If P is made a party to the proceedings the Official Solicitor may act as P's litigation friend, if so appointed by the court. He may also act as advocate to the court if invited to do so by it. This is particularly relevant in serious medical treatment cases concerning incapacitated adults.

There are reproduced at the conclusion of this Chapter two documents specifically relating to the Official Solicitor. The first is the Practice Note published by the Official Solicitor of March 2013 as to his appointment in proceedings relating to both incapacitated adults and children. The second is the Ministry of Justice document of the 12 August 2013 entitled 'Court of Protection – health care and welfare cases'. This document makes reference to PD9E and the types of serious medical treatment issues mentioned within the latter. This second Ministry of Justice document indicates accordingly the circumstances in which the Official Solicitor will be likely to act for P in serious medical treatment cases, if appointed by the court to do so.

In relation to determining whether P lacks the capacity to conduct proceedings (namely, whether he or she lacks litigation capacity) in many cases the evidence will be clear and undisputed. In other cases there may be a material issue in this regard which will need to be determined by the court. A party or intended party is entitled to dispute an opinion that they lack litigation capacity. In some cases there may be a dispute between medical experts on the issue of litigation capacity, which will need to be determined by the court. The court may if necessary, where there is any such dispute or disputes, make a formal finding on the issue of litigation capacity.

8.1.6 Vulnerable persons falling outside the scope of the MCA 2005

The Practice Note of the Official Solicitor published in March 2013 includes reference to those cases where the Family Division of the High Court is invited to exercise its inherent jurisdiction in relation to a vulnerable adult. The note defines a 'vulnerable adult' as a person who has mental capacity in respect of the decisions in question but who lacks litigation capacity.

There is a line of legal authorities concerning 'vulnerable adults', including the cases of *Re SK (An Adult) (Forced Marriage: Appropriate Relief)* [2005] 2 FLR 230, *Re SA (Vulnerable Adult with Capacity: Marriage)* [2006] 1 FLR 867 and *Westminster City Council v IC, KC and NNC* [2007] EWHC 3096 (Fam). In the latter case Wood J stated that: 'Save where it would be demonstrably inconsistent with the will of Parliament, the inherent jurisdiction remains alive, in appropriate cases, where it is necessary, lawful and proportionate, to meet circumstances unmet by the scope of the Mental Capacity Act 2005.' In the case of *R (Muhammad) v Secretary of State for the Home Department* [2013] EWHC 3157 (Admin), the claimants were in immigration detention and were challenging the lawfulness of that detention. They contended that their mental health was such that they were not fit for detention, and specifically they relied upon the fact that they were refusing food and drink. It was accepted that the claimants had the capacity both to litigate and to make decisions about refusing food and/or medical treatment. In the circumstances, the claimants could not come within the definition of 'vulnerable adults'.

The inherent jurisdiction of the High Court accordingly will remain available to protect suitably vulnerable persons who are determined to require the court's protection but who fall outside the scope of the MCA 2005.

In relation to the procedure to be adopted in those cases where the Family Division is invited to exercise its inherent jurisdiction in relation to a vulnerable adult falling outside the scope of the MCA 2005, the Civil Procedure Rules 1998 will apply; the claim will be a Part 8 claim and Part 21 of those Rules relating to protected parties will apply. It is to be noted that Rule 9 of Part 3 of the Court of Protection Rules 2007 provides that 'in any case not expressly provided for by these Rules ... The Civil Procedure Rules 1998 ... may be applied ... in so far as is necessary to further the overriding objective'.

8.1.7   Transparency: hearings in private or in public

Reproduced at the conclusion of this Chapter is the Practice Guidance issued by the President of the Court of Protection on the 16 January 2014 entitled 'Transparency in the Court of Protection'.

Part 13 of the Court of Protection Rules 2007 and Practice Direction A supplementing it (PD13A) concern the nature of hearings in the Court of Protection including reporting restrictions.

Rule 90 provides the general rule that a hearing is to *be held in private.* Aside from those entitled to attend a hearing, the court may make an order '(a) authorising any person, or class of persons, to attend the hearing or part of it; or (b) excluding any person, or class of persons, from attending the hearing or a part of it'.

Those persons may include the press, relatives or interested groups. All or any may be authorised to attend a hearing or part of it; all or any similarly may be excluded from attending a hearing or part of it.

Rule 91 permits the court to make orders authorising the publication of such information relating to the proceedings as it may specify, or the publication of the text or a summary of the whole or part of a judgment or order made by the court. In so doing, the court may impose terms including restrictions on the publication of the identities of some or all of those involved in the case, as well as such other restrictions on the publication of information relating to the proceedings as the court sees fit.

Rule 92 gives the court powers to order that a hearing or part of the hearing *be held in public*. The court may exclude any person or class of persons from attending a public hearing or a part of it. The Rule gives the court wide powers to impose restrictions on the publication of identities of some or all of those involved in the case, as well as to impose such other restrictions on the publication of information relating to the proceedings as it sees fit.

Rule 93 provides that an order under rule 90, 91 or 92 may be made only where it appears to the court that there is good reason for making the order; may be made at any time and either on the Court's own initiative or on an application made by any person in accordance with Part 10 of the Rules.

8.2   JURISDICTION: PROCEDURE IN RELATION TO CHILDREN

8.2.1   The twofold jurisdiction: Children Act 1989; inherent jurisdiction of the High Court

The jurisdiction governing children's cases is twofold: first there is the Children Act 1989 (CA 1989) (as amended by the Children and Families Act 2014) jurisdiction; secondly, there is the Inherent Jurisdiction of the High Court.

Children Act 1989

By s 105(1) of CA 1989 a 'child' means a person under the age of 18. Medical treatment issues may arise during the course of private law proceedings or public law proceedings under the Act. In private law proceedings these may include applications for specific issue orders under s 8 of the Act, where there is a dispute usually between parents over proposed medical treatment of the child. In public law proceedings the court may be invited to give directions under s 38(6) of the Act as it considers appropriate with regard to the medical or psychiatric examination of the child; but if the child is of sufficient understanding to make an informed decision he may refuse to submit to the examination or other assessment.

The new Practice Direction 12B supplementing Part 12 of the Family Procedure Rules 2010 (FPR 2010) is entitled 'Child Arrangements Programme'. This programme (the CAP) applies where a dispute arises between separated parents and/or families about arrangements concerning children, including any specific issues over medical treatment.

Where any such issue is before the court under this Act, the appropriate terms of the 1989 Act (as amended by the Children and Families Act 2014) are to be considered and weighed, in order to be able to determine what is in the best interests of the child or children in question, taking into account the checklist factors under s 1 of the Act.

Inherent Jurisdiction of the High Court

The High Court is able to step into the shoes of the parents and to approve or not approve, on behalf of the child, the medical treatment proposed for him or her. This Inherent Jurisdiction of the High Court in relation to children – the parens patriae jurisdiction – is equally exercisable whether the child is or is not a ward of court *(Re M and N (Minors) (Wardship: Publication of Information)* [1990] Fam 211, at 223G).

As was stated by Balcombe LJ in the case of *Re W (A Minor)* [1992] 3 WLR 758, at 773:

> '... It had long been recognised that wardship was only machinery and the Court's inherent jurisdiction could be exercised whether or not the child was a ward: see, for example, *In Re L (An Infant)* [1968] P 119, 157 ...'.

The Inherent Jurisdiction is not derivative from the parents' rights and responsibilities but derives from, or is, the delegated performance of the duties of the Crown to protect its subjects, and particularly children, who are the generations of the future *(Re C (A Minor) (Wardship: Medical Treatment) (No 2)* [1990] Fam 39, at 46, [1990] 1 FLR 263, at 266).

In *Re Z (A Minor) (Identification: Restrictions on Publication)* [1997] Fam 1, the Court of Appeal helpfully analysed the High Court's jurisdiction in relation to wardship and the Inherent Jurisdiction in respect of children.

In practical terms, the court, when exercising the parens patriae jurisdiction, takes over the rights and duties of the parents. The wishes and views of the parents will be important. However, in the end, the responsibility for the decision will be that of the court alone.

Within its parens patriae jurisdiction, the court will be able to approve or not approve medical treatment for and on behalf of the minor, dependent upon whether such treatment is or is not in the minor's best interests.

The powers of the High Court, under its Inherent Jurisdiction with respect to minors, are 'theoretically limitless' *(Re W (A Minor) (Medical Treatment: Court's Jurisdiction)* [1992] 3 WLR 758, at 769). To this extent, for example, the court has power to override a minor's refusal to submit to a medical examination directed under s 38(6) of CA 1989 and to direct that the minor is medically examined, assessed or treated.

The following provisions apply to applications by local authorities for the court to exercise its inherent jurisdiction.

By s 100(3) of CA 1989, a local authority has to seek and obtain leave of the court to be able to apply for the exercise of the court's Inherent Jurisdiction with respect to children.

By s 100(4) of the Act, the court may only grant leave if it is satisfied that:

- the result which the authority wished to achieve could not be achieved through the making of any order of a kind to which subs (5) applies; and
- there is reasonable cause to believe that, if the court's inherent jurisdiction is not exercised with respect to the child, he is likely to suffer significant harm.

Section 100(5) applies to any order:

- made otherwise than in the exercise of the court's Inherent Jurisdiction; and
- which the local authority is entitled to apply for (assuming, in the case of any application which may only be made with leave, that leave is granted).

8.2.2 Practice and procedure under the Family Procedure Rules 2010

The procedure governing applications under both CA 1989 and the Inherent Jurisdiction is set out within Part 12 of FPR 2010. By rule 12.1, the rules in Part 12 apply to private law proceedings, public law proceedings and proceedings relating to the exercise of the court's Inherent Jurisdiction (other than applications for the court's permission to start such proceedings). Part 12 is supplemented by a raft of Practice Directions from Practice Direction 12A through to Practice Direction 12P. PD12A is applicable to public law proceedings and PD12B to private law proceedings.

In relation to particular provisions concerning the Inherent Jurisdiction, Part 5 of Part 12 of FPR 2010 is entitled 'Special provisions about Inherent Jurisdiction Proceedings'. By rule 12.36(1), an application for proceedings under the Inherent Jurisdiction of the court must be started in the High Court.

Practice Direction 12D is entitled 'Inherent jurisdiction (including wardship) proceedings'. It is reproduced at the end of this Chapter. This document elucidates the purpose and remit of the Inherent Jurisdiction concerning children, which includes the duty of the court to ensure that a child who is the subject of proceedings is protected and properly taken care of.

The court may, in exercising its Inherent Jurisdiction, make any order or determine any issue in respect of a child unless limited by case law or statute. Proceedings under the Inherent Jurisdiction should not be commenced unless it is clear that the issues concerning the child cannot be resolved under CA 1989. Paragraph 1.2 of the Practice Direction sets out the wide powers of the court under its Inherent Jurisdiction including making a wide range of injunctions for child protection, including orders relating to medical treatment and orders to restrain publicity.

The Practice Direction includes reference to disputes about medical treatment, and medical treatment cases of very significant difficulty are likely to be considered appropriate for the Inherent Jurisdiction of the High Court.

The court's wardship jurisdiction is a part of and not separate from the court's Inherent Jurisdiction. One characteristic of the wardship jurisdiction is that custody of the child is vested in the court, with no important step being able to be taken in the child's life without the consent of the court.

In the majority of serious medical treatment cases suitable for the High Court under the Inherent Jurisdiction, wardship will not be relevant or applicable. The court will be concentrating on a particular issue or issues concerning medical treatment in relation to the child and determining what is in his or her best interests.

8.2.3 Expert evidence; medical examination of children

In both CA 1989 proceedings and proceedings under the Inherent Jurisdiction of the High Court, a significant feature of the case may sometimes be a physical or psychological illness of the child.

If proceedings are instituted, permission must be sought from the court before any further proposed medical examination of the subject child or children may occur.

By s 13(1) of the Children and Families Act 2014:

'A person may not without the permission of the court instruct a person to provide expert evidence for use in children proceedings.'

By s 13(3) of the 2014 Act:

'A person may not without the permission of the court cause a child to be medically or psychiatrically examined or otherwise assessed for the purposes of the provision of expert evidence in children proceedings.'

By s 13(6) of the 2014 Act the court may give permission 'only if the court is of the opinion that the expert evidence is necessary to assist the court to resolve the proceedings justly'.

8.2.4 The legal status of the child who is the subject of any medical treatment issue/s

By s 41 of CA 1989, in 'specified proceedings' the subject child will automatically be a party to the proceedings and a children's guardian will be appointed, unless the court is satisfied that it is not necessary to do so in order to safeguard the child's interests. Section 41(6) defines specified proceedings, which include care proceedings.

Leaving aside specified proceedings as above, otherwise in proceedings brought both under CA 1989 and the Inherent Jurisdiction the subject child is not automatically a party to the proceedings. In both instances, by rule 16.2 of FPR 2010 the court may make a child a party to proceedings if it considers it is in the best interests of the child to do so.

The Practice Direction 16A at Part 4, Section 1 is entitled 'When a child should be made a party to proceedings'. The document indicates that making the child a party to the proceedings will only occur in a minority of cases involving issues of significant difficulty. It offers guidance as to the circumstances which may justify the joining of the child as a party, including where there are complex medical or mental health issues to be determined or there are other unusually complex issues that necessitate separate representation of the child.

In medical treatment cases presenting issues of very significant difficulty it is likely that the subject child will be joined as a party. Certainly a child of sufficient understanding to instruct his or her own solicitor should be made a party and given notice of any application.

By rule 12.37 of FPR 2010 the child who is the subject of wardship proceedings must not be made a party to those proceedings unless the court gives permission following an application.

8.2.5 Children's guardian

By FPR 2010, rule 16.4 the court must appoint a children's guardian for a child who is the subject of proceedings if the court has made the child a party in accordance with rule 16.2. Section 2 of Part 4 of PD16A sets out the duties of a children's guardian appointed under rule 16.4.

By rule 16.24 of FPR 2010 and indeed Practice Direction 16A, the first port of call (in relation to proceedings brought under both CA 1989 and the inherent jurisdiction when the court has joined the subject child) will be the appointment of a Cafcass Officer as children's guardian. Provision is made in rule 16.24, however, for the appointment – if Cafcass for whatever reason are unable to be utilized – if they consent, of 'a person other than the Official Solicitor' or 'the Official Solicitor'. The Official Solicitor may act for the child in exceptional circumstances.

By rule 16.6, other than in 'specified proceedings' a child may conduct proceedings without a children's guardian in proceedings both under CA 1989 and the Inherent Jurisdiction where the child has obtained the court's permission or a solicitor considers that the child is able, having regard to his or her understanding, to give instructions in relation to the proceedings and has accepted instructions from that child to act for that child in the proceedings and, if the proceedings have begun, the solicitor is already acting.

8.2.6   The representation of parents lacking capacity

By rule 2.3 of FPR 2010 a 'protected party' means a party, or an intended party, who lacks capacity (within the meaning of the 2005 Act) to conduct proceedings.

Where a parent or parents who are parties to proceedings lack capacity to conduct proceedings, by FPR 2010, rule 15.2 they must have a litigation friend to conduct proceedings on their behalf. The Official Solicitor may act for parents who lack mental capacity (within the meaning of MCA 2005) to instruct their own solicitor (or are under 18) who are involved in court proceedings concerning their children. In the case of *An NHS Trust v KH* [2013] 1 FLR 1471, the Trust sought declarations in relation to the best interests of a 3-year-old boy who was very seriously ill. The parents had difficulties of their own and lacked capacity to make decisions about their son's medical treatment or to conduct the proceedings on their own behalf. They were represented by the Official Solicitor.

8.2.7   Transparency: hearings in private

Reproduced at the conclusion of this Chapter is the Practice Guidance issued by the President of the Family Division on 16 January 2014 entitled 'Transparency in the Family Courts, Publication of Judgments'.

By FPR 2010, rule 27.10, proceedings to which these rules apply are to be held in private 'except where the court directs otherwise'.

Rule 27.11 sets out provisions concerning those who are able to be in attendance at a private hearing. Leaving aside the excepted category of proceedings defined at rule 27.11(1), otherwise in proceedings concerning children rule 27.11(2) entitles duly accredited representatives of newsgathering and reporting organisations to be present, as well as any other person whom the court permits to be present. Rule 27.11(3) allows the court to direct, in the circumstances there set out, that such news and reporting representatives shall not attend the proceedings or a part of such proceedings.

Practice Direction 27B concerns itself in detail with the attendance of media representatives at hearings in Family Proceedings.

Whilst there are no express provisions in FPR 2010 in relation to the power of the court to order a hearing concerning children to be heard in public, nevertheless it is clear from the words 'except where the court directs otherwise' in rule 27.10 that the court may indeed order a hearing or part of the hearing concerning a child to be heard in public.

In the case of *NHS Trust v A (A Child)* [2007] EWHC 1696 (Fam) concerning a seriously ill 7-month-old baby, Holman J said that at the outset of the hearing the applicant hospital and the parents both strongly urged the court to hear the whole case and to give judgment in private. The parents desperately wished to avoid any publicity or intrusion into the lives of themselves and their family. The hospital wished to avoid intrusion into their vital sensitive work for their patient and other patients. The court exercised its discretion to hear the evidence and arguments in private, stating that to do otherwise would have been very unfair on the parents in particular who were already suffering greatly from the illness of their child, who did not initiate the proceedings, and had done nothing whatsoever to court any publicity into an intensely private matter. The court decided, however, that it would announce its decision and reasoning publicly because the public are entitled to know what decisions courts take in this field and why. The restraints of s 12 of the Administration of Justice Act 1960 and all other relevant reporting restraints would apply.

On the other hand the following two medical treatment cases concerning very seriously ill young children were heard in public, and the contrasting comments by the two respective judges as to the impact of this are illuminating.

In the case of *Portsmouth NHS Trust v Wyatt* [2005] EWHC 693 (Fam) the judge said at paragraph 23:

> 'This case has for reasons earlier explained been heard throughout in public. I recognise that it is the family and the medical and nursing staff who have borne the brunt of that publicity. Whilst the reporting of the case and comments on it have, so far as I can see, been uniformly fair and balanced, some other publicity has been found hurtful and has added to the stress borne by individuals linked to the child. It is of course essential that the public should understand the workings of this jurisdiction and that there should be full and open debate about it. I only wanted to say that I recognise and acknowledge that this has come at a price to those most closely involved in the childcare which, as all the expert evidence has asserted, has been uniformly of the highest standard.'

In the case of *An NHS Trust v MB* [2006] EWHC 507 (Fam) the judge said at paragraph 1 of his judgment:

> 'since the second day of this hearing I have sat in public with a number of journalists and others present. I am in no doubt that it was appropriate

that this case, not just this judgment but almost the whole of the evidence, be heard in public and I am glad that the BBC made their application. I have not personally felt that the presence of the media has been intrusive in the court room; nor, so far as I could observe, has it been oppressive to or added to the burden upon the parents, even when giving their evidence. I thank the media for the sensitivity they have shown, at any rate within the court room.'

It is to be noted that in the case of *Re OT* [2009] EWHC 633 (Fam), again a case concerning a seriously unwell young child, the judge sat in public throughout the case where possible.

8.3 THE TRANSFER OF PROCEEDINGS BETWEEN THE COURT OF PROTECTION AND A COURT HAVING JURISDICTION UNDER CHILDREN ACT 1989

Section 21 of MCA 2005 makes provision for the transfer of cases concerning persons under the age of 18 from the Court of Protection to a court having jurisdiction under CA 1989 and vice versa from a court having jurisdiction under CA 1989 to the Court of Protection.

At the end of this Chapter is reproduced the Mental Capacity Act 2005 (Transfer of Proceedings) Order 2007, SI 2007/1899, setting out the factors each court must take into account in determining whether proceedings concerning a person under the age of 18 should be transferred to the other court. Those factors can be seen on the face of the statutory instrument, save only to say that, in a serious medical treatment case affecting a 16-year-old or 17-year-old who lacks capacity, art 3(3)(c) may be relevant in considering a transfer to the Court of Protection from a court having jurisdiction under CA 1989 where any order is likely to continue to have a manifest effect when that person reaches the age of 18 and thereafter.

APPENDICES TO CHAPTER 8

PRACTICE DIRECTION E – APPLICATIONS RELATING TO SERIOUS MEDICAL TREATMENT (PD9E)

This practice direction supplements Part 9 of the Court of Protection Rules 2007

General

1. Rule 71 enables a practice direction to make additional or different provision in relation to specified applications.

Applications to which this Practice Direction applies

2. This practice direction sets out the procedure to be followed where the application concerns serious medical treatment in relation to P.

Meaning of 'serious medical treatment' in relation to the Rules and this practice direction

3. Serious medical treatment means treatment which involves providing, withdrawing or withholding treatment in circumstances where:

(a) in a case where a single treatment is being proposed, there is a fine balance between its benefits to P and the burdens and risks it is likely to entail for him;

(b) in a case where there is a choice of treatments, a decision as to which one to use is finely balanced; or

(c) the treatment, procedure or investigation proposed would be likely to involve serious consequences for P.

4. 'Serious consequences' are those which could have a serious impact on P, either from the effects of the treatment, procedure or investigation itself or its wider implications. This may include treatments, procedures or investigations which:

(a) cause, or may cause, serious and prolonged pain, distress or side effects;

(b) have potentially major consequences for P; or

(c) have a serious impact on P's future life choices.

Matters which should be brought to the court

5. Cases involving any of the following decisions should be regarded as serious medical treatment for the purpose of the Rules and this practice direction, and should be brought to the court:

(a) decisions about the proposed withholding or withdrawal of artificial nutrition and hydration from a person in a permanent vegetative state or a minimally conscious state;

(b) cases involving organ or bone marrow donation by a person who lacks capacity to consent; and

(c) cases involving non-therapeutic sterilisation of a person who lacks capacity to consent.

6. Examples of serious medical treatment may include:

(a) certain terminations of pregnancy in relation to a person who lacks capacity to consent to such a procedure;

(b) a medical procedure performed on a person who lacks capacity to consent to it, where the procedure is for the purpose of a donation to another person;

(c) a medical procedure or treatment to be carried out on a person who lacks capacity to consent to it, where that procedure or treatment must be carried out using a degree of force to restrain the person concerned;

(d) an experimental or innovative treatment for the benefit of a person who lacks capacity to consent to such treatment; and

(e) a case involving an ethical dilemma in an untested area.

7. There may be other procedures or treatments not contained in the list in paragraphs 5 and 6 above which can be regarded as serious medical treatment. Whether or not a procedure is regarded as serious medical treatment will depend on the circumstances and the consequences for the patient.

Consultation with the Official Solicitor

8. Members of the Official Solicitor's staff are prepared to discuss applications in relation to serious medical treatment before an application is made. Any enquiries about adult medical and welfare cases should be addressed to a family and medical litigation lawyer at the Office of the Official Solicitor, 81 Chancery Lane, London WC2A IDD, ph: 020 7911 7127, fax: 020 7911 7105, email: enquiries@offsol.gsi.gov.uk.

Parties to proceedings

9. The person bringing the application will always be a party to proceedings, as will a respondent named in the application form who files an acknowledgment of service. In cases involving issues as to serious medical treatment, an organisation which is, or will be, responsible for providing clinical or caring services to P should usually be named as a respondent in the application form (where it is not already the applicant in the proceedings).

(Practice Direction B accompanying Part 9 sets out the persons who are to be notified that an application form has been issued.)

10. The court will consider whether anyone not already a party should be joined as a party to the proceedings. Other persons with sufficient interest may apply to be joined as parties to the proceedings and the court has a duty to identify at as early a stage as possible who the parties to the proceedings should be.

Allocation of the case

11. Where an application is made to the court in relation to:

    (a) the lawfulness of withholding or withdrawing artificial nutrition and hydration from a person in a permanent vegetative state, or a minimally conscious state; or

    (b) a case involving an ethical dilemma in an untested area,

the proceedings (including permission, the giving of any directions, and any hearing) must be conducted by the President of the Court of Protection or by another judge nominated by the President.

12. Where an application is made to the court in relation to serious medical treatment (other than that outlined in paragraph 11) the proceedings (including permission, the giving of any directions, and any hearing) must be conducted by a judge of the court who has been nominated as such by virtue of section 46(2)(a) to (c) of the Act (ie the President of the Family Division, the Chancellor or a puisne judge of the High Court).

Matters to be considered at the first directions hearing

13. Unless the matter is one which needs to be disposed of urgently, the court will list it for a first directions hearing.

(Practice Direction B accompanying Part 10 sets out the procedure to be followed for urgent applications.)

14. The court may give such directions as it considers appropriate. If the court has not already done so, it should in particular consider whether to do any or all of the following at the first directions hearing:

    (a) decide whether P should be joined as party to the proceedings, and give directions to that effect;

    (b) if P is to be joined as a party to the proceedings, decide whether the Official Solicitor should be invited to act as a litigation friend or whether some other person should be appointed as a litigation friend;

    (c) identify anyone else who has been notified of the proceedings and who has filed an acknowledgment and applied to be joined as a party to proceedings, and consider that application; and

(d) set a timetable for the proceedings including, where possible, a date for the final hearing.

15. The court should also consider whether to give any of the other directions listed in rule 85(2).

16. The court will ordinarily make an order pursuant to rule 92 that any hearing shall be held in public, with restrictions to be imposed in relation to publication of information about the proceedings.

Declarations

17. Where a declaration is needed, the order sought should be in the following or similar terms:

- That P lacks capacity to make a decision in relation to the (proposed medical treatment or procedure).
  Eg 'That P lacks capacity to make a decision in relation to sterilisation by vasectomy'; and

- That, having regard to the best interests of P, it is lawful for the (proposed medical treatment or procedure) to be carried out by (proposed healthcare provider).

18. Where the application is for the withdrawal of life-sustaining treatment, the order sought should be in the following or similar terms:

- That P lacks capacity to consent to continued life-sustaining treatment measures (and specify what these are); and
- That, having regard to the best interests of P, it is lawful for (name of healthcare provider) to withdraw the life-sustaining treatment from P.

MINISTRY OF JUSTICE
COURT OF PROTECTION – HEALTHCARE AND WELFARE CASES

The Official Solicitor is a litigation friend of last resort. If the person who lacks capacity ('P') is a party to the proceedings the Official Solicitor may act as 'P''s litigation friend of, if so appointed by the court. He may also act as advocate to the court if invited to do so by the court.

Some healthcare matters are so serious that they must be brought to the court for a decision, for example

- applications to withhold or withdraw artificial nutrition and hydration from a person in a permanent vegetative state or a minimally conscious state

- application for the non-therapeutic sterilisation of a person who lacks capacity to consent

- application involving organ or bone marrow donation by a person who lacks capacity to consent

Other cases involving serious medical treatment may be brought to court if there is serious doubt or disagreement about whether a particular treatment will be in P's best interests (see PD 9E for further examples).

Serious medical treatment cases must be heard by a judge of the court who has been nominated as such by virtue of section 46(2)(a) to (c) of the Act (ie, the President of the Court of Protection, the chancellor or a puisne judge of the High Court) PD 12A.

Applications may also be made in a wide range of other healthcare and welfare disputes, usually in respect of residence and contact matters, when there is a serious justiciable issue requiring a decision by the court.

A number of practice directions have been issued in relation to the Mental Capacity Act 2005. These can be found on the Judiciary website.

PRACTICE NOTE
MARCH 2013
THE OFFICIAL SOLICITOR TO THE SENIOR
COURTS: APPOINTMENT IN FAMILY PROCEEDINGS
AND PROCEEDINGS UNDER THE INHERENT
JURISDICTION IN RELATION TO ADULTS

Introduction

1 This Practice Note replaces the Practice Note dated 2 April 2001 issued by the Official Solicitor.

2 It concerns:

(a) the appointment of the Official Solicitor as "litigation friend" of a "protected party" or child in family proceedings or where the Family Division of the High Court is being invited to exercise its inherent jurisdiction in relation to a vulnerable adult[1];

(b) requests by the court to the Official Solicitor to conduct *Harbin v Masterman*[2] enquiries; and

(c) requests by the court to the Official Solicitor to act as, or appoint counsel to act as, an advocate to the court[3].

The Note is intended to be helpful guidance, but is always subject to legislation including the Rules of Court, to Practice Directions, and to case law.

3 For the avoidance of doubt, the Children and Family Court Advisory and Support Service (Cafcass) has responsibilities in relation to a child in family proceedings in which their welfare is or may be in question (Criminal Justice and Court Services Act 2000, section 12). Since 1 April 2001 the Official Solicitor has not represented a child who is the subject of family proceedings (other than in very exceptional circumstances or where a transfer to the Court of Protection is being considered see paragraph 7 below).

In cases of doubt or difficulty, staff of the Official Solicitor's office will liaise with staff of Cafcass Legal Services to avoid duplication and ensure the most suitable arrangements are made.

---

[1] In this context a 'vulnerable adult' is a person who has mental capacity in respect of the decisions in question but who lacks litigation capacity.

[2] [1896] 1 Ch 351.

[3] Pursuant to the Memorandum "Requests for the appointment of an advocate to the court" of the Attorney General and the Lord Chief Justice of 19 December 2001.

Children and Protected Parties who require a litigation friend in proceedings

4 Adults: a "protected party" requires a litigation friend. In family proceedings this requirement appears in Part 15 of the Family Procedure Rules 2010 ("FPR 2010") and in proceedings in the Family Division of the High Court of Justice under the court's inherent jurisdiction it appears in Part 21 of the Civil Procedure Rules 1998 ("CPR 1998"). In family proceedings, a "protected party" means a party, or an intended party, who lacks capacity (within the meaning of the Mental Capacity Act 2005) to conduct the proceedings: FPR 2010, rule 2.3; and in proceedings under the inherent jurisdiction the expression has the same meaning: CPR 1998, rule 21.2. The following should be noted:

(a) there must be undisputed evidence that the party, or intended party, lacks capacity to conduct the proceedings;

(b) that evidence, and what flows from the party, or intended party, being a protected party, should have been disclosed to, and carefully explained to, the party or intended party;

(c) the party, or intended party, is entitled to dispute an opinion that they lack litigation capacity and there may be cases where the party's, or intended party's, capacity to conduct the proceedings is the subject of dispute between competent experts. In either case a formal finding by the court under FPR 2010, rule 2.3, or CPR 1998, rule 21.2 is required.

5 Non-subject child: a child whose own welfare is not the subject of family proceedings may nevertheless be a party. The most common examples are:

(a) a child who is also the parent of a child, and who is a respondent to a Children Act 1989 or Adoption and Children Act 2002 application;

(b) a child who wishes to make an application for a Children Act 1989 order naming another child (typically a contact order naming a sibling);

(c) a child witness to some disputed factual issue in a children case and who may require intervenor status;

(d) a child party to an application for a declaration of status under Part III of the Family Law Act 1986;

(e) a child intervenor in financial remedy proceedings;

(f) a child applicant for, or respondent to, an application for an order under Part IV (Family Homes and Domestic Violence) or Part 4A (Forced Marriage) of the Family Law Act 1996.

6 FPR 2010 Part 16 makes provision for the representation of children. Rule 16.6 sets out the circumstances in which a child does not need a children's guardian or litigation friend. Any child party to proceedings under the Children Act 1989, Part 4A Family Law Act 1996, applications in adoption, placement and related proceedings, or proceedings relating to the exercise of the court's inherent jurisdiction with respect to children may rely on the provisions of rule 16.6.

7 Children aged 16–17 years: the Mental Capacity Act 2005 (Transfer of Proceedings) Order 2007 (SI 2007/1899) makes provision for the transfer of proceedings from the Court of Protection to a court having jurisdiction under the Children Act 1989. The Order also makes provision for the transfer of the whole or part of the proceedings from a court having jurisdiction under the Children Act 1989 to the Court of Protection where it considers that in all circumstances, it is just and convenient to transfer the proceedings. Article 3(3) of the Order lists those factors to which the court must have regard when making a determination about transfer either on an application or of its own initiative. Court of Protection proceedings are not family proceedings and therefore transfer of proceedings into the Court of Protection will mean that any involvement by Cafcass in those proceedings will end.

8 The Court of Protection Rules 2007 apply to proceedings in the Court of Protection. Rule 141(4)–(6) of those Rules make provision for a child to be permitted to conduct proceedings in the Court of Protection without a litigation friend. However if the child is 'P' within the meaning of rule 6 of the Court of Protection Rules 2007 reference should be made to rule 141(1) and rule 147 of those Rules in relation to the appointment of a litigation friend.

The role of a litigation friend

9 The case law and the Rules provide that a litigation friend must fairly and competently conduct the proceedings in the protected party's or child's best interests, and must have no interest in the proceedings adverse to that of the protected party or child. The procedure and basis for the appointment of a litigation friend and the duty of a litigation friend are contained in Part 15 (Representation of Protected Parties) FPR 2010 and Part 16 (Representation of Children and Reports in Proceedings Involving Children) FPR 2010 and the associated Practice Directions.

The Official Solicitor's criteria for consenting to act as litigation friend

10 The Official Solicitor is the litigation friend of last resort. No person, including the Official Solicitor, can be appointed to act as litigation friend without their consent. The Official Solicitor will not accept appointment where there is another person who is suitable and willing to act as litigation friend. The Official Solicitor's criteria for consenting to act as litigation friend are:

(a) in the case of an adult that the party or intended party is a protected party[4];

(b) there is security for the costs of legal representation of the protected party which the Official Solicitor considers satisfactory. Sources of security may be

   (i) the Legal Aid Agency where the protected party or child is eligible for public funding;

   (ii) the protected party's or child's own funds where they have financial capacity or where they do not where the Court of Protection has given him authority to recover the costs from the adult's or child's funds;

   (iii) an undertaking from another party to pay his costs;

(c) the case is a last resort case.

Invitations to the Official Solicitor: new cases

11 Solicitors who have been consulted by a child or a protected party (or by someone acting on their behalf, or concerned about their interests) should write to the Official Solicitor setting out the background to the proposed case and explaining the basis on which the Official Solicitor's criteria for acting are met.

Invitations to the Official Solicitor: pending proceedings

12 Where a case is already before the court, an order inviting the Official Solicitor to act should be expressed as being made subject to his consent. The Official Solicitor aims to provide an initial response to any invitation within 10 working days. But he cannot consent to act unless and until he is satisfied both that his criteria are met and that he has a member of his staff to whom the case can be allocated as the case's case manager. So from time to time there will be a waiting list of cases which meet the Official Solicitor's acceptance criteria but in respect of which, because he has no case manager available to take the case, he cannot

---

4 The Official Solicitor is able to provide a pro forma certificate of capacity to conduct proceedings and notes for guidance.

accept appointment as litigation friend. Save in exceptional circumstances, cases will be accepted in strict chronological order starting with the earliest placed on the waiting list of cases which have met the criteria for acceptance. What constitutes exceptional circumstances will be fact specific; the decision to expedite acceptance of a case is one for the Official Solicitor.

13 To enable the Official Solicitor to consider the invitation to him to act, he should be provided with the following as soon as possible:

(a) the sealed court order inviting him to act as litigation friend (with a note of the reasons approved by the Judge if appropriate);

(b) a copy of the letter of instruction to the expert by which an opinion was sought as to the party's capacity to conduct the proceedings whether in the form of the Official Solicitor's certificate of capacity to conduct the proceedings or otherwise;

(c) (adult party) the opinion on capacity (the Official Solicitor's pro forma certificate of capacity to conduct proceedings may be requested from his office for the purpose of obtaining an opinion);

(d) confirmation that there is satisfactory security for the costs of legal representation (including any relevant supporting documents); it is a matter for the Official Solicitor whether the proposed security for costs is satisfactory;

(e) confirmation that there is no other person suitable and willing to act as litigation friend (including the enquiries made to this end);

(f) the court file (provision of the court file may not be necessary if the court directs a party to provide a full indexed copy of the bundle to the Official Solicitor on a timely basis).

Litigants in person

14 If one or more parties is or are litigants in person, and there is reason to believe that any litigant in person may lack capacity to conduct the proceedings, the court will need to consider, and if necessary give directions as to:

(a) who is to arrange for the assessment of capacity to conduct the proceedings;

(b) how the cost of that assessment is to be funded;

(c) how any invitation to act as litigation friend is to be made to either any suitable and willing person or the Official Solicitor so as to provide him with the documents and information (including information to enable him to make the enquiries necessary to establish whether or not there is funding available);

(d) any resulting timetabling and, where the Official Solicitor is being invited to be litigation friend, having regard to the Official Solicitor's need to investigate whether his acceptance criteria are met, the need for him to have a case manager available to deal with the case and the possibility that an application to the Court of Protection (for authority to pay the costs out of the protected party's or child's funds) may be necessary.

15 The Official Solicitor will notify the court in the event he expects a delay in accepting appointment either because it is not evident that his criteria are met or for any other reason. The court may wish to consider:

(a) making enquiries of the parties as to the steps being taken by them to establish that the Official Solicitor's criteria for acting are met in the particular case;

(b) whether directions should be made to ensure that such enquiries are progressed on a timely basis;

(c) fixing a further directions appointment.

16 If, at any time, another litigation friend is appointed before the Official Solicitor is in a position to accept the invitation to him to act, the Official Solicitor should be notified without delay.

Where the Official Solicitor has accepted appointment as litigation friend

17 Once the Official Solicitor is able to accept appointment as litigation friend he will need time to prepare the case on behalf of the protected party or child and may wish to make submissions about any substantive hearing date.

18 To avoid unnecessary delay in progression of the case, he will require from the solicitors he appoints for the protected party or child:

(a) a reading list identifying the material which the solicitors consider will assist by way of introduction to the case in obtaining an overview of the issues from the perspective of the protected party or child;

(b) a summary of the background to the proceedings, of any major steps that have occurred within the proceedings, and identification of the issues in the proceedings;

(c) advice as to the steps the Official Solicitor should now take in the proceedings on behalf of the protected party or child;

(d) copies of all notes of attendance on the protected party or child so that the Official Solicitor is properly informed as to the views and wishes expressed by the protected party or child to date;

(e) confirmation of the protected party's or child's present ascertainable views and wishes in relation to the proceedings.

Advising the court: *Harbin v Masterman* **enquiries and Advocate to the Court**

19 Where the Official Solicitor is invited, with his consent, to conduct enquiries under *Harbin v Masterman* and it appears to the Official Solicitor that any public body wishes to seek the assistance of the court but is unwilling to carry out the enquiries itself, the Official Solicitor may seek an undertaking from that public body to indemnify him in respect of his costs of carrying out those enquiries.

20 As noted at paragraph 2(c) above, the Official Solicitor may be invited, with his consent, to act or instruct counsel as a friend of the court (advocate to the court) if it appears to the court that such an invitation is more appropriately addressed to him rather than (or in addition to) Cafcass Legal Services or to the Attorney-General.

Contacting the Official Solicitor

21 It may be helpful to discuss the question of appointment with the Official Solicitor or one of his staff by telephoning 020 7911 7127 (family litigation) or 020 7911 7233 (divorce litigation), in particular:

(a) if in doubt about whether his criteria for acting are met, or

(b) to request a copy of the Official Solicitor's pro forma certificate of capacity to conduct proceedings and notes for guidance.

The Official Solicitor's certificate of capacity to conduct proceedings, a sample letter of instruction, other precedent documents and further guidance in relation to the appointment of the Official Solicitor are also available at www.justice.gov.uk (follow the links to the Official Solicitor).

22 Enquiries about the appointment of the Official Solicitor as litigation friend should be addressed:

(a) (in divorce and financial remedy proceedings) to the Divisional Manager, Divorce Litigation;

(b) (in children proceedings or proceedings under Part IV Family Law Act 1996) to the Divisional Manager, Family Litigation;.

All other enquiries should be addressed to a family lawyer.

The contact details are:

81 Chancery Lane,
London WC2A 1DD.
DX 0012 London Chancery Lane
Fax: 020 7911 7105
E-mail address: enquiries@offsol.gsi.gov.uk

Alastair Pitblado
Official Solicitor

PRACTICE DIRECTION 12D –
INHERENT JURISDICTION (INCLUDING WARDSHIP) PROCEEDINGS

FPR Pt 12, Ch 5

This Practice Direction supplements FPR Part 12, Chapter 5

The nature of inherent jurisdiction proceedings

1.1 It is the duty of the court under its inherent jurisdiction to ensure that a child who is the subject of proceedings is protected and properly taken care of. The court may in exercising its inherent jurisdiction make any order or determine any issue in respect of a child unless limited by case law or statute. Such proceedings should not be commenced unless it is clear that the issues concerning the child cannot be resolved under the Children Act 1989.

1.2 The court may under its inherent jurisdiction, in addition to all of the orders which can be made in family proceedings, make a wide range of injunctions for the child's protection of which the following are the most common –

    (a)   orders to restrain publicity;
    (b)   orders to prevent an undesirable association;
    (c)   orders relating to medical treatment;
    (d)   orders to protect abducted children, or children where the case has another substantial foreign element; and
    (e)   orders for the return of children to and from another state.

1.3 The court's wardship jurisdiction is part of and not separate from the court's inherent jurisdiction. The distinguishing characteristics of wardship are that –

    (a)   custody of a child who is a ward is vested in the court; and
    (b)   although day to day care and control of the ward is given to an individual or to a local authority, no important step can be taken in the child's life without the court's consent.

Transfer of proceedings to family court

2.1 Whilst the family court does not have jurisdiction to deal with applications that a child be made or cease to be a ward of court, consideration should be given to transferring the case in whole or in part to the family court where a direction has been given confirming the wardship and directing that the child remain a ward of court during his minority or until further order.

2.2 The family court must transfer the case back to the High Court if a decision is required as to whether the child should remain a ward of court.

2.3 The following proceedings in relation to a ward of court will be dealt with in the High Court unless the nature of the issues of fact or law makes them more suitable for hearing in the family court –

(a) those in which an officer of the Cafcass High Court Team or the Official Solicitor is or becomes the litigation friend or children's guardian of the ward or a party to the proceedings;

(b) those in which a local authority is or becomes a party;

(c) those in which an application for paternity testing is made;

(d) those in which there is a dispute about medical treatment;

(e) those in which an application is opposed on the grounds of lack of jurisdiction;

(f) those in which there is a substantial foreign element;

(g) those in which there is an opposed application for leave to take the child permanently out of the jurisdiction or where there is an application for temporary removal of a child from the jurisdiction and it is opposed on the ground that the child may not be duly returned.

Amendments—FPR Update 9.

Parties

3.1 Where the child has formed or is seeking to form an association, considered to be undesirable, with another person, that other person should not be made a party to the application. Such a person should be made a respondent only to an application within the proceedings for an injunction or committal. Such a person should not be added to the title of the proceedings nor allowed to see any documents other than those relating directly to the proceedings for the injunction or committal. He or she should be allowed time to obtain representation and any injunction should in the first instance extend over a few days only.

Removal from jurisdiction

4.1 A child who is a ward of court may not be removed from England and Wales without the court's permission. Practice Direction 12F (International Child Abduction) deals in detail with locating and protecting children at risk of unlawful removal.

Criminal Proceedings

5.1 Where a child has been interviewed by the police in connection with contemplated criminal proceedings and the child subsequently becomes a ward of court, the permission of the court deciding the wardship proceedings ("the wardship court") is not required for the child to be called as a witness in the criminal proceedings.

5.2 Where the police need to interview a child who is already a ward of court, an application must be made for permission for the police to do so. Where permission is given the order should, unless there is some special reason to the contrary, give permission for any number of interviews which may be required by the prosecution or the police. If a need arises to conduct any interview beyond the permission contained in the order, a further application must be made.

5.3 The above applications must be made with notice to all parties.

5.4 Where a person may become the subject of a criminal investigation and it is considered necessary for the child who is a ward of court to be interviewed without that person knowing that the police are making inquiries, the application for permission to interview the child may be made without notice to that party. Notice should, however, where practicable be given to the children's guardian.

5.5 There will be other occasions where the police need to deal with complaints, or alleged offences, concerning children who are wards of court where it is appropriate, if not essential, for action to be taken straight away without the prior permission of the wardship court, for example –

(a) serious offences against the child such as rape, where a medical examination and the collection of forensic evidence ought to be carried out promptly;

(b) where the child is suspected by the police of having committed a criminal act and the police wish to interview the child in respect of that matter;

(c) where the police wish to interview the child as a potential witness.

5.6 In such instances, the police should notify the parent or foster parent with whom the child is living or another 'appropriate adult' (within the Police and Criminal Evidence Act 1984 – Code of Practice C for the Detention, Treatment and Questioning of Persons by Police Officers) so that that adult has the opportunity of being present when the police interview the child. Additionally, if practicable the child's guardian (if one has been appointed) should be notified and invited to attend the police interview or to nominate a third party to attend on the guardian's behalf. A record of the interview or a copy of any statement made by the child should be supplied to the children's guardian. Where the child has been interviewed without the guardian's knowledge, the guardian should be informed at the earliest opportunity of this fact and (if it be the case) that the police wish to conduct further interviews. The wardship court should be informed of the situation at the earliest possible opportunity thereafter by the children's guardian, parent, foster parent (through the local authority) or other responsible adult.

Applications to the Criminal Injuries Compensation Authority

6.1 Where a child who is a ward of court has a right to make a claim for compensation to the Criminal Injuries Compensation Authority ("CICA"), an application must be made by the child's guardian, or, if no guardian has been appointed, the person with care and control of the child, for permission to apply to CICA and disclose such documents on the wardship proceedings file as are considered necessary to establish whether or not the child is eligible for an award plus, as appropriate, the amount of the award.

6.2 Any order giving permission should state that any award made by CICA should normally be paid into court immediately upon receipt and, once that payment has been made, application should made to the court as to its management and administration. If it is proposed to invest the award in any other way, the court's prior approval must be sought

The role of the tipstaff

7.1 The tipstaff is the enforcement officer for all orders made in the High Court. The tipstaff's jurisdiction extends throughout England and Wales. Every applicable order made in the High Court is addressed to the tipstaff in children and family matters (eg "The Court hereby directs the Tipstaff of the High Court of Justice, whether acting by himself or his assistants or a police officer as follows...").

7.2 The tipstaff may effect an arrest and then inform the police. Sometimes the local bailiff or police will detain a person in custody until the tipstaff arrives to collect that person or give further directions as to the disposal of the matter. The tipstaff may also make a forced entry although there will generally be a uniformed police officer standing by to make sure there is no breach of the peace.

7.3 There is only one tipstaff (with two assistants) but the tipstaff can also call on any constable or bailiff to assist in carrying out the tipstaff's duties.

7.4 The majority of the tipstaff's work involves locating children and taking them into protective custody, including cases of child abduction abroad.

MENTAL CAPACITY ACT 2005 (TRANSFER OF PROCEEDINGS) ORDER 2007

SI 2007/1899

1 Citation and commencement

(1) This Order may be cited as the Mental Capacity Act 2005 (Transfer of Proceedings) Order 2007.

(2) This Order shall come into force on 1 October 2007.

(3) In this Order 'the Children Act' means the Children Act 1989.

2 Transfers from the Court of Protection to a court having jurisdiction under the Children Act

(1) This article applies to any proceedings in the Court of Protection which relate to a person under 18.

(2) The Court of Protection may direct the transfer of the whole or part of the proceedings to a court having jurisdiction under the Children Act where it considers that in all the circumstances, it is just and convenient to transfer the proceedings.

(3) In making a determination, the Court of Protection must have regard to –

- (a) whether the proceedings should be heard together with other proceedings that are pending in a court having jurisdiction under the Children Act;
- (b) whether any order that may be made by a court having jurisdiction under that Act is likely to be a more appropriate way of dealing with the proceedings;
- (c) the need to meet any requirements that would apply if the proceedings had been started in a court having jurisdiction under the Children Act; and
- (d) any other matter that the court considers relevant.

(4) The Court of Protection –

- (a) may exercise the power to make an order under paragraph (2) on an application or on its own initiative; and
- (b) where it orders a transfer, must give reasons for its decision.

(5) Any proceedings transferred under this article –

- (a) are to be treated for all purposes as if they were proceedings under the Children Act which had been started in a court having jurisdiction under that Act; and

(b)   are to be dealt with after the transfer in accordance with directions given by a court having jurisdiction under that Act.

3 Transfers from a court having jurisdiction under the Children Act to the Court of Protection

(1) This article applies to any proceedings in a court having jurisdiction under the Children Act which relate to a person under 18.

(2) A court having jurisdiction under the Children Act may direct the transfer of the whole or part of the proceedings to the Court of Protection where it considers that in all circumstances, it is just and convenient to transfer the proceedings.

(3) In making a determination, the court having jurisdiction under the Children Act must have regard to –

(a)   whether the proceedings should be heard together with other proceedings that are pending in the Court of Protection;
(b)   whether any order that may be made by the Court of Protection is likely to be a more appropriate way of dealing with the proceedings;
(c)   the extent to which any order made as respects a person who lacks capacity is likely to continue to have effect when that person reaches 18; and
(d)   any other matter that the court considers relevant.

(4) A court having jurisdiction under the Children Act –

(a)   may exercise the power to make an order under paragraph (2) on an application or on its own initiative; and
(b)   where it orders a transfer, must give reasons for its decision.

(5) Any proceedings transferred under this article –

(a)   are to be treated for all purposes as if they were proceedings under the Mental Capacity Act 2005 which had been started in the Court of Protection; and
(b)   are to be dealt with after the transfer in accordance with directions given by the Court of Protection.

4 Avoidance of double liability for fees

Any fee paid for the purpose of starting any proceedings that are transferred under article 2 or 3 is to be treated as if it were the fee that would have been payable if the proceedings had started in the court to which the transfer is made.

TRANSPARENCY IN THE COURT OF PROTECTION PUBLICATION OF JUDGMENTS PRACTICE GUIDANCE ISSUED ON 16 JANUARY 2014 BY SIR JAMES MUNBY, PRESIDENT OF THE COURT OF PROTECTION

The purpose of this Guidance

1 This Guidance (together with similar Guidance issued at the same time for the family courts) is intended to bring about an immediate and significant change in practice in relation to the publication of judgments in family courts and the Court of Protection.

2 In both courts there is a need for greater transparency in order to improve public understanding of the court process and confidence in the court system. At present too few judgments are made available to the public, which has a legitimate interest in being able to read what is being done by the judges in its name. The Guidance will have the effect of increasing the number of judgments available for publication (even if they will often need to be published in appropriately anonymised form).

3 In July 2011 Sir Nicholas Wall P issued, jointly with Bob Satchwell, Executive Director of the Society of Editors, a paper, The Family Courts: Media Access & Reporting (Media Access & Reporting), setting out a statement of the current state of the law. In their preface they recognised that the debate on increased transparency and public confidence in the family courts would move forward and that future consideration of this difficult and sensitive area would need to include the questions of access to and reporting of proceedings by the media, whilst maintaining the privacy of the families involved. The paper is to be found at:

http://www.judiciary.gov.uk/Resources/JCO/Documents/Guidance/
family-courtsmedia-july2011.pdf

4 In April 2013 I issued a statement, View from the President's Chambers: the Process of Reform, [2013] Fam Law 548, in which I identified transparency as one of the three strands in the reforms which the family justice system is currently undergoing. I said:

> 'I am determined to take steps to improve access to and reporting of family proceedings. I am determined that the new Family Court should not be saddled, as the family courts are at present, with the charge that we are a system of secret and unaccountable justice. Work, commenced by my predecessor, is well underway. I hope to be in a position to make important announcements in the near future.'

5 That applies just as much to the issue of transparency in the Court of Protection.

6 Very similar issues arise in both the Family Court (as it will be from April 2014) and the Court of Protection in relation to the need to protect the personal privacy of children and vulnerable adults. The applicable rules differ, however, and this is something that needs attention. My starting point is that so far as possible the same rules and principles should apply in both the family courts (in due course the Family Court) and the Court of Protection.

7 I propose to adopt an incremental approach. Initially I am issuing this Guidance. This will be followed by further Guidance and in due course more formal Practice Directions and changes to the Rules (the Court of Protection Rules 2007 and the Family Procedure Rules 2010). Changes to primary legislation are unlikely in the near future.

8 As provided in paragraph 14 below, this Guidance applies only to judgments delivered by certain judges. In due course consideration will be given to extending it to judgments delivered by other judges.

The legal framework

9 The effect of section 12 of the Administration of Justice Act 1960 is that it is a contempt of court to publish a judgment in a Court of Protection case unless either the judgment has been delivered in public or, where delivered in private, the judge has authorised publication. In the latter case, the judge normally gives permission for the judgment to be published on condition that the published version protects the anonymity of the person who is subject of the proceedings and members of their family.

10 In every case the terms on which publication is permitted are a matter for the judge and will be set out by the judge in a rubric at the start of the judgment.

11 The normal terms as described in paragraph 9 may be appropriate in a case where no-one wishes to discuss the proceedings otherwise than anonymously. But they may be inappropriate, for example, where family members wish to discuss their experiences in public, identifying themselves and making use of the judgment. Equally, they may be inappropriate in cases where findings have been made against a person and someone else contends and/or the court concludes that it is in the public interest for that person to be identified in any published version of the judgment.

12 If any party wishes to identify himself or herself, or any other party or person, as being a person referred to in any published version of the judgment, their remedy is to seek an order of the court and a suitable modification of the rubric: Media Access & Reporting, paragraph 82; *Re RB (Adult) (No 4)* [2011] EWHC 3017 (Fam), [2012] 1 FLR 466, paras [17], [19].

13 Nothing in this Guidance affects the exercise by the judge in any particular case of whatever powers would otherwise be available to regulate the publication of material relating to the proceedings. For example, where a judgment is likely to be used in a way that would defeat the purpose of any anonymisation, it is open to the judge to refuse to publish the judgment or to make an order restricting its use.

Guidance

14 This Guidance takes effect from 3 February 2014. It applies to all judgments in the Court of Protection delivered by the Senior Judge, nominated Circuit Judges and High Court Judges.

15 The following paragraphs of this Guidance distinguish between two classes of judgment:
(i)   those that the judge must ordinarily allow to be published (paragraphs 16 and 17); and
(ii) those that may be published (paragraph 18).

16 Permission to publish a judgment should always be given whenever the judge concludes that publication would be in the public interest and whether or not a request has been made by a party or the media.

17 Where a judgment relates to matters set out in the Schedule below and a written judgment already exists in a publishable form or the judge has already ordered that the judgment be transcribed, the starting point is that permission should be given for the judgment to be published unless there are compelling reasons why the judgment should not be published.

SCHEDULE

Judgments arising from:
(i)   any application for an order involving the giving or withholding of serious medical treatment and any other hearing held in public;
(ii) any application for a declaration or order involving a deprivation or possible deprivation of liberty;

(iii) any case where there is a dispute as to who should act as an attorney or a deputy;

(iv) any case where the issues include whether a person should be restrained from acting as an attorney or a deputy or that an appointment should be revoked or his or her powers should be reduced;

(v) any application for an order that an incapacitated adult (P) be moved into or out of a residential establishment or other institution;

(vi) any case where the sale of P's home is in issue

(vii) any case where a property and affairs application relates to assets (including P's home) of £1 million or more or to damages awarded by a court sitting in public;

(viii) any application for a declaration as to capacity to marry or to consent to sexual relations;

(ix) any application for an order involving a restraint on publication of information relating to the proceedings.

18 In all other cases, the starting point is that permission may be given for the judgment to be published whenever a party or an accredited member of the media applies for an order permitting publication, and the judge concludes that permission for the judgment to be published should be given.

19 In deciding whether and if so when to publish a judgment, the judge shall have regard to all the circumstances, the rights arising under any relevant provision of the European Convention on Human Rights, including Articles 6 (right to a fair hearing), 8 (respect for private and family life) and 10 (freedom of expression), and the effect of publication upon any current or potential criminal proceedings.

20 In all cases where a judge gives permission for a judgment to be published:

(i) public authorities and expert witnesses should be named in the judgment approved for publication, unless there are compelling reasons why they should not be so named;

(ii) the person who is the subject of proceedings in the Court of Protection and other members of their family should not normally be named in the judgment approved for publication unless the judge otherwise orders;

(iii) anonymity in the judgment as published should not normally extend beyond protecting the privacy of the adults who are the subject of the proceedings and other members of their families, unless there are compelling reasons to do so.

21 Unless the judgment is already in anonymised form, any necessary anonymisation of the judgment shall be carried out as the judge orders. The version approved for publication will contain such rubric as the judge specifies. Unless the rubric specified by the judge provides expressly to the contrary every published judgment shall be deemed to contain the following rubric:

> "This judgment was delivered in private. The judge has given leave for this version of the judgment to be published on condition that (irrespective of what is contained in the judgment) in any published version of the judgment the anonymity of the incapacitated person and members of their family must be strictly preserved. All persons, including representatives of the media, must ensure that this condition is strictly complied with. Failure to do so will be a contempt of court."

22 The judge will need to consider who should be ordered to bear the cost of transcribing the judgment. Unless the judge otherwise orders:

(i) in cases falling under paragraph 18, the cost of transcribing the judgment shall be borne by the party or person applying for publication of the judgment;

(ii) in other cases, the cost of transcribing the judgment shall be at public expense.

23 In all cases where permission is given for a judgment to be published, the version of the judgment approved for publication shall be made available, upon payment of any appropriate charge that may be required, to any person who requests a copy. Where a judgment to which paragraph 16 or 17 applies is approved for publication, it shall as soon as reasonably practicable be placed by the court on the BAILII website. Where a judgment to which paragraph 18 applies is approved for publication, the judge shall consider whether it should be placed on the BAILII website and, if so, it shall as soon as reasonably practicable be placed by the court on the BAILII website.

PART IV

OTHER SPECIFIC AREAS IN RELATION TO MEDICAL TREATMENT AND THE LAW

CHAPTER 9

ADULT REFUSAL OF MEDICAL TREATMENT: NON-CONSENSUAL TREATMENT

9.1 THE PRESUMPTION OF CAPACITY TO DECIDE

The thrust of this chapter is to consider the capacity or lack of capacity of an adult patient to consent to or refuse medical treatment.

By s 1(2) of the Mental Capacity Act 2005 (MCA 2005), 'a person must be assumed to have capacity unless it is established that he lacks capacity'. By s 1(3) of the Act, 'a person is not to be treated as unable to make a decision unless all practicable steps to help him to do so have been taken without success'. By s 1(4) of the Act, 'a person is not to be treated as unable to make a decision merely because he makes an unwise decision'.

Prima facie, every adult has the right and capacity to decide whether or not he or she will accept medical treatment, even if a refusal may risk permanent injury to his or her health or even lead to premature death. This is so, notwithstanding the very strong public interest in preserving the life and health of all citizens. This has been described as the conflict of principle between two interests. The first interest is that of the patient, and consists of his right to self-determination, even if it will damage his health or lead to premature death. The second interest is that of society in upholding the concept that all human life is sacred and that it should be preserved, if at all posssible. It is established that the right of the individual is paramount.

Such a principle is evidenced, in stark terms, in the three cases below.

First, *Secretary of State for the Home Department v Robb* [1995] 1 FLR 412 concerned a prisoner on hunger strike. He was of sound mind and understanding. It was held that the principle of self-determination required that effect be given to the patient's wishes; that a patient who refused treatment and in consequence died did not commit suicide nor did a doctor who complied with the patient's wishes aid and abet a suicide.

In *St George's Healthcare NHS Trust v S* [1998] 2 FLR 728, a pregnant woman suffering from pre-eclampsia rejected the advice of a doctor that she needed urgent attention and admission to hospital for an induced delivery and that, without such treatment, her health and life and the life of the baby were in danger. She was admitted to a mental hospital against her will for assessment under s 2 of the Mental Health Act 1983 (MHA 1983). A judge was then requested to grant, and did grant, a declaration to the NHS trust dispensing with her consent to treatment and later that same evening her baby was born by Caesarean section. The Court of Appeal, in upholding her appeal against the declaration granted, held that, even though her own life and that of the baby were in danger, she was entitled to reject the advice offered and that the removal of the baby from within the body of the mother under physical compulsion amounted to trespass to the person.

In the case of *Ms B v An NHS Hospital Trust* [2002] EWHC 429 (Fam), the 62-year-old claimant, Miss B, sought declarations from the High Court claiming that the invasive treatment which she was currently being given by the hospital trust by way of artificial ventilation was an unlawful trespass. The claimant had become tetraplegic, suffering complete paralysis from the neck down. She began to experience respiratory problems, and was treated with a ventilator, upon which she had been entirely dependent ever since.

At the time of the court hearing the claimant's situation was that she was paralysed from the neck down. She was conscious and capable of speech with the assistance of a speaking valve. She could move her head and use some of her neck muscles, but could not move her torso, arms or legs at all. She was able to eat and drink. She was totally dependent on her carers, to feed, clothe and wash her and assist with bodily functions. Her life was supported by artificial ventilation through a tracheostomy, a tube in her windpipe. Without the help of artificial ventilation, according to the medical evidence, she would have a less than 1% chance of independent ventilation, and death would almost certainly follow.

The main issue in the case was whether the claimant had the mental capacity to choose whether to accept or refuse medical treatment, in circumstances in which her refusal would, almost inevitably, lead to her death.

As the judge said, it was important to underline that she was not being asked directly to decide whether the claimant lived or died but whether the claimant was legally competent to make that decision. Equally important was the significant point in the case that, if the claimant was competent to accept or refuse medical treatment, then the best interests test would not be relevant or applicable at all. The choice would be entirely that of the claimant.

Counsel for the claimant submitted that the evidence conclusively proved that the claimant had the requisite mental capacity to make her own decision about her future medical care, and in particular, to decide whether artificial ventilation should be withdrawn. Counsel for the hospital trust sought to persuade the judge that the claimant did not have legal capacity, despite the conclusions of the treating clinicians. Counsel for the Official Solicitor submitted that the claimant was legally competent and would be so for the foreseeable future.

The claimant provided two written statements and gave oral evidence, giving a clear account of her wishes and feelings. She made it clear that she had never changed her view that she wanted the ventilator withdrawn. She said that she found the idea of living as she was intolerable.

The judge was entirely satisfied that the patient was legally competent to make all relevant decisions about her medical treatment including the decision whether to seek to withdraw from artificial ventilation. Her mental competence was determined to be commensurate with the gravity of the decision she might wish to make.

In the light of the decision of the judge that the claimant had mental capacity she was also prepared to grant an appropriate declaration that, during a certain period, the claimant had been treated unlawfully by the hospital trust.

9.1.1   Advance decisions, deputies and lasting powers of attorney

It is not lawful to treat a patient who has capacity and refuses that treatment. Nor is it lawful to treat a patient who lacks capacity if he has made a valid and applicable advance decision to refuse it: see the Mental Capacity Act 2005 (MCA 2005), ss 24 to 26. Nor is it lawful to treat such a patient if he has granted a lasting power of attorney (under s 10) or the court has appointed a deputy (under s 16) with the power to give or withhold consent to that treatment and that consent is withheld; but an attorney only has power to give or withhold consent to the carrying out or continuation of life-sustaining treatment if the instrument expressly so provides (s 11(8)) and a deputy cannot refuse consent to such treatment (s 20(5)).

9.2 ADULTS LACKING THE CAPACITY TO DECIDE

The presumption that an adult has the capacity to decide can be rebutted. A small number of the population lack the necessary mental capacity, due to mental illness or retarded development. This connotes a long-term or permanent lack of capacity to decide. There are, however, many adults who are ordinarily competent and of sound mind whose capacity may be diminished or extinguished by reason of temporary factors, such as pain, severe fatigue, drugs being used in their treatment, confusion or other effects of shock or unconsciousness. Those adults with learning difficulties or mental illness may or may not lack capacity, whether generally or in relation to specific issues.

By s 2(1) of the MCA 2005, 'For the purposes of this Act, a person lacks capacity in relation to a matter if at the material time he is unable to make a decision for himself in relation to the matter because of an impairment of, or disturbance in the functioning of, the mind or brain.' By s 2(2) of the Act, 'it does not matter whether the impairment or disturbance is permanent or temporary'.

If the patient does not have the required capacity to decide, the medical practitioner may treat the patient in what he or she believes to be in the patient's best interests. In these circumstances, s 1(5) and s 5 of the Act are applicable.

9.3 ADJUDGING WHETHER OR NOT AN ADULT PATIENT HAS THE CAPACITY TO DECIDE

If the patient has the requisite capacity to decide, the doctor is bound by the patient's decision. If, on the other hand, the patient does not have the requisite capacity to decide, the doctor may treat the patient in what he or she believes to be the patient's best interests. In the circumstances, MCA 2005, ss 1(5) and 5 are applicable.

This distinction can present a particular dilemma for doctors, particularly in urgent and life-threatening circumstances. In cases of doubt as to the effect of a purported refusal of treatment, where failure to treat threatens the patient's life or threatens irreparable damage to his or her health, doctors and health authorities should not hesitate to apply to the courts for assistance *(Re T (An Adult) (Consent to Medical Treatment)* [1992] 2 FLR 458, at 474.

In the above case of *Re T*, the Court of Appeal set out the principles to be applied where an adult patient is refusing the treatment being medically advised according to the doctor's clinical judgment and the consequences of such refusal may have far-reaching consequences, including permanent injury or death ([1992] 2 FLR 458, at 473):

'1.   Prima facie every adult has the right and capacity to decide whether or not he will accept medical treatment, even if a refusal may risk permanent injury to his health or even lead to premature death. Furthermore, it matters not whether the reasons for the refusal were rational or irrational, unknown or even non-existent. This is so notwithstanding the very strong public interest in preserving the life and health of all citizens. However the presumption of capacity to decide, which stems from the fact that the patient is an adult, is rebuttable.

2.   An adult patient may be deprived of his capacity to decide either by long-term medical incapacity or retarded development or by temporary factors such as unconsciousness or confusion or the effects of fatigue, shock, pain or drugs.

3.   If an adult patient did not have the capacity to decide at the time of the purported refusal and still does not have that capacity, it is the duty of the doctors to treat him in whatever way they consider, in the exercise of their clinical judgment, to be in his best interests.

4.   Doctors faced with a refusal of consent have to give very careful and detailed consideration to what was the patient's capacity to decide at the time when the decision was made. It may not be a case of capacity or no capacity. It may be a case of reduced capacity. What matters is whether at that time the patient's capacity was reduced below the level needed in the case of a refusal of that importance, for refusals can vary in importance. Some may involve a risk to life or of irreparable damage to health. Others may not.

5.   In some cases doctors will not only have to consider the capacity of the patient to refuse treatment, but also whether the refusal has been vitiated because it resulted not from the patient's will, but from the will of others. It matters not that those others sought, however strongly, to persuade the patient to refuse, so long as in the end the refusal represented the patient's independent decision. If, however, his will was overborne, the refusal will not have represented a true decision. In this context the relationship of the persuader to the patient – for example, spouse, parents or religious adviser – will be important, because some relationships more readily lend themselves to overbearing the patient's independent will than do others.

6.   In all cases doctors will need to consider what is the true scope and basis of the refusal. Was it intended to apply in the circumstances which have arisen? Was it based upon assumptions which in the event have not been realised? A refusal is only effective within its true scope and is vitiated if it is based upon false assumptions.

7.   Forms of refusal should be redesigned to bring the consequence of a refusal forcibly to the attention of patients.

8.   In cases of doubt as to the effect of a purported refusal of treatment, where failure to treat threatens the patient's life or threatens irreparable damage to his health, doctors and health authorities should not hesitate to apply to the courts for assistance.'

At p 470 of *Re T*, Lord Donaldson confronted the difficult task of medical practitioners in adjudging capacity as follows:

'Doctors faced with a refusal of consent have to give very careful and detailed consideration to the patient's capacity to decide at the time when the decision was made. It may not be the simple case of the patient having no capacity because, for example, at that time he had hallucinations. It may be a more difficult case of a temporarily reduced capacity at the time when his decision was made. What matters is that the doctors should consider whether at that time he had a capacity which was commensurate with the gravity of the decision which he purported to make. The more serious the decision, the greater the capacity required. If the patient had the requisite capacity, they are bound by his decision. If not, they are free to treat him in what they believe to be his best interests.'

Assessment of Mental Capacity (published by the British Medical Association) is a report of the British Medical Association and The Law Society which incorporates guidance for doctors and lawyers on adjudging capacity. It provides practical guidance to both professions on circumstances where it may be necessary to assess a person's capacity, on how to assess capacity and highlighting any professional or ethical dilemmas that may arise.

9.3.1   *Re C* and the common law three-stage decision-making test as to capacity to decide

In *Re C (Refusal of Medical Treatment)* [1994] 1 FLR 31, the adult patient in question was unwilling to countenance the amputation of his leg, which was suffering from gangrene. He (the patient) sought from the hospital and was refused an undertaking that they would not amputate the leg in any future circumstances without his consent. The overall question was whether it had been established that the patient's capacity was so reduced by his chronic mental illness that he did not understand the nature, purpose and effects of the proposed treatment. Thorpe J, as he then was, accepted the medical evidence to the court that the decision-making process could be analysed in three stages. First, comprehending and retaining treatment information; secondly, believing it and, thirdly, weighing it in the balance to arrive at a choice. The judge determined that the patient had met, on the evidence, the three-stage test and granted him the relief he sought by ruling that he was capable of refusing consent to medical treatment.

9.3.2 The statutory test

By s 3(1) of MCA 2005:

'a person is unable to make a decision for himself if he is unable –
(a) to understand the information relevant to the decision,
(b) to retain that information,
(c) to use or weigh that information as part of the process of making the decision, or
(d) to communicate his decision (whether by talking, using sign language or any other means).'

The full terms of s 3, including s 3(2), s 3(3) and s 3(4) are also significant and are to be scrutinised carefully.

9.4 WHETHER TO OVERRIDE A REFUSAL OF CONSENT TO TREATMENT THROUGH LACK OF CAPACITY

The patient's right of choice exists, whether the reasons for making that choice are rational, irrational, unknown or even non-existent. Nevertheless, an adult patient, in refusing consent to medical treatment, may lack capacity for the following reasons.

9.4.1 Non-competence

At the time of an apparent refusal of treatment, the patient may not, for the time being, be a competent adult. His or her understanding and reasoning powers may be seriously reduced by drugs or other circumstances, although he or she is not actually unconscious. It is vital to consider, in adjudging capacity or lack of capacity, whether the patient has a capacity commensurate with the gravity of the situation. In *Re MB (Medical Treatment)* [1997] 2 FLR 426, the patient fully consented to and sought a Caesarean section operation. However, she could not bring herself to undergo the Caesarean section, since her fear of needles impeded the doctors in proceeding with the operation. On the evidence, it was determined by the court that the patient was temporarily incompetent. Her capacity was not commensurate with the gravity of the decision to be taken. A vaginal delivery would have posed a serious risk of death or brain damage to the baby. Her fear of needles and the panic it caused dominated her mind to the extent that she was incapable of making a decision at all.

9.4.2 Undue influence

A patient's refusal of consent may be invalid and vitiated through undue influence if it results, not from the patient's will, but from the will of others. The fundamental question is whether a refusal represents a patient's independent decision. There will not be undue influence simply because a patient is influenced and advised strenuously in his or her decision by others, provided that, in the end, the refusal represents his or her own independent decision. If, however, the will of the patient is overridden, the refusal will not have represented a true decision. The facts of each case need to be considered and the relationship between the patient and the adviser, whether a spouse, parents or religious adviser.

Re T (An Adult) (Consent for Medical Treatment) [1992] 2 FLR 458 concerned a patient whose mother was a Jehovah's Witness. The patient was 34 weeks pregnant and was involved in a car accident. While the patient's mother was with her, the patient had indicated to a staff nurse that she did not want a blood transfusion. The patient signed a pro forma refusal of consent to blood transfusions. When her condition deteriorated and she became unconscious, her father and another person applied to the court for a declaration that it would be lawful to administer a blood transfusion. The hospital had been abiding by the patient's refusal. It was held by the Court of Appeal that the patient's refusal was not a valid refusal and was not a genuine decision of the patient's, vitiated as it was by undue influence and varying other factors.

9.4.3 Changed circumstances

Another reason why an apparent refusal of consent may not be a true refusal is that it may not have been made with reference to the particular circumstances in which it turns out to be relevant. A patient who refuses consent in some circumstances does not necessarily give a true refusal of consent to treatment in any different circumstances which may arise. In all cases, doctors will need to consider the true scope and basis of the refusal – whether it was intended to apply in the circumstances which have arisen, whether it was based on assumptions which in the event have not been realised. A refusal can only be effective within its true scope and is vitiated if it is based upon false assumptions. In the case of *Re T*, the patient had refused consent to a blood transfusion in circumstances where she had been reassured that a blood transfusion was not often necessary, after a Caesarean section. Further, there was discussion with her as to alternative treatment available other than a blood transfusion. It was held that it could not be said that T understood the consequences of a continuing refusal to a blood transfusion in her changed deteriorating circumstances, given that there had been discussion earlier as to alternatives to a blood transfusion.

9.4.4 Specific circumstances

Induced delivery: Caesarean section operation

The guidelines from the Royal College of Obstetricians and Gynaecologists entitled 'A Consideration of the Law and Ethics in relation to Court-Authorised Obstetric Intervention' give advice to members of the medical profession. The Committee concluded that:

> 'It is inappropriate and unlikely to be helpful or necessary to invoke judicial intervention to overrule an informed and competent woman's refusal of a proposed medical treatment, even though her refusal might place her life and that of her foetus at risk.'

The Court of Appeal has examined in much detail, in *Re MB (Medical Treatment)* [1997] 2 FLR 426 and *St George's Healthcare NHS Trust v S* [1998] 2 FLR 728, the circumstances in which it may or may not be lawful to carry out a Caesarean section operation on a patient if she is unwilling to consent to such an operation.

The High Court too has considered within the remit of the MCA 2005 the approach to the issue of the lawfulness of carrying out a Caesarean section in the case of *The Mental Health Trust, The Acute Trust and The Council v DD* [2014] EWHC 11 (COP).

In *Re MB*, the patient had been willing to have a Caesarean section operation, as was advised to be medically necessary, but panicked at the last moment through her needle phobia when attempts were made to carry out the operation. She withdrew her consent to the operation. In circumstances where the patient was in labour and refused to agree to anaesthesia, the health authority applied for and was granted a declaration by the High Court judge that it would be lawful for the consultant gynaecologist to operate on her using reasonable force if necessary. The Court of Appeal dismissed the patient's appeal against the decision at first instance.

The Court of Appeal ruled that a competent adult patient has an absolute right to refuse to consent to medical treatment for any reason or for no reason at all, even where that decision might lead to his or her death. It is lawful, however, for doctors to be able to medically intervene in the absence of consent from the patient only where two circumstances pertain. First, the patient must lack competence. Secondly, the proposed treatment must be in the patient's best interests. On the particular facts of *Re MB*, the patient was, at the critical time, the court determined, suffering from an impairment of her mental functioning and was thereby temporarily incompetent.

The case of *St George's Healthcare NHS Trust v S* [1998] 2 FLR 728 sharply illustrates the presumption of capacity to decide and the principles of self-determination and autonomy of the patient; questions arose of unlawful admission to and detention in hospital. The patient, S, was 36 weeks pregnant. She had not sought ante-natal care. She was diagnosed as having pre-eclampsia, and advised that she needed urgent attention and admission to hospital for an induced delivery. Without this treatment, her health and life, and the health and life of her baby were in real danger. She fully understood the potential risks and rejected the advice. She was admitted to hospital against her will under MHA 1983. An ex parte declaration was sought, and granted, by a judge, dispensing with her consent to treatment. Later that evening, she was delivered of a baby girl by Caesarean section. On appeal, the declaration by the judge at first instance was set aside.

It was held that the patient was entitled not to be forced to submit to an invasion of her body against her will, notwithstanding the serious risks to her own life and that of her unborn child. Her right was not reduced or diminished, it was held, merely because her decision to exercise it might appear to be morally repugnant. The declaration of the judge at first instance involved the removal of the baby from within the body of the mother under physical compulsion. Unless lawfully justified, this amounted to an infringement of the mother's autonomy. Of themselves, the perceived needs of the foetus did not provide the necessary justification. The unlawful admission and detention of S under the MHA 1983 in this case is considered in Chapter 10 of this book.

In *Norfolk and Norwich Healthcare NHS Trust v W* [1996] 2 FLR 613, the patient arrived at hospital in labour. Throughout the day, she continued to deny she was pregnant. The obstetrician sought authority from the court to bring the patient's labour to an end by forceps delivery and, if necessary, a Caesarean section. It was held that, although the patient was not suffering from a mental disorder, she lacked the capacity and mental competence to make a decision about the proposed treatment because she was incapable of weighing up the considerations that were involved. Leave was granted to bring the labour to an end by forceps delivery and, if necessary, a Caesarean section.

In *Tameside and Glossop Acute Services NHS Trust v CH (A Patient)* [1996] 1 FLR 762, the pregnant patient suffered from paranoid schizophrenia. She was resistant to treatment. Because of an intra-uterine growth retardation of the foetus, if the pregnancy was allowed to continue the foetus might have died in the womb. The trust applied to the court for authorisation to perform a Caesarean section, should it become necessary, if an induced labour was not successful, and to restrain the patient, if need be. The patient overwhelmingly lacked the capacity to consent to or refuse treatment. It was held that the proposed treatment, including the use of restraint, if clinically necessary, was within s 63 of MHA 1983 and thus could be administered without her consent.

In the case of *Re S (Adult: Surgical Treatment)* [1993] 1 FLR 26, it was held that the Health Authority could lawfully perform an emergency Caesarean section operation on the patient on the grounds that it was in her and the unborn child's vital interests, despite the patient's refusal to give her consent and a declaration was granted to that effect.

In *Rochdale Healthcare (NHS) Trust v C* [1997] 1 FCR 274, the patient, who was in hospital for the birth of her child, would not agree to a Caesarean section as she had had a previous delivery in this way and subsequently suffered backache and pain around the resulting scar. She said she would rather die than have a Caesarean section again. The operation was required urgently and an application was made to the court less than an hour before it would need to be carried out. The consultant in charge was of the opinion that the patient seemed to be fully competent. It was held that an essential element in assessing a patient's capacity to decide whether or not to accept treatment was whether she was capable of weighing up the information she was given. In this case, the patient was in the throes of labour, with all that involved in terms of pain and emotional stress.

The judge determined that a patient who, in those circumstances, could speak in terms which seemed to accept the inevitability of her own death, was not a patient who was able properly to weigh up the considerations that arose so as to make any valid decision. The court held that it would be in the best interests of the patient for the proposed procedure to be performed. Whilst the court was considering and determining the urgent application, it became apparent that the patient had in fact changed her mind and given her consent to the medical procedure. The operation, accordingly, was, in fact, performed with her consent and was successful for both the patient and the child.

The overall principles and effects flowing from the two major cases, *Re MB* and *St George's Healthcare NHS Trust v S*, already referred to, are as follows:

(a) A pregnant woman, who is an adult of sound mind, has an absolute right to refuse medical treatment, even if her own life and that of the unborn child depends on such treatment.

(b) Invasive surgery under physical compulsion cannot be justified on the basis of the needs of the foetus.

(c) A patient's right not to be forced to submit to an invasion of her body against her will is not reduced or diminished merely because her decision to exercise it may appear morally repugnant.

(d) The Mental Health Act 1983 cannot be used to detain a person against her will merely because her thinking process is unusual, even apparently bizarre and irrational, and contrary to the views of the overwhelming majority of the community at large. In *St George's Healthcare NHS Trust v S*, S was determined by the Court of Appeal to have been unlawfully admitted to, and detained in, hospital. This aspect of the case is further scrutinised in Chapter 10 of this book.

(e) Even where lawfully detained under MHA 1983, a patient is not deprived of all autonomy and cannot be forced into medical procedures, such as a Caesarean section operation unconnected with her mental condition, unless her capacity to consent to such treatment is diminished.

(f) It is a criminal or tortious assault to perform physically invasive medical treatment without a patient's consent. In *St George's Healthcare NHS Trust v S*, the Caesarean section operation (together with the accompanying medical procedures) amounted to trespass on S. Whilst it might be available to defeat any claim based on aggravated or exemplary damages, the judge's decision at first instance, which was set aside by the Court of Appeal, would provide no defence to S's claim for damages for trespass against the relevant hospital.

(g) It is lawful for doctors to intervene and carry out physically invasive treatment such as a Caesarean section operation without a patient's consent if the patient lacks the capacity to decide and is thus incompetent and the proposed medical treatment is in the best interests of the patient.

(h) The Court of Appeal in *St George's Healthcare NHS Trust v S* set out guidelines to be followed in circumstances including where the possible need for Caesarean surgery is diagnosed and there is serious doubt about the patient's capacity to accept or decline treatment.

The High Court case of *The Mental Health Trust, The Acute Trust and The Council v DD* [2014] EWCOP 11 requires scrutiny.

The court was concerned with an urgent case concerning DD, a 36-year-old woman expecting a baby and at an advanced stage of her pregnancy. This was to be her sixth child. DD had mild to borderline learning difficulties: she had a full-scale IQ between 67 and 75. The medical evidence was that she had an autistic spectrum disorder. This caused her to be very rigid in her thinking.

The pregnancy was viewed as high risk because the mother had had a previous pre-term baby; she had had more than four pregnancies; she had had three previous Caesarean sections; she had had previous thrombo-embolic disease. There was a history of DD suffering acute medical conditions associated with pregnancy and childbirth; there had previously been concealment by her of her condition, and at the time she had not sought medical attention.

The mother's wishes, and indeed those of the father, were for a home birth without social or health care assistance. Their wishes are considered in detail at paragraphs 122 and 124 of the judgment, and included the mother wanting to have the baby naturally, in peace, and that it was her body and she did not want anyone doing anything with it. In relation to antenatal care, she had wished to be left alone.

In relation to the issue of the mother's capacity, there was no real question that the mother had the ability to understand the information, retain it, and communicate her decision. It was her ability to weigh the relevant information which caused the most material concern. The court had to consider both whether she had litigation capacity but also whether or not she had the capacity to decide on the mode and timing of delivery of the baby.

The judge, in deciding that she lacked capacity in both regards, said at paragraph 86 of his judgment:

> 'Her decision-making is undoubtedly unwise, but it is not, in my judgment, just "*unwise*"; it lacks the essential characteristic of discrimination which only comes when the relevant information is evaluated, and weighed. I am satisfied that in relation to each of the matters under consideration her impairment of mind (essentially attributable to her autistic spectrum disorder, overlaid with her learning disability) prevents her from weighing the information relevant to each decision.'

The court then went on to consider what course of action was in the best interests of DD.

The judge held that it was plainly in the mother's best interests (both physically and mentally) that her baby was born alive, healthy and safely.

Within the judgment, the court weighed and balanced the advantages and disadvantages of the options of a vaginal delivery and that of a Caesarean operation. Amongst other factors, the court felt that there was little prospect of the mother providing the level of co-operation, compliance and acquiescence that would enable plans to be made for the baby to be delivered by spontaneous vaginal delivery in hospital. The mother had undergone successfully three previous Caesarean sections. A Caesarean section was regarded as the safest mode of delivery for such a high-risk pregnancy.

The judge concluded that it was in the mother's best interest, and therefore lawful, for her to be conveyed to the hospital in order for there to be carried out a planned Caesarean section procedure and all necessary antenatal care. The judge required the applicants to take all reasonable steps to minimise distress to the mother and to maintain their dignity.

There then arose the material issue of the measures necessary to give effect to the court's determination. The judge authorised the applicants to take such necessary, reasonable and proportionate measures to give effect to the best interests of DD to include if necessary forced entry into her home, restraint and sedation.

The reasoning and determination of the judge in this respect was as follows:

> '129. I am conscious that steps may need to be taken to give effect to the decision which I make, if compelled attendance at hospital is required (for caesarean or induced vaginal delivery) in the face of DD's objection. The extent of reasonable force, compulsion and/or deprivation of liberty which may become necessary can only be judged in each individual case and by the health professionals.

> 130. On two recent occasions forcible entry has had to be made to DD's home in order to achieve some form of assessment: once with the authorisation of the lay justices (section 135 MHA 1983: 8 April 2014) and once pursuant to an order of Pauffley J (section 48 MCA 2005: 19 June 2014).

> 131. Any physical restraint or deprivation of liberty is a significant interference with DD's rights under Articles 5 and Article 8 of the ECHR and, in my judgment, as such should only be carried out:

i)   by professionals who have received training in the relevant techniques and who have reviewed the individual plan for DD;

ii)   as a last resort and where less restrictive alternatives, such as verbal de-escalation and distraction techniques, have failed and only when it is necessary to do so;

iii) in the least restrictive manner, proportionate to achieving the aim, for the shortest period possible;

iv)   in accordance with any agreed Care Plans, Risk Assessments and Court Orders;'

The remaining issue in the significant case was in relation to obtaining the most reliable current evidence of DD's capacity to make decisions about contraception. The applicants sought that the mother should be conveyed to a community Healthcare centre to receive relevant information and education about contraception and thereafter should be assessed as to her capacity to weigh the relevant information on contraception. The Official Solicitor referred to the Mental Capacity Act Code of Practice, which says: 'Nobody can be forced to undergo an assessment of capacity.'

The judge determined that there were reasonable grounds to believe that the mother lacked capacity to consent to an assessment of her capacity to make decisions in relation to contraception. The judge then further determined that whilst he considered that a court could exceptionally direct an assessment in P's best interests, notwithstanding the Mental Capacity Act 2005 Code of Practice, he did not regard it to be in the mother's best interest that she should be subject to a one-day assessment of her capacity to make decisions about contraception at that stage.

Fear of needles

In *Re MB (Medical Treatment)* [1997] 2 FLR 426, 40 weeks into the patient's pregnancy, it was found that the foetus was in the breach position. It was explained to the mother that a vaginal delivery would pose a serious risk of death or brain damage to the baby. She agreed to have a Caesarean section and was admitted to hospital and she and her partner agreed to the operation and signed a consent form.

In the case of *Re L (Patient: Non-Consensual Treatment)* [1997] 2 FLR 837, the patient was 8 hours into her labour and her cervix had not dilated. The consultant obstetrician reached the view that, without intervention, the baby would die. The mother was keen to have her baby. She agreed in principle to a Caesarean section.

In each of the two cases above, however, the patients suffered a fear of needles which prevented the operations taking place. In each case, the health authority/trust applied for a declaration that it would be lawful to effect the treatment required by insertion of a needle for the purposes of anaesthesia and performance of an emergency Caesarean operation. The court held, in each instance, that the fear of needles and the panic involved impaired and disabled the patients' mental functioning. In each instance, the patient was held to be temporarily incompetent. Accordingly, in both cases the relief sought was acceded to by the court.

Blood transfusions

In *Re T (An Adult) (Consent to Medical Treatment)* [1992] 2 FLR 458, the patient was 34 weeks pregnant and suffered a road accident. Her mother was a practising Jehovah's Witness. While the mother was with her, the patient indicated that she did not want a blood transfusion. She signed a pro forma refusal of consent to such a blood transfusion. She was reassured that blood transfusions were often not necessary and that alternative options to a transfusion were available. The baby was stillborn. The patient's condition then deteriorated and she became unconscious. The consultant anaesthetist had wished to administer a blood transfusion but was inhibited from doing so by the patient's expressed wishes. The patient's father and friend applied to the court for a declaration that it was lawful for the hospital to administer a blood transfusion.

The Court of Appeal held that the patient's refusal was not a valid and genuine decision, vitiated, as it was, by varying factors – the road accident, the ordeal and confusion she had been through and likely undue influence from her own mother. Nor could it be said that T understood the consequences of any continuing refusal in her changed deteriorating circumstances, given that there had been discussion earlier as to the alternatives to a blood transfusion. The declaration authorising a lawful blood transfusion was upheld.

In the case of *Nottinghamshire Healthcare NHS Trust v RC* [2014] EWHC 1317 (COP), RC was 23 and had been diagnosed with antisocial and emotionally unstable personality disorders. He had a repeated history of grave self-harm. In August 2013, serving a prison sentence for sexual assault, he became a Jehovah's Witness.

In February 2014 he slashed the major artery in his arm and was admitted to a secure psychiatric hospital, where he repeatedly attempted to re-open the wound. He refused to consent to blood transfusions on religious grounds and in April 2014 signed an advance decision to that effect, found to be compliant with MCA 2005, ss 24–26.

The NHS Trust sought the following three declarations from the Court of Protection:

(1) RC had the capacity to refuse blood transfusions and to self-harm;

(2) the advance decision was valid and operative should RC become incapable of issuing a decision to refuse treatment; and

(3) the treating physician's decision not to impose a blood transfusion was lawful.

The judge made those declarations (save that it was unnecessary and inappropriate to declare RC capable of self-harm).

At paragraph 42 of his judgment, the judge said:

'In my judgment, conducting, as I must, a full merits review, I conclude that the decision made by Dr S is completely correct. In my judgment it would be an abuse of power in such circumstances even to think about imposing a blood transfusion on RC having regard to my findings that he presently has capacity to refuse blood products and, were such capacity to disappear for any reason, the advance decision would be operative. To impose a blood transfusion would be a denial of a most basic freedom. I therefore declare that the decision of Dr S is lawful and that it is lawful for those responsible for the medical care of RC to withhold all and any treatment which is transfusion into him of blood or primary blood components (red cells, white cells, plasma or platelets) notwithstanding the existence of powers under section 63 MHA.'

Amputation

In *Re C (Refusal of Medical Treatment)* [1994] 1 FLR 31, surgeons at a hospital considered the patient would die imminently if his leg was not amputated below the knee. He had gangrene in his right foot. C refused to consider amputation. Alternative treatment was being tried and was successful but there was a likelihood of the gangrene recurring. C requested an undertaking from the hospital that it would not amputate the leg in any further circumstances. The hospital refused and C sought an injunction to restrain the hospital from amputating his right leg then or in the future without his expressed consent. It was held that, although his general capacity was impaired by schizophrenia, he had sufficiently understood the nature, purpose and effects of the treatment. He had understood and made a clear choice and, accordingly, relief would be granted in his favour.

In the case of *Heart of England NHS Foundation Trust v JB (by her litigation friend, the Official Solicitor)* [2014] EWHC 342 (COP), the case concerned a patient suffering from paranoid schizophrenia who was suffering with a gangrenous right foot which came off leaving an unresolved wound; the issue then arising being over the patient's unwillingness to agree to the medical advice that an amputation was necessary to allow the wound to be closed and to prevent it becoming infected.

The hospital trust applied to the court for a declaration that the patient JB lacked capacity to make a decision about serious medical treatment. It sought a declaration that it would be in her best interests to have a through-knee amputation and for her to be sedated if she resisted. During the hearing, the trust accepted the medical view that the appropriate operation would be a below-knee amputation.

The judge, Jackson J, said:

> 'The right to decide whether or not to consent to medical treatment is one of the most important rights guaranteed by law. Few decisions are as significant as the decision about whether to have major surgery. For the doctors, it can be difficult to know what recommendation to make. For the patient, the decision about whether to accept or reject medical advice involves weighing up the risks and benefits according to the patient's own system of values against a background where diagnosis and prognosis are rarely certain, even for doctors. Such decisions are intensely personal. They are taken in stressful circumstances. There are no right or wrong answers. The freedom to choose for oneself is a part of what it means to be a human being. For this reason, anyone capable of making decisions has an absolute right to accept or refuse medical treatment, regardless of the wisdom or consequences of the decision. The decision does not have to be justified to anyone. In the absence of consent, any invasion of the body will be a criminal assault. The fact that the intervention is well-meaning or therapeutic makes no difference.'

There was a conflict on the medical evidence as to whether or not JB lacked capacity: the hospital trust maintained that she did not, and the Official Solicitor contended that she did. The judge emphasised that it was for the trust to displace the presumption that JB had capacity on the balance of probabilities, and he did not accept the submission of the trust that incapacity could be deduced from isolated instances of eccentric reasoning on the part of JB.

The judge said:

'The temptation to base a judgement of a person's capacity upon whether they seem to have made a good or bad decision, and in particular upon whether they have accepted or rejected medical advice, is absolutely to be avoided. That would be to put the cart before the horse or, expressed another way, to allow the tail of welfare to wag the dog of capacity. Any tendency in this direction risks infringing the rights of that group of persons who, though vulnerable, are capable of making their own decisions. Many who suffer from mental illness are well able to make decisions about their medical treatment, and it is important not to make unjustified assumptions to the contrary.'

Nor did the judge accept the submission on behalf the Official Solicitor that the issue was whether JB had the capacity to consent to a below-knee amputation, as opposed to the operations no longer proposed by the trust namely a through-knee or above-knee amputation. The judge determined that what was required was an understanding by JB of the nature, purpose and effects of the proposed treatment: in that sense, the proposed treatment was surgical treatment for a potentially gangrenous limb, and was not limited to one of the possible operations. Treating each type of amputation as different was an impractical and unnecessary distinction that would diminish the scope of JB's capacity and potentially lead to unprofitable reassessments with every change in the treatment program.

The judge concluded that JB undoubtedly had a disturbance in the functioning of a mind in the form of paranoid schizophrenia (as to which she lacked insight), but that it had not been established that she thereby lacked the capacity to make a decision about surgery for herself. On the contrary, he determined that the evidence established that she did have capacity to decide whether to undergo an amputation of whatever kind. Accordingly, whether the operation would proceed or not would be entirely a matter for the patient JB to decide.

Dialysis treatment

Re JT (Adult: Refusal of Medical Treatment) [1998] 1 FLR 48, concerned a woman of 25 suffering from mental disability. She developed renal failure. Eleven attempts were made to give her dialysis treatment. She resisted and then refused the treatment altogether. She made clear that she objected to dialysis and wanted to die. The judge carefully applied the three-stage test in *Re C*. It was clear that, notwithstanding her mental disability, she realised the consequences of refusal to continue treatment and that she had the capacity to decide to refuse the medical treatment in question.

In *Re D (Medical Treatment: Mentally Disabled Patient)* [1998] 2 FLR 22, the patient suffered from a long-standing psychiatric illness. He lacked the capacity to consent, or not consent, to treatment. He had developed a serious kidney complaint and required dialysis. He was, however, unable to co-operate with that treatment. The hospital authority sought the protection of the court in the form of a declaration that it was lawful not to impose treatment on D in the likely event that they continued to be unable to treat him. D was represented by the Official Solicitor. Declaratory relief was granted by the court in terms that, notwithstanding D's inability to consent to or refuse medical treatment, it would be lawful as being in his best interests for the hospital authority not to impose dialysis on him in circumstances in which it was not reasonably practicable so to do.

Hunger strikes

The general law is that an adult person of full mental capacity has the right to choose whether to eat or not. Even if the refusal to eat is tantamount to suicide, as in the case of a hunger strike, the adult in question cannot be compelled to eat or be forcibly fed. On the other hand, if a person lacks the mental capacity to choose, in common law the medical practitioner who has him in his care may treat him according to his clinical judgment of the patient's best interests (*B v Croydon Health Authority* [1995] 1 FLR 470).

Secretary of State for the Home Department v Robb [1995] 1 FLR 412, concerned a prisoner on hunger strike. He was 27 years old and had spent half his life in custody for criminal offences. It was agreed by all the medical and psychiatric experts assessing him that he was of sound mind and understanding. The patient's right of self-determination, it was held, was not diminished in the case of the defendant by his status as a detained prisoner. The principle of self-determination required that effect be given to his wishes and that a patient who refused treatment and, in consequence, died did not commit suicide, nor did a doctor who complied with the patient's wishes aid or abet a suicide. Declaratory relief was granted, as sought by the Home Secretary, that he could lawfully abide by the refusal of the defendant to receive nutrition and could lawfully abstain from providing hydration and nutrition whether by artificial means or otherwise for so long as the defendant retained the capacity to refuse the same.

The decision to force-feed Ian Brady was held to be within s 63 of MHA 1983. His hunger strike, ostensibly in protest at the decision to move him to another ward, was held to be a manifestation or symptom of his very profound personality disorder (he was additionally found to be incapacitated): see *Ex parte Brady* [2000] Lloyd's Rep Med 355. In *B v Croydon Health Authority* [1995] Fam 133 the court declared that it was lawful to force-feed a patient who would otherwise die from self-starvation which was the result of her borderline personality disorder. By contrast, in *An NHS Trust v A* [2014] 2 WLR 607 a hunger strike by a detained Iranian doctor protesting about the impoundment of his passport was held to be not a manifestation or symptom of his mental disorder.

Anorexia and force-feeding

In the case of *A Local Authority v E* [2012] EWHC 1639 (COP) the judge determined that it was lawful and in E's best interests for her to be fed, forcibly if necessary. He found that the resulting interference with her rights under Articles 3 and 8 of the European Convention on Human Rights (ECHR) was proportionate and necessary in order to protect her right to life under Article 2.

E's parents were sceptical and had grave misgivings about the likely outcome of further treatment. They did not want E to die, but after years of supporting her through a series of unsuccessful treatments they believed that, unless further medical intervention had a real prospect of making a difference, her wishes should be respected. The medical staff were highly doubtful about further coercive treatment, and the health authority adopted a neutral position. The Official Solicitor, having initially taken a different view, advised that treatment which might return E to a relatively normal life was available, had not so far been tried, and that E should receive it. The Official Solicitor accordingly sought a declaration that forcible feeding was in E's best interests. The expert medical evidence was that E would have perhaps a 20–30% chance of full recovery.

The judge said there were two only possible courses of action.

The first was that there should be no intervention, with E remaining in the Trinity Hospital being provided with care and pain relief until her death from the effects of starvation.

The second option was E's immediate transfer to a specialist hospital where she would be stabilised and fed with calorific material through a nasogastric tube or a tube inserted through her stomach wall. Any resistance would be overcome by physical restraint or by chemical sedation. The process would continue for a year or more. Once her weight had been restored, she would be offered therapies for her eating disorder and for other physical and psychological problems. By these means, she might overcome her feeling that her life was not worth living.

In *NHS Trust v L* [2012] EWHC 2741 (COP), L was a highly intelligent 29-year-old who, because of serious anorexia nervosa, had spent 90% of her previous 16 years in inpatient units, often under MHA 1983. She also suffered from severe obsessive compulsive disorder. In January 2012, her detention under s 3 of the Act was rescinded after all treatment options had been exhausted and compulsory treatment had been shown only to reinforce her mental disorder and to increase her disability.

The NHS Trust sought a declaration that it was not in her best interests to be the subject of forcible feeding or medical treatment, notwithstanding that she would inevitably die without it. Although L told her mother that she did not want to die and still hoped to become strong enough to move to a nursing home, she was critically ill, refusing all food by mouth and wanting to make an advance decision to refuse treatment for hypoglycaemia. The judge granted the relief sought by the Trust.

The judge held that L lacked capacity to make decisions in relation to serious medical treatment, in particular nutrition and hydration and the administration of dextrose for hypoglycaemic episodes, because her profound and illogical fear of weight gain prevented her from being able to weigh up the risks and benefits. However, she did have capacity to decide on antibiotic treatment and analgesia and treatment for pressure sores. This was because the latter treatments were not calorific.

The judge noted that L's seemingly rational desire to get stronger and to move to a nursing home was 'completely overwhelmed by her terror of gaining weight and by her fear of calories'. Her mother did not consider compulsory feeding to be in her best interests. The expert in the case concluded: 'there comes a point in the treatment of any patient where, regardless of the diagnosis, the slavish pursuit of life at any cost becomes unconscionable. I believe, sadly, this point has been reached in L's treatment.'

After noting that the strong presumption to preserve life is not absolute, the judge held:

> '68 In my judgment this is one of those few cases where the only possible treatment, namely force feeding under sedation, is not to be countenanced in L's best interests: to do so would be futile, carrying with it a near

certainty that it would cause her death in any event. Such a course would be overly burdensome in that every calorie that enters her body is an enemy to L.

69 Ms L would I am satisfied by appallingly distressed and resistant to any suggestion that she was to be force fed and to what purpose? Her poor body is closing down, organ failure has begun, she can no longer resist infection and she is, at all times, in imminent danger of cardiac arrest. Even if she could, by some miracle, agree to some minuscule increase in her nutrient intake her organ failure is nevertheless irreversible and her anorexia so severe and deep rooted that there could be no real possibility of for maintaining her co-operation ...'

9.5   THE USE OF REASONABLE FORCE AS A NECESSARY INCIDENCE OF TREATMENT

In *Norfolk and Norwich Healthcare (NHS) Trust v W* [1996] 2 FLR 613, the facts of which have been previously raised, it was held that the court did have power at common law in the circumstances arising to authorise the use of reasonable force as a necessary incidence of treatment.

In *Tameside and Glossop Acute Services Trust v CH* [1996] 1 FLR 762, the judge's view was that where, at common law, the question of the lawfulness of using restraint on a patient arose, an application should be made to the court seeking a determination that such treatment would be lawful.

In *Re MB (Medical Treatment)* [1997] 2 FLR 426, all that was involved, in this context, was the prick of a needle to enable the first part of anaesthesia to be given to the patient. In the event, no problem arose, since, following the court's determination, the patient finally co-operated and signed the consent form. However, in relation to the use of reasonable force, Butler-Sloss LJ, at 439 said as follows:

'In a number of first instance decisions the declarations have included that it would be lawful for reasonable force to be used in the course of such treatment That declaration was granted ... in the present case and is criticised ... It would however follow, in our view, from the decision that a patient is not competent to refuse treatment, that such treatment may have to be given against her continued objection if it is in her best interests that the treatment be given despite those objections. The extent of force or compulsion which may become necessary can only be judged in each individual case and by the health professionals. It may become for them a balance between continuing treatment which is forcibly opposed and deciding not to continue with it. This is a difficult issue which may have to be considered in greater depth on another occasion.'

Such procedural advice and guidance has been developed and expanded in the case of *St George's Healthcare NHS Trust v S* [1998] 2 FLR 728. In that case, the Court of Appeal, after consultation with the President of the Family Division and the Official Solicitor, at 758, 759 and 760 of the judgment set out detailed guidelines as to the practice and procedure then to be followed in these type of cases. For example, the guidelines apply when the possible need for Caesarean surgery is diagnosed and there is serious doubt about the pregnant woman's capacity to accept or decline treatment. The guidelines further apply more generally to any other cases where surgical or invasive treatment may be needed by a patient whether male or female but there is real doubt as to the patient's capacity to accept or decline treatment.

It is important to emphasise, however, under guideline [vii] that the hearing before the court should be inter partes. An order made in the patient's absence will not be binding on the patient unless he or she is represented either by a guardian ad litem (if incapable of giving instructions) or (if capable) by counsel or solicitor. Accordingly, a declaration granted ex parte without the patient being so represented will be of no assistance to the health authority or NHS trust. In the case of *St George's Healthcare NHS Trust v S*, the judge at first instance had erred in making a declaratory order on an ex parte application in proceedings which had not been instituted by the issue of the summons, without the patient's knowledge or even any attempt to inform her or her solicitor of the application, without any evidence, and without any provision to vary or discharge the order. This appeal against the grant of the declaration at first instance was allowed. It is important to emphasise and the guidelines themselves remind legal and medical practitioners that there may be occasions when there may be a serious question about the competence of a patient and the situation facing the authority may be so urgent and the consequences so desperate that it will be impracticable to attempt to comply with the guidelines. As it is put in the conclusion to the guidelines, 'where delay may itself cause serious damage to the patient's health or put her life at risk then formulaic compliance with these guidelines would be inappropriate'.

The terms of s 15 of MCA 2005 in relation to the power of the court now to make declarations under the statute are wide, including under s 15(1)(c) the court may make declarations as to 'the lawfulness or otherwise of any act done, or yet to be done, in relation to that person'.

This would enable the court to consider any issues arising as to the limited use of reasonable force as a necessary incidence of treatment of a person lacking capacity.

So far as carers and clinicians are concerned in relation to any act of restraint of a patient reasonably believed to be lacking capacity, s 6 of the MCA 2005 makes s 5 of the Act applicable to any such act of restraint if two conditions are satisfied: the first is that the person carrying out the restraint reasonably believes that it is necessary to do the act in order to prevent harm to the patient; the second is that the act is a proportionate response to the likelihood of the patient suffering harm, and the seriousness of that harm.

The case of *The Mental Health Trust, The Acute Trust and The Council v DD* [2014] EWCOP 11 evinces the wide powers available to the court in this area; as indicated in more detail at **9.4.4**, the judge gave leave if necessary for there to be forced entry into DD's home, for her to be conveyed to hospital and for her to be restrained and sedated.

CHAPTER 10

MEDICAL TREATMENT AND MHA 1983; RESTRICTION ON DEPRIVATION OF LIBERTY UNDER THE MCA 2005; THE INTERFACE BETWEEN MHA 1983 AND MCA 2005

10.1 SELF-DETERMINATION AND THE MENTALLY ILL

In relation to those suffering from mental illness, as with those who are not, consent is required from a patient before medical treatment can be given.

It was emphasised by the Law Commission in its report on Mental Incapacity (Law Com No 231) that, wherever possible, and particularly in relation to the vulnerable, who are or may be mentally ill, the principle of self-determination and autonomy of the individual must apply and be further encouraged.

As was stated by Jackson J in the case of *Heart of England NHS Foundation Trust v JB (by her litigation friend, the Official Solicitor)* [2014] EWHC 342 (COP) at paragraph 6 of the judgment:

> 'furthermore, the Mental Capacity Act 2005 provides (section 1(6)) that even where a person lacks capacity, any interference with their rights and freedom of action must be the least restrictive possible: this acknowledges that people who lack capacity still have rights and that their freedom of action is as important to them as it is to anyone else.'

The Mental Health Act 1983 (MHA 1983) Code of Practice, issued by the Department of Health and Welsh Office, stresses the necessity of providing patients with sufficient information to enable them to understand the nature, purpose and likely effect of the treatment and to inform the patient of any viable alternatives. The Code goes further and says the patient should be advised of his or her right to withdraw consent at any time during the period of treatment.

10.1.1   The common law test as to capacity to consent

In *Re C (Refusal of Medical Treatment)* [1994] 1 FLR 31, an adult patient who was suffering from gangrene in one of his legs was advised by doctors that there was a large chance of imminent death if the leg was not amputated. The adult patient was unwilling to countenance the amputation of the leg and sought assurances from the hospital that his wishes would be respected then and in the future. In determining whether an adult patient does or does not have the capacity to decide, the judge applied a three-stage test:

(1) whether the adult patient could comprehend and retain the treatment information;

(2) whether the adult patient believed it;

(3) whether the adult patient could weigh it in the balance to arrive at a choice.

10.1.2   A person suffering from mental disorder is not necessarily incapable of giving or refusing consent to treatment

The fact that a person is suffering from mental illness does not automatically mean that he or she lacks the capacity to decide. To ascertain the common law position in this regard, it is helpful to scrutinise briefly four cases, in each of which it was held that doctors were bound by the decision of the patient to refuse treatment, notwithstanding any mental health problems they had.

In *Re C* [1994] 1 FLR 31, which has been referred to previously, the adult patient in question had been diagnosed as suffering from chronic paranoid schizophrenia and had been transferred to Broadmoor, where he was treated with drugs and ECT. This had resulted in some improvement and he was on an open ward. Notwithstanding his mental health difficulties and background, it was held that he had the capacity to refuse the medical treatment advised. The patient was quite content to follow medical advice and co-operate with treatment as long as his rejection of amputation was respected.

In *Re JT (Adult: Refusal of Medical Treatment)* [1998] 1 FLR 48, the court was concerned with a patient, a woman of 25, who suffered from mental disability involving learning difficulties and extremely severe behavioural disturbance. She was found to have developed renal failure. Eleven attempts were made to give her dialysis treatment, most of them resisted by the patient, and, thereafter, she refused any further treatment. There was no feasible alternative treatment. The patient consistently told the doctor and both psychiatrists concerned with the case and members of her family that she objected to dialysis and wanted to die. It was held to be clear on the evidence that the patient understood the information given to her as to the purpose of dialysis treatment and its nature, that she believed it, that she realised the consequences of refusal to continue treatment, and that she had the capacity to make a decision about giving or refusing agreement to treatment in accordance with the three-stage test laid down in *Re C*. Declarations were granted by the court that the patient was capable of refusing medical treatment and also that it was lawful for the hospitals in question to abide by her refusal and not perform renal dialysis on her.

The case of *Home Secretary v Robb* [1995] 1 FLR 412 concerned a prisoner on hunger strike. He was then aged 27 and had spent at least half his life in custody for criminal offences and suffered from a personality disorder evidenced by a number of factors including addiction to drugs and violent tendencies. It was agreed, however, by all the medical and psychiatric experts assessing him that he was of sound mind and understanding. Relief was granted by the court to the effect that the Home Secretary might lawfully observe and abide by the refusal of the prisoner to receive nutrition, and further that the Home Secretary might lawfully abstain from providing hydration and nutrition, whether by artificial means or otherwise, for so long as the prisoner retained the capacity to refuse food or drink. The court emphasised again the principle of self-determination which required that effect be given to a patient's wishes providing that he or she has the capacity to make a choice. It was further held that a patient who refuses treatment and in consequence dies does not commit suicide nor does a doctor who complies with the patient's wishes aide or abet a suicide.

In *St George's Healthcare NHS Trust v S; R v Collins and Others ex parte S* [1998] 2 FLR 728 a woman who was 36 weeks pregnant was admitted to hospital under MHA 1983 against her will in circumstances where she was suffering from pre-eclampsia and refusing voluntarily to be admitted to hospital for an induced delivery or Caesarean section. She had been advised that without hospital treatment her health and life, and the life of her baby, were in danger. Notwithstanding such advice, and fully understanding the potential risks, the patient rejected such advice since she wanted her baby to be born naturally. It was held in the Court of Appeal that the fact that she was jeopardising her own life and that of the baby did not connote any form of mental illness. Even though her choice might appear to most either morally repugnant or irrational, she was fully entitled, the Court of Appeal held, not to be treated in hospital against her wishes, even if she was thereby risking her own life and that of the unborn child. She was determined by the court to have the capacity to make a choice.

The Code of Practice under MHA 1983 states at paragraph 15.11:

> 'A person suffering from a mental disorder is not necessarily incapable of giving consent. Capacity to consent is variable in people with mental disorder and should be assessed in relation to the particular patient, at the particular time, as regards the particular treatment proposed. Not everyone is equally capable of understanding the same explanation of a treatment plan. A person is more likely to be able to give valid consent if the explanation is appropriate to the level of his assessed ability.'

At common law, a person who ordinarily has the capacity to consent or refuse to consent to treatment, notwithstanding that he or she may suffer from mental illness, may be given medical treatment in the absence of his or her consent in the circumstances of a medical emergency. Section 1(5) and s 5 of the Mental Capacity Act 2005 (MCA 2005) pertain here.

10.1.3 Caesarean section operations and MHA 1983

The basic facts of the *St George's Healthcare NHS Trust v S* case have been set out above. S was rejecting medical treatment which was advised to be urgently necessary for her own health and that of the unborn child.

S was admitted to hospital – the Springfield Psychiatric Hospital – under MHA 1983, s 2.

Section 2(2) of the Act is as follows:

> 'An application for admission for assessment may be made in respect of a patient on the grounds that –
> (a) he is suffering from mental disorder of a nature or degree which warrants the detention of the patient in a hospital for assessment (or for assessment followed by medical treatment) for at least a limited period; and
> (b) he ought to be so detained in the interests of his own health and safety or with a view to the protection of other persons.'

The Court of Appeal determined that the application for admission under s 2 was unlawful and appropriate declaratory relief was granted by the court in S's favour. While satisfied that the requirements of s 2(2)(b) might well have been fulfilled, the cumulative grounds prescribed in s 2(2)(a), the Court of Appeal held, were not established. Those involved in the decision to make an application for admission under s 2 had failed to maintain the distinction between the urgent need of S for treatment arising from her pregnancy and the separate question whether her mental disorder (in the form of depression) warranted her detention in hospital. There was no evidence that S had been detained in order to assess or treat any such mental disorder. Rather, she had been detained in order that adequate provision could be made to deal with S's pregnancy and the safety of her unborn child.

It was further held that S's transfer to, and the period while she was detained at, St George's Hospital, where the child was born, were both unlawful. S was, therefore, wrongly detained throughout the period when she was in St George's Hospital and throughout the operative procedures which were carried out on her, in accordance with the declaration granted by the judge at first instance.

Important principles emanate from *St George's Healthcare NHS Trust v S* in relation to the use, or possible use, of the provisions of MHA 1983 where invasive surgery such as that of a Caesarean section operation may be necessary.

First, MHA 1983 cannot be deployed to achieve the detention of an individual against her will merely because her thinking process is unusual, even apparently bizarre and irrational, and contrary to the views of the overwhelming majority of the community at large.

Secondly, even where a person is lawfully detained under MHA 1983, she is not deprived of all autonomy and cannot be forced into medical procedures such as a Caesarean section operation unconnected with her mental condition unless her capacity to consent to such treatment is diminished. This aspect is further examined when considering s 63 of the MHA 1983 later in this chapter.

10.2   MHA 1983

MHA 1983, as amended by the Mental Health Act 2007 (MHA 2007), is principally concerned with the admission of patients to hospital for assessment and treatment for their mental disorder. However, MHA 2007 extends powers of compulsion by introducing compulsory community treatment orders (also referred to as supervised community treatment) for patients previously detained in hospital who are then living in the community, but who continue to need treatment for their mental disorder.

Mental disorder is defined as any disorder or disability of the mind: MHA 1983, s 1(2), as amended by MHA 2007.

By s 1(2A) of the Act:

'a person with learning disability shall not be considered by reason of that disability to be (a) suffering from mental disorder for the purposes of the provisions mentioned in subsection (2B) below; or (b) requiring treatment in hospital for mental disorder for the purposes of sections 17E and 50 to 53 below, unless that disability is associated with abnormally aggressive or seriously irresponsible conduct on his part.'

By s 1(2B) of the Act the provisions are:

(a)   ss 3, 7, 17A, 20, and 20A;

(b)   ss 35 to 38,45A, 47, 48 and 51; and

(c)   s 72(1)(b) and (c) and (4).

MHA 1983 enables compulsory powers for admission to hospital for assessment or treatment when the statutory conditions for 'sectioning' the patient are met.

In the case of admission for assessment under s 2, the patient must be suffering from mental disorder of a nature or degree which warrants the detention of the patient in a hospital for assessment, and: '... he ought to be so detained in the interests of his own health or safety or with a view to the protection of other persons'.

In the case of admission for treatment under s 3, the grounds need to be established that:

> '(a)   he is suffering from mental disorder of a nature or degree which makes it appropriate for him to receive medical treatment in a hospital:
>
> ...
>
> (c)   it is necessary for the health or safety of the patient or for the protection of other persons that he should receive such treatment and it cannot be provided unless he is detained under this section; and
>
> (d)   appropriate medical treatment is available for him.'

10.2.1   The meaning of medical treatment

The test for 'medical treatment' in s 145(1) of MHA 1983 now reads: 'medical treatment includes nursing, psychological intervention and specialist mental health habilitation, rehabilitation and care'.

Section 145(4) reads:

> 'any reference in this Act to medical treatment, in relation to mental disorder, shall be construed as a reference to medical treatment the

purpose of which is to alleviate, or prevent a worsening of, the disorder or one or more of its symptoms or manifestations.'

In relation to the 'appropriate treatment' test, by MHA 1983 s 3(4) it is provided:

'In this Act, references to appropriate medical treatment, in relation to a person suffering from mental disorder, are references to medical treatment which is appropriate in his case, taking into account the nature and degree of the mental disorder and all the circumstances of his case.'

10.2.2 Part IV of MHA 1983: 'consent to treatment'

By MHA 1983, s 63, the consent of the patient shall **not** be required for any medical treatment given to him for the mental disorder from which he is suffering, not being a form of treatment to which s 57, 58 or 58A applies, if the treatment is given by or under the direction of the approved clinician in charge of the treatment.

Section 63 covers a wide range of therapeutic activities involving a variety of professional staff and includes, in particular, psychological and social therapies.

In practice, medical staff will seek the consent of the patient and it is unlikely that most of these activities could be undertaken without the patient's acceptance and active co-operation. Indeed, as predicated at paragraph 16.4 of the Code of Practice: 'For all treatments proposed for a detained patient and which may be lawfully given under the Act it is necessary *first* to seek the patient's agreement and consent.'

In the case of *Tameside and Glossop Acute Services Trust v CH* [1996] 1 FLR 762, the defendant patient was aged 41 at the time and had suffered from paranoid schizophrenia since 1983. In 1995, she was admitted to the psychiatric wing of the hospital under s 3 of the Act and it was discovered that she was pregnant. She wished to have the baby but was apt to resist treatment. She clearly lacked capacity. An intra-uterine growth retardation of the foetus was discovered and the medical view taken was that if the pregnancy was allowed to continue the foetus might die in the womb. The doctors wished to induce labour and, given that the patient lacked capacity and might actively resist, the trust applied to the court for authorisation to perform a Caesarean section should it become necessary, restraining the patient if need be.

The court held that the proposed treatment, including the use of restraint if clinically necessary, was treatment given for the mental disorder from which she was suffering within s 63 of the Act. Accordingly, by virtue of that section, the treatment could be administered without her consent. The reasons for the proposed treatment falling within s 63 were as follows. First, an ancillary reason for the induction and, if necessary, the Caesarean section, was to prevent a deterioration of the patient's mental state. Secondly, for the treatment of her schizophrenia to be effective, it was necessary for her to give birth to a live baby. Thirdly, her treatment required her to receive strong anti-psychotic medication which had been interrupted by pregnancy and could not be resumed until the child was born.

Whether and to what extent the reasoning in the *Tameside* case in relation to s 63 is still applicable must be cast into doubt by the case of *St George's Healthcare NHS Trust v S; R v Collins ex parte S* [1998] 2 FLR 728. There, the Court of Appeal reasoned that s 63 may apply to the treatment of any condition which is 'integral' to the mental disorder of the patient. The question is whether a Caesarean section can be viewed as treatment for a patient's mental disorder. The view of the Court of Appeal was that, in the final analysis, a woman detained under the Act for mental disorder cannot be forced into medical procedures unconnected with her mental condition unless her capacity to consent to such treatment is diminished. It would appear, accordingly, to be the case that, where a woman patient is detained under the Act and the question arises as to whether an induced delivery and/or Caesarean section should be carried out, the essential consideration will be her capacity to decide. When she retains her capacity, her consent will remain an essential pre-requisite and whether she does or does not have the capacity to decide will have to be determined on the basis of the circumstances in each individual case.

In *B v Croydon Health Authority* [1995] 1 FLR 470, the patient, a woman of 24, was detained in hospital under s 3 of the Act suffering from a psychopathic disorder with symptoms including a compulsion to self-harm. She virtually stopped eating and was threatened with feeding by naso-gastric tube. An application was made on her behalf for an injunction restraining the health authority from feeding the patient by tube without her consent. It was held that she could be lawfully fed in such a manner without her consent under s 63 of the Act. Given the wide definition of s 145(1), namely that 'treatment' included nursing and care concurrent with the core treatment or as a necessary pre-requisite to such treatment, it was held by the court that it must follow that the term 'medical treatment ... for the mental disorder' in s 63 included treatment given to alleviate the symptoms of the disorder as well as treatment to remedy its underlying cause.

The relationship between s 63 and the definition of 'medical treatment' contained within s 145(4) was considered by the High Court in the case of *Nottinghamshire Healthcare NHS Trust v RC* [2014] EWCOP 1317.

RC was 23 and had been diagnosed with antisocial and emotionally unstable personality disorders. He had a repeated history of grave self-harm. In August 2013, serving a prison sentence for sexual assault, he became a Jehovah's Witness. In February 2014 he slashed the major artery in his arm and was admitted to a secure psychiatric hospital, where he repeatedly attempted to re-open the wound. He refused to consent to blood transfusions on religious grounds and in April 2014 signed an advance decision to that effect, found to be compliant with ss 24–26 of MCA 2005.

The expert medical disagreement was whether the administration of a blood transfusion amounted to treatment which prevented the worsening of a symptom or manifestation of RC's mental disorder. One doctor was of the opinion that it plainly was. The other doctor disagreed.

At paragraph 24 of his judgment, the judge said:

> 'The cases have drawn a distinction between a condition which is, on the one hand, a consequence of the disorder, and, on other hand, a condition which is a symptom or manifestation of it. The former is not within section 63, the latter is. I confess to finding the distinction intellectually challenging. At all events a wide (but not always consistent) interpretation has been given to section 145(4). Thus the decision to force-feed Ian Brady was held to be within section 63. His hunger strike, ostensibly in protest at the decision to move him to another ward, was held to be a manifestation or symptom of his very profound personality disorder (he was additionally found to be incapacitated): see *Ex parte Brady* [2000] Lloyd's Rep Med 355. In *B v Croydon Health Authority* [1995] Fam 133 the court declared that it was lawful to force-feed a patient who would otherwise die from self-starvation which was the result of her borderline personality disorder. By contrast in *A NHS Trust v Dr A* [2014] 2 WLR 607 a hunger strike by a detained Iranian doctor protesting about the impoundment of his passport was held to be not a manifestation or symptom of his mental disorder. In *Tameside and Glossop Acute Services v CH* [1996] 1 FLR 762 it was held that section 63 could be used to restrain a patient to enforce a Caesarean section upon her; while in *St George's Healthcare NHS Trust v S* the opposite conclusion was reached.'

The judge determined that a proper interpretation of the authorities must lead to a conclusion that a blood transfusion would plainly amount to treatment of a symptom or manifestation of the underlying mental disorder.

In reaching such a view, he said at paragraph 31 of his judgment:

> 'On reflection I am in agreement with Mr Francis QC's analysis. It cannot be disputed that the act of self harming, the slashing open of the brachial artery, is a symptom or manifestation of the underlying personality disorder. Therefore to treat the wound in any way is to treat the manifestation or symptom of the underlying disorder. So, indisputably, to suture the wound would be squarely within section 63. As would be the administration of a course of antibiotics to prevent infection. A consequence of bleeding from the wound is that haemoglobin levels are lowered. While it is strictly true, as Dr Latham says, that "low haemoglobin is not wholly a manifestation or symptom of personality disorder", it is my view that to treat the low haemoglobin by a blood transfusion is just as much a treatment of a symptom or manifestation of the disorder as is to stitch up the wound or to administer antibiotics.'

A positive decision to impose non-consensual medical treatment pursuant to MHA 1983, s 63

A positive decision to impose non-consensual medical treatment pursuant to s 63 of MHA 1983 is a public law decision susceptible to judicial review: see *R (on the application of B) v Haddock (Responsible Medical Officer)* [2006] MHLR 306. Paragraphs 13 and 14 of that decision make clear that Convention rights will be in play and therefore a 'full merits review' must be undertaken on the evidence, with the court making the decision de novo, but placing considerable weight on the initial decision made under s 63 by the approved clinician in charge of the treatment.

A positive decision not to impose treatment under MHA 1983, s 3

A decision made by an approved clinician in charge of the treatment in respect of a patient detained under MHA 1983 not to impose any treatment on him or her is not accompanied by any procedure for judicial scrutiny of it. This is surprising, especially as Article 2 of the European Convention on Human Rights (ECHR) is (as here) likely to be engaged. As is well-known this protects the right to life. It is the most fundamental of the Convention rights. Countless authorities have emphasised the imperative duty on public authorities to give effect to this right where detained persons are concerned. So if the approved clinician in charge of the treatment decides not to impose potentially life-saving treatment one can see the important need for judicial scrutiny to determine whether the patient has, with a full awareness of the implications elected to opt-out of the right to life granted to him by Article 2. And one would expect, as has happened here, that a second medical opinion would be commissioned concerning the approved clinician's decision.

In drawing such a distinction in the above terms in the *Nottinghamshire* case, the judge concluded at paragraph 21 of his judgment in relation to the procedure to be adopted by NHS Trusts in this context:

> 'In my judgment where the approved clinician makes a decision not to impose treatment under section 63, and where the consequences of that decision may prove to be life-threatening, then the NHS trust in question would be well advised, as it has here, to apply to the High Court for declaratory relief. The hearing will necessarily involve a "full merits review" of the initial decision. It would be truly bizarre if such a full merits review were held where a positive decision was made under section 63, but not where there was a negative one, especially where one considers that the negative decision may have far more momentous consequences (i.e. death) than the positive one.'

MHA 1983, s 57 refers to forms of medical treatment for mental disorder including any surgical operation for destroying brain tissue or for destroying the functioning of the brain tissue. Any such medical treatment requires the patient's consent as well as a second opinion.

MHA 1983, s 58 requires the consent of the patient or a second opinion, and includes reference to medical treatment for mental disorder involving the administration of medicine to a patient by any means in terms set out in detail within the statutory provision.

MHA 1983, s 58A refers to the medical treatment for mental disorder including involving electro-convulsive therapy. Generally speaking, a patient is not to be given any form of treatment to which this section applies unless he falls within subs (3), (4) or (5) of the section.

MHA 1983, s 62 sets out that in certain circumstances the provisions of ss 57, 58 and 58A will not apply where urgent medical treatment is required within the terms set out in the section.

10.3 PATIENTS LACKING THE CAPACITY TO GIVE OR REFUSE CONSENT TO MEDICAL TREATMENT

In relation to a patient who fails the test as to capacity, and in the absence of consent, a doctor may only treat such a patient as is permitted by the MCA 2005 unless the MHA 1983 must be used.

In the case of *Re F (Mental Patient: Sterilisation)* [1990] 2 AC 1, it was held that treatment of a patient in common law is lawful if it is in his or her best interests. Such treatment would be in his or her best interests, as Lord Brandon said at p 55:

'If it is carried out to save lives or ensure improvement or prevent deterioration in their physical or mental health.'

The standard by which to measure whether or not a doctor is acting in the best interests of the incapacitated patient is the test laid down in *Bolam v Friern Hospital Management Committee* [1957] 1 WLR 582, namely that he or she must act in accordance with a practice accepted at the time by a responsible body of medical opinion skilled in the particular form of treatment in question. In the case of *Re F*, the House of Lords rejected the view of the Court of Appeal in the case that a more stringent test was required than the *Bolam* test for adults lacking capacity. A more stringent test for those adults who are incompetent, the House of Lords held, could result in such adults being deprived, in some circumstances, of the benefit of medical treatment which adults who are competent to give consent, enjoy.

The case of *Re F* further decided that, in the absence of parens patriae jurisdiction for adults, any jurisdiction to approve or disapprove of medical treatment for and on behalf of an incapacitated adult does not exist. No one, including the court, accordingly can give consent or refuse consent to treatment for those mentally ill adults who lack capacity.

In the case of *Re F* at p 69, Lord Griffiths summarised the position as follows:

'In a civilised society the mentally incompetent must be provided with medical and nursing care and those who look after them must do their best for them. Stated in legal terms the doctor who undertakes responsibility for the treatment of the mental patient who is incapable of giving consent to treatment must give the treatment that he considers to be in the best interests of his patient and the standard of care required of the doctor will be that laid down in *Bolam* ...'

The court is now able, however, to declare under MCA 2005, s 15 that proposed medical treatment is lawful as being in a patient's best interests, or not lawful as not being in the patient's best interests, providing only that the patient lacks capacity.

The jurisdiction for a doctor to be able to treat, without his or her consent, an adult who lacks capacity used to lie in the common law principle of necessity (*Re F* [1990] 2 AC 1 and *R v Bournewood Community and Mental Health NHS Trust ex parte L* [1998] 2 FLR 550).

10.3.1   Lasting Powers of Attorney

By s 9(1) of the MCA 2005 a lasting power of attorney is a power of attorney under which the donor confers on the donee authority to make decisions about all or any of the following: (a) the patient's personal welfare or specified matters concerning the patient's personal welfare and (b) the patient's property and affairs or specified matters concerning the patient's property and affairs, and which includes authority to make such decisions in circumstances where the patient no longer has capacity.

Sections 9 to 14 of the Act provide the legal framework for lasting powers of attorney, whereby one person, the donor, can confer authority on a donee by a power of attorney to make decisions. The formalities for making a lasting power of attorney are dealt with at Sch 1 to the Act. Since a lasting power of attorney is a power of attorney, accordingly the common law principles governing the relationship between a principal and his or her agent apply to a lasting power of attorney.

10.3.2   The appointment of a deputy

By s 16 of the MCA 2005 the court may make the decision or decisions on the patient's behalf in relation to the matter or matters in issue, or may appoint a person (a deputy) to make decisions on the patient's behalf in relation to the matter or matters in issue. By s 16(4) of the Act when deciding whether it is in the patient's best interests to appoint a deputy, the court must have regard (in addition to ss 1 and 4 of the Act) to the principles that (a) a decision by the court is to be preferred to the appointment of a deputy to make a decision, and (b) the powers conferred on a deputy should be as limited in scope and duration as is reasonably practicable in the circumstances.

10.4   INFORMALITY OF DECISION MAKING IN RELATION TO ADULTS LACKING CAPACITY

Regular decisions are taken by medical practitioners or other health carers, day-to-day, for and on behalf of those adults lacking capacity, without any recourse to the courts. Many patients suffering from mental illness who lack capacity do so for a long period or permanently. Many of the medical decisions taken are mundane, some less than mundane. Issues of capacity to decide from the patient's point of view may never arise or be tested and there must be a grey area as to the legal basis on which some of these decisions are made and as to whether, on occasions and unwittingly, doctors or other health carers may be exceeding their authority to treat the patient.

The MHA 1983 Code of Practice states at paragraph 15.20:

> 'The administration of medical treatment to people incapable of taking their own treatment decisions is a matter of much concern to professionals and others involved in their care. It is the personal responsibility of professionals to ensure that they understand the relevant law.'

Section 5 of the MCA 2005 states in terms that a person who does an act in connection with the care or treatment of another person will be put in the same position as if dealing with someone who had capacity to consent and had consented, and therefore will not incur any liability in doing the act, if: before doing the act he or she had taken reasonable steps to establish whether the person lacks capacity; and he or she reasonably believes the person lacks capacity and it is in that person's best interests for the act to be done.

This replaces, in possibly somewhat wider terms, the common law doctrine of necessity. It provides the basis upon which the vast majority of medical treatment decisions in relation to adults lacking capacity can be taken without seeking any court authorisation. The act must be connected to the person's care or treatment. This term of the statute will not protect from negligence. It will allow restraint of the person lacking capacity provided that there is a reasonable belief that it is necessary to do the act to prevent harm to him or her and the act is a proportionate response: MCA 2005, s 6.

10.5   INFORMAL ADMISSIONS TO HOSPITAL UNDER MHA 1983

Patients may be admitted to hospital under MHA 1983, either informally or formally. The informal admission of patients is under s 131 of the Act. What fell for decision in the case of *R v Bournewood Community and Mental Health NHS Trust ex parte L* [1998] 2 FLR 550, was what category or categories of patients come within s 131 as being suitable for informal admission.

The Court of Appeal had held that those who, though lacking capacity to consent, do not object to admission to hospital ('compliant incapacitated patients') do not fall within s 131 and are not within the category of an informal patient.

The House of Lords, in allowing the appeal from the Court of Appeal and having more background to the intention which lay behind the passing into legislation of the statutory provision in question, held that s 131 of the Act should be so construed that such patients described above, namely those who are 'compliant incapacitated patients', do fall within s 131 and can be admitted as informal patients to hospital.

The Percy Commission and its consequent report had pointed the way in suggesting that there would be less stigma for patients and their families, and thus more incentive and encouragement for them to receive medical help, if patients could be readily admitted to hospital without a formal admission and the consequences flowing from that. The Court of Appeal, however, had pointed out that one of the consequences – and a significant one – for those patients admitted informally was that they were not able to avail themselves of all the statutory safeguards in MHA 1983 available to those formally admitted.

The case of *L* clarified the common law legal basis, in the absence then of any statutory provision, for the medical treatment of those adult patients informally admitted to hospital. The justification for such medical treatment lies in the common law principle of necessity.

Lord Steyn at the end of his judgment in the case of *L* at p 569 said this:

> 'The common law principle of necessity is a useful concept, but it contains none of the safeguards of the Act of 1983. It places effective and unqualified control in the hands of the hospital psychiatrist and other healthcare professionals. It is, of course, true that such professionals owe a duty of care to patients and that they will almost invariably act in what they consider to be the best interests of the patient. But neither habeas corpus nor judicial review are sufficient safeguards against misjudgements and professional lapses in the case of compliant incapacitated patients. Given that such patients are diagnostically indistinguishable from compulsory patients, there is no reason to withhold the specific and affective protection of the Act of 1983 from a large class of vulnerable mentally incapacitated individuals. Their moral right to be treated with

dignity requires nothing less. The only comfort is that Counsel for the Secretary of State have assured the House that reform of the law is under active consideration.'

10.6   RESTRICTION ON DEPRIVATION OF LIBERTY UNDER MCA 2005

Article 5 of the ECHR provides:

'1 Everyone has the right to liberty and security of person. No one shall be deprived of his liberty save in the following cases and in accordance with a procedure prescribed by law—...
(e)   the lawful detention ... of persons of unsound mind ...

4 Everyone who is deprived of his liberty by ... detention shall be entitled to take proceedings by which the lawfulness of his detention shall be decided speedily by a court and his release ordered if the detention is not lawful.'

In the case of *HL v UK* (2005) 81 BMLR 131 the European Court of Human Rights was concerned with a 48-year-old autistic man lacking capacity who for some months was an informal patient, not compulsorily detained under MHA 1983, in the intensive behavioural unit of Bournewood Hospital.

The court held that he had been deprived of his liberty in breach of Article 5. The court identified accordingly 'the Bournewood gap' in our legal framework for control over the deprivation of liberty in the case of an incapable person affected otherwise than pursuant to the Act of 1983. Parliament sought to fill the gap by making insertions into MCA 2005 which, by s 4A(5) and Sch A1, set up a framework for such control in the case of a person receiving care or treatment in a hospital or a care home and which, by s 4A(1) and (3), rendered any other such deprivation lawful only if made pursuant to a court order that was in his or her best interests.

The terms of s 4A of MCA 2005 are as follows:

'4A Restriction on deprivation of liberty

(1) This Act does not authorise any person ("D") to deprive any other person ("P") of his liberty.

(2) But that is subject to –
(a)   the following provisions of this section, and
(b)   section 4B.

(3) D may deprive P of his liberty if, by doing so, D is giving effect to a relevant decision of the court.

(4) A relevant decision of the court is a decision made by an order under section 16(2)(a) in relation to a matter concerning P's personal welfare.

(5) D may deprive P of his liberty if the deprivation is authorised by Schedule A1 (hospital and care home residents: deprivation of liberty).'

The overall effect of the above statutory section is that it is lawful to deprive any person of their liberty either if it is a consequence of giving effect to an order of the Court of Protection on a personal welfare matter or, if the deprivation of liberty is in a hospital or care home, if a standard or urgent authorisation is in force. Schedule A1 is very detailed and encompasses whether and how authorisation may be given by a hospital or care home to deprive a person lacking capacity of their liberty by detaining them for the purpose of being given care or treatment.

The Mental Capacity Act 2005: Deprivation of Liberty Safeguards Code of Practice (supplementing the main Mental Capacity Act 2005 Code of Practice) is also very detailed and understandably so, given the sensitivity surrounding the issue of deprivation of liberty.

At the end of this chapter the joint guidance from the President of the Court of Protection and OFSTED entitled 'Deprivation of liberty-guidance for providers of children's homes and residential special schools' is reproduced.

10.6.1   The distinction between restriction of liberty and deprivation of liberty

The Strasbourg case law shows that it is not every restriction on freedom of movement and association which will amount to a deprivation of liberty and will engage Article 5.

The European Court of Human Rights (in *Storck v Germany* (2005) 43 EHRR 96) has made clear that a deprivation of liberty has three elements:
(a) 'the objective element of a person's confinement to a certain limited place for a not negligible length of time';
(b) the 'additional subjective element that they have not validly consented to the confinement in question':
(c) the confinement must be 'imputable to the State'.

In *Guzzardi v Italy* (1981) EHRR 333 it is said as follows:

> '... the starting point must be his concrete situation and account must be
> taken of a whole range of criteria such as the type, duration, effects and
> manner of implementation of the measure in question. The difference
> between deprivation of and restriction upon liberty is nonetheless merely
> one of degree or intensity, and not one of nature or substance ... the
> process of classification into one or other of these categories sometimes
> proves to be no easy task in that some borderline cases are a matter of
> pure opinion ...'

In the case of *P and Q v Surrey County Council*, the very issue before
Parker J and then the Court of Appeal ([2011] EWCA Civ 190) was
whether the arrangements for two sisters amounted to a deprivation of
their liberty. The Official Solicitor for the sisters appealed against the
declaration made by Parker J that their arrangements did not amount to
a deprivation of their liberty. The County Council sought to maintain
and uphold the declaration made. The Court of Appeal upheld the view
that the living arrangements of the sisters did not amount to a
deprivation of liberty. As will be indicated shortly, the Supreme Court
took a very different view, and declared that their living arrangements at
the relevant time constituted a deprivation of liberty within the meaning
of s 64(5) of MCA 2005. P was 19 and had a mental age of 2½, and Q
was 18 and had a mental age of 4 to 5 years of age. The children were
unable to live with their mother for the reasons set out in the judgment.
At the time of the hearing at first instance P was living in a foster home
and Q was placed in a small residential home for adolescents. The
appeal was dismissed.

In relation to the three elements mentioned above relating to a
deprivation of liberty, neither sister was in a position to give a valid
consent to any arrangements for their care; their arrangements were
imputable both to the County Council and, for that matter, also to the
orders of the judge; the enquiry in the case accordingly was as to an
objective analysis of their circumstances, including whether or not they
were being confined in such way as to amount to a deprivation of their
liberty.

Counsel for the sisters maintained that in essence the Council exercised
complete and effective control over their placements. The Court of
Appeal set out the varying factors relating to the cases of each of the
sisters, including the fact that whilst they were not free to leave their
respective accommodation, they were not under close confinement
within their accommodation, did not object to the arrangements and did
not seek to leave.

The court indicated that a valid factor to be borne in mind was the level of conflict, if any, engendered by the placement, and in this particular case neither sister was objecting at all to the arrangements.

The Court of Appeal also indicated that the administration to a person of medication, at any rate of antipsychotic drugs and other tranquillizers, would need to be considered as to whether they might suppress a person's liberty to express himself or herself as they might otherwise wish. P was not in receipt of medication. Q was in receipt of medication, albeit not forcibly administered, for control of her anxiety; but she would have required such medication whatever the circumstances and neither its purpose nor its effect was to restrain her from trying to leave the home or from pursuing any other activity.

P's living conditions in the foster home appeared to be overall normal and balanced. More borderline were the living circumstances of Q in the small residential home, as was stated in the Court of Appeal judgment:

> 'The small size of the home for adolescents in which she lived; her lack of objection to life there: her attendance at the educational unit; her good contact with such members of her family as were significant for her; and her other, fairly active, social life: such were the main factors which have kept her case outside of Article 5.'

In the case of *Cheshire West and Chester Council v P*, P was 38 years of age at the time of the Court of Protection hearing. He was born with cerebral palsy and Down's syndrome, and required 24-hour-care to meet his personal care needs. When his health began to deteriorate, the local social services authority obtained orders from the Court of Protection that it was in P's best interests to live in accommodation arranged by the local authority.

P was placed in Z house, not a care home, but a spacious bungalow shared with two other residents with staff on duty during the day and overnight. Baker J at the final hearing held that P could not go anywhere, or do anything, without the support and assistance of staff at Z house. He determined further that the steps required to deal with P's challenging behaviour led to a clear conclusion that, looked at overall, P was being deprived of his liberty. The Court of Appeal substituted a declaration that the arrangements did not involve a deprivation of liberty: [2011] EWCA Civ 1257. As indicated shortly, the Supreme Court took a very different view from the Court of Appeal and restored the determination of the judge at the final hearing.

The Supreme Court judgment ([2014] UKSC 19) is very significant in considering the meaning of 'deprivation of liberty'. It considered appeals from both of the above cases of *P and Q v Surrey County Council*, and *Cheshire West and Chester Council v P*. Both appeals were allowed. In both cases there was determined to be deprivations of liberty.

The Supreme Court reiterated that MCA 2005, s 64(5) states that: 'In this Act, references to a deprivation of a person's liberty have the same meaning as in Article 5(1) of the Human Rights Convention.'

The Supreme Court stated that the first and most fundamental question was whether the concept of physical liberty protected by Article 5 is the same for everyone, regardless of whether or not they are mentally or physically disabled.

Lady Hale said that the whole point about human rights is the universal character. She said:

> '45. In my view, it is axiomatic that people with disabilities, both mental and physical, have the same human rights as the rest of the human race. It may be that those rights have sometimes to be limited or restricted because of their disabilities, but the starting point should be the same as that for everyone else. This flows inexorably from the universal character of human rights, founded on the inherent dignity of all human beings, and is confirmed in the United Nations Convention on the Rights of Persons with Disabilities. Far from disability entitling the state to deny such people human rights: rather it places upon the state (and upon others) the duty to make reasonable accommodation to cater for the special needs of those with disabilities.

> 46. Those rights include the right to physical liberty, which is guaranteed by article 5 of the European Convention. This is not a right to do or to go where one pleases. It is a more focussed right, not to be deprived of that physical liberty. But, as it seems to me, what it means to be deprived of liberty must be the same for everyone, whether or not they have physical or mental disabilities. If it would be a deprivation of my liberty to be obliged to live in a particular place, subject to constant monitoring and control, only allowed out with close supervision, and unable to move away without permission even if such an opportunity became available, then it must also be a deprivation of the liberty of a disabled person. The fact that my living arrangements are comfortable, and indeed make my life as enjoyable as it could possibly be, should make no difference. A gilded cage is still a cage.'

The court rejected the 'relative normality' approach of the Court of Appeal in the case of *P*, and confirmed other factors which are not relevant in determining whether there is a deprivation of liberty. A person's compliance or lack of objection is not relevant; the reason or purpose behind a particular placement is also not relevant.

The acid test is whether a person is under the complete supervision and control of those caring for him or her and is not free to leave the place where he or she lives. The key factor is whether the person is, or is not, free to leave. Another material factor is whether the person lacks capacity to consent to these arrangements. The confinement in question too must be 'imputable to the State'. As was pointed out in the judgment, similar constraints would not necessarily amount to a deprivation of liberty for the purpose of Article 5 if imposed by parents in the exercise of their ordinary parental responsibilities and outside the legal framework governing state intervention in the lives of children or people who lack the capacity to make their own decisions.

At the end of this chapter, guidance published by the Department of Health dated 28 March 2014 drawing attention to the above judgment of the Supreme Court to help to ensure that health and social care organisations continue to comply with the law following the revised test determined by the Supreme Court as to the meaning of deprivation of liberty is reproduced.

10.6.2 Challenging a deprivation of liberty authorised by Sch A1 to MCA 2005

Section 21A of MCA 2005 sets out the powers of the court in relation to Sch A1, including varying or terminating a standard authorisation and determining whether an urgent authorisation should have been given.

At the end of this chapter, Practice Direction A (supplementing Part 10A of the Court of Protection Rules 2007) in relation to the procedure to be adopted in deprivation of liberty applications is reproduced. By their nature, such applications are of special urgency and therefore will be dealt with by the court according to the special procedure set out in the Practice Direction.

In the case of *Re M (Best Interests: Deprivation of Liberty)* [2013] EWHC 3456 (COP) a 67-year-old lady named M successfully challenged a deprivation of liberty standard authorisation made soon after she entered a care home in June 2012. She wished to return home and to share time with her partner of 30 years who maintained his own property but spent a few days each week with her in her home. M had very substantial medical needs, the most prominent being control of her diabetes. The group responsible for providing services to her opposed the application due to the need she had, as they maintained, to remain in the care home to receive suitable support and control of her medical needs.

Peter Jackson J determined that the question of capacity was not in dispute: arising from her medical condition M had an impairment of the functioning of the mind or brain which was relatively mild but crossed the diagnostic threshold. Further, she lacked capacity to decide whether she should live. Material to this was an appropriate appreciation of the risks arising from the lower level of supervision of the diabetes management that a home placement entailed compared with the 24-hour professional oversight of her medical needs if she remained in the care home. The judge determined M had an inflexible but mistaken belief that she could manage her own diabetes and consequently could not be aware of the serious risks involved in a reduction in the level of supervision.

The manager of the care home gave evidence as to M's refusal to accept support within her own home (as identified by district nurses and care agencies), which could have devastating consequences on her health if she returned home; her refusal to access care services would be highly likely. M was assessed by a consultant psychiatrist who on balance recommended to the court that the return home should be attempted. He described her current quality of life as being significantly adversely affected by her deprivation of liberty.

The judge clearly set out the factors to be weighed in determining under s 4 of the Act what course would be in M's best interests, and accepted that she had been greatly accommodated in the care home in 2012 despite her objections, and that the standard authorisations were rightly granted in the early stages. However, in the past year her physical condition had improved as a result of the care she had received, and the committed support her partner would provide was also a significant factor. The strength of her wishes and feelings to return home, which was consistent, was also material to the court's decision. The judge said that M's views were quite understandable bearing in mind the restricted and impoverished quality of her life in the care home: this was no fault at all of the care home.

At paragraph 38 of the judgment, the judge stated:

> 'In the end, if M remains confined in a home she is entitled to ask "what for?" The only answer that could be provided at the moment is:"to keep you alive as long as possible." In my view that is not a sufficient answer. The right to life and the state's obligation to protect it is not absolute and

the court must surely have regard to the person's own assessment of her quality of life. In M's case there is little to be said for a solution that attempts, without any guarantee of success, to preserve for her a daily life without meaning or happiness and which she, with some justification, regards as insupportable.'

10.6.3   Section 4B of MCA 2005

Providing the conditions set out within s 4B are met, a person may be deprived of their liberty to save their life or prevent a serious deterioration in their condition whilst a decision is sought from the Court of Protection on any question as to whether they may lawfully be deprived of their liberty.

10.7   THE INTERFACE BETWEEN MHA 1983 AND MCA 2005

The purpose of MHA 1983 is to provide the statutory framework for the compulsory care and treatment of people for their mental disorder when they are unable or unwilling to consent to the care and treatment, and when it is necessary for that care and treatment to be given to protect themselves or others from harm.

As already seen from the case-law and commentary above, as well as patients detained under the Act who lack capacity, it is possible for someone detained under MHA 1983 to have capacity in relation to a treatment decision. The question whether an individual patient has or does not have decision-making capacity is not the key determinant of whether the powers conferred by MHA 1983 should be used.

MCA 2005, however, is based entirely on a capacity test in the sense that its statutory provisions have no application to those persons who have the capacity to make their own decisions. The 2005 Act applies only in relation to those who lack capacity, and to no others.

Those adults who are in a persistent vegetative state or who are minimally conscious lack capacity but would not ordinarily come within the ambit of the exercise of compulsory powers under MHA 1983. Adults with learning difficulties who may lack capacity, or similarly with dementia who lack capacity, also generally speaking will not be subject to such compulsory powers under the 1983 Act: they will be more likely to be subject to the terms of MCA 2005 in its wider decision-making for those lacking capacity. Under s 1(5) of the 2005 statute, 'any act done, or decision made, under this Act for or on behalf of a person who lacks capacity must be done, or made, in his best interests'.

The emphasis of MHA 1983 is to a large degree directed towards decisions concerning medical treatment for mental disorder. Of course there will be some overlap, for example if a patient with dementia whose daily life has been managed at home in accordance with MCA 2005 deteriorates in the sense of becoming seriously or abnormally aggressive, then the statutory test under MCA 1983 may become met requiring the compulsory admission of that person to hospital.

It is to be noted that MCA 2005, s 28(1) provides that nothing in the 2005 Act authorises anyone to give a patient medical treatment for mental disorder, or to consent to a patient being given medical treatment for mental disorder, if at the time his treatment is regulated by Part IV of the 1983 Act, which regulates the medical treatment for mental disorder of patients who are 'liable to be detained' in hospital under the 1983 Act (s 56(1)), including patients who are actually detained.

APPENDICES TO CHAPTER 10

DEPRIVATION OF LIBERTY – GUIDANCE FOR PROVIDERS OF CHILDREN'S HOMES AND RESIDENTIAL SPECIAL SCHOOLS

1. This is guidance, issued jointly by the President of the Court of Protection and Ofsted, on the deprivation of liberty under the Mental Capacity Act 2005.

2. There are two ways in which a deprivation of liberty can be authorised and so in which a person can be deprived of their liberty under the Mental Capacity Act 2005:

- An urgent or standard authorisation which can only be given by a supervisory body on the request of a managing authority of a hospital or care home[1] in respect to a person who has reached 18. This specifically excludes an establishment which is a children's home. An urgent or standard authorisation cannot be given in respect of a children's home. Nor can an urgent or standard authorisation be made in relation to a person under the age of 18 years old.

- By order of the Court of Protection[2]: orders and declarations of the Court of Protection are made in relation to a person who is over the age of 16 and lacks capacity. The order may authorise (not require) the detention of that person. Any such order is a decision on behalf of the person who lacks capacity – it is not like an injunction aimed at requiring third parties to take steps to facilitate the detention of that young person.

3. The Court of Protection should be reminded by the parties of the Regulations that apply to children's homes and residential special schools. The Court of Protection does not have the jurisdiction to require any home or school to act in breach of such Regulations or to authorise any such breach. Accordingly, the Court of Protection should not make an order authorising a plan for the care and supervision involving the detention of a person, where to do so would involve the children's home or a residential special school breaching the regulations that apply to it. If compliance with an Order of the Court of Protection would involve such a breach of the relevant Regulations it cannot be

---

[1] Such authorisations are granted under Schedule A1 of the Mental Capacity Act 2005. The meaning of a care home is provided by section 3 of the Care Standards Act 2000 (Para. 178 of Schedule A1 to 2005 Act).

[2] Sections 4A(3) and (4) and section 16(2)(a) of the 2005 Act.

relied on to justify breach of the Regulations or enforced in a manner that would involve such a breach.[3] The most relevant Regulations are referred to below.

Children's homes and residential special schools registered as children's homes

4. All children's homes must meet the Children's Home Regulations (2001). In this instance, the relevant regulations are: regulation 11 (Promotion of welfare), regulation 17 (Behaviour management and discipline) and regulation 17A (Restraint). As restraint can only be used to prevent a child from leaving a secure children's home, there is no purpose to be served in seeking an order of the Court of Protection authorising such restraint by a non-secure children's home because the Court of Protection has no jurisdiction to order or authorise a breach of these Regulations.

Non-maintained residential special schools[4]

5. These schools must comply with the Education (Non-Maintained Special Schools) (England) Regulations 2011 which require the school to comply with the National Minimum Standards in relation to safeguarding the welfare of children[5]. NMS 12.7 states that:

> 'No school restricts the liberty of any child as a matter of routine or provides any form of secure accommodation.'

6. As this type of school is unable to deprive a young person of their liberty the Court of Protection has no jurisdiction to make an order that requires or authorises it to do so in breach of that regulation.

Independent residential special schools

7. These schools must comply with the Education (Independent School Standards) (England) Regulations 2010, which provide that the schools must have regard to the National Minimum Standards for residential special schools[6] and so NMS 12.7 is relevant. If the school does not meet NMS 12.7 it must have good reason for not doing so. It is not the

---

[3] The effect of these orders does not **require** the deprivation of the person's liberty, but rather **permits** the deprivation of their liberty in certain circumstances and mitigates liability in terms of potential breaches of Article 5 of the European Convention of Human Rights (right to liberty of person).

[4] As defined in section 337 of Education Act 1996.

[5] Regulation 3 and paragraph 13(2) of the Schedule to the 2011 Regulations.

[6] Regulation 3(1) and paragraph 8 of Schedule 1 to the 2010 Regulations.

spirit of the NMS that there are different applicable standards for independent and non-maintained residential special schools.

8. Accordingly, such schools are not entitled to deprive children of their liberty and the Court of Protection should not authorise a deprivation of liberty by this type of school.

The Mental Health Act Code of Practice 1983

9. In *R (on the application of C) v A Local Authority* [2011] EWHC 1539 (Admin) and [2011] 14 CCLR 471 and [2100] Med LR 415 "the blue room case" the Court considered the need to have regard to the Mental Health Code of Practice 1983 in a case involving seclusion. This approach is one which should be followed. However, the need to have regard to the Mental Health Code of Practice 1983 in cases involving seclusion does not mean that Regulations and Guidance expressly directed towards children's homes should not be followed. The primary focus of all children's homes should be on the Regulations and Guidance which relates to such homes, and in the case of residential special schools the Regulations which apply, albeit in the exceptional case, such as the blue room case, assistance can also be derived from the Mental Health Code of Practice. The position is similar in relation to the Mental Capacity Act 2005 and the Code of Practice and Guidance relating to it.

Good practice in the event providers are aware of an application to the Court of Protection

10. Should the providers of children's homes or residential special schools become aware of an application to the Court of Protection and be aware of a reason why it is not possible or appropriate for the incapacitated person to be detained at the home or school (whether because it is in breach of regulations or for other reason) it is good practice to advise the Court of Protection and parties to the application that this is the position and to give reasons why this is the case as soon as possible.

In Summary:

11. No application should be made to the Court of Protection in relation to any child under the age of 16 years old.

12. Standard and urgent authorisations under Schedule A1 Mental Capacity Act have no application to children's homes as they only apply to hospitals and care homes and only apply to those over the age of 18 years old.

13. Orders of the Court of Protection authorising a deprivation of liberty by nonsecure children's homes or residential special schools should not be sought or made and they should not be advanced or relied on to permit such homes and schools to act in breach of the Regulations that apply to them.

14. The Mental Health Act Guidance and other Guidance may be relevant but do not override the Regulations and Guidance directed towards children's homes and schools.

Dated the 12th February 2014

President of the Court of Protection
National Director Social Care Ofsted

DEPARTMENT OF HEALTH (28 MARCH 2014) DEPRIVATION OF LIBERTY SAFEGUARDS (DOLS)

Judgment of the Supreme Court
P v Cheshire West and Chester Council and another
P and Q v Surrey County Council

The contents of this note are specifically addressed to all those who are

- involved in the assessment and/or authorisation of a deprivation of liberty
- involved in the care of individuals who may lack capacity
- responsible for policies and procedures relating to the care of individuals who may lack capacity.

Mental Capacity Act (MCA) and Deprivation of Liberty Safeguard (DoLS) leads should ensure this note is cascaded to all relevant staff.

Background

On 19 March 2014, the Supreme Court handed down its judgment in the case of *P v Cheshire West and Chester Council and another* and *P and Q v Surrey County Council*. The full judgment can be found on the Supreme Court's website at the following link:

http://supremecourt.uk/decided-cases/docs/UKSC_2012_0068_Judgment.pdf

The accompanying press release with a short description of the cases under consideration can be found at the following link:

http://supremecourt.uk/decided-cases/docs/UKSC_2012_0068_PressSummary.pdf

The judgment is significant in the determination of whether arrangements made for the care and/or treatment of an individual lacking capacity to consent to those arrangements amount to a deprivation of liberty.

A deprivation of liberty for such a person must be authorised in accordance with one of the following legal regimes: a deprivation of liberty authorisation or Court of Protection order under the Deprivation of Liberty Safeguards (DoLS) in the Mental Capacity Act 2005, or (if applicable) under the Mental Health Act 1983.

Key points from the Supreme Court judgment

Revised test for deprivation of liberty

The Supreme Court has clarified that there is a deprivation of liberty for the purposes of ECHR Article 5 in the following circumstances:

> The person is under continuous supervision and control and is not free to leave, and the person lacks capacity to consent to these arrangements.

The Supreme Court held that factors which are NOT relevant to determining whether there is a deprivation of liberty include the person's compliance or lack of objection and the reason or purpose behind a particular placement[7]. It was also held that the relative normality of the placement, given the person's needs, was not relevant. This means that the person should not be compared with anyone else in determining whether there is a deprivation of liberty. However, young persons aged 16 or 17 should be compared to persons of a similar age and maturity without disabilities.

Deprivation of liberty in "domestic" settings

The Supreme Court has held that a deprivation of liberty can occur in domestic settings where the State is responsible for imposing such arrangements. This will include a placement in a supported living arrangement in the community. Hence, where there is, or is likely to be, a deprivation of liberty in such placements that must be authorised by the Court of Protection.

Suggested actions

Relevant staff should

- Familiarise themselves with the provisions of the Mental Capacity Act, in particular the five principles and specifically the 'least restrictive' principle.
- When designing and implementing new care and treatment plans for individuals lacking capacity, be alert to any restrictions and restraint which may be of a degree or intensity that mean an individual is being, or is likely to be, deprived of their liberty (following the revised test supplied by the Supreme Court).

---

[7]   Nb, these factors (compliance/objection and the reason or purpose for the placement) are of course still relevant to assessment of best interests and consideration of Article 8 rights.

- Take steps to review existing care and treatment plans for individuals lacking capacity to determine if there is a deprivation of liberty (following the revised test supplied by the Supreme Court).
- Where a potential deprivation of liberty is identified, a full exploration of the alternative ways of providing the care and/or treatment should be undertaken, in order to identify any less restrictive ways of providing that care which will avoid a deprivation of liberty.
- Where the care/treatment plan for an individual lacking capacity will unavoidably result in a deprivation of liberty judged to be in that person's best interests, this MUST be authorised.

Local authorities should in addition

- Review their allocation of resources in light of the revised test given by the Supreme Court to ensure they meet their legal responsibilities.

Although local authorities are the supervisory body for DoLS for both care home and hospital settings, the NHS (commissioners and providers) have a vital role to play in correctly implementing DoLS (and the wider MCA). We expect that the NHS and local authorities will continue to work closely together on this.

Authorising a deprivation of liberty

The DoLS process for obtaining a standard authorisation or urgent authorisation can be used where individuals lacking capacity are deprived of their liberty in a hospital or care home.

The Court of Protection can also make an order authorising a deprivation of liberty; this is the only route available for authorising deprivation of liberty in domestic settings such as supported living arrangements. This route is also available for complex cases in hospital and/or care home settings.

Individuals may also be deprived of their liberty under the Mental Health Act if the requirements for detention under that Act are met.

Further information

In the first instance professionals should contact their organisation's MCA-DoLS lead for further information.

In the meantime the Government is preparing its response to the House of Lords Select Committee report into the MCA and DoLS. We expect to issue this response by the summer.

The attached annex provides some additional background.

Annex – Further background and steps for consideration

It is difficult to predict the number of individuals who lack capacity whose arrangements should be assessed in light of the Supreme Court judgment and the number of additional individuals for whom deprivation of liberty will need to be authorised.

Local authorities submit information on the number of assessments undertaken for deprivation of liberty authorisations under the Mental Capacity Act 2005 and the number of authorisations approved to the Health and Social Care Information Centre. The Department of Health and the Care Quality Commission will explore how best to monitor the evolving situation to assist in determining the practical impact of the Supreme Court's revised test.

Professionals must remember that the deprivation of liberty authorisations and Court of Protection orders under the Deprivation of Liberty Safeguards (DoLS) in the Mental Capacity Act 2005 are rooted in the principles of that Act. DoLS exist to provide protection to individuals – to safeguard these individuals when a deprivation of liberty is an unavoidable part of a best interests care plan. Individuals who are identified as potentially deprived of their liberty must be considered on a case-by-case basis and all appropriate steps taken to remove the risk of a deprivation of liberty where possible. The emphasis should be on empowerment and enablement.

Further steps that Local Authorities could consider taking are:
- Ensuring awareness of the Supreme Court judgment among care providers
- Ensuring awareness of the need to reduce restraint and restrictions and promote liberty in care plans
- Mapping any additional requirements for Best Interest Assessors (BIAs) and working collaboratively with other Local Authorities to reduce training costs
- Reviewing information on the number of individuals in supported living arrangements to identify those individuals whose arrangements should be reviewed

PRACTICE DIRECTION AA – DEPRIVATION OF LIBERTY APPLICATIONS (PD10AA)

This practice direction supplements Part 10A of the Court of Protection Rules 2007

Introduction

1. This practice direction sets out the procedure to be followed in deprivation of liberty ("DoL") applications. "DoL applications", for these purposes, means applications to the court for orders under section 21A of the Mental Capacity Act 2005 relating to a standard or urgent authorisation under Schedule A1 of that Act to deprive a person of his or her liberty; or proceedings (for example, relating to costs or appeals) connected with or consequent upon such applications. By their nature, such applications are of special urgency and therefore will be dealt with by the court according to the special procedure described here. Other applications may, while not being DoL applications within the meaning of the term explained above, raise issues relating to deprivation of liberty and require similarly urgent attention; and while the special DoL procedure will not apply to such applications, they should as explained in paragraph 3.4 be raised with the DoL team at the earliest possible stage so that they can be handled appropriately. The key features of the special DoL procedure are:

(a) special DoL court forms ensure that DoL court papers stand out as such and receive special handling by the court office;

(b) the application is placed before a judge of the court as soon as possible – if necessary, before issue of the application – for judicial directions to be given as to the steps to be taken in the application, and who is to take each step and by when;

(c) the usual Court of Protection Rules (for example, as to method and timing of service of the application) will apply only so far as consistent with the judicial directions given for the particular case;

(d) a dedicated team in the court office ("the DoL team") will deal with DoL applications at all stages, including liaison with would-be applicants/other parties;

(e) the progress of each DoL case will be monitored by a judge assigned to that case, assisted by the DoL team.

Before issuing an application

2. Potential applicants should contact the DoL team at the earliest possible stage before issuing a DoL application. Where this is not possible, the applicant should liaise with the DoL team at the same time

as, or as soon as possible after, lodging the application. The DoL team can be contacted by telephone in the first instance and by fax.

3. The information that the DoL team needs, with as much advance warning as possible, is (1) that a DoL application is to be made; (2) how urgent the application is (i.e., by when should the Court's decision, or interim decision, on the merits be given); and (3) when the Court will receive the application papers. In extremely urgent cases, the DoL team can arrange for a telephone application to be made to the judge for directions and/or an interim order even before the application has been issued. Further brief details should be given which may include:

(a) the parties' details
(b) where the parties live
(c) the issue to be decided
(d) the date of urgent or standard authorisation
(e) the date of effective detention
(f) the parties' legal representatives
(g) any family members or others who are involved
(h) whether there have been any other court proceedings involving the parties and if so, where.

4. Contact details for the DoL team are:

Court of Protection
DoLs Application Branch
Court of Protection
The Royal Courts of Justice
Thomas More Building
Strand
London
WC2A 2LL
DX 44450 Strand
Telephone: 0300 456 4600

5. The court office is open for personal attendance between the hours of 10 a.m. to 4.00 p.m. on working days. The DoL team can receive telephone calls and faxes between the same hours. Faxes transmitted after 4.00 p.m. will be dealt with the next working day.

6. When in an emergency it is necessary to make a telephone application to a judge outside normal court hours, the security office at the Royal Courts of Justice should be contacted on 020 7947 6000. The security officer should be informed of the nature of the case. In the Family

Division, the out-of-hours application procedure involves the judge being contacted through a Family Division duty officer, and the RCJ security officer will need to contact the duty officer and not the judge's clerk or the judge.

7. Intending applicants/other parties may find it helpful to refer to:

(a) the Code of Practice Deprivation of Liberty Safeguards (June 2008), ISBN 978-0113228157, supplementing the main Mental Capacity Act 2005 Code of Practice: in particular Chapter 10, What is the Court of Protection and who can apply to it?; and

(b) the judgment of Mr Justice Munby in *Salford City Council v GJ, NJ and BJ (Incapacitated Adults)* [2008] EWHC 1097 (Fam); [2008] 2 FLR 1295. Although this case was decided before the coming into force of the DoL amendments to the Mental Capacity Act 2005, it sets out helpful guidance on the appropriate court procedures for cases relating to the deprivation of liberty of adults.

8. The DoL team will be pleased to explain the court's procedures for handling DoL cases. Please note that the team (as with all court staff) is not permitted to give advice on matters of law. Please do not contact the DoL team unless your inquiry concerns a deprivation of liberty question (whether relating to a potential application, or a case which is already lodged with the Court).

DoL court forms

9. The special DoL court forms are as follows:

(a) DLA: Deprivation of Liberty Application Form: to be used for all DoL applications;

(b) DLB: Deprivation of Liberty Request for Urgent Consideration: this short form allows applicants to set out the reasons why the case is urgent, the timetable they wish the case to follow, and any interim relief sought. A draft of any order sought should be attached. Ideally, the DLB (plus any draft order) should be placed at the top of the draft application and both issued and served together;

(c) DLC: Deprivation of Liberty Permission Form: P (the person who is being, or may be, deprived of his/her liberty); and P's appointed representative, attorney or deputy do not need the court's permission to make a DoL application. Anyone else (including family members) needs permission.

Where the applicant needs permission to make a DoL application, the DLC form should be lodged and served together with a draft of the DLA and, where appropriate, the DLB. The DLB should always be placed at the top of the papers and (where this is so) mention that permission is required and that a completed DLC is attached;

(a) DLD: Deprivation of Liberty Certificate of Service/non-service and Certificate of notification/non-notification;

(b) DLE: Deprivation of Liberty Acknowledgement of service/ notification.

These forms can be obtained from the Court of Protection office or downloaded from the court's website www.justice.gov.uk/global/forms/hmcts/index.htm

10. To ensure that papers relating to DoL applications are promptly directed to the DoL team at the court, it is essential that the appropriate DoL court forms are used.

11. The DoL court forms should be used for, and only for, DoL applications. If in such a case it is anticipated that other issues may arise, the DoL forms should identify and describe briefly those issues and any relief which may be sought in respect of them: sections 3.5 and 5 of form DLA, the Deprivation of Liberty Application Form, offer an opportunity to do this. "Other issues" are perhaps most likely to arise in the event that the court decides the DoL application in the applicant's favour. In such a case, if the applicant has already identified the "other issues" in his/her form DLA, the court will be able to address these, either by dealing with them immediately or by giving directions for their future handling.

12. Accordingly, unless the court expressly directs, applicants should not issue a second and separate application (using the standard court forms) relating to any "other issues".

13. Where an application seeks relief concerning a deprivation of P's liberty other than under section 21A in respect of a standard or urgent authorisation (for example, where the application is for an order under section 16(2)(a)), the dedicated DoL court forms should not be used. Rather the standard court forms should be used for such an application, but it should be made clear on them that relief relating to a deprivation of P's liberty is being sought, and the proposed applicant should contact the DoL team to discuss handling at the earliest possible stage before issuing the application.

How to issue a DoL application

14. To issue a DoL application, the following forms should be filed at court:

(a) form DLA

(b)   form DLB (plus draft order)
(c)   form DLC if appropriate
(d)   court fee of £400.00

Where a draft order is lodged with the court, it would be helpful – although not compulsory – if an electronic version of the order could also be lodged on disc, if possible.

15. In cases of extreme emergency or where it is not possible to attend at the court office, for example during weekends, the court will expect an applicant to undertake to file forms DLA and DLC and to pay the court fee unless an exemption applies.

Inviting the court to make judicial directions for the handling of the application

16. The following is a sample list of possible issues which the court is likely to wish to consider in judicial directions in a DoL case. It is intended as a prompt, not as a definitive list of the issues that may need to be covered:

(a)   upon whom, by when and how service of the application should be effected;
(b)   dispensing with acknowledgement of service of the application or allowing a short period of time for so doing, which in some cases may amount to a few hours only;
(c)   whether further lay or expert evidence should be obtained;
(d)   whether P/the detained person should be a party and represented by the Official Solicitor and whether any other person should be a party;
(e)   whether any family members should be formally notified of the application and of any hearing and joined as parties;
(f)   fixing a date for a First Hearing and giving a time estimate;
(g)   fixing a trial window for any final hearing and giving a time estimate;
(h)   the level of judge appropriate to hear the case;
(i)   whether the case is such that it should be immediately transferred to the High Court for a High Court Judge to give directions;
(j)   provision for a bundle for the judge at the First Hearing.

17. If you are an applicant without legal representation, and you are not sure exactly what directions you should ask for, you may prefer simply to invite the judge to make appropriate directions in light of the nature and urgency of the case as you have explained it on the DLB form. In exceptionally urgent cases, there may not be time to formulate draft

directions: the court will understand if applicants in such cases (whether or not legally represented) simply ask the judge for appropriate directions.

After issue of the application

18. The DoL team will immediately take steps to ensure that the application is placed before a judge nominated to hear Court of Protection cases and DoL applications. During working hours, the application will be placed before a Judge at Archway Tower. Out of hours, at weekends and on public holidays, the application will be placed before the judge who is most immediately available.

19. As soon as the court office is put on notice of a DoL application, the DoL team will notify a judge to put the judge on stand-by to deal with the application. The judge will consider the application on the papers and make a first order.

Steps after the judge's first order

20. The DoL team will:

    (a)   action every point in the judge's note or instruction;
    (b)   refer any query that arises to the judge immediately or, if not available, to another judge;
    (c)   make all arrangements for any transfer of the case to another court and/or for a hearing.

21. The applicant or his/her legal representative should follow all steps in the judge's order and:

    (a)   form DLD should be filed with the court if appropriate; and
    (b)   form DLE should be included in any documents served unless ordered otherwise.

The First Hearing

22. The First Hearing will be listed for the court to fix a date for any subsequent hearing(s), give directions and/or to make an interim or final order if appropriate. The court will make such orders and give such directions as are appropriate in the case.

23. The court will aim to have the First Hearing before a judge of every DoL application within 5 working days of the date of issue of the application.

24. Applicants can indicate on the DLB form if they think that the application needs to be considered within a shorter timetable, and set

out proposals for such a timetable. On the first paper consideration the court will consider when the First Hearing should be listed.

25. If time allows and no specific direction has been made by the court, an indexed and paginated bundle should be prepared for the judge and any skeleton arguments and draft orders given to the court as soon as they are available. A copy of the index should be provided to all parties and, where another party appears in person, a copy of the bundle should be provided.

Hearing in private

26. Part 13 of the Court of Protection Rules 2007 provides at rule 90, as supplemented by Practice Direction A to Part 13, that the general rule is that a hearing is held in private. Rule 92 allows the court to order that a hearing be in public if the criteria in rule 93 apply.

Costs

27. The general rule, in rule 157 of the Court of Protection Rules 2007, is that in a health and welfare case there will be no order as to costs of the proceedings. The general rule applies to DoL applications.

Appeals

28. Part 20 of the Court of Protection Rules 2007 applies to appeals. Permission is required to appeal (rule 172) and this will only be granted where the court considers that the appeal would have a real prospect of success or there is some other compelling reason why the appeal should be heard (rule 173).

CHAPTER 11

CHILDREN: CONSENT OR REFUSAL OF CONSENT TO MEDICAL TREATMENT

11.1 DEFINITION OF A CHILD

A minor is a person who has not attained the age of 18 years (s 1(1) of the Family Law Reform Act 1969). The corresponding definition of a child is set out in s 105 of the Children Act 1989 (CA 1989). There 'child means ... a person under the age of eighteen'. The use of the wording 'an immature child' below refers to a child who is not 'Gillick-competent'. That a child is 'immature' will ordinarily be obvious by reason of his or her age. The relevant test as to competency in respect of the older minor is considered in due course in this chapter.

11.2 PARENTAL CONSENT TO MEDICAL TREATMENT FOR AND ON BEHALF OF THE IMMATURE CHILD

11.2.1 The general requirement of consent before treatment

> 'It is trite law that, in general, a doctor is not entitled to treat a patient without the consent of someone who is authorised to give that consent. If he does so, he will be liable in damages for trespass to the person and may be guilty of a criminal assault ...'

(Re R (A Minor) (Wardship: Medical Treatment) [1992] 1 FLR 190 at 196).

In the European Court case of *Glass v UK* (App 61827/000) [2004] 1 FLR 1019 (*Glass No 2*) the European Court of Human Rights held that the decision to impose treatment on a minor child in defiance of the objections of his mother, and in the absence of authorisation by a court, gave rise to an interference with the child's right to respect for his private life and in particular his right to physical integrity. In the case a 'do not resuscitate' notice had been placed on the notes of a disabled child who was thought to be about to die, and diamorphine was administered contrary to his mother's wishes. The court concluded that the decision of the authorities to override the mother's objection to the proposed treatment in the absence of authorisation by a court resulted in a breach of Article 8 of the European Convention on Human Rights (ECHR).

11.2.2 Emergencies

In an emergency or exceptional circumstances (such as abandonment of the child or inability to find the parent), a doctor may treat a child without parental knowledge and consent.

11.2.3 Parental responsibility

A parent or parents or other person or body with parental responsibility will ordinarily consent to treatment for and on behalf of the minor, unless and until such minor himself or herself has the capacity to consent.

'Parental responsibility' means 'all the rights, duties, powers, responsibilities and authority which by law a parent of a child has in relation to the child and his property' (CA 1989, s 3). That section of the Act includes the right of a person with parental responsibility to consent to medical treatment for and on behalf of a child. Valid consent to medical treatment of the immature minor is, accordingly, obtained from a person who has parental responsibility for that minor. The position of the mother and father of a child in relation to parental responsibility may be seen in ss 2 and 4 of the 1989 Act. Attention is drawn too to the new statutory provisions as to parental responsibility within s 12 of the 1989 Act. A local authority which has a care order in relation to a child will have parental responsibility for such child pursuant to CA 1989, s 33(3)(a).

Section 2(9) of the Act permits a person with parental responsibility 'to arrange for some or all of it to be met by one or more persons acting on his behalf'. This statutory provision does not permit a person with parental responsibility to surrender or transfer any part of his or her parental responsibility but might envisage, for example, a mother who is abroad for a period to delegate her authority to consent to medical treatment for the child to a relative. To what extent a consent to treatment by such a person would be treated by a medical practitioner as valid is untested and might depend, for example, on the scope of the arrangement between the mother and relative, the proof in writing or otherwise of such arrangement and the type of treatment required. Again, in relation to s 3(5) of CA 1989, it is untested as to what extent, if at all, a person who does not have parental responsibility for a child but has de facto care may consent to any medical treatment for and on behalf of the child or have any such consent accepted as valid.

It would certainly appear to be reasonable within s 3(5) for someone caring for a child, where the parent or parents are absent, to arrange routine medical treatment. In circumstances where the child may require more significant medical treatment, however, questions would inevitably arise as to whether the parents' permission could be sought and obtained. The consequences to the child of delaying any medical treatment would also, no doubt, be a factor for consideration. If the health of a child were seriously at risk and whether or not the terms of s 3(5) applied, the common law principles of necessity would entitle medical practitioners in the absence of parental consent to effect treatment which was in the best interests of the child. The agreement of the de facto carers to the medical treatment advised to be taken by the doctors in those circumstances would undoubtedly assist the child and doctors to reduce the scope for any controversy upon the re-appearance of the parent or parents with parental responsibility.

11.2.4   Disagreement between parents

A mother of a child – whether or not she and the father were married at the date of birth of the child – will have parental responsibility for that child. The father of a child will have parental responsibility for that child if, at the date of birth, he and the mother were married (CA 1989, s 2). If they were not so married, the father will acquire parental responsibility by his name being on the child's birth certificate as from the designated date, or may acquire parental responsibility by the mother and father entering into a 'parental responsibility agreement', as designated under the appropriate regulations or by the father applying to the court for an order granting him parental responsibility under s 4 of the Act. If the father has parental responsibility, he and the mother of the child may disagree as to proposed medical treatment for their child. As a matter of law, the consent of either parent will authorise such medical treatment. As was said in *Re R (A Minor) (Wardship: Medical Treatment)* [1992] 1 FLR 190 at 196:

> 'If the parents disagree, one consenting and the other refusing, the doctor will be presented with a professional and ethical but not with a legal problem because, if he has the consent of one authorised person, the treatment will not without more constitute a trespass or a criminal assault.'

11.3 PARENTAL REFUSAL OF MEDICAL TREATMENT FOR AND ON BEHALF OF THE IMMATURE CHILD: OVERRIDING SUCH REFUSAL IF IN THE BEST INTERESTS OF THE CHILD

A parent or parents or other person or body with parental responsibility will ordinarily be entitled to consent to or refuse treatment for and on behalf of the child, unless and until such minor achieves the necessary capacity himself or herself under the test in *Gillick v West Norfolk and Wisbech Area Health Authority* [1986] AC 112.

Although doctors/clinicians owe no legal duties of care to parents, they have legal obligations to give effect to their wishes unless superseded by the court. As was stated by Lord Donaldson in the case of *Re W* [1992] 3 WLR 758, co-operation between doctor and patient is at the heart of medical treatment if it is to be successful, and treatment which is imposed against the will of the patient is surely to be avoided wherever possible. Where there is, however, an issue/disagreement between the clinicians and parents over a medical treatment issue, the issue in question will need to be determined by the court. Until the court has ruled the views of the parents take precedence.

Thus, in the period between the issue of proceedings and the judgment the usual situation is that the views of the parents prevail unless clinicians cannot, consistent with their professional views, follow the parents' instructions: *Portsmouth NHS Trust v Wyatt* [2005] 1 WLR 3995. The latter judgment was that given by the Court of Appeal in that case.

In one of the judgments at first instance in the above case of *Wyatt*, reported at [2005] EWHC 693 (Fam), Hedley J was required to consider the contention that it was simply neither right nor practicable to give or withhold medical treatment against the wishes of parents. The judge's determination was as follows:

> 'I do not doubt that many will have sympathy with that view. It is not, however, the law. The best interests decision and thus its consequences in terms of treatment is committed to the judge where parents and professionals cannot agree. That means there must always be a real possibility of an outcome at variance with parental wishes. Of course, as I emphasised ... in my earlier judgment, the views of the parents must be accorded profound respect and given weight but they cannot be decisive.'

As can be seen in the following paragraphs below, where there is a disagreement between parents and clinicians over medical treatment the court's independent view, depending on the facts of the particular case, may sometimes coincide with the views of the parents or sometimes coincide with the views of the clinicians.

The court accordingly has the power under its parens patriae jurisdiction to overrule, if required, the refusal of a parent or parents to consent to medical treatment for and on behalf of an immature child.

11.3.1 The test for the court

The court's prime and paramount consideration will be the best interests of the minor (*Re J (A Minor) (Wardship: Medical Treatment)* [1991] 1 FLR 366 at 381). The court will scrutinise and balance the evidence presented to reach a decision in the best interests of the child.

In the decision in *Wyatt v Portsmouth NHS Trust* [2006] 1 FLR 554, the Court of Appeal set out the 'intellectual milestones' for the court to consider. They are:

(1) the judge must decide what is in the best interests of the child;

(2) in doing so, the child's welfare is a paramount consideration;

(3) the judge must look at it from the assumed point of view of the patient;

(4) there is a strong presumption in favour of the course of action that would prolong life but that presumption is not irrebuttable;

(5) the term 'best interests' encompasses medical, emotional and all other welfare issues; and

(6) the court must conduct a balancing exercise in which all relevant factors are weighed.

The court performs accordingly a balancing act bringing all the relevant expert evidence and other evidence before it so as to enable the court to decide whether the proposed treatment is or is not in the minor's best interests.

11.3.2 The views of the parents and the court's balancing exercise

Since it is the parents' view which may or may not be overruled by the court, necessarily their views and the reasons for their refusal of proposed medical treatment for their child must be carefully considered. Per Sir Thomas Bingham MR in *Re Z (A Minor) (Identification: Restrictions on Publication)* [1997] Fam 1 at 32–33:

'I would for my part accept without reservation that the decision of a devoted and responsible parent should be treated with respect. It should certainly not be disregarded or lightly set aside. But the role of the Court is to exercise an independent and objective judgment. If that judgment is in accord with that of the devoted and responsible parent, well and good. If it is not, then it is the duty of the Court, after giving due weight to the view of the devoted and responsible parent, to give effect to its own judgment. That is what it is there for. Its judgment may of course be wrong. So may that of the parent. But once the jurisdiction of the Court is invoked its clear duty is to reach and express the best judgment it can.'

Liver transplant operation

In *Re T (A Minor) (Wardship: Medical Treatment)* [1997] 1 FLR 502, T was born in April 1995 with a life-threatening liver defect and an operation when he was 3½ weeks old was unsuccessful. The unanimous medical prognosis was that he would not live beyond the age of 2 to 2½ years without a liver transplant. It was equally the unanimous clinical opinion of the consultants that it was in his best interests to undergo the operation when a donor liver became available. The parents, healthcare professionals, had gone with their baby son to live and work abroad. They did not wish him to undergo a transplant and refused consent to an operation should a suitable liver become available. The doctors in England treating T referred the matter to the relevant local authority, which applied, pursuant to CA 1989, s 100(3), for the court to exercise its inherent wardship jurisdiction. The court at first instance overruled the parents' refusal. The Court of Appeal allowed the parents' appeal and refused to overrule the parents' decision. They held that the judge at first instance had erred in categorising the mother as unreasonable simply because the clinical evidence was to the effect that the child was a good candidate for a transplant with good prospects of a favourable outcome. The deep rooted concern of the mother was as to the benefits to her son of the major invasive surgery and post-operative treatment, the dangers of failure, long-term as well as short-term, the possibility of the need for further transplants, the likely length of life and the effect upon her of all these concerns. The judge had not, it was held, sufficiently taken into account the relevance or the weight of such considerations in his final balancing exercise.

There were broader factors beyond the clinical evidence as to the prospects of success of a transplant to be taken into account. First, the doctor involved and his team, while strongly recommending the operation, wished to respect the decision of the mother and were not willing to perform the operation without her consent. Coercing the mother, so to speak, would not assist the child, given the importance of the total co-operation of the mother with the operation and the consequent treatment. Secondly, there were all manner of difficulties in implementing the order with the child and parents abroad – not because the parents would not comply with a court order but because of the disturbance to their lives and the re-adjustments that would be required to have to come back to this country. It was not disputed that the parents were loving and caring parents. Butler-Sloss LJ, at p 510, took the view that 'this mother and this child were one for the purpose of an unusual case'. Whilst it has been suggested that *Re T* places greater weight and emphasis on the parental view, the Court of Appeal made quite clear that each case would turn on its own facts, that the case was unusual and that the test remained the same: namely, the paramount consideration was the welfare and best interests of the child.

Downs syndrome

In *Re B (A Minor) (Wardship: Medical Treatment)* [1981] 1 WLR 1421, the parents' refusal to consent to an operation on their baby girl suffering from Downs syndrome was overruled by the Court of Appeal. They held that the operation was to go ahead against the parents' wishes. The parents took the view that the kindest course in their daughter's best interests was for her not to have the operation. The local authority felt she could have a happy and settled home life through long-term fostering or adoption.

The baby girl was born suffering from Down's syndrome and had an intestinal blockage from which she would die within a very short period of time unless she had an operation. If she had the operation, there was a considerable risk that she would suffer from heart trouble and die within 2 or 3 months. If, on the other hand, the operation was successful, she would have a life expectancy of some 20–30 years, during which time she would be very handicapped mentally and physically. The child was made a ward of court.

The local authority contended that the operation should go ahead, adding that provision would be made, if necessary, for the child to be cared for through long-term fostering or adoption. The parents opposed the operation, feeling that it was in their daughter's best interests to let nature take its course. The judge at first instance decided that it was in the child's best interests that she should not have the operation. The Court of Appeal disagreed and overruled the parents' refusal, stating that the operation should proceed.

Blood transfusions: Jehovah's Witnesses

In *Re S (A Minor) (Medical Treatment)* [1993] 1 FLR 376, the child, aged 4½ years, was diagnosed as suffering from T-cell leukaemia with a high risk of death. His parents were dedicated Jehovah's Witnesses and his family records and instructions had always opposed blood transfusions. The parents were supportive of any form of medical or scientific intervention, provided it did not breach the veto upon the use of blood. The evidence established that either the doctors in whose care the child was had the authority to treat S intensively with the discretion to administer blood, or there was no medical treatment which held any prospect of care for the child. An argument contended on the parents' behalf was that, if the treatment was applied in the face of parental opposition, this would act to the child's detriment in years to come since he would be being parented by parents who believed his life was prolonged by 'an ungodly act'. Thorpe J, as he then was, took the view that such an argument had little foundation in reality and, by his decision, the family were to recognise that responsibility for the consent to the blood transfusion was taken by the court and absolved their conscience of responsibility. Other 'Jehovah's Witnesses cases' involving overruling parental opposition are: *Re E (A Minor)* (1990) 9 BMLR 1; *Re R (A Minor) (Blood Transfusion)* [1993] 2 FLR 757; *Re S (A Minor) (Consent to Medical Treatment)* [1994] 2 FLR 1065 and *Re L (Medical Treatment: Gillick Competence)* [1998] 2 FLR 810. There is also the transfusion case of *X NHS Trust v T (Adult Patient: Refusal of Medical Treatment)* [2004] EWHC 1279 (Fam).

For legal and medical practitioners involved in any such case (both adults and minors), the handbook entitled *Family Care and Medical Management for Jehovah's Witnesses* sets out in detail the approach of Jehovah's Witnesses, founded on deep religious convictions, to their refusal of blood transfusions, yet their acceptance of most medical and surgical treatments available as well as their willingness to accept alternative treatments to blood transfusions such as 'non-blood expanders'.

Bone marrow transplant

In *An NHS Trust v A (A Child)* [2007] EWHC 1696 (Fam), the court was concerned with a baby of 7 months of age whose medical condition had caused her to be very ill; without treatment it was medically certain that she would die, probably by about the age of one. The only effective treatment was a bone marrow transplant. In the circumstances of the case, doctors estimated that such a transplant had about a 50% prospect of effecting a lasting cure so that she would then have a normal life expectancy. There was also about a 10% prospect that she would die during and as a direct result of the treatment; a 30% prospect that the treatment would not be successful and she would still die from the underlying condition she had; there was a 10% prospect that although surviving she might have some significant impairment. The treatment would be lengthy, painful and distressing. The child's parents believed that their daughter should enjoy the quality of such life as remained to her and not undergo the treatment. They felt their daughter had already suffered greatly as they had witnessed. They wished to spare her further suffering and to prolong as long as possible the quality of life she currently had. They believed too that God might yet cure her. The doctors strongly disagreed with the views and perspectives of the parents and asked the court, in place of the parents, to give the necessary permission or consent for the treatment to take place.

The judge, Holman J, said he had become convinced having heard the evidence that it was in the overall best interests of the baby to undergo a bone marrow transplant. He said as follows:

> 'If a bone marrow transplant could only prolong by a relatively short period her life; or if it would leave her alive but probably seriously impaired (e.g. significantly brain damaged) then I would or might take a different view. But in my view a 50% prospect of a full, normal life (even though infertile) when set against the certainty of death before the age of one or one and a half, does in this case outweigh all other considerations and disadvantages. If the opportunity of a bone marrow transplant is not taken, a very real prospect of a full life, weighed against certain death, will have been lost for a few more months of babyhood. A is more than merely a baby. She is a living human being, with a future as well as a present, to whom, despite her disease, modern medicine and science may be able to give a full life. In a case which includes a strong reference to God and religion, I am deeply conscious of my fallibility. But I am convinced that A should be given that opportunity. I hope that the parents will feel able to accept my judgment. Whatever her future and outcome, A and her family will remain deeply in my thoughts.'

MMR vaccine

In the case of *F v F (MMR Vaccine)* [2013] EWHC 2683 (Fam) the father applied for a declaration and a specific issue order concerning his daughters L and M, who were 15 years and 11 years of age respectively. He sought an order that they both receive the MMR vaccination. This was opposed by the mother.

This was the type of issue concerning the exercise of parental responsibility, that in most cases is negotiated between parents and their decision is then put into effect. It will often involve discussion and explanation by parents of their decision to their children which may sometimes be against their wishes and feelings.

In this particular case the parents could not agree and thus it was for the court to determine the issue. The legal framework was not in issue. The paramount consideration of the court was the welfare of each of the two children. In considering their welfare the court was necessarily guided by the matters set out in the welfare checklist in CA 1989, s 1(3).

The older child, L, had been inoculated by agreement between the parents soon after the birth. Later on following the public debate on the alleged concerns over the vaccine, the parents decided in consultation with their GP that L should not receive a booster and M should not be vaccinated at all. The parents separated, and the context of the application was that the father had become increasingly concerned that the girls had not been immunised and were not protected. He was concerned about the serious consequences of contracting measles, mumps and rubella. The need for children to have protection had been brought into sharper focus following the recent outbreak of measles in Wales.

The father claimed he was a reluctant participant in the joint decision not to inoculate. The mother in opposing the application contended she was concerned about the side-effects of vaccination; the father's change of position; the impact of the vaccination as being undertaken against her children's wishes; and the fact that L was a vegan whose objection was based partly on the fact that the vaccine contained animal-based ingredients. The judge, Theis J, reached the conclusion that it was in the best interests of each of the children that they receive the MMR vaccination. Amongst the detailed reasons given, the judge said:

> 'Obviously in reaching this decision I am aware this is against the girls' wishes, but that is not the only factor. It is of course an important factor, particularly bearing in mind their ages but the court also has to consider their level of understanding of the issues involved and what factors have influenced their views. In this case I do not consider there is a balanced level of understanding by them of the issues involved, the focus has been on the negative aspects in a somewhat unfocused way ... The medical advice is for the children to receive the vaccine even though it is accepted there are risks of side effects of the vaccine. The health risk of getting any of the diseases the vaccine prevents is clear. They are serious diseases that could have long-term health consequences.'

Radiotherapy and chemotherapy

In the case of *An NHS Trust v SR* [2012] EWHC 3842 (Fam) before Bodey J, the court was concerned with a young boy aged 7 who was suffering from a malignant brain tumour. The consultant paediatric oncologist and the multidisciplinary team of child cancer experts at the hospital treating him were of the opinion that following surgery the child required radiotherapy and chemotherapy. Generally speaking such a treatment package has about an 80% success rate, sometimes put at 86%. The father, the NHS trust and the Guardian contended that the radiotherapy and chemotherapy should be delivered to the child as soon as possible. The mother strongly opposed the treatment proposed, believing that there were alternative methods of treatment which should be used and which would avoid or reduce the undoubtedly detrimental long-term side-effects of the treatment package being proposed. The judge acceded to the application by the NHS Trust for the treatment to proceed, determining that such course was in the best interests of the child. In considering the application the judge accepted that the advantages of the proposed treatment had to be balanced against the disadvantages of which there were several. Those disadvantages are considered within the judgment as well as, of course, the countervailing advantages. The judge heard evidence, including from the consultant paediatric oncologist with hands-on responsibility for the treatment of the child. He told the court how his team strove to strike the necessary balance in giving their child patients treatment which had the best possible rate of survival, but with the least possible detrimental side effects. There was plainly insufficient evidence in relation to the possible benefits of any credible alternative therapies which might work for such very young children.

11.4 A CHILD'S RIGHTS TO CONSENT TO MEDICAL TREATMENT

11.4.1 A child's common law right to consent

At common law, a child of sufficient intelligence and understanding (a '*Gillick*-competent' child) can consent to medical treatment, notwith-standing absence of the parents' consent or any express prohibition by them (*Re W (A Minor) (Medical Treatment: Court's Jurisdiction)* [1992] 3 WLR 758 at 764G–H).

In *Gillick v West Norfolk and Wisbech Area Health Authority* [1986] AC 112, the central issue was whether parents could effectively impose a veto on medical treatment for a child patient under the age of 16 years by failing or refusing to consent to treatment to which the child might consent. Mrs Gillick was not challenging the right of a Wardship Court to exercise its parens patriae jurisdiction. She asserted an absolute right of veto on the part of parents generally and herself in particular on medical advice and treatment in relation to their children under the age of 16. The House of Lords decisively rejected her contentions, holding that a child of sufficient intelligence and understanding could consent to medical treatment, notwithstanding any refusal of consent by his or her parents.

The facts of the Gillick case

The case was based on Mrs Victoria Gillick's concern to challenge the legality of a 'Memorandum of Guidance' issued by the Department of Health and Social Security which advised that:

(1) there was a clear need for contraceptive services to be available for, and accessible to, young people at risk of pregnancy irrespective of age;

(2) it was for the doctor to decide whether to provide contraceptive advice and treatment; and

(3) the Medical Defence Union had advised that the parents of a child, of whatever age, independently seeking advice and treatment should not be contacted by any staff without the permission of that child.

None of Mrs Gillick's daughters, then aged 13, 12, 10 and 5, contemplated engaging in sexual intercourse in the immediate future or had sought or were likely independently to seek contraceptive advice or treatment. However, Mrs Gillick, in the absence of assurances she requested, sought declarations that the 'Memorandum of Guidance' was unlawful and against the authority that no doctor was entitled, as a matter of law, to give contraceptive advice and/or abortion advice to any of her children under the age of 16 without her consent.

The Gillick competency test

It was held in the *Gillick* case that a child can consent to treatment on his or her own behalf when he or she achieves a sufficient understanding and intelligence to enable him or her to understand fully what is proposed.

It is a question of fact in each case whether a child seeking advice or 'consenting' to treatment has sufficient understanding of what is involved to give a consent valid in law.

In the case of *Re R (A Minor) (Wardship: Medical Treatment)* [1992] 1 FLR 190, the court was concerned with a minor of 15 years with problems of mental health and disturbed behaviour. The court at first instance and in the Court of Appeal accepted that she lacked the necessary capacity to consent or refuse consent to the proposed treatment. At p 200, Lord Donaldson said:

> 'But even if she was capable, on a good day, of a sufficient degree of understanding to meet the *Gillick* criteria, her mental disability, to the cure or amelioration of which the proposed treatment was directed, was such that on other days she was not only '*Gillick*-incompetent', but actually sectionable. No child in that situation can be regarded as '*Gillick*-competent' and the Judge was wholly right in so finding in relation to R.'

In *Re K, W and H (Minors) (Medical Treatment)* [1993] 1 FLR 854 at 859, Thorpe J, as he then was, said:

> '*Gillick* competency is a developmental concept and will not be lost or acquired on a day to day or week to week basis.'

In *Re W (A Minor) (Medical Treatment: Court Jurisdiction)* [1992] 3 WLR 758, the court was concerned with a girl who had attained 16 years of age and suffered from anorexia nervosa of a serious nature. The Court of Appeal doubted whether the child had sufficient understanding to make the medical choice she had. It was said in the Court of Appeal that 'it is a feature of anorexia nervosa that it is capable of destroying the ability to make an informed choice'.

In *Re L (Medical Treatment: Gillick Competency)* [1998] 2 FLR 810, it was vital for the 14-year-old female patient who had suffered severe burns and was in a life-threatening condition to receive a blood transfusion or transfusions. Her sincere and strong wish was not to have a blood transfusion on the basis of her religious beliefs as a Jehovah's Witness. The President of the Family Division, Sir Stephen Brown, determined, on the evidence, that she was not '*Gillick*-competent', in that she had not been provided with sufficient information as to the grave consequences, including the manner of her death, flowing from her refusal to have been able to make a suitably informed choice. The judge made an order permitting the medical treatment required, despite the fact that L did not consent.

The right of a Gillick-competent minor to consent to treatment can be overridden by the court

A minor of any age who is '*Gillick*-competent' in the context of a particular treatment has a right to consent to that treatment, which cannot be overridden by those with parental responsibility, but can be overridden by the court (*Re W* [1992] 3 WLR 758 at 772).

11.4.2 A child's statutory right to consent

Section 8 of the Family Law Reform Act 1969 gives children who have attained the age of 16 years a right to consent to surgical, medical or dental treatment. Such a consent cannot be overridden by those with parental responsibility for the minor. It can, however, be overridden by the court.

11.4.3 Donation of organs or blood

Section 8 of the 1969 Act does not extend to permit a minor who has attained 16 years to consent to the donation of organs or blood. The common law right of a child of any age who is '*Gillick*-competent' to consent to treatment extends to the donation of blood or organs. It is uncontroversial that a *Gillick*-competent child of any age would be able to consent to give blood under the common law. In relation, however, to so serious a procedure as the donation of an organ by a child of whatever age, it is most unlikely, for one, or both, of two reasons, that medical practitioners would act solely on the consent of the child and without the full consent of the child's parents. First, it would be hard for a doctor to be satisfied that any child under the age of 18 was *Gillick*-competent in the context of so serious a procedure which could not benefit the child. Secondly, as a matter of ethics and professional duty in respect of the best interests of the minor, it is 'inconceivable', to use the words of Lord Donaldson in *Re W* [1992] 3 WLR 758 at 767:

> 'that he (the doctor) would proceed in reliance solely upon the consent of an underage patient, however *Gillick*-competent in the absence of supporting parental consent ...'

11.5   A CHILD'S RIGHTS TO REFUSE CONSENT TO MEDICAL TREATMENT

11.5.1   No absolute right of any minor to refuse medical treatment

Unlike an adult, any child of any age, including one who is '*Gillick*-competent' does not have an absolute right to refuse medical treatment.

11.5.2   The parental right to consent to treatment on behalf of a child who is refusing treatment

If a child of any age refuses treatment, a parent or parents, or other person or body with parental responsibility, may consent to such treatment for and on the child's behalf and thus override the child's refusal. This applies even if the minor is '*Gillick*-competent'. A parent or parents, or other person or body with parental responsibility, may consent to treatment against the child's wishes and, as a matter of law, the doctor is then authorised and able to treat the minor according to his or her clinical judgment.

In *Re K, W and H (Minors) (Medical Treatment)* [1993] 1 FLR 854, a highly specialised unit for adolescents with disturbed behaviour sought relief from the court under s 8 of the Children Act 1989 in circumstances where three patients had complained about and refused the provision in the unit to them of medication in an emergency. Two of the girls in question were 15 years old and evinced highly disturbed behaviour. The third girl was not quite 15 years old and suffered from mental illness. The parent or parents of each of the three minors consented to the medical treatment provided, including the emergency medication. Thorpe J, as he then was, repeated the principle that where a child, including one who is *Gillick*-competent refused medical treatment, consent can be given by someone else who has parental responsibility:

> '... None of these three is *Gillick*-competent and even if they were *Gillick*-competent it is manifest that their refusal of consent would not expose doctor B ... to the risk of criminal or civil proceedings if he proceeded to administer medication in emergency and in the face of such refusal since in each instance he has a parental consent ...'.

The judge was unwilling to make any orders on the unit's applications and emphasised that applications to the court should be discouraged since it was established that a parental consent would suffice to authorise medical treatment, even if a minor was refusing, as in that case, medication.

Given the principles set out above as to parental consent in the face of a minor's refusal of treatment, 'hair-raising possibilities' were canvassed before the court in *Re W (A Minor) (Medical Treatment: Court's Jurisdiction)* [1992] 3 WLR 758 at 767 as to abortions being carried out by doctors, in reliance upon the consent of parents and despite the refusal of consent by 16- and 17-year-olds. It seems a remote proposition that a doctor would, in these circumstances, be willing to exercise his or her clinical judgment so as to overrule the minor's wishes, notwithstanding the parents' consent. It is to be emphasised that the parental consent, on general principles, only authorises or permits the doctor to treat if he or she sees fit, according to his or her clinical judgment. Lord Donaldson, at p 767 said that:

> 'Whilst this may be possible as a matter of law, I do not see any likelihood taking account of medical ethics, unless the abortion was truly in the best interests of the child.'

He further said that a safeguard was that:

> 'The inherent jurisdiction of the court could still be invoked in such a case to prevent an abortion which was contrary to the interests of the minor.'

11.6 THE POWER OF THE COURT TO OVERRULE A CHILD'S REFUSAL OF CONSENT TO TREATMENT

11.6.1 The wide powers of the court to overrule a child's refusal

In the absence of parental consent or otherwise, the court has power to override, if it sees fit, a refusal to consent to treatment of a child over 16 years of age, or under that age but *Gillick*-competent (*Re W (A Minor) (Medical Treatment: Court's Jurisdiction)* [1992] 3 WLR 758 at 769):

> 'There is ample authority for the proposition that the inherent powers of the Court under its parens patriae jurisdiction are theoretically limitless and that they certainly extend beyond the powers of a natural parent ... There can therefore be no doubt that it has power to override the refusal of a minor, whether over the age of sixteen or under that age but "*Gillick*-competent". It does not do so by ordering the doctors to treat which, even if within the Court's powers, would be an abuse of them or by ordering the minor to accept treatment, but by authorising the doctors to treat the minor in accordance with their clinical judgment, subject to any restrictions which the Court may impose.'

11.6.2   The child's views

The refusal of the child and his or her age, maturity and understanding and wishes and feelings will weigh importantly:

(a)   in any decision by the parent whether to consent to the treatment, notwithstanding the minor's refusal;

(b)   concerning whether or how the medical practitioner chooses to treat the minor notwithstanding any consent by the parent or court;

(c)   concerning whether the court should grant leave for the treatment to occur against the minor's wishes.

In relation to the law, in the words of Balcombe LJ in *Re W* [1992] 3 WLR 758 at 776:

> 'As children approach the age of majority they are increasingly able to take their own decisions concerning their medical treatment ... it will normally be in the best interests of a child of sufficient age and understanding to make an informed decision that the court should respect its integrity as a human being and not lightly override its decision on such a personal matter as medical treatment. All the more so if that treatment is invasive.'

11.6.3   Whether or not the child lacks capacity

It is axiomatic, in cases of refusal of treatment by minors, that the court will wish to scrutinise whether or not the minor has the capacity to refuse within the requisite test. The test to be applied will be either the '*Gillick*-competency' test or the three-stage test of Thorpe J, as he then was, set out in the case of *Re C (Adult: Refusal of Medical Treatment)* [1994] 1 FLR 31.

Re L (Medical Treatment: Gillick Competence) [1998] 2 FLR 810, concerned a 14-year-old female patient who had suffered severe burns and was in a life-threatening condition. As a Jehovah's Witness, she was refusing consent to a blood transfusion on the grounds of her sincerely-held religious beliefs. The court applied the '*Gillick*-competency' test and, for reasons already indicated in relation to this case, determined her to be not '*Gillick*-competent'. In *A Metropolitan Borough Council v DB* [1997] 1 FLR 767, Cazalet J was concerned with a female minor aged 17 years. She was described as 'a simple soul' with a large number of difficulties. The judge applied the three-stage test of *Re C* and found that she failed each of the three stages.

Consent will be more readily given by the court, it appears, for medical treatment of a child against his or her wishes, and notwithstanding his or her refusal, if the child is determined by the court to be lacking in capacity. In *Re R (A Minor) (Wardship: Medical Treatment)* [1992] 1 FLR 190 and in *Re W (A Minor)* [1992] 3 WLR 758, the children in question were viewed to be lacking in capacity. So also was the case in *Re K, W and H (Minors) (Medical Treatment)* [1993] 1 FLR 854 and in *Re L (Medical Treatment: Gillick Competency)* [1998] 2 FLR 810. In the latter case of *Re L*, however, the court made clear that, even if the patient was '*Gillick*-competent', the court would still have overriden her refusal to consent to medical treatment since such treatment was determined by the court to be in her best interests.

11.6.4 Serious medical treatment cases where child near to the age of majority is refusing treatment for a life-threatening condition

Two separate cases before Johnson J illustrate the dilemma for the court in serious medical treatment cases where the child is near to the age of majority and refusing treatment for a life-threatening condition.

In *Re M (Medical Treatment: Consent)* [1999] 2 FLR 1097, a 15-year-old girl refused to consent to the heart transplant which was needed to save her life. The girl's reasons for refusing consent were that she did not want to have someone else's heart, and did not wish to take medication for the rest of her life. The hospital, which had obtained the mother's consent to the treatment, sought leave from the court to carry out the heart transplant. The court authorised the hospital to get medical treatment according to the doctors' clinical judgment, including a heart transplant. The court determined that the girl was an intelligent young person, whose wishes carried considerable weight, but that she had been overwhelmed by the circumstances and the decision she was being asked to make. Her severe condition had developed only very recently, she had had only a few days to consider her situation. While recognising the risk that for the rest of her life she would carry resentment about what had been done to her, the court weighed that risk against the certainty of death if the order were not made.

In the case of *Re P (A Minor)* [2003] EWHC 2327 (Fam) the child was nearly 17 years of age and was steadfastly refusing the wish of doctors to administer blood or blood products to seek to remedy severe bleeding rising from his inherited condition called 'hypermobility syndrome'. He was a staunch and committed Jehovah's Witness. The immediate medical crisis passed but the clinicians felt the risk remained because the precise cause of the child's medical difficulties remained unidentified. The doctors had made every attempt possible to prevent further bleeding and to improve the child's blood count without giving him any blood products. However it remained possible that there would be a further episode (such as that which had recently occurred) and in the opinion of the doctors, the child might well not survive without the administration of blood or blood products.

The doctors made it clear that they were not planning to give blood unless there were signs of acute bleeding and imminent deterioration in the child's condition which would be irreversible. The hospital sought leave from the court to administer blood if the child's situation became 'immediately life-threatening'. The judge acceded to the application, notwithstanding the child's age and opposition, making clear that such leave would be granted providing there was no reasonable practical alternative treatment. The judge was mindful of the reality that when a child reaches 18, as an autonomous adult then he or she is entirely able to refuse any medical treatment, whatever the consequences, providing of course that they have capacity. However he took the view that the proposed medical treatment, if required, was in the 17-year-old child's best interests.

11.6.5   The 'best interests of the child' test

Beyond the question of capacity, the court will wish to scrutinise all the evidence and make a decision as to whether it is in the best interests of the minor to overrule his or her refusal to accept treatment. In *Re R (A Minor) (Wardship: Medical Treatment)* [1992] 1 FLR 190, the 15-year-old minor who suffered from disturbed behaviour said she did not want or need the drugs prescribed. Within wardship proceedings, the local authority applied for leave for the unit to administer such medication as was necessary without the girl's consent. The application was granted. In *Re W (A Minor)* [1992] 3 WLR 758, the minor had attained 16 years and was suffering from severe anorexia nervosa. The court held that her best interests required the court to direct her immediate transfer to and treatment at a new unit without her consent.

11.6.6   Power of the court to order the detention of a child for treatment and the use of reasonable force incidental to treatment

The powers of the court under the inherent jurisdiction are extremely wide and the court will not hesitate to give leave for medical treatment to be effected against the minor's wishes if that is required in the minor's best interests, including authorising the use of force. In the case of *Re C (Detention: Medical Treatment)* [1997] 2 FLR 180, the extent of the court's powers under the inherent jurisdiction was considered by Wall J. The 16-year-old minor suffered from anorexia nervosa. The local authority funded her treatment at a private specialist clinic, yet C absconded from the clinic many times. Her behaviour had become disturbed and suicidal. Doctors at the clinic in question regarded the minor's enforced presence at the clinic under an order of the court as an essential component of her treatment and were not prepared to treat her without such an order. The local authority obtained leave to invoke the court's inherent jurisdiction and sought orders authorising C's detention at the clinic and the administration of medical treatment without her consent. Residence at the clinic was an essential component of her treatment. It was clearly in the minor's best interests to be treated. The court directed that the child should be detained as an in-patient at the clinic for the purposes of medical treatment, using reasonable force if necessary. Notwithstanding that the clinic did not constitute secure accommodation and that, accordingly, the provisions of CA 1989, s 25 could not apply, detention of the minor against her wishes could be so authorised by the court within the parameters of its inherent jurisdiction. Given the safeguards applying to any order made under CA 1989, s 25, the court was anxious to provide similar safeguards, and the order provided for C to be discharged from the clinic if the doctors judged that the reasons for her detention no longer applied, and required the clinic to consult with C's parents and the local authority on its treatment plans. It also gave liberty for all parties to apply on short notice to a High Court judge.

In *A Metropolitan Borough Council v DB* [1997] 1 FLR 767, the 17-year-old girl in question, who had a crack cocaine addiction, was in a hospital ward and currently agreeing to necessary treatment. The real concern was that, if she later refused treatment, her condition could deteriorate and a crisis situation could develop which could be fatal if she was not treated within hours. The order made by Cazalet J was in these terms:

> 'Upon it being determined that [the minor] is competent neither to consent to nor to refuse medical treatment, such reasonable force may be authorised by the local authority to be used to implement such medical treatment to [the minor] as may be considered necessary by the doctors concerned for her to prevent her death or serious deterioration in her health.'

11.6.7   Abortion and young persons

The case of *Re X (A Child)* [2014] EWHC 1871 (Fam) concerned a 13-year-old child who was 14 weeks pregnant by a boy aged 14. The child was at the time the subject of ongoing care proceedings. The issue before the court was whether or not the pregnancy should be terminated.

The 13-year-old pregnant child lacked *Gillick* capacity and could not in law give a valid consent. Notwithstanding this, it was still important, in relation to such a personal and intimate issue as pregnancy, to attach such weight as was possible to the wishes and feelings of the child in her qualified autonomy.

The judge agreed with the medical expert that it would not be right to subject X to a termination unless she was both compliant and accepting. Whilst she could not give a valid consent, something 'of the nature of consent or agreement, using those words in the colloquial sense, is required. The consultant's word "accepting" in my judgment captures the nuance very well'.

The judge declared that it would be lawful, as being in X's best interests, for a doctor treating her to carry out a termination in accordance with the criteria set out in s 1 of the Abortion Act 1967 notwithstanding her incapacity to provide legal consent, subject to her being compliant and accepting of such medical procedure.

At paragraph 9 of the judgment the court gave the following guidance:

> 'I leave on one side cases where the mother has for whatever reason so little appreciation of what is going on as not to be able to express any wishes and feelings. This, I emphasise, is not such a case. The point is very simple and profoundly important. This court in exercise of its inherent jurisdiction in relation to children undoubtedly has power to authorise the use of restraint and physical force to compel a child to submit to a surgical procedure: see *Re C (Detention: Medical Treatment)* [1997] 2 FLR 180 and *Re PS (Incapacitated or Vulnerable Adult)* [2007] EWHC 623 (Fam), [2007] 2 FLR 1083. I say nothing about how this power should appropriately be exercised in the case of other forms of medical or surgical intervention. In the case of the proposed termination of a pregnancy, however, the point surely is this. Only the most compelling arguments could possibly justify compelling a mother who wished to carry her child to term to submit to an unwanted termination. It would be unwise to be too prescriptive, for every case must be judged on its own unique facts, but I find it hard to conceive of any case where such a drastic form of order – such an immensely invasive procedure – could be appropriate in the case of a mother who does not want a termination, unless there was powerful evidence that allowing the pregnancy to continue would put the mother's life or long-term health at very grave risk. Conversely, it would be a very strong thing indeed, if the mother wants a termination, to require her to

continue with an unwanted pregnancy even though the conditions in section 1 of the 1967 Act are satisfied.'

The power of the court to override a child's refusal to submit to medical examination under CA 1989, s 38(6) and to direct the child to be medically examined, assessed and treated

In *South Glamorgan County Council v W and B* [1993] 1 FCR 626, the court was concerned with a girl aged 15 years. She had long-standing behavioural problems. She had confined herself to the front room of her father's house with curtains drawn for approximately 11 months, and had had hardly any contact with the outside world. The local authority commenced care proceedings. The judge made an interim care order with the direction under CA 1989, s 38(6) for her to receive psychiatric examination and assessment and, if necessary, to be treated at an adolescent unit and to remain there during assessment. In the event, the minor did not consent to go to the unit. Leave was granted to the local authority under s 100(3) of the 1989 Act to bring proceedings to invoke the exercise of the inherent jurisdiction on the grounds that the result which the local authority wished to achieve could not be so achieved through the making of any order to which s 100(5) applied and there was real cause to believe that, if the inherent jurisdiction of the court was not exercised with respect to the child, she was likely to suffer significant harm. It was held that there was inherent power under the parens patriae jurisdiction to override the refusal of a minor, whether over the age of 16 or under that age, to submit to assessment and medical examination and treatment if it was in her best interests and notwithstanding that she might be of sufficient understanding to make an informed decision about a medical examination or psychiatric examination or assessment.

The court further determined that, in an appropriate case where other remedies under CA 1989 had been exhausted and found not to bring about the desired result, there was jurisdiction to resort to other remedies, and the particular remedy was to provide the authority for doctors to treat the child and authority, if it was needed, for the local authority to take all necessary steps to bring the child to the doctors so that she could be assessed and treated properly. On the facts, it was directed that the child should be admitted to the adolescent unit in her own interests without any further delay.

11.7   THE UNBORN CHILD

The legal status of the unborn child has arisen and been considered in the courts in differing applications and circumstances.

11.7.1   Applications by a father to prevent a mother having an abortion

In *Paton v The British Pregnancy Advisory Service Trustees* [1979] QB 276, a father made an unsuccessful attempt to obtain an injunction in the High Court to prevent his wife having an abortion. It was held that the foetus, in English law, does not have a right of its own, at least until it is born and does not have a separate existence from its mother until it is born.

In *C v S* [1987] 2 FLR 505, a High Court judge refused relief to an unborn child on that occasion named as the 'second plaintiff', in an attempt by the father to prevent the mother having an abortion. The judge referred to a number of decisions in Canada stating that an unborn child was not a person and any rights accorded to the foetus were held contingent upon its subsequent birth alive.

11.7.2   Applications toward an unborn child

In *Re F (In Utero) (Wardship)* [1988] 2 FLR 307, a local authority attempted to make the unborn child of a mentally disturbed mother a ward of court. The Court of Appeal upheld the judge at first instance, in determining that the court did not have power to ward a foetus. Balcombe LJ, in his judgment, considered s 1 of the Infant Life (Preservation) Act 1929 and Article 2 of the ECHR and found that neither supported the local authority on the issue of the wardship of the unborn child. He said, at p 325C:

> 'Approaching the question as one of principle, in my judgment, there is no jurisdiction to make an unborn child a ward of court. Since an unborn child has, ex hypothesi, no existence independent of its mother, the only purpose of extending the jurisdiction to include a foetus is to enable the mother's actions to be controlled. Indeed that is the purpose of the present application.'

11.7.3   The interests of the unborn child where the mother refuses medical intervention

Where a pregnant mother is determined by the court, as in *Re MB (Medical Treatment)* [1997] 2 FLR 426, to be not competent, medical intervention will occur in the best interests of the adult patient and consequently the interests of the unborn child will be protected.

Two cases have considered at length the position in law of the unborn child. In both, the mothers required Caesarean operations. In *Re MB (Medical Treatment)*, the mother was agreeable to a Caesarean operation but, at the last moment, was overwhelmed by a fear of needles and withdrew her consent to the operation. Without the anaesthetic, the Caesarean operation could not occur. A declaration was granted that it would be lawful for the consultant in question to operate on her using reasonable force if necessary. The Court of Appeal held that, at the time of her refusal, the patient was temporarily incompetent. The Court of Appeal considered at length the status of the unborn child:

> 'The law is, in our judgment, clear that a competent woman who has the capacity to decide may, for religious reasons, other reasons, or for no reasons at all, choose not to have medical intervention, even though, as we have already stated, the consequence may be the death or serious handicap of the child she bears or her own death. She may refuse to consent to the anaesthesia injection in the full knowledge that her decision may significantly reduce the chance of her unborn child being born alive. The foetus up to the moment of birth does not have any separate interests capable of being taken into account when a court has to consider an application for a declaration in respect of a Caesarean section operation. The court does not have the jurisdiction to declare that such medical intervention is lawful to protect the interests of the unborn child even at the point of birth.'

In *St George's Healthcare NHS Trust v S* [1998] 2 FLR 728, the mother, a veterinary nurse, wanted a natural birth. She underwent no ante-natal care. At 36 weeks of her pregnancy she was found to be suffering from pre-eclampsia and was advised that she needed to be admitted to hospital for an induced delivery and that, without such treatment, her health and life and the life of her baby were in danger. She fully understood the potential risks but rejected the advice. She was admitted to hospital against her will. A judge was asked to and did grant a declaration dispensing with her consent to treatment and, thereafter, her baby was born by Caesarean section. She applied to the Court of Appeal, who allowed her appeal, holding that, as a competent adult at the time, her refusal of treatment was fully justified on the grounds of her right of self-determination and should not have been overridden, notwithstanding that such refusal jeopardised the life not only of herself but also that of her unborn child. In relation to the status of the unborn child and protection to be afforded to it, at p 746 of that authority, the Court of Appeal summarised the position as follows:

'In our judgment while pregnancy increases the personal responsibilities of a woman it does not diminish her entitlement to decide whether or not to undergo medical treatment. Although human, and protected by the law in a number of different ways set out in the judgment in *Re MB*, an unborn child is not a separate person from its mother. Its need for medical assistance does not prevail over her rights. She is entitled not to be forced to submit to an invasion of her body against her will, whether her own life or that of her unborn child depends on it. Her right is not reduced or diminished merely because her decision to exercise it may appear morally repugnant. The declaration in this case involved the removal of the baby from within the body of her mother under physical compulsion. Unless lawfully justified, this constituted an infringement of the mother's autonomy. Of themselves the perceived needs of the foetus did not provide the necessary justification.'

In the assisted reproduction case of *Evans v Amicus Healthcare* [2003] EWHC 2161 (Fam), considered in detail in Chapter 13 of this book, a part of the applicant's case was that the embryos in issue were entitled to protection under Articles 2 and 8 of the ECHR. This aspect of her claim was never upheld by the number of courts considering the case, including the Grand Chamber of the European Court.

11.8   MEDICAL EXAMINATIONS AND INTERVIEWS OF CHILDREN

11.8.1   Medical examinations prior to or in the absence of legal proceedings

The position in law commensurate with the principles set out in this chapter on consent is that, save in exceptional circumstances, such as an emergency, no doctor may examine an immature minor without the consent of a parent or parents, or other person or body with parental responsibility. Where a full care order has been made in respect of an immature minor and there are no continuing legal proceedings, consent to a medical examination of the immature minor will be sought of the local authority who exercise parental responsibility for the minor. If the minor has sufficient understanding to meet the criteria of the '*Gillick* test', he or she may consent to an examination on his or her own behalf.

11.8.2   Medical examinations during the currency of family proceedings

If family proceedings are instituted, permission must be sought from the court before any further proposed medical examination of the subject child or children may occur.

By s 13(1) of the Children and Families Act 2014:

'A person may not without the permission of the court instruct a person to provide expert evidence for use in children proceedings.'

By s 13(3) of the 2014 Act:

'A person may not without the permission of the court cause a child to be medically or psychiatrically examined or otherwise assessed for the purposes of the provision of expert evidence in children proceedings.'

By s 13(6) of the 2014 Act the court may give permission 'only if the court is of the opinion that the expert evidence is necessary to assist the court to resolve the proceedings justly'.

It is necessary to scrutinise succinctly the provisions as to medical or psychiatric examination of children in 'public law' cases. By s 44(6)(b) of CA 1989, where the court makes an emergency protection order, it may give such directions (if any) as it considers appropriate with respect to the medical or psychiatric examination or other assessment of the child.

Under s 44(8) of the Act, a direction under subs (6)(b) may be to the effect that there is to be:

(a) no such examination or assessment; or

(b) no such examination or assessment unless the court directs otherwise.

Where a direction is given by the court for the medical or psychiatric examination of a child, the child may, by s 44(7) of the Act, refuse to submit to the examination or other assessment if he or she is of sufficient understanding to make an informed decision.

When the court makes an interim care order or interim supervision order under CA 1989, s 38, or, at any time while such an order is in force, the court may give such directions, if any, as it considers appropriate with regard to the medical or psychiatric examination or other assessment of the child, but if the child is of sufficient understanding to make an informed decision, he or she may refuse to submit to the examination or other assessment: CA 1989, s 38(6).

By s 38(7) of the Act, a direction under s 38(6) may be to the effect that there is to be either no such examination or assessment, or no such examination or assessment unless the court directs otherwise.

Sections 38(7A) and (7B), inserted by s 13(11) of the 2014 Act, provide as follows:

'(7A) A direction under subsection (6) to the effect that there is to be a medical or psychiatric examination or other assessment of the child may be given only if the court is of the opinion that the examination or other assessment is necessary to assist the court to resolve the proceedings justly.

(7B) When deciding whether to give a direction under subsection (6) to that effect the court is to have regard in particular to –
(a) any impact which any examination or other assessment would be likely to have on the welfare of the child, and any other impact which giving the direction would be likely to have on the welfare of the child,
(b) the issues with which the examination or other assessment would assist the court,
(c) the questions which the examination or other assessment would enable the court to answer,
(d) the evidence otherwise available,
(e) the impact which the direction would be likely to have on the timetable, duration and conduct of the proceedings,
(f) the cost of the examination or other assessment, and
(g) any matters prescribed by Family Procedure Rules.'

11.8.3   Medical examinations and interviews of children in respect of allegations of sexual or other abuse

The Report of the Inquiry into Child Abuse in Cleveland 1987 remains the touchstone for practice and procedure in this field and, since then, procedures have been developed involving co-operation between agencies in investigating allegations of sexual abuse in respect of minors.

The report of a working party of the Royal College of Physicians entitled 'Physical Signs of Sexual Abuse in Children', now in a subsequent edition, but originally published in 1997, is, and has been, widely used by the legal profession, the medical profession and within the courts.

In respect of issues raised in relation to consents to medical examination, practitioners are referred to Chapter 11 of the Cleveland Report and, in particular, to paragraphs 11.31 to 11.40.

Assuming an appropriate consent has been forthcoming, medical practitioners who have examined a minor for suspected sexual abuse and disagree in their findings and conclusions should discuss their reports and resolve their differences, where possible, and, in the absence of agreement, should identify the areas of dispute between them, recognising that their purpose is to act in the best interests of the child: see 6.f at p 248 of the Cleveland Report under the heading 'Recommendations to the Medical Profession'.

In the case of *Re D (Minors) (Child Abuse: Interviews)* [1998] 2 FLR 10, the Court of Appeal reviewed the practice to be adopted in interviewing children where allegations of sexual abuse are made. The thrust of the decision was to confirm again that social workers and medical and other health professionals should be on guard against prompting or leading children to provide information in these cases. The court referred to the detailed recommendations in Chapter 12 of the Cleveland Report and subsequent decisions of the Court of Appeal and the Family Division in this regard, together with the principles laid down in the Memorandum of Good Practice.

The Court of Appeal determined that, for the purposes of civil proceedings in the family context, the guidelines set out in the Memorandum, required for criminal trials, may not have to be strictly adhered to, but its underlying principles are equally applicable to care or private family law cases. It was reiterated in the judgment of Butler-Sloss LJ that spontaneous information provided by a child is obviously more valuable than information fed to the child by leading questions or prompting. Whilst some children have to be helped to give evidence, the greater the help provided by facilitating the answers, the less reliable the answers will be. Legal practitioners advising in this field and medical practitioners and social workers involved in the difficult task of questioning young children where allegations of sexual abuse arise will be well served by considering carefully the full judgment of the Court of Appeal in this case.

The achieving best evidence (ABE) interviews of children, conducted usually by specialist police officers, are now a familiar part of practising life within the remit particularly of proceedings under s 31 of CA 1989, and are often of much assistance to the courts and practitioners both in the process of fact finding and weighing the best interests of children.

In the case of *Re A-H (Children)* [2013] EWCA Civ 282, the father appealed a finding that he had sexually abused the 12-year-old child of the family on a number of occasions between the ages of 11 and 13. The central aspect of the father's appeal was that the consultant paediatrician who had examined the child had, in her report, cited passages from the guidance of the Royal College of Paediatrics and Child Health (2008) in a partial way.

The complaint was that the paediatrician had quoted headline statements from the research which seemed to establish that penetrative sexual intercourse with a minor may result in no physical signs on subsequent paediatric investigation without drawing attention to the fact that research findings suggest that in cases of repeated penile penetration the absence of any resulting physical signs is unusual.

The final paragraph of the paediatrician's report stated: 'There are no ano-genital signs to either support or negate [T's] report of sexual abuse. It is well recognised that a high proportion of children who have been sexually abused have no ano-genital signs at examination.'

In oral evidence she further said: '... in somebody who is physically mature – and [T] was at the time I saw her physically very mature – then intercourse could have occurred on any number of occasions without there being any signs physical. What we are looking for, when we are examining children, is signs that intercourse has caused damage to tissues.'

Baker J found that the father had perpetrated the sexual abuse of which the child complained. The father appealed to the Court of Appeal.

Thorpe LJ dismissed the appeal. He held that the additional material contained in the Royal College of Paediatrics and Child Health guidance would not have altered the flavour of the expert's citation. Although no copy of the Royal College of Paediatrics and Child Health guidance was available at the trial (which, it was said by counsel for the father, had hampered his ability to effectively cross examine the expert), Thorpe LJ noted that its disclosure had not been sought before the trial and in any event it was a public document.

Further, what Thorpe LJ held to be the key point, ie whether or not it made a difference that the child complained not of a single act but of an unspecified number of irregular acts over a period of 2 years had been put to the paediatrician in oral evidence. She had explained clearly that it did not make any difference to her opinion. Thorpe LJ concluded by saying that the report had in fact been a model one of its kind. The other two judges agreed.

CHAPTER 12

ADVANCE DECISIONS OR 'LIVING WILLS'

12.1 ADVANCE DECISIONS TO REFUSE TREATMENT

Generally it is the patient's consent which makes medical treatment lawful. It is not lawful to treat a patient who has capacity and refuses that treatment. Nor is it lawful to treat a patient who lacks capacity if he or she has made a valid and applicable advance decision to refuse it.

12.2 THE STATUTORY PROVISIONS

The relevant statutory provisions of the Mental Capacity Act 2005 (MCA 2005) are as follows:

'24 Advance decisions to refuse treatment: general

(1) "Advance decision" means a decision made by a person ("P"), after he has reached 18 and when he has capacity to do so, that if –
(a) at a later time and in such circumstances as he may specify, a specified treatment is proposed to be carried out or continued by a person providing health care for him, and
(b) at that time he lacks capacity to consent to the carrying out or continuation of the treatment,
the specified treatment is not to be carried out or continued.

(2) For the purposes of subsection (1)(a), a decision may be regarded as specifying a treatment or circumstances even though expressed in layman's terms.

(3) P may withdraw or alter an advance decision at any time when he has capacity to do so.

(4) A withdrawal (including a partial withdrawal) need not be in writing.

(5) An alteration of an advance decision need not be in writing (unless section 25(5) applies in relation to the decision resulting from the alteration).

25 Validity and applicability of advance decisions

(1) An advance decision does not affect the liability which a person may incur for carrying out or continuing a treatment in relation to P unless the decision is at the material time –
(a)   valid, and
(b)   applicable to the treatment.

(2) An advance decision is not valid if P –
(a)   has withdrawn the decision at a time when he had capacity to do so,
(b)   has, under a lasting power of attorney created after the advance decision was made, conferred authority on the donee (or, if more than one, any of them) to give or refuse consent to the treatment to which the advance decision relates, or
(c)   has done anything else clearly inconsistent with the advance decision remaining his fixed decision.

(3) An advance decision is not applicable to the treatment in question if at the material time P has capacity to give or refuse consent to it.

(4) An advance decision is not applicable to the treatment in question if –
(a)   that treatment is not the treatment specified in the advance decision,
(b)   any circumstances specified in the advance decision are absent, or
(c)   there are reasonable grounds for believing that circumstances exist which P did not anticipate at the time of the advance decision and which would have affected his decision had he anticipated them.

(5) An advance decision is not applicable to life-sustaining treatment unless –
(a)   the decision is verified by a statement by P to the effect that it is to apply to that treatment even if life is at risk, and
(b)   the decision and statement comply with subsection (6).

(6) A decision or statement complies with this subsection only if –
(a)   it is in writing,
(b)   it is signed by P or by another person in P's presence and by P's direction,
(c)   the signature is made or acknowledged by P in the presence of a witness, and
(d)   the witness signs it, or acknowledges his signature, in P's presence.

(7) The existence of any lasting power of attorney other than one of a description mentioned in subsection (2)(b) does not prevent the advance decision from being regarded as valid and applicable.

26 Effect of advance decisions

(1) If P has made an advance decision which is –

(a) valid, and

(b) applicable to a treatment,

the decision has effect as if he had made it, and had had capacity to make it, at the time when the question arises whether the treatment should be carried out or continued.

(2) A person does not incur liability for carrying out or continuing the treatment unless, at the time, he is satisfied that an advance decision exists which is valid and applicable to the treatment.

(3) A person does not incur liability for the consequences of withholding or withdrawing a treatment from P if, at the time, he reasonably believes that an advance decision exists which is valid and applicable to the treatment.

(4) The court may make a declaration as to whether an advance decision –

(a) exists;

(b) is valid;

(c) is applicable to a treatment.

(5) Nothing in an apparent advance decision stops a person –

(a) providing life-sustaining treatment, or

(b) doing any act he reasonably believes to be necessary to prevent a serious deterioration in P's condition,

while a decision as respects any relevant issue is sought from the court.'

12.3   ADVANCE DECISIONS GENERALLY

There is no set form for advanced decisions, because the contents will inevitably vary, depending on the person's wishes and situation. The Mental Capacity Act 2005 Code of Practice includes guidance on what should be included in an advance decision at paragraphs 9.10–9.23.

At paragraph 9.19, the Code lists matters that it is helpful to include in an advanced decision.

They are set out below:

- full details of the person making the advance decision including the date of birth, home address and any distinguishing features;
- the name and address of the person's GP and whether they have a copy of the document;
- a statement that the document should be used if the person ever lacks capacity to take treatment decisions;

- a clear statement of the decision, the treatment to be refused and the circumstances in which the decision will apply;
- the date the document was written;
- the person's signature (or the signature of someone the person has asked to sign on their behalf and in their presence);
- the signature of the person witnessing the signature, if there is one;
- where the treatment contemplated is one that is not life sustaining, then no formality is required in order for it to be considered potentially valid or applicable.

Indeed, the advance decision may not be in writing. The potential difficulties that that poses in terms of establishing its validity and applicability at a later date are addressed at paragraph 9.23 of the Code of Practice where the suggestion is made that healthcare professionals should, wherever possible, record a verbal decision in a person's Health Care Record. That note should include details both of the decision, and also those present (and in what role they were present, and whether they heard it, took part in it or are just aware that it exists).

12.4   ADVANCE DECISIONS TO REFUSE LIFE-SUSTAINING TREATMENT

The Code of Practice also lists matters in relation to advance decisions dealing with life-sustaining treatment at paragraphs 9.24–9.28.

They are fully set out below:

> '9.24 The Act imposes particular legal requirements and safeguards on the making of advance decisions to refuse life sustaining treatment. Advance decisions to refuse life-sustaining treatment must meet specific requirements:
> - They must be put in writing. If the person is unable to write, someone else should write it down for them. For example, a family member can write down the decision on their behalf, or a healthcare professional can record it in the person's healthcare notes.
> - The person must sign the advance decision. If they are unable to sign, they can direct someone to sign on their behalf in their presence.
> - The person making the decision must sign in the presence of a witness to the signature. The witness must then sign the document in the presence of the person making the advance decision. If the person making the advance decision is unable to sign, the witness can witness them directing someone else to sign on their behalf. The witness must then sign to indicate that they have witnessed the nominated person signing the document in front of the person making the advance decision.

- The advance decision must include a clear, specific written statement from the person making the advance decision that the advance decision is to apply to the specific treatment even if life is at risk.
- If this statement is made at a different time or in a separate document to the advance decision, the person making the advance decision (or someone they have directed to sign) must sign it in the presence of a witness, who must also sign it.

9.25 Section 4(10) states that life-sustaining treatment is treatment which a healthcare professional who is providing care to the person regards as necessary to sustain life. This decision will not just depend on the type of treatment. It will also depend on the circumstances in which the healthcare professional is giving it.

9.26 Artificial nutrition and hydration (ANH) has been recognised as a form of medical treatment. ANH involves using tubes to provide nutrition and fluids to someone who cannot take them by mouth. It bypasses the natural mechanisms that control hunger and thirst and requires clinical monitoring. An advance decision can refuse ANH. Refusing ANH in an advance decision is likely to result in the person's death, if the advance decision is followed.

9.27 It is very important to discuss advance decisions to refuse life-sustaining treatment with a healthcare professional. But it is not compulsory. A healthcare professional will be able to explain:
- what types of treatment may be life-sustaining treatment, and in what circumstances
- the implications and consequences of refusing such treatment (see also paragraph 9.14).

9.28 An advance decision cannot refuse actions that are needed to keep a person comfortable (sometimes called basic or essential care). Examples include warmth, shelter, actions to keep a person clean and the offer of food and water by mouth. Section 5 of the Act allows healthcare professionals to carry out these actions in the best interests of a person who lacks capacity to consent (see chapter 6). An advance decision can refuse artificial nutrition and hydration.'

In the life-sustaining treatment case of *An NHS Trust v D* [2012] EWHC 885 (COP), it was determined and accepted that patient D's advance decision in writing could not be effective or relied upon because of the absence of a witness to such decision.

12.5 THE JURISDICTION OF THE COURT

The court may make a declaration as to whether an advance decision exists, is valid or is applicable to a treatment pursuant to s 26(4) of the

Act. Accordingly, if there is any doubt or disagreement over whether an advance decision exists, is valid or is applicable to a treatment, an application can be made to the Court of Protection for it to make a declaration.

In the case of *X Primary Care Trust v XB* [2012] EWHC 1390 (Fam), Theis J said:

> 'In the event that there is an issue raised about an advance decision, it is important that it is investigated by the relevant health authorities or relevant bodies as a matter of urgency. This will clarify issues at an early stage. It will enable relevant primary evidence to be gathered (for example, by taking statement) and, if required, an application made to this court. The judges who sit in the Court of Protection are experienced in dealing with urgent applications, as this case has demonstrated.'

In the case of *Re E (Medical Treatment)* [2012] EWHC 1639 (COP), Peter Jackson J said:

> 'Where there is a genuine doubt or disagreement about the validity of an advance decision, the Court of Protection can make a decision: MCA Code of Practice at 9.67.'

It is necessary to emphasise that the first port of call in considering the validity or applicability of advance decision is to determine whether the person in question had capacity at the time of making such decision. If the person in question lacked capacity at the time of making the advance decision, then the validity of the advance decision falls at the first hurdle.

There may be potential evidential difficulties here if, for example, the advance decision was made a long time before any issue over its applicability or validity at the time when a question arises over whether medical treatment should be carried out or continued. There needs to be borne in mind in this regard, however, the presumption that a person has and retains capacity, unless and until it is proved otherwise.

The second port of call is then to determine whether the person in question lacks capacity at the time the question arises and whether the treatment in question should be carried out or continued. If the person in question at this time has capacity to give or refuse consent to such treatment, then the advance decision cannot be valid: s 25(3) of the MCA 2005.

In the case of *X Primary Care Trust v XB* (above), XB suffered from motor neurone disease. As a patient with long-term invasive ventilation he was unable to talk. He had been able, however, to communicate by varying different means, most latterly by movement of his eyes to the right to indicate that he agreed with the question that was being asked of him.

On 2 November 2011, XB made an advance decision to refuse treatment. There will be set out below in detail the circumstances in which decision was made by him because they are very illuminating as to the care that was taken by him and the others involved to meet the necessary requirements concerning a valid and applicable refusal of life-sustaining treatment.

It suffices to say at once that Theis J was entirely satisfied that XB had capacity to make the advance decision on 2 November, 2011, and that it complied with all the necessary formalities to be an effective advance decision.

The question of what life-sustaining treatment XB wished to receive had been discussed with him on a number of occasions, dating back to at least 2010, and appropriate advice had been taken at various stages by XW, the general practitioner, and others. At points in 2010 and 2011, XB had indicated that he wished to have such treatment withdrawn, but he had not expressed such a wish in what was considered to be a consistent form.

On 2 November 2011, he made an advance decision to refuse treatment. XW, who has been his general practitioner since 1993, made a statement and gave oral evidence to the court about the build-up to this being done, and the discussions he had had with XB and others about this. For example, at a meeting in August 2011, XB had expressed the wish for his ventilation device to be removed that day. It was explained to him that that could not be done, but that arrangements would be made to prepare an advance decision. This was initially drafted by AW, a mental capacity co-ordinator who had been contacted by the general practitioner, following the general practitioner attending a talk AW had given. The draft was discussed with YB and XW. It was felt it needed simplifying to enable it to be explained to XB. A further simpler document was prepared, using a pro forma template that YB had been able to locate on the internet.

This background in relation to the advance decision being made on 2 November 2011 was independently confirmed in the statements before the court from YB from AW. The relevant part of the advance decision reads as follows:

'I have been diagnosed with motor neurone disease (MND-ALS). I am becoming progressively weaker. This has affected my respiratory system. I need support from NIV. Feeding I have a PEG. Stoma/catheter for elimination, and most importantly my ability to communicate, which I now do with my eyes + communication board. I have discussed with my family my feelings and this is the right time to make a decision about the way I die. I know my condition is terminal. I wish to express my choices.'

A little later in the document, it continues under the part entitled 'I would wish to refuse life-sustaining treatment, even if my life was at risk'. Firstly, in the left-hand box it states 'Removal of non-invasive ventilation (NIV)', and records that this should be done in the following circumstances:

'In the event that my disease progresses to a stage where I am unable to communicate my needs and lose the ability to have any control over my decisions of my care and management. I fully understand the implication of the advance decision, and appreciate the consequences and it would put my life at risk. I consent to have relevant treatment before and after NIV removal to prevent me from becoming distressed or experiencing pain. However, apart from the above, I would not wish to have any life prolonging treatment, including my PEG feed.'

This document was agreed to by XB, with his wife YB, XW, his general practitioner, and AW, the mental capacity co-ordinator, in attendance on 2 November 2011. One of the carers was also there. It is thought it was a carer called L, but the evidence demonstrates that the carer took no active part in the preparation or involvement of this document.

On 2 November 2011, seeking XB's views in relation to this document was done as a collaborative process by those who were there, whereby it was read out to him, and then each part was dealt with and questions were asked in a way to find out if XB consented. His consent was communicated by movement of his eyes.

It is to be noted that there was no issue before Theis J, at the point of time she was considering the validity and applicability in court, that XB by this time was lacking capacity to communicate his views as to the continuation of life support or to conduct the litigation.

It is to be further noted that the advance decision of XB had complied in particular with the requirement of s 25(5)(a) of the MCA 2005, with him making clear that his decision to refuse treatment recognised this 'would put his life at risk'.

In the case of *Re E (Medical Treatment)* [2012] EWHC 1639 (COP) referred to above, the judge was not satisfied that E had capacity on the two separate occasions she had made advance decisions. He determined accordingly that such advanced decisions could not be relied upon because at the time she made them E lacked capacity. The ability for those advance decisions to be considered as applicable accordingly fell at the first hurdle.

The case of *W v M* [2011] EWHC 2443 (Fam) is helpful in relation to considering a patient's wishes and feelings and those of her family under s 4(6) and (7) of the Act, in circumstances where the patient, M, had made no formal advance decision as to medical treatment.

Section 4(6) of the MCA 2005 requires the court to consider, so far as reasonably ascertainable, the patient's past and present wishes and feelings. Section 4(7) requires the court to take into account the views of anyone engaged in caring for the patient or interested in their welfare.

In the case of *Nottinghamshire Healthcare NHS Trust v RC* [2014] EWHC 1317 (COP), RC was 23 and had been diagnosed with antisocial and emotionally unstable personality disorders. He had a repeated history of grave self-harm. In August 2013, serving a prison sentence for sexual assault, he became a Jehovah's Witness. In February 2014 he slashed the major artery in his arm and was admitted to a secure psychiatric hospital, where he repeatedly attempted to re-open the wound. He refused to consent to blood transfusions on religious grounds and in April 2014 signed an advance decision to that effect, found to be compliant with ss.24–26 of MCA 2005.

Amongst the declarations sought by the NHS Trust declarations from the Court of Protection was one asserting that the advance decision was valid and operative should RC become incapable of issuing a decision to refuse treatment. The judge acceded to the making of this declaration.

Attached at the end of this Chapter are sample 'living wills'.

APPENDICES TO CHAPTER 12

ADVANCE DECISIONS PRECEDENTS

1 Standard advance decision

THIS ADVANCE DECISION is made on

by me

of

of

born on

I WISH these instructions to be acted upon if two registered medical practitioners are of the opinion that I am no longer capable of making and communicating a treatment decision AND that I am:

- unconscious, and it is unlikely that I shall ever regain consciousness; or

- suffering from an incurable or irreversible condition that will result in my death within a relatively short time; or

- so severely disabled, physically or mentally, that I shall be totally dependent on others for the rest of my life.

I REFUSE any medical or surgical treatment if:

- its burdens and risks outweigh its potential benefits; or

- it involves any research or experimentation which is likely to be of little or no therapeutic value to me; or

- it will needlessly prolong my life or postpone the actual moment of my death.

I CONSENT to being fed orally, and to any treatment that may:

- safeguard my dignity; or

- make me more comfortable; or

- relieve pain and suffering;

even though such treatment might unintentionally precipitate my death.

I confirm that this advance decision shall apply even if my life is at risk and results in my death.

SIGNED by me

in the presence of:

2 Advance decision which the maker defines an intolerable condition

THIS ADVANCE DECISION is made on

by me

of

born on

(1)   If two registered medical practitioners are of the opinion that I am no longer capable of making and communicating a medical treatment decision, and that I am suffering from an intolerable condition, as defined below:

      (a)   I REFUSE any medical treatment which is designed simply to keep me alive, even if my life is at risk and results in my death; but

      (b)   I CONSENT to being fed orally, and to any treatment that may relieve my pain and suffering, even though it might unintentionally shorten my life.

(2)   An intolerable condition is one in which I will almost certainly spend the rest of my life:

      (a)   being mentally incapable of making or communicating a treatment decision for myself; or

      (b)   in constant, unremitting pain; or

      (c)   in a coma; or

      (d)   with severe disfigurement to my face or head; or

      (e)   permanently confined to bed.

(3)   An intolerable condition is also one in which I will suffer from any [two or more] of the following disabilities for the rest of my life:

      (a)   unable to communicate sensibly;

(b)   unable to recognise my family and friends;

(c)   unable to feed, dress and wash myself;

(d)   unable to control my bladder and bowel;

(e)   (*specify any other disabilities which the maker believes would make his or her life intolerable*).

SIGNED by me

in the presence of:

3 Advance decision: any supervening illness is not to be actively treated

THIS ADVANCE DECISION is made on

by me

of

of

born on

(1)   I HAVE been diagnosed as suffering from (*state diagnosis*),

and I am fully aware of:

(a)   the course the illness may take;

(b)   the extent to which its symptoms can and cannot be alleviated by medical treatment and nursing care; and

(c)   the consequences of refusing treatment.

(2)   I WANT these instructions to be implemented if I am no longer capable of making and communicating a decision about my health care, even if my life is at risk and it results in my death.

(3)   IF I sustain an injury, or suffer from any separate illness, condition or disease, which, if it were left untreated, would probably be the cause of my death:

(a)   I REFUSE any active treatment of that injury, illness, condition or disease; but

(b)   I CONSENT to being fed orally, and to any treatment which may relieve pain or be considered necessary for the health, safety and protection of others.

(4)   IF, for any reason, these instructions are not clear or not applicable in the circumstances, I WOULD LIKE my (*state relationship, if any*):

Name:

Address:

Address:

Telephone:

to be consulted before any irrevocable decision is made about my health care.

SIGNED by me

in the presence of:

4 Advance statement: maximum treatment

THIS ADVANCE STATEMENT is made on

by me

of

born on

(1)   IF I am no longer capable of making and communicating a decision about my health care, I WISH to be kept alive for as long as reasonably possible using any form of treatment available, regardless of:

•   my condition;

•   the prognosis;

•   the cost – provided I have sufficient resources to pay for such treatment.

(2)   I CONSENT to any medical, surgical or nursing treatment or care that may:

- save or sustain my life;

- make me more comfortable;

- relieve pain and suffering;

- be necessary for the health, safety or protection of others.

(3) I AGREE to take part in any therapeutic or non-therapeutic research or experiment, provided that:

- it does not involve any substantial risk to my health;

- it does not defeat my overall objective to remain alive for as long as I reasonably can.

(4) I DO NOT REQUIRE anyone who is responsible for my care to:

- do anything unlawful;

- give me any treatment they regard as futile;

- do anything they consider to be clinically inappropriate;

- act otherwise than a responsible and competent body of relevant professional opinion would act.

SIGNED by me

in the presence of:

5 Advance decision: treatment preferences

THIS ADVANCE DECISION is made on

by me

of

born on

IF I AM UNABLE TO MAKE AND COMMUNICATE DECISIONS ABOUT MY HEALTH CARE FOR MYSELF, AND:

(1) IF I AM CRITICALLY ILL, in other words, very ill but not terminally ill, and my condition could improve with medical treatment:

- I want to be hospitalised.

- I want to go into intensive care.

- I want to be resuscitated if my heart stops.

- I want to have surgery.

- I want to be put on a breathing machine.

(2)   IF I AM TERMINALLY ILL, in other words, dying and my condition cannot be improved by medical treatment, no matter what is done:

- I want to be hospitalised.

- I want my family to [decide] [be consulted on] whether I should go into intensive care [after they have discussed the matter with my doctor].

- I want my doctor to decide whether to resuscitate me if my heart stops.

- I want my family to [decide][be consulted on] whether I should have surgery [after they have discussed the matter with my doctor].

- I want my family to [decide] [be consulted on] whether I should be put on a breathing machine [after they have discussed the matter with my doctor].

(3)   IF I AM IN AN IRREVERSIBLE COMA, and it is unlikely that I shall ever regain consciousness:

- I want to be hospitalised.

- I want my family to [decide] [be consulted on] whether I should go into intensive care [after they have discussed the matter with my doctor].

- I want my doctor to decide whether to resuscitate me if my heart stops.

- I want my family to [decide] [be consulted on] whether I have surgery [after they have discussed the matter with my doctor].

- I do not want to be put on a breathing machine.

- I want my family to [decide] [be consulted on] whether I should be fed through a tube [after they have discussed the matter with my doctor].

SIGNED by me

in the presence of:

6 People to be consulted before a treatment decision is made

THIS ADVANCE STATEMENT is made on

by me

of

born on

IF I AM NO LONGER CAPABLE OF MAKING AND COMMUNI-CATING A DECISION ABOUT MY HEALTH CARE

I would like the following person to be consulted before any decision about my treatment or care is made:

Relationship, if any:

Full name:

Address:

Telephone (home):

Telephone (work):

If that person is not reasonably available, or is incapacitated, or is unwilling to be consulted, I would like the following person to be consulted instead:

Relationship, if any:

Full name:

Address:

Telephone (home):

Telephone (work):

SIGNED by me

in the presence of:

7 Letter registering an advance decision with a client's GP/Consultant

(*Date*)

Dear Dr (*GP or consultant's name*),

(*Full name, address, and date of birth of client*)

I am enclosing a photocopy of the advance decision recently signed by your patient, (*client's name*), who is also one of my clients.

Please would you:

- acknowledge receipt by signing and dating the duplicate copy of this letter, and returning it to me in the enclosed pre-paid envelope;

- ensure that the advance decision is placed in (*client's*) medical records and is clearly visible;

- add this information to my client's NHS Summary Care Records and

- bring it to the attention of the authorities if (he)/(she) is hospitalised.

The original document is being held for safe custody in our strongroom, and a copy has been retained by (*client*) (and (his)/(her) family)/(and the person in charge of the care home where (he)/(she) resides). (He)/(She) has been advised to review the document at regular intervals and whenever there is a major change in (his)/(her) personal circumstances.

If, for any reason, you consider that the instructions could be inapplicable in the situation which is likely to arise in (his)/(her) case, please would you let (him)/(her) and me know as soon as possible so that we can consider amending the document accordingly.

Yours sincerely

Enclosures:

- Copy of advance medical decision

- Duplicate copy of this letter

- Pre-paid envelope

Miscellaneous clauses

1 Address

TO MY FAMILY, MY FRIENDS AND THOSE WHO ARE RESPONSIBLE FOR MY MEDICAL CARE

2 Age-related instructions

I do not wish to be resuscitated if:

- I suffer a cardiac arrest; and

- I am aged (90) or over.

3 Attestation clause

I CERTIFY that (*maker's name*) signed this advance decision in my presence. To the best of my knowledge, I am not currently entitled to any part of (his)/(her) estate under (his)/(her) Will, or the law relating to intestacy, or by right of survivorship.

4 Chemotherapy and radiotherapy

If I have incurable cancer, and there is no likelihood that my condition will improve, and any further chemotherapy and radiotherapy will merely extend my life for a little longer, I wish that all chemotherapy and radiotherapy be withheld or discontinued, unless it is absolutely essential to alleviate pain and distress.

5 Competence

I understand the nature and effect of this advance decision and am [emotionally and] mentally competent to make it.

6 Conscientious objection

Any doctor or nurse who is unwilling to comply with these wishes should take reasonable steps as soon as possible to transfer the responsibility for my care to another doctor or nurse who is willing to comply with these wishes.

7 Dementia

IF I AM SUFFERING FROM MILD DEMENTIA, for example:

I am able to have meaningful conversations, but I am forgetful, and have a poor short-term memory.

I am able to carry out most routine daily activities, such as housework, dressing, eating, bathing and using the toilet.

I have bladder and bowel control.

I am able to live at home with someone caring for me for a few hours each day.

My wishes are as follows: (*specify instructions*)

IF I AM SUFFERING FROM MODERATE DEMENTIA, for example:

I am not always able to recognise family and friends.

I can engage in conversation, but may not always make sense.

I need help with my daily routines.

I may still have bladder and bowel control.

I could possibly live at home with someone caring for me throughout the day, but probably should be in a residential care home or nursing home.

My wishes are as follows: (*specify instructions*)

IF I AM SUFFERING FROM SEVERE DEMENTIA, for example:

I cannot recognise my family and friends.

I am unable to have a meaningful conversation.

I am unable to carry out any routine daily activities.

I cannot feed myself.

I no longer have bladder and bowel control.

I need to be cared for day and night.

My wishes are as follows: (*specify instructions*)

8 Diabetes

I am a diabetic.

I do not wish to be treated if my blood sugar level rises above (25) mm/vol and continues for (10) days, and if I am at risk of losing my sight.

I am aware that in future I may have circulatory and other problems which could involve a decision about major surgery.

I refuse to undergo any major surgery, such as the amputation of a limb, even though such refusal may jeopardise my life.

9 Discussion with doctor

I have discussed this advance medical decision with my GP/ Consultant.

(*Name*)

(*Address*)

(*Telephone*)

10 Feeding

I (consent to)/(refuse) enteral feeding (through the gastro-intestinal tract with the aid of a naso-gastric tube).

I (consent to)/(refuse) parenteral nutrition (the intravenous provision of carbohydrate, fat and proteins).

11 Organ donation

If brain stem death has occurred, and any part of my body is needed for the treatment of others, I consent to being kept on a ventilator for no more than (24 *hours*) in order to preserve the part(s) for transplantation.

12 Place of death

If it is practicable in the circumstances, I would rather die at home than in a hospital, hospice, or nursing home.

13 Presence of relative or friend

If my death is imminent I would like:

(*Name*)

(*Address*)

(*Telephone*)

to be contacted and given the chance to be with me before I die.

14 Revocation of earlier wishes

These wishes supersede any earlier written or spoken statements about my health care.

15 Severability clauses

If any part of this advance decision is unlawful, invalid or unenforceable, it can be severed from the parts that are lawful, valid and enforceable.

16 Specific interventions

(Describe the clinical situations in which these instructions are to apply)

I [DO NOT] WANT:

- Cardiopulmonary resuscitation

- Mechanical breathing

- Artificial nutrition and hydration

- Major surgery

- Kidney dialysis

- Chemotherapy

- Minor surgery

- Radiotherapy

- Invasive diagnostic tests

- Blood or blood products

- Antibiotics

- Simple diagnostic tests

- Pain medications, even if they dull consciousness and indirectly shorten my life

17 Stroke

If I am suffering from a mild stroke, for example:

I have mild paralysis on one side of my body.

I can walk unaided, or with a stick or frame.

I am able to have meaningful conversations, but might have speech difficulties.

I can carry out most routine daily activities, such as work, household tasks, dressing, eating, bathing and using the toilet.

I have bowel and bladder control.

I could live at home with someone caring for me for a few hours each day.

My instructions are: (*specify instructions*)

If I am suffering from a moderate stroke, for example:

I have moderate paralysis on one side of my body.

I am unable to walk and need a wheelchair.

I can carry out conversations, but might not always make sense.

I need help with routine daily activities.

I may have bowel and bladder control.

I could live at home with someone caring for me throughout the daytime; otherwise I would probably need to live in a residential care home or nursing home.

My instructions are: (*specify instructions*)

If I am suffering from a severe stroke, for example:

I have severe paralysis on one side of the body.

I am unable to walk, and need to be in a chair or in bed.

I am unable to have meaningful conversations.

I am unable to carry out routine daily activities.

I may need to be fed through a tube.

I do not have control over my bowel or bladder.

I could live at home with someone caring for me all day and night; otherwise I would probably need to be cared for in a nursing home.

My instructions are as follows: (*specify instructions*)

18 Values history

I am not afraid of death but I am afraid of having no control over my bodily and mental functions until I die [because ...]

[*OR*]

What I fear most is ...

CHAPTER 13

MEDICAL TREATMENT OTHER THAN FOR PURELY MEDICAL REASONS

13.1 STERILISATION

13.1.1 Prior sanction of the High Court required

There is, understandably, concern and anxiety in relation to proposed sterilisation operations on either minors or mentally incapacitated adults. Such an operation involves the deprivation of a woman's basic human right to reproduce. A major concern has been to be vigilant that a sterilisation operation should not occur for any reasons of convenience in relation to a minor or adult who is difficult to care for.

Sterilisation of a girl under 18 should only be carried out with the leave of a High Court judge: *Re B (A Minor) (Wardship: Sterilisation)* [1988] AC 199, HL.

In relation to adults, a sterilisation operation should never be carried out upon a woman incapable of giving her own consent, unless there has been prior approval of a High Court judge that the procedure was one which was in the best interests of the woman: *Re S (Medical Treatment: Adult Sterilisation)* [1998] 1 FLR 944.

13.1.2 The special features of a sterilisation operation

The operation will in most cases be irreversible. By reason of the general irreversibility of the operation, the almost certain result of it will be to deprive the woman concerned of what is widely and properly regarded as one of the fundamental rights of a woman, namely, the right to bear children. The deprivation of that right gives rise to moral and emotional considerations to which many people attach great importance.

If the question whether the operation is in the best interests of the adult or minor is left to be decided without the involvement of the court, there may be a greater risk of it being decided wrongly or at least of it being thought to have been decided wrongly. If there is no involvement of the court, there is a risk of the operation being carried out for improper reasons or with improper motives. The involvement of the court in the decision to operate, if that is the decision reached, will serve to protect the doctor or doctors who performed the operation and any others who may be concerned in it from subsequent adverse criticism or claims. Lord Griffiths, in the case of *Re F (Mental Patient: Sterilisation)* [1990] AC 1, HL, at 68, summarised the reason for the caution and concern in relation to these operations as follows:

> '... The argument in this appeal has ranged far and wide in search of a measure to protect those who cannot protect themselves from the insult of an unnecessary sterilisation. Every judge who has considered the problem has recognised that there should be some control mechanism imposed upon those who have the care of infants or mentally incompetent women of child bearing age to prevent or at least inhibit them from sterilising the women without approval of the High Court. I am, I should make clear, speaking now and hereafter of an operation for sterilisation which is proposed not for the treatment of diseased organs but an operation on a woman with healthy reproductive organs in order to avoid the risk of pregnancy. The reasons for the anxiety about a sterilisation which it is proposed should be carried out for other than purely medical reasons, such as the removal of the ovaries to prevent the spread of cancer, are readily understandable and are shared throughout the common law world.'

13.1.3   Children and sterilisation

It is helpful to contrast two cases involving the sterilisation of minors.

In the case of *Re D (A Minor) (Wardship: Sterilisation)* [1976] 2 WLR 279, the girl involved, D, was aged 11 years and suffering from an unusual syndrome of which the symptoms were accelerated growth during infancy, epilepsy, general clumsiness and emotional instability, as well as an impairment of mental function. She had, however, a dull normal intelligence and her clumsiness was lessening and her behaviour was improving. It was not possible to predict her future role in society, but the likelihood was that she would have sufficient capacity to marry. Her widowed mother, worried in case D might give birth to a baby for which she was incapable of caring and which might also be abnormal, wanted D to be sterilised. The consultant paediatrician, under whose care D was, recommended a sterilisation operation and a consultant gynaecologist agreed to perform it.

Certain persons concerned with D's welfare, including the plaintiff, an educational psychologist, challenged the decision to operate. In the case of D, it was left to the educational psychologist as plaintiff to apply to make D a ward of court. The Official Solicitor was appointed as D's guardian ad litem at the plaintiff's request. It was held that the court would not risk the incurring of damage which it could not repair but would rather prevent the damage being done; the operation could be delayed or prevented if D were to remain a ward of court and, accordingly, the court should exercise its protective functions in regard to D and continue her wardship. The judge took the view that a decision to perform an operation, such as that proposed, for non-therapeutic purposes on a minor could not be within a doctor's sole clinical judgment.

The facts of *Re B (A Minor) (Wardship: Sterilisation)* [1988] AC 199 are very different. B, a girl aged 17 years, suffered from a moderate degree of mental handicap but had a very limited intellectual development. Although 17, her ability to understand speech was that of a 6-year-old and her ability to express herself was that of a 2-year-old. Her mother and staff at the council residential institution where she lived became aware that she was beginning to show signs of sexual awareness, exemplified by provocative approaches to male members of staff and other residents. The local authority applied by originating summons for an order making B a ward of court and for leave to be given for her to undergo a sterilisation operation.

Evidence was adduced that B could not be placed on any effective contraceptive regime and that she was not capable of knowing the causal connection between intercourse and childbirth, the nature of pregnancy or what was involved in delivery. She would panic and require heavy sedation during a normal delivery, which carried the risk of injury to the child, and delivery by Caesarean section was deemed to be inappropriate as there was the likelihood of B opening up her post-operative wounds, thus preventing the healing of the scar. She had no maternal instincts and was unlikely ever to desire or be able to care for a child. The judge at first instance gave leave for the operation to be carried out. The Official Solicitor, as guardian ad litem, appealed to the Court of Appeal. The Court of Appeal dismissed the appeal, thereby endorsing that the operation should be carried out as being in her best interests. It was held that a court, exercising wardship jurisdiction, when reaching a decision on an application to authorise an operation for the sterilisation of the ward, was concerned with only one primary and paramount consideration, namely the welfare and best interests of the ward. The conclusion of the Court of Appeal was that, on the totality of the evidence, the operation would be in the patient's best interests.

13.1.4   Adults and sterilisation

It is an obvious point, yet nevertheless important to emphasise, that the court will have different facts, and, perhaps, different considerations, in each particular case of this nature that comes before it. Accordingly, the court will in each and every case of this nature carefully and exhaustively examine the evidence presented.

In the case of *Re LC (Medical Treatment: Sterilisation)* [1997] 2 FLR 258, the judge at first instance indicated that, both on the wider implications of the question of whether a severely handicapped person should be subjected to non-consensual invasive surgery, and on the facts of the individual case, the balance could be argued one way or another. In the end, his decision was based, understandably in the circumstances, on very practical and pragmatic considerations. The patient was mentally handicapped with an intellectual age of about 3½. She was born in 1972. In 1991, in the care of a residential home, she was indecently assaulted by a member of staff. She had thereafter been moved to another home with an infinitely superior standard of care. It was a small home with dedicated staff. The local authority, supported by the mother of the patient, contended that the patient was vulnerable in the future to the possibility of sexual abuse, the risk of which could not be eliminated and hence it would be in her best interests for the court to sanction the proposed sterilisation operation. The Official Solicitor, as well as a key social worker, held the view that such an operation was not in the patient's best interests. The judge held that the evidence established that the level of care at the home now was of such exceptionally high quality that, whilst it continued, it would not be in the patient's best interests to impose upon her the surgical procedure, which was not without risks or painful consequences. Accordingly, no order was made on the originating summons.

In the case of *Re X (Adult Patient: Sterilisation)* [1998] 2 FLR 1124, however, the conclusion of the court on the evidence before it was that permanent sterilisation was in the best interests of the patient. The patient X was 31 years of age, physically able but severely mentally incapacitated. She regularly attended an adult training centre and appeared to enjoy physical contact with men. She had a particularly close relationship with one male user of the centre. She had been fitted with a contraceptive coil but when that needed to be replaced, X's parents, supported by the Official Solicitor, sought and obtained declaratory relief on the basis that permanent sterilisation involving only one operation was in X's best interests. There was a real risk that X would have a sexual relationship and might become pregnant. Although X said she would like a baby, she was incapable of caring for a child whose birth and inevitable removal from her would be frightening and upsetting to her. Some reliable form of contraception was therefore essential to prevent the psychological damage which would probably result from pregnancy. The only realistic alternative to sterilisation was the contraceptive coil which, because it would need to be replaced regularly, would involve three further operations and the risk of infection.

In the case of *Re F* [1990] 2 AC 1, the view of the judge at first instance was confirmed in both the Court of Appeal and the House of Lords that a sterilisation was in the best interests of the patient. F was a 36-year-old, mentally handicapped woman residing in a mental hospital and with the mental age of a small child. The question of her being sterilised had arisen because of a relationship which she had formed with a male patient at the same hospital. The relationship was of a sexual nature and probably involved sexual intercourse, or something close to it, about twice a month. The relationship was entirely voluntary on the patient's part and it was likely that she obtained pleasure from it. There was no reason to believe that she had other than the ordinary fertility of a woman of her age. Because of her mental disability, however, she could not have coped at all with pregnancy, labour or delivery, the meaning of which she would not have understood. Nor could she have cared for a baby, if she had ever had one. In those circumstances, it would have been, on the evidence, from a psychiatric point of view, disastrous for her to conceive a child. There was a serious objection to each of the ordinary methods of contraception. So far as the varieties of the pill were concerned, she would not have been able to have used them effectively, and there was a risk of their causing damage to her physical health. So far as an intra-uterine device was concerned, there would be danger of infection arising, the symptoms of which she would not have been able to describe so that remedial measures could not have been taken in time. It was in those circumstances, and upon such evidence, that the court concluded the sterilisation operation to be in F's best interests.

Whereas in the above case of *Re F* the patient had formed a sexual relationship with someone else, in the case of *Re S (Medical Treatment: Adult Sterilisation)* [1998] 1 FLR 944, the essential issue for the court was the risk in the future of the patient being 'sexually exploited'. The patient S was 22. She was described by the judge as a charming and attractive young woman and, to all outward appearances, entirely normal. However, her mental and emotional state was such that she was quite unable to look after herself. She had virtually no ability to communicate, except by making some very basic noises. She required help in dressing and looking after her own basic physical needs. She could not be left to walk alone along a street. More particularly, she had no understanding of sexuality.

The patient's mother sought a declaration that it would be lawful for her daughter to be sterilised to eliminate the risk of pregnancy. The issue before the court was whether the risk of pregnancy was such as to require sterilisation, with the consequent imposition on S of necessary invasive procedures which carried a risk of fatality. The assessment of the future risk involved a degree of speculation which had to be based on circumstances that existed, or could be reasonably foreseen to exist. In the absence of any identifiable, rather than speculative risk, the court adjudged that the mother's application should be refused. Importantly, the thrust of the submission made on behalf of the official solicitor was that, if, in the circumstances of the case of re S, the court was to declare sterilisation to be lawful, then it would be difficult to envisage any factual situation in which the relief would be refused.

In the case of *Re A (Male Sterilisation)* [2000] 1 FLR 549, an application was made for a declaration that a non-therapeutic male sterilisation was lawful. The application was refused at first instance and again on appeal. The application was predicated on the basis that a man suffering from Downs Syndrome might have a sexual relationship in the future. The psychiatrist for the Official Solicitor judged the risk of sexual intercourse to be very small, and the judge at first instance found that the man was unlikely to enter into any casual sexual relationship with a woman.

13.1.5   Recent cases on sterilisation

In the case of *An NHS Trust v DE* [2013] EWHC 2562 (Fam) the Trust applied to the Court of Protection for relief, including for a declaration that it was lawful and in DE's best interests that he should undergo a non-therapeutic vasectomy. DE was 37 years old and suffering from a life-long learning disability. He had an IQ of 40, with an adult mental age of between 6 and 9 years. He was wholly dependent on the exceptional commitment and care of his parents with whom he lived. He had a girlfriend who suffered from learning disabilities too and lived with her parents; this relationship was long-standing over some 10 years and was of much importance and benefit to them both. They had developed a sexual relationship leading to the birth of their child in June 2010. This occurrence intensely disturbed the routines and stability of DE and his girlfriend, as well as both families generally. DE was distressed as were his parents.

The Court of Protection proceedings having been instituted, an interim declaration was granted by the court that DE lacked capacity to engage in sexual relations. The overall circumstances then led to the girlfriend temporarily ending her relationship with DE. Care proceedings were instituted leading to the baby being cared for by the maternal grandparents under a special guardianship order. As matters thereafter transpired, work was carried out with DE and it was accepted by the parties that DE had capacity to engage in sexual relations.

Whilst accordingly DE could consent to having a sexual relationship, it was accepted by all parties that he did not have capacity to consent to contraception and would not regain the necessary capacity. It therefore remained for the court to determine whether or not it was in DE's best interests to have a vasectomy. Whilst DE's wishes and feelings in relation to a vasectomy were taken into account, the judge treated them with the utmost caution. It was agreed that DE lacked the capacity to weigh up the competing arguments for and against having a vasectomy. Whilst his relationship with his girlfriend was restored, DE sustained a loss in his confidence and indeed in his autonomy, given the overall upheaval and the supervision still required of the relationship, in the context of the concerns over another pregnancy.

It was material in the case that DE had clearly expressed throughout the wish to have no more children. He was clear that he wished to continue to live with his parents. The evidence supported the view that his relationship with his girlfriend was both important and beneficial to him.

His parents actively supported him undergoing a vasectomy. The judge referred to s 4(6)(c) of the Mental Capacity Act 2005 (MCA 2005) which requires the court to take into account other factors which DE would be likely to consider if he were able to do so. The court could take into account the benefits to the parents of DE of his having a vasectomy if it was a factor DE would consider if he had capacity. She said it was likely that DE would consider the benefit to his parents of relieving them of anxiety and strain: such a benefit to the parents would be of significant benefit to DE, not only because he would benefit from them being happier and less anxious but also because – relieved of the anxiety of a second pregnancy through a vasectomy – they would feel able to relax the supervision of the relationship that otherwise would be necessary to avoid another pregnancy.

The court carefully weighed up the matters in favour and against the use of condoms. Whilst accepting the medical opinion that vasectomy is a routine safe form of long term contraception, the court had at the forefront of its mind throughout the seriousness of the consequences of such a medical procedure, which would be to sterilise DE and render him infertile.

On the medical evidence the judge was satisfied that with DE's likely unreliability in the use of condoms; despite the work done with him in this regard and other factors there was a substantive risk of a further pregnancy by reliance on that method of contraception. She found there was a high (over 18%) chance of pregnancy using condoms; DE's technique was poor and he could not be relied upon consistently to use them. A medical expert in the case summarised DE's position as follows: vasectomy – no babies; condom – might be babies.

The court reminded itself that the procedure sought was non therapeutic. The court carefully considered the terms of s 4 of the MCA 2005.

In relation to Article 8 of the European Convention on Human Rights and Fundamental Freedoms (ECHR), the court considered that the application of DE's right to respect for his private life involved competing rights which it had to balance. On the one hand if DE underwent a vasectomy the likelihood was that he would lose or significantly reduce his ability to make the choice to become a genetic parent in the future. On the other hand, under Article 8 he had a right to respect for his autonomy which included his decision not to have any more children and his wish to develop a sexual relationship with his girlfriend which should be as anxiety free as possible. The judge held that DE's right to respect for family life under Article 8 was not violated by a decision that would reduce the likelihood of him becoming a genetic father in the future.

The determination of the court was that it was overwhelmingly in DE's best interests to have a vasectomy. This would enable DE to maintain an enduring and loving relationship with his girlfriend without the anxiety and distress of another pregnancy; it would permit the relationship to proceed without the supervision of it that might otherwise be required; it would allow the relationship to be restored to the way it was prior to his girlfriend having become pregnant. If another child was born not only would DE be deeply distressed but a removal of the child from his girlfriend would be likely to result in the breakdown of their relationship. The carrying out of the procedure would be in tune with DE's clear and consistent wish not to have any more children. DE's parents and thereby DE too would benefit from the procedure being carried out, as discussed above. Moreover, DE's confidence and autonomy was likely to be enhanced and improved by his re-establishing and maintaining the routines and activities he had previously enjoyed. Overall his having the procedure would enhance DE's private life, his relationship with his parents and his own independence.

In the case of *A Local Authority v K* [2013] EWHC 242 (COP) before Cobb J, the case concerned K, who was 21 years old and born with Down's syndrome, with an associated mild/moderate learning disability. There was no issue between the parties that K lacked capacity in respect of the issues before the court. K resided at home and it was accepted that she received a high level of care from her family. Her parents sought medical advice about contraception for K and requested that she be sterilised. Following a consultant gynaecologist initially acceding to such parental request, a 'best interests' meeting was held which concluded that non therapeutic sterilisation was not in her best interests. Her parents indicated that they planned to remove K from the jurisdiction and make arrangements for her to be sterilised abroad. The local authority issued proceedings to prevent her removal from the jurisdiction and for declarations in relation to contraception and sterilisation.

The judge considered in his judgment K's capacity as follows:

'Capacity:

23. The first issue for me to consider is K's capacity. In assisting me to make a determination under section 2 and section 3 of the MCA 2005, I have seen a report from Dr. D. Having reviewed the material, and met with K, he concluded that K has a significant mental impairment, with a full scale IQ of less than 70 and Down's Syndrome. Specifically, he comments, K lacks capacity to deal with the specific issues of contraception and sterilisation which are before the court. Rightly, no party raises an issue in these proceedings about capacity.

24. In evaluating capacity in circumstances concerning sterilisation and contraceptive treatment, I remind myself of the test formulated by Bodey J in *A Local Authority v A* [2010] EWHC 1549 (COP); [2010] COPLR Con Vol 138 at para.64. The test for capacity to be applied to ascertain a woman's ability to understand and weigh up the immediate medical issues surrounding contraceptive treatment includes consideration of:
(a) the reason for contraception and what it does (which includes the likelihood of pregnancy if it is not in use during sexual intercourse);
(b) the types available and how each is used;
(c) the advantages and disadvantages of each type;
(d) the possible side-effects of each and how they can be dealt with;
(e) how easily each type can be changed; and
(f) the generally accepted effectiveness of each.

25. There is no doubt, having regard to the report of Dr. D, that K would not have capacity to understand and weigh up the immediate medical issues identified above. I find that she lacks capacity in this regard and that I should therefore consider making a decision in her best interests.'

An expert report was commissioned within the proceedings which concluded that sterilisation was not in the best interests of K. This led to a consensus between the parties that K should not receive any form of contraception and should not be subject to a non- therapeutic sterilisation.

The Local Authority, supported by the Official Solicitor, asked the court to grant a declaration that it was not in K's best interests to be sterilised so that there was clarity should a 'best interests' determination have to be made 'on the ground'. K's parents opposed this on the basis that such a procedure could not be excluded as a necessary action in the future.

The judge considered that the case engaged important considerations under both the ECHR, Article 8 (right to respect for private and family life) and Article 12 (right to found a family) rights of K. He concluded that it was in K's best interests that he bring as much clarity to medical treatment issues as he could, and he granted a declaration that sterilisation would be a disproportionate, and not the least restrictive, step to achieve contraception for K in the future (absent significant change in the circumstances).

In weighing the best interests of K there was particular consideration of s 1(6), 4(2) and 4(7) of the MCA 2005. In this respect it is helpful to set out here exactly what the judge said on best interests:

> '**Best interests:**
>
> 26. Any decision made or endorsed by the Court in a case such as this must, by statute, be taken in the best interests of K (section 1(5) MCA 2005), with regard to the fact that the decision should be the "least restrictive" of K's rights and freedom of action (section 1(6)). In reaching a conclusion on her best interests, I have had regard to the provisions of section 4 MCA 2005, and to "all the relevant circumstances" (section 4(2)). Those circumstances include all "medical, emotional and all other welfare issues" concerning K (borrowing the language of the pre-MCA 2005 Court of Appeal decisions of *Re MB (Medical Treatment)* [1997] 2 FLR 426 at 429, and *R-B v Official Solicitor: Re A (Medical Sterilisation)* (1999) 53 BMLR 66). In this respect, I have of course had regard to the method of achieving the sterilisation (involving the necessary hospitalisation of K), the likely permanence of the procedure, and the interference with K's physical integrity.

27. In reaching a decision I have also paid significant attention to the views of K's parents (section 4(7)). They appeared in person in court before me; bravely and emotionally, Mrs K spoke for the couple in advancing to me why they believe that sterilisation is (or may well be) the right procedure for K. In particular, I have noted, and understand, Mrs K's plea that in the event that K has to undergo general anaesthetic for any contraceptive procedure (which would be indicated for the insertion of an IUCD), then it would be fairer to K for her to be sterilised so that the issue of future contraception is resolved once and for all". I have no doubt that Mr and Mrs K are deeply concerned to do what is best for K, and that the views expressed by them sincerely reflect what they believe to be best for K.

28. In reaching my conclusions, I have also had regard to the statements of the social worker; these reflect an intuitive understanding of the issues, and proper acknowledgement of the important role of the parents in K's life.'

13.1.6   Practice and procedure

In relation to the procedure to be adopted in relation to non- therapeutic sterilisation cases, Cobb J stated in the same case as follows:

'Practice/Procedure:

36. Referral to the Court of Protection in a case such as this could and should always be considered at the earliest moment in accordance with the Rules (see in particular Practice Direction 9E to the Court of Protection Rules 2007, and Para.6.18 and Paras.8.18-8.29 of the Mental Capacity Act 2005 Code of Practice). I take this opportunity to remind medical (and, where relevant, legal) practitioners of the Court of Protection's role in considering a question of non-therapeutic sterilisation. Such a treatment decision is so serious that the Court has to make it. In particular I advise that particular note is made of the process as follows:

(a)   The decision of whether someone who lacks capacity to consent should have a non-therapeutic sterilisation is a question involving "serious medical treatment" (see Practice Direction E (PD9E) – Applications relating to serious medical treatment). Non-therapeutic sterilisation is specifically identified in this category (see Paragraph 5(c));

(b)   A question concerning non-therapeutic sterilisation of a person who lacks capacity to give consent "should be brought to the court" (Para.5 ibid.);

(c)   Where a question arises as to non-therapeutic sterilisation of a person who lacks capacity to consent, the proposed applicant (whether it be carer, local authority or trust), can (indeed I suggest should) usefully discuss the application with the Official Solicitor's department before the application is made (see PD9E para.8): such cases should be addressed to a family and medical litigation lawyer at the Office of the Official Solicitor;

(d) The organisation which is, or will be, responsible for providing clinical or caring services to P should usually be named as a respondent in the application form (where it is not already the applicant in the proceedings);

(e) Proceedings of this kind must be conducted by a judge of the Court of Protection who has been nominated as such by virtue of section 46(2)(a) to (c) of the Act (i.e. the President of the Family Division, the Chancellor or a puisne judge of the High Court) (Para.12 PD9E);

(f) At the first hearing of the application the Court will consider
    i)   whether P should be joined as party to the proceedings, and give directions to that effect;
    ii)   if P is to be joined as a party to the proceedings, decide whether the Official Solicitor should be invited to act as a litigation friend or whether some other person should be appointed as a litigation friend;
    iii) identify anyone else who has been notified of the proceedings and who has filed an acknowledgment and applied to be joined as a party to proceedings, and consider that application; and
    iv)   set a timetable for the proceedings including, where possible, a date for the final hearing.

(g) Note that the hearing will generally be in public, given the nature of the application, although the Court will ordinarily make an order pursuant to Rule 92 that restrictions be imposed in relation to publication of information about the proceedings.

37. Where a declaration is needed, the order sought should be in the following or similar terms:

(a) That P lacks capacity to make a decision in relation to the [proposed medical treatment or procedure]. e.g. 'That P lacks capacity to make a decision in relation to sterilisation by [named procedure]'; and

(b) That, having regard to the best interests of P, it is lawful for the [proposed medical treatment or procedure] to be carried out by [proposed healthcare provider]; or

(c) That it is not in the best interests of P to undergo [the proposed medical treatment or procedure].'

13.2 HUMAN TISSUE ACT 2004

The UK Human Tissue Act 2004 (HT Act 2004) is designed to regulate all activity involving human tissue, organs, or bodies. It was introduced in the House of Commons in December 2003 and received Royal Assent on 15 November 2004.

This Act repealed and replaced the Human Tissue Act 1961, the Anatomy Act 1984, and the Human Organ Transplants Act 1989. It also repealed and replaced the Human Tissue Act (Northern Ireland) 1962, the Human Organ Transplants (Northern Ireland) Order 1989 and the Anatomy (Northern Ireland) Order 1992.

The Act had its origins in events of serious public concern, namely the retained organs scandals at Bristol Royal Infirmary and the Royal Liverpool Childrens' Hospital. The Act is correspondingly dominated by regulation of post-mortem examinations and retention of human tissue, with consistent emphasis on the need for fully informed consent. Compliance with these requirements is mandatory with the risk of up to 3 years' imprisonment and/or fines for any deviation.

The Act has the broad purpose of regulating the storage and use of human tissue from the living, and the removal, storage and use of tissue from the deceased.

Human tissue can be defined as material which has come from the human body which consists of, or includes, human cells.

Cell lines are excluded, as are hair and nails from living people. Live gametes and embryos are excluded as they are already covered by the Human Fertilisation and Embryology Act 1990.

The Act is in three parts and has seven schedules:

Part 1 is about consent. It sets out the requirement to obtain appropriate consent to carry out activities regulated under the Act: storage and use of whole bodies, removal, storage and use of human material (organs, tissues and cells) from the bodies of deceased persons, and storage and use of material from living people, for purposes set out in Sch 1. It defines appropriate consent by reference to who may give it, and provides for a 'nominated representative' who may make decisions about regulated activities after a person's death. Part 1 makes it an offence to carry out regulated activities without appropriate consent, makes it unlawful to use bodies or human material, once donated, for purposes other than those set out in Sch 1 and establishes penalties.

Part 1 also sets out what should happen to 'existing holdings' of human material obtained before the consent provisions take effect. This Part also exempts coroners from the requirements of Part 1 of the Act, and allows storage and use of human material, obtained from living persons, for specified purposes without consent.

Part 1 does not apply to the removal (as opposed to the storage and use) of human material from living persons. The current law will continue to apply to that. Nor does Part 1 affect the existing law on storage and use of human material for purposes other than those mentioned in Part 1.

Section 2 sets out the meaning of 'appropriate consent' in relation to activities regarding the body of a deceased child, or relevant material from living or deceased children. For the purposes of this section, children are people under the age of 18.

Section 3 sets out the meaning of 'appropriate consent', in relation to activities concerning the body of a deceased adult or relevant material from a person who is (at the time of the activity) a living or deceased adult. If the adult is alive his own consent is required. Subsections (3) to (5) provide that after death, the adult's consent, given in advance in writing and witnessed, is required for purposes of anatomical examination or public display. Anatomical examination is relevant only in relation to a whole body or material which has come from a whole body during an anatomical examination. For other scheduled purposes, if the adult made no prior decision, a person nominated by him in accordance with s 4 to make decisions after his death or, failing that, someone in a 'qualifying relationship' (as listed in s 54(9) and dealt with further at s 27(4)) may give consent.

Part 2 is about the regulatory system to be established to make sure that regulated activities are carried out in a proper manner. It sets up the Human Tissue Authority (HTA) with a remit covering removal, storage, use and disposal of human material. It also sets out the range of activities for which a licence from the HTA is required. It prohibits the conduct of those activities without a licence and establishes penalties for so doing. This Part also sets out who will be responsible for a licence, their duties under a licence and related procedures. It provides for the HTA to issue codes of practice concerning the proper conduct of activities within its remit, to issue directions and make reports. Part 2 brings the regulation of transplants between living persons under the HTA and prohibits commercial dealing in human material.

Part 3 deals with various important supplementary issues and general provisions.

Section 43 makes it clear that it is lawful for hospital authorities to take the minimum steps to preserve the organs of deceased persons whilst appropriate consent to transplantation is sought. Section 44 provides for disposal of human material which is no longer to be kept.

Section 45 makes it an offence, with specified exceptions, for a person to have human material with a view to analysing its DNA without consent. Section 47 creates a power for certain national museums to transfer human remains out of their collections if they think it appropriate to do so. This Part also contains general provisions including powers of inspection, entry, search and seizure, the power to make regulations and orders by way of statutory instruments, interpretation and consequential changes to existing statutes.

The HTA has published nine Codes of Practice providing practical guidance to professionals carrying out activities which lie within the HTA's remit.

13.2.1   Code of Practice 1: Consent

The Code is divided into two main sections.

The first section highlights the importance of consent as the central tenet of the Act.

The second section provides guidance on the requirements for consent and is divided into three parts. Part 1 sets out in detail the general provisions on consent. There are then different consent requirements which apply when dealing with tissue from the deceased and tissue from the living; these are set out in Parts 2 and 3. Parts 2 and 3 are further divided into consent requirements for adults and children.

Consent requirements for the living in relation to the storage and use of human tissue fall under the Act; removal of tissue is a common law matter. Consent to treatment and examination is covered by the common law and MCA 2005.

The guidance outlined in the first section of the Code highlights the importance of consent, which underpins the HT Act 2004. The following issues are central to the application of the consent provisions of the Act: is consent required?; appropriate consent; valid consent; scope of consent; duration of consent; and withdrawal of consent.

Consent under the Act relates to the purposes for which material might be removed, stored or used. These purposes are set out in Sch 1 to the HT Act 2004 and are called scheduled purposes.

In broad terms, the Act and the codes of practice require that consent is required to: store and use relevant material from the living; store and use dead bodies; and remove, store and use relevant material from a dead body.

Anyone removing, storing or using material in circumstances for which the Act requires consent must be satisfied that consent is in place.

Consent to treatment and examination is covered by the common law and the Mental Capacity 2005.

Appropriate consent

The Act is clear about what constitutes 'appropriate consent'. Appropriate consent is defined in terms of the person who may give consent. This is either the consent of the person concerned, their nominated representative or (in the absence of either of these) the consent of a person in a 'qualifying relationship' with them immediately before they died.

Valid consent

In relation to 'valid consent' the giving of consent is a positive act. For consent to be valid it must be given voluntarily, by an appropriately informed person who has the capacity to agree to the activity in question. For consent to be valid, the person should understand what the activity involves and, where appropriate, what the risks are. When seeking consent, healthcare professionals or other suitably experienced people should ensure that it is appropriate for the intended purpose.

To ensure that the removal, storage or use of any tissue is lawful, it is important to establish clearly that consent has been given. Consent may be expressed in various ways, and does not necessarily need to be in writing, unless the Act requires it to be.

Obtaining valid consent presupposes that there is a process in which individuals, including their families where appropriate, may discuss the issue fully, ask questions and make an informed choice.

When seeking consent to store umbilical cord blood for potential use for transplantation, establishments should provide balanced information to the mother about the options available, including the benefits and risks, to enable them to make a fully informed choice. This may include guidelines from the Royal College of Obstetricians and Gynaecologists.

Scope of consent

In relation to the 'scope of consent' consent may differ in scope as it may be generic or specific. Generic consent typically only applies to research. If conducting research on samples of tissue, it is good practice to request a generic consent because this avoids the need to obtain further consent in the future. It is still important, however, that the consent is valid. Consent may differ in its duration. It may be enduring or time-limited.

Enduring consent means that it remains in force unless consent is withdrawn. A person may, however, specify a time limit for how long they wish their consent to remain in force. In both cases, the decision should be clearly documented in the patient's records, the laboratory records or both.

Withdrawal of consent

In relation to 'withdrawal of consent' consent may be withdrawn at any time whether it is generic or specific. Withdrawal should be discussed at the outset when consent is being sought. The practicalities of withdrawing consent and the implications of doing so should be made clear, for example, for potential recipients if the donated tissue is for clinical use. Withdrawal of consent cannot be effective where tissue has already been used.

If someone gives consent for their tissue to be stored or used for more than one scheduled purpose and then withdraws consent for a particular scheduled purpose (e.g. research), this does not necessarily mean that the sample or samples have to be removed or destroyed. However, the samples may no longer be stored or used for the particular purpose for which consent has been withdrawn. In addition, if someone withdraws consent for samples to be used in any future projects, this does not mean that information research data should be withdrawn from any existing projects.

13.2.2 Code of Practice 2: Donation of organs for transplantation

This Code sets out the HTA's requirements for living donation of organs for transplantation. It includes specific information on the requirements of the HT Act 2004 and about the HTA's role in approving donations.

This Code also includes guidance on deceased organ donation. It sets out the legislative requirements for seeking consent to donation and information about the roles of the HTA and NHS Blood and Transplant (NHSBT) in the deceased donation process.

The paragraph numbers below refer to some of those set out within Code of Practice 2.

Living organ donation

'29. The Human Tissue Act governs consent for the storage and use of organs or part organs taken from a living person for the purpose of transplantation.

30. Consent for the removal of organs from living donors, whether for transplantation or otherwise, is outside the scope of the HT Act. It is instead covered by the common law and the Mental Capacity Act (MC Act) 2005.

31. The requirements for living donor transplantation are set out in sections 33 and 34 of the HT Act.

32. It is an offence to remove or use any organ or part organ from the body of a living person for transplantation unless the requirements of the HT Act and the Regulations are met.'

Paragraphs 27 and 28 of the Code set out the forms of living organ donation that may be made.

Paragraph 27 sets out the differing forms of donation where a healthy person donates to a recipient an organ (usually a kidney) or part organ (for example, liver or lung lobe).

'28. Domino donation is a further form of living donation where an organ or part organ is removed for the primary purpose of a person's medical treatment.

58. As required by the Human Tissue Act 2004 (Persons who Lack Capacity to Consent and Transplants) Regulations 2006, the HTA must assess all cases of living organ donation (except domino donations) for transplantation. The HTA undertakes this role through an independent assessment process.

33. The Regulations require that, with the exception of domino donations (defined in paragraph 27), all living organ donations for transplantation must be approved by the HTA before the donation can take place.

34. Before the HTA can approve such cases, the Regulations require that the Authority must be satisfied that:
i.　　no reward has been, or is to be, given
ii.　　consent to removal for the purpose of transplantation has been given (or removal for that purpose is otherwise lawful) an Independent

Assessor (IA) (see paragraphs 60–64) has conducted separate interviews with the donor (and if different from the donor, the person giving consent) and the recipient (or the person acting on behalf of the recipient) and submitted a report of their assessment to the HTA

iii. an Independent Assessor (IA) (see paragraphs 60–64) has conducted separate interviews with the donor (and if different from the donor, the person giving consent) and the recipient (or the person acting on behalf of the recipient) and submitted a report of their assessment to the HTA

44. The HTA requires that checks are made to ensure that no other payment or reward is made and that the donor does not profit from the donation.

45. The HT Act also prohibits commercial dealings in human material, including organs or part organs, for the purposes of transplantation. A person is committing an offence if they:

i. give, offer or receive any type of reward for the supply or offer of supply of any organ or part organ

ii. look for a person willing to supply any organ or part organ for reward

iii. offer to supply any organ or part organ for reward

iv. initiate or negotiate any arrangement involving the giving of a reward for the supply of, or for an offer to supply, any organ or part organ

v. take part in the management or control of any type of group whose activities consist of or include the initiation or negotiation of such arrangements

vi. cause to be published or distributed, or knowingly publish or distribute, an advertisement inviting people to supply, or offering to supply, any organ or part organ for reward, or indicate that the advertiser is willing to initiate or negotiate any such arrangements. This covers all and any types of advertising

46. This offence carries the risk of a fine and up to three years imprisonment. No offence is committed, however, where payments relate to reimbursement of the donor's expenses as discussed above, or reimbursement is for relevant expenses connected with transporting, removing, preparing, preserving, or storing human material for the purpose of transplantation.'

Adults – special considerations

'50. Where an adult lacks the capacity to consent to the removal of an organ or part organ, the case must be referred to a court for a declaration that the removal would be lawful. Donation may then only proceed if court approval has been obtained and following court approval the case is referred to, and approved by, an HTA panel (see paragraphs 69–70).'

Children – special considerations

'47. Children can be considered as living organ donors only in extremely rare circumstances. In accordance with common law and the Children Act 1989 before the removal of a solid organ or part organ from a child for donation, court approval should be obtained. Appendix A to this code provides further guidance on requirements for court approval.

48. Living donation by a child under the HT Act can only go ahead with the approval of an HTA panel (see paragraphs 69–70). The HT Act defines a child as being under 18 years old. Such cases should only be referred to the HTA for decision after court approval to the removal has been obtained.

85. The HT Act requires consent be given for the storage and use of organs for transplantation. Where a child is deemed competent to consent to that decision, the necessary consent will be their own. A person who has parental responsibility for the child can consent to the storage and use of organs for transplantation on the child's behalf if there is no decision by the child either to, or not to, consent, and:
i.   the child is not competent to deal with the issue of consent to donation
ii.   even though the child is competent to do so, they have not made a decision about consent to donation

86. A person who has parental responsibility will usually, but not always, be the child's parent. The category of persons with parental responsibility is as set out in the Children Act 1989.'

Deceased organ donation

'The requirements of the legislation and consent

92. The removal, storage and use of organs or part organs from a deceased person for transplantation is governed by the HT Act. Before they can be removed, stored or used for transplantation, appropriate consent must be obtained (see paragraphs 96–103 and 115–118).

93. The code of practice on Consent sets out guiding principles on how the law should be applied to consent for removal, storage and/or use of tissue, including organs, from the body of a deceased person. It should be consulted and read in conjunction with this code of practice.

Consent – adults

95. The HT Act makes clear that where an adult made a decision to, or not to, consent to organ donation taking place after their death, then that consent is sufficient for the activity to be lawful.

96. In cases of potential deceased donation, the transplant coordinator or delegated person should be approached at an early stage and asked to determine whether the deceased person had consented to donate their organs after death. This should be done before partners, relatives or close friends are approached.

97. Trained staff should determine whether the deceased person had given consent for organ donation by checking relevant sources, such as the Organ Donor Register. If consent is established, those close to the deceased should be told.

98. If no records are held, an approach should be made to the deceased person's partner, relatives or close friends by a transplant coordinator or a member of the team who cared for the person, or both together, to establish any known decision of the deceased person to consent (or not) to donation.

99. Once it is known that the deceased person consented to donation, the matter should be discussed sensitively with those close to the deceased. They should be encouraged to recognise the wishes of the deceased and it should be made clear, if necessary, that they do not have the legal right to veto or overrule their wishes. There may nevertheless be cases in which donation is considered inappropriate and each case should be assessed individually.

100. If the deceased person's wishes are unknown and donation is a possibility, trained healthcare professionals should raise the subject of donation with the appropriate partner, relative/s or close friend/s. This approach should be made as sensitively as possible and provide enough information to allow a decision to be reached. Once a decision has been made, it must be respected.

101. If the deceased person's wishes are not known and they were an adult who had appointed a person to deal with the use of their body after death, then consent can be given by that nominated representative (see paragraphs 104–108).

102. If the deceased person's wishes are not known, and they had not appointed a nominated representative, consent can be given by a person who was in a qualifying relationship immediately before the death (see paragraphs 109–114).

Nominated representatives

103. Under the HT Act, adults may appoint one or more people to represent them after death and provide a decision on consent on their behalf. The trained healthcare professionals should make reasonable enquiries at the hospital, with the prospective donor's GP or with those

close to the deceased person to ask whether a nominated representative was appointed to take those decisions.

104. The appointment of a nominated representative and its terms and conditions may be made orally or in writing. The HT Act sets out the requirements for a valid appointment. The appointment of a nominated representative may be revoked at any time.

105. If the deceased person appointed more than one nominated representative, only one of them needs to give consent, unless the terms of the appointment specify that they must act jointly.

106. The nominated representative's consent cannot be overridden by other individuals, including family members. It is advisable, nevertheless, to ensure that appropriate consultation and discussion takes place between all those involved.

107. The nomination may be disregarded if no one is able to give consent under it. This includes situations where it is not practicable to communicate with the nominated representative within the time available if the consent is to be acted upon. In the event that a nomination is disregarded, consent may be given by a person in a 'qualifying relationship' (see paragraphs 109–114).

Qualifying relationships

108. If the deceased person has not indicated their consent (or refusal) to the use of their organs for transplantation or, in the case of an adult, appointed a nominated representative, then the appropriate consent may be given by someone who was in a 'qualifying relationship' with the deceased person immediately before their death. Those in a qualifying relationship are found in the HT Act in the following order (highest first)

1. spouse or partner (including civil or same sex partner). The HT Act states that for these purposes a person is another person's partner if the two of them (whether of different sexes or the same sex) live as partners in an enduring family relationship.
2. parent or child (in this context a child can be any age and means a biological or adopted child)
3. brother or sister
4. grandparent or grandchild
5. niece or nephew
6. stepfather or stepmother
7. half-brother or half-sister
8. friend of long standing

109. Consent is needed from only one person in the hierarchy of qualifying relationships and should be obtained from the person ranked highest. If a person high up the list refuses to give consent, it is not

possible to act on consent from someone further down the list. For example, if a spouse refuses but others in the family wish to give consent, the wishes of the spouse must be respected. However, the guidance in paragraphs 111 and 113 should be observed in line with this principle. If there is no one available in a qualifying relationship to make a decision on consent (and consent had not been indicated by the deceased person or a nominated representative), it is unlawful to proceed with removal, storage or use of the deceased's persons organs or part organs for transplantation.

110. While the HT Act is clear about the hierarchy of consent, the person giving consent should be encouraged to discuss the decision with other family members – this may include people not on the list, for example, an aunt or uncle.

111. Relationships listed together, for example 'brother or sister', are accorded equal ranking, in which case it is sufficient to obtain consent from just one of them, provided they are ranked equal highest. For example, if the deceased person has no spouse or partner, but has several children, the consent of only one child is required.

112. Where there is a conflict between those accorded equal ranking, then this needs to be discussed sensitively with all parties, whilst explaining clearly that so far as the HT Act is concerned, the consent of one of those ranked equally in the hierarchy is sufficient for the procedure to go ahead.

113. In applying the principles set out above, a person's relationship shall be left out of account if:

This means a person may be omitted from the hierarchy if they cannot be located in reasonable time for the activity in question to be addressed, declines to deal with the matter or is unable to do so, for example, because they are a child or lack capacity to consent. In such cases, the next person in the hierarchy would become the appropriate person to give consent.

Consent – children

114. The position for a child, who was competent to reach a decision before they died and consented to organ donation taking place after their death, is legally no different from that of an adult. The child's consent is sufficient to make the removal, storage or use of their organs for transplantation lawful.

115. Clearly, in any case where a child has given consent to donation, especially if the child has self-registered on the Organ Donor Register it is essential to discuss this with the child's family, and take their views and wishes into account before deciding how to proceed. In some cases it may also be advisable to establish with the person who had parental responsibility for the deceased child, whether the child was competent to

make the decision. A person who has parental responsibility will usually, but not always, be the child's parent.

116. If a child did not make a decision, or was not competent to make a decision, the HT Act makes clear that in this instance the appropriate consent will be that of a person with parental responsibility for the child immediately before they died. The consent of only one person with parental responsibility is necessary.

117. If there is no person with parental responsibility (e.g., if the parents have also died, perhaps at the same time as the child), then consent for organ donation should be sought from someone in a qualifying relationship, as set out in paragraphs 109–114. Under the HT Act, children cannot appoint nominated representatives and therefore provisions relating to seeking consent from nominated representatives do not apply.'

13.2.3   Bone marrow transplant

A question which has arisen and been considered by the court is the donation of bone marrow by a donor who is incapable of giving consent, where a significant benefit will flow to another person. What is distinct here (as opposed to, for example, proposed sterilisation operations) is that there is a third party who is intended to benefit from the proposed medical treatment on the patient. Notwithstanding such distinction, pursuant to *Re F (Mental Patient: Sterilisation)* [1990] 2 AC 1, the lawfulness of taking bone marrow from an adult donor who is incapable of giving consent will depend upon whether the treatment is in the best interests of the patient. The court will thereby have to be satisfied that the procedure envisaged will benefit the patient and, accordingly, benefits which may flow to the third party are relevant only insofar as they have a positive effect on the best interests of the patient.

It is helpful to scrutinise in this regard the case of *Re Y (Mental Incapacity: Bone Marrow Transplant)* [1996] 2 FLR 787. In that case, the patient was a severely mentally and physically handicapped young woman aged 25. Since birth she had suffered from hydrocephalus and required assistance in all her daily needs, except feeding. She was incapable of understanding what was said to her and understood her own basic needs only but not the needs of others. The plaintiff was the eldest of the patient's sisters and suffered from pre-leukaemic bone marrow disorder, myelodispastic syndrome. She urgently required a bone marrow transplant, preferably from sibling transplantation which, according to medical opinion, produced the best results for a significant prolongation of life. Although the patient had lived away from the family since the age of 10, first in a residential school and then in a community home, the family were closely knit and over the years had kept in touch with the patient, especially her mother who visited regularly and with whom the patient had the closest relationship. The mother also suffered from ill-health, had had a recent coronary by-pass operation and suffered from angina. Her condition was further exacerbated by her anxieties over the health of the sister. With the agreement of the family and the support of the Official Solicitor, the guardian ad litem of the patient, the sister applied for a declaration that blood tests and a bone marrow harvesting operation under general anaesthetic could lawfully be performed upon the patient, despite the fact that she (the patient) was unable to give an informed consent for such procedures.

The appropriate test applied, as previously indicated, was whether the evidence showed that it was in the best interests of the patient for the procedures to take place. The findings of the court were as follows. The fact that the process would significantly benefit the sister was not relevant, unless, as a result of the patient helping her sister in that way, the best interests of the patient were served. The evidence showed that the patient benefited from the visits of her family and her occasional involvement in family events, since they maintained a link with the outside world which was helpful to her. Further, the patient showed an obvious affection with her mother which demonstrated that her mother held a special place in the patient's world. If the application was unsuccessful, the chances of the plaintiff sister not surviving were materially increased, which would have an adverse effect on her mother's health and the mother would be unable to maintain regular contact with the patient. In those circumstances, the defendant patient would clearly be harmed by the reduction in or loss of contact with her mother. Accordingly, the court held, it was to the benefit of the patient that she should act as a donor to her sister because her positive relationship with both her mother and sister would be prolonged and improved. Since the disadvantages to the patient were very small and no real long-term risk from a bone marrow harvesting would be caused, it was to the defendant's emotional, psychological and social benefit to grant the declaration sought.

The *Code of Practice* 6 to the HT Act 2004 issued by the HTA provides that transplantation falls within the Authority's statutory remit. This particular Code of Practice is a Code on donation of bone marrow for transplantation. By paragraph 22 of the Code consent for the storage and use of bone marrow taken from a living person for the purpose of transplantation is governed by the HT Act 2004. Consent for the removal of bone marrow from a living person, whether for transplantation or otherwise, is outside the scope of the HT Act and is instead governed by common law.

The HT Act 2004 requires the consent be obtained to store and use tissue, such as bone marrow transplantation. Whilst consent for removal is governed by the common law, by paragraph 58 of the Code the necessary consents should ideally be sought in a single process.

Under the HT Act 2004 and the Human Tissue Act 2004 (Persons who Lack Capacity to Consent and Transplant) Regulations 2006 (SI 2006/1659) donation of bone marrow both by adults with capacity and children competent to give consent may be approved locally. The HT Act 2004 defines a child as a person under 18 years of age. The Regulations require, however, that donations of bone marrow from children who are not competent to give consent, or from adults lacking capacity, must be approved by the HTA.

Paragraphs 74 to 81 of the Code deal with 'Children and the consent process'. These provisions consider the position of children who are assessed to be legally competent to consent to the donation. The provisions then consider the necessity to obtain consent from those with parental responsibility for the non-*Gillick* competent child.

By paragraph 78:

> 'in these cases, a person with parental responsibility can consent to storage and use of bone marrow for transplantation on behalf of the child, if the donation is assessed as being in the child's overall best interests, taking into account not only the medical but also the emotional, psychological and social aspects of the donation, as well as the risks. The consent of any one person with parental responsibility is necessary.'

It is important to note paragraph 81 of the Code which states: 'where there is any dispute between people with parental responsibility or any doubt as to the child's best interests, the matter should be referred to the court for approval'. In such instances, the HTA would then only consider the case for approval if the court was of the view that donations in the best interests of the donor child.

By paragraph 87 of the Code, in relation to the case of donation of bone marrow by adults who lack capacity to consent, cases must be referred to a court for a declaration that the proposed intervention is lawful before them referring the case to the HTA for a decision on the donation.

13.3   THE HUMAN FERTILISATION AND EMBRYOLOGY ACT 1990

13.3.1   Meaning of 'embryo' and 'gamete'

Section 1 of the Human Fertilisation and Embryology Act 2008 (the 2008 Act) amends s 1 of the Human Fertilisation and Embryology Act 1990 (the 1990 Act) so as to ensure that the Act applies to all live human embryos regardless of the manner of their creation, and to all live human gametes (eggs and sperm).

An embryo will continue to be defined under the new s 1(1) in broad terms as a 'live human embryo' but the definition no longer assumes that an embryo can only be created by fertilisation. This brings the term 'embryo' up to date with technologies that have been developed since the time of enactment of the 1990 Act.

The definition of an 'embryo' in the amended s 1(1)(a) of the 1990 Act excludes certain types of embryos created by combining together human and animal gametes, or human embryos altered using animal DNA or animal cells. Such entities are defined as 'human admixed embryos' by s 4A of the 1990 Act (as inserted by s 4 of the 2008 Act).

The term 'gametes' under s 1(4) of the 1990 Act has been amended to expressly encompass not only mature eggs and sperm, but also immature gametogenic cells such as primary oocytes, and spermatocytes.

A regulation-making power has been taken to expand the definitions of 'embryo', 'eggs', 'sperm' or 'gametes', where this is considered by the Secretary of State to be necessary or desirable in light of developments in science or medicine (see new s 1(6)).

Section 3: prohibitions in connection with embryos

Section 3 of the 2008 Act amends s 3 of the 1990 Act, which covers prohibitions connected with embryos. Section 3(2) prohibits the placing in any woman of any embryo other than a permitted embryo or any gametes other than permitted eggs or permitted sperm.

A permitted embryo is defined as an embryo which has been formed by the fertilisation of a permitted egg by a permitted sperm, whose nuclear or mitochondrial DNA has not been altered and which has not had cells added (except by division of the embryo's own cells). Permitted eggs are defined as eggs produced by or extracted from the ovaries of a woman and permitted sperm as sperm produced by or extracted from the testes of a man. These eggs and sperm must also not have been subject to any alterations to their nuclear or mitochondrial DNA. This section ensures embryos created by artificial gametes or genetically modified gametes could not be placed in a woman. Similarly, genetically modified embryos or embryos created by cloning cannot be placed in a woman. This prevents reproductive cloning and supersedes the Human Reproductive Cloning Act 2001.

A regulation-making power is provided under s 3ZA(5) of the 1990 Act to allow the meaning of permitted eggs and permitted embryos to be extended to include eggs or embryos that have been treated in such a way as specified in regulations to prevent the transmission of serious mitochondrial disease. In the future, it may be possible to create embryos using an affected woman's egg, her partner's sperm and healthy donated mitochondria. This regulation-making power will enable such embryos and eggs to be implanted in a woman if the technology became available and was proven safe. Further provision regarding mitochondrial donation is made in s 26 of the 2008 Act, which inserts s 35A into the 1990 Act.

13.3.2 Consent to use or storage of gametes, embryos and human admixed embryos etc.

Section 13 of the 2008 Act introduces Sch 3 to the Act which amends Sch 3 to the 1990 Act, relating to consent to store or use embryos or gametes to create an embryo in vitro.

Formalities of consent

Schedule 3 to the 1990 Act states that consent for the storage and use of gametes and embryos is required in writing. This requirement for written consent is retained; there is now an express requirement that the consent must be signed.

Physical incapacity

People who have suffered an injury resulting in a condition such as quadriplegia or a similar condition may lack the physical ability to sign the consent form although they have the capacity to consent. Paragraph 1(2) of Sch 3 to the 1990 Act will allow a physically incapacitated person, who is unable to write and therefore give consent in writing, to direct another to sign on their behalf, in the presence of a witness.

Purpose of consent

Under the 1990 Act, consent must specify the purposes for which any gamete or embryos are to be used. The 2008 Act amends paragraph 2(1) of Sch 3 so that, in addition to being able to consent to the use of embryos for treatment or research, a person may now also specify that an embryo can be used in the training of embryologists.

The collection and storage of embryos and gametes

The guiding principles and practicalities in relation to the collection and storage of embryos and gametes to be used at a later date to create a child are set out as follows.

From reading the relevant sections of the Act, and the relevant 2009 Regulations a number of matters are apparent:

(1) As long ago as 1990 Parliament accepted that gametes and embryos could legally and properly be collected and stored to be used at a later date to create a child.

(2) That such activities needed to be prescribed and regulated by statute and regulations. Safeguards and prohibitions were required to ensure that proper arrangements were in place and managed and such have been in place under the Act and relevant Regulations.

(3) Since 1990 the Act and Regulations have been amended, and in particular s 28 was amended by the Human Fertilisation and Embryology (Deceased Fathers) Act 2003. By those amendments it was specifically envisaged, and provided for, that the sperm of a man collected before his death could be used to create an embryo, and that any child born of that creation could be recognised and registered as the child of the deceased. The importance of the amendment is that Parliament accepted that medical science had progressed, and thought fit to enable with safeguards to make it lawful to create an embryo using the sperm of a deceased man.

(4) There are basic agreed issues:
   (i) gametes cannot be stored without consent of the provider;
   (ii) consent for storage of gametes must be given in writing and signed by the gamete provider. There is no prescribed form;
   (iii) there is a statutory storage period (10 years) but a gamete provider must specify the maximum period of storage if less than 10 years;

(iv) the consent must also include what is to happen to the gametes in the event of his death, or mental incapacity, whether they should perish at the end of the stated period or remain in storage;

(v)   the 2009 Regulations provided circumstances in which gametes could be stored beyond 10 years from first storage with a maximum of 55 years;

(vi) gametes may only be used for treatment purposes but only if the provider gives consent, in which case he may identify a particular person to receive the treatment;

(vii) before a person gives consent he must be given the opportunity to receive proper counselling, and be provided with such relevant information as is proper. That is set out in the statute, and provision made for guidance on this subject to licence holders in the Code of Practice.

13.3.3   Withdrawal of consent to the storage/usage of gametes

Paragraph 4 of Sch 3 to the 1990 Act requires that a person withdrawing their consent to the storage and/or use of gametes or embryos gives notice of this to the establishment holding the gametes or embryos. New paragraph 1(1) of Sch 3 requires this notice to be provided in writing and signed by the person withdrawing consent.

Paragraph 7 of Sch 3 to the 2008 Act inserts paragraph 4A into Sch 3 to the 1990 Act and introduces a 'cooling off period' where one person in a couple seeking fertility treatment withdraws their consent to the storage of an embryo or, where donated gametes are used, where the gamete donor withdraws consent. This provision does not alter the requirement that the consent of both parties is required to store the embryos but it is intended to provide a year-long 'cooling off' period during which the embryos will not be destroyed unless all interested persons (see paragraph 4A(3)) consent. There is also to be a 'cooling off' period where a single woman seeks fertility treatment and the gamete donor or donors withdraw consent.

This provision allows embryos to remain lawfully stored while the parties, if they wish, attempt to reach a private resolution on the future of the embryos. If the interested persons do not agree to the embryos being removed from storage or simply do not respond to the notification, the embryos will remain in storage until the one-year period expires after which they would be allowed to perish.

The case of *Evans v Amicus Healthcare Ltd* [2003] EWHC 2161 (Fam) pertains to the issue of withdrawal of consent. The case was heard at first instance before Wall J. The applicant Natalee Evans ('the applicant') and her partner Howard Johnston ('J') commenced treatment at an assisted conception clinic. They were informed that the applicant had tumours in both ovaries, and that her ovaries would have to be removed. They were told that because the tumours were growing slowly it would be possible first to extract some eggs for in vitro fertilisation, but this would have to be done quickly.

It was explained to them by the clinic that the applicant and her partner would each have to sign a form consenting to the IVF treatment and that, in accordance with the provisions of the 1990 Act, it would be possible for either to withdraw his or her consent at any time before the embryos were implanted in the applicant's uterus. The applicant asked whether it would be possible to freeze her unfertilised eggs but was informed that this procedure was not performed at the clinic. At that point J reassured her that they were not going to split up, that she did not need to consider the freezing of her eggs, that she should not be negative and that he wanted to be the father of her child. J ticked the boxes which recorded his consent to use his sperm to fertilise the applicant's eggs in vitro and the use of the embryos thus created for the treatment of himself and the applicant together. The applicant signed a form which referred to eggs rather than sperm, and essentially replicated that signed by her partner; she ticked the boxes providing for the treatment of herself and for the treatment 'of myself with a named partner'.

The couple thereafter attended the clinic: 11 eggs were harvested and fertilised; six embryos were created and consigned to storage. The applicant underwent an operation to remove her ovaries. She was told she should wait 2 years before attempting to implant any of the embryos in her uterus.

Thereafter the relationship between the couple broke down. The future of the embryos was discussed between them. J then wrote to the clinic to notify it of the separation and to state that the embryos should be destroyed.

The applicant commenced proceedings in the High Court seeking an injunction requiring her ex-partner to restore his consent to the use and storage of the embryos and a declaration that he had not varied and could not vary his consent. Additionally she sought a declaration of incompatibility under the Human Rights Act 1998 to the effect that s 12 of, and Sch 3 to, the 1990 Act breached her rights under Articles 8, 12 and 14 of the ECHR. She also pleaded that the embryos were entitled to protection under Articles 2 and 8. Interim orders were made requiring the clinic to preserve the embryos until the end of the proceedings.

The trial judge, Wall J, dismissed the applicant's claims. He concluded that under the terms of the 1990 Act, and as a matter of public policy, it had not been open to J to give an unequivocal consent to the use of the embryos irrespective of any change of circumstance, and that, as a matter of fact, J had only ever consented to his treatment 'together' with the applicant, and not to her continuing treatment on her own in the event that their relationship ended.

The case was then heard in the Court of Appeal ([2004] EWCA Civ 727). The court held that the clear policy of the 1990 act was to ensure the continuing consent of both parties from the commencement of treatment to the point of implantation of the embryo, and that 'the court should be extremely slow to recognise or to create a principle of waiver that would conflict with the Parliamentary scheme'.

Leave to appeal to the House of Lords was refused, and the applicant took her case to the European Court of Human Rights (ECtHR). On 7 March 2006 the Chamber of the European Court comprising a panel of seven judges delivered a majority 5–2 ruling against the applicant. The Court, like the national courts, had great sympathy for the plight of the applicant who, if implantation did not take place, would be deprived of the ability to give birth to her own child. However, the panel majority found that, even in such exceptional circumstances, the right to a family life – enshrined in Article 8 of the ECHR – could not override J's withdrawal of consent. The panel also ruled unanimously that the issue of when the right to life begins 'comes within the margin of appreciation which the Court generally considers that states should enjoy in this sphere', and thus rejected the claim that the right to life of the embryos was being threatened.

The case was then referred to the Grand Chamber of the ECtHR. On 10 April 2007 the Grand Chamber ruled against the applicant's appeal under three articles of the Convention. The court unanimously ruled that there had been no breach of the right to life; on the right to respect for private and family life and on the prohibition of discrimination the 17 judges ruled 13 to 4. At paragraph 90 of the judgment it is said:

'As regards the balance struck between the conflicting Article 8 rights of the parties to the IVF treatment, the Grand Chamber, in common with every other court which has examined this case, has great sympathy for the applicant, who clearly desires a genetically related child above all else.

However ... It does not consider that the applicant's right to respect for the decision to become a parent in the genetic sense should be accorded greater weight than J's right to respect for his decision not to have a genetically related child with her.'

13.3.4   Parenthood in cases involving assisted reproduction

(1)   Section 33 of the 2008 Act considers and determines the meaning of 'the mother' of the child.

Section 33 re-enacts s 27 of the 1990 Act. It will remain the case that the woman who carries a child following assisted reproduction (anywhere in the world) is the child's mother, unless the child is subsequently adopted or parenthood is transferred through a parental order.

2.   Section 35 of the 2008 Act considers and determines the meaning of the married man as father of the child.

By s 35 there is no change to the existing position in relation to a child conceived as a result of treatment with donor sperm by a married woman. Her husband will be treated as the child's father, unless it is shown that he did not consent to his wife's treatment. This provision (and others which operate to determine legal parenthood) is subject to the common law presumption that a child is the legitimate child of a married couple, as to which see the note on s 38 below.

3.   Sections 36 and 37 of the 2008 Act consider and determine the meaning of the unmarried man as father of the child.

The existing provisions of the 1990 Act which enabled an unmarried man to be the father of a donor-conceived child if he is 'treated together' with the mother in a licensed clinic were replaced by ss 36 and 37. The provisions require the couple to be treated in a UK licensed clinic, as before, to ensure there is clear evidence of the parents' intentions about fatherhood. However, for the man to be the father at the time the embryo or gametes have been placed in the woman or at the time she is artificially inseminated, the couple must each have given notice of consent to him being treated as the father. Neither of them must have given notice withdrawing that consent and the woman to be treated must not have given notice of consent to another man or woman being treated as the child's parent. The notices of consent do not necessarily have to be drawn up in the clinic, but they must be provided to the 'person responsible' at the clinic. This is the person under whose supervision licensed activities are carried out. If, for example, a woman were to give notice of consent to several people being the father of a child, and corresponding notices were given by the other persons, the latest set provided to the clinic would apply. A notice under s 37 must be in writing and signed by the person giving their consent. The requirement for written notice is waived, however, if any of the parties involved is unable to sign because of illness, injury or physical disability.

After the transfer of the gametes or embryo, neither the man nor the woman can withdraw their consent to the man being treated as the child's father unless the woman does not conceive and a new cycle of treatment has to begin. Changes to the conditions which must be included in all treatment licences, which are made by s 14(3), will require that, if the man withdraws his consent at an earlier stage, the woman must be told before the treatment proceeds. She will therefore have the opportunity to decide whether she wishes to go ahead in these circumstances. If the woman withdraws her agreement to the man being the father, he must be told as soon as possible but he would not, through these provisions, be able to stop her going ahead if she wished to do so. Notices may not validly be given by two people who are within the prohibited degrees of relationship. This is defined in s 58(2) of the 2008 Act to include parents and children, siblings and uncles or aunts and their nephew or nieces. Close relatives of this kind may not jointly be treated as a child's parents.

The Act will maintain the situation that if an unmarried couple carry out self-insemination with donor sperm at home or elsewhere, not as part of licensed treatment, the male partner would not be the legal parent. He would have to take steps to acquire formal parental responsibility, for example by adopting the child. An unmarried man cannot become a parent where donor sperm is provided under a licence under paragraph 1A of Sch 2 to the 1990 Act (non-medical fertility services) unless also used in treatment services.

Section 38(1) provides that where a person is treated as a child's father under the preceding sections, no other person is to be treated as the father. A sperm donor, for example, would not have this status.

13.3.5   Parenthood and the use of sperm, or transfer of embryo, after death of man providing sperm

The full terms below of s 39 of the 2008 Act enable a sperm provider to be treated as a father even if the sperm was used after his death.

'**Section 39 Use of sperm, or transfer of embryo, after death of man providing sperm**

(1) If—

(a) the child has been carried by W as a result of the placing in her of an embryo or of sperm and eggs or her artificial insemination,

(b) the creation of the embryo carried by W was brought about by using the sperm of a man after his death, or the creation of the embryo was brought about using the sperm of a man before his death but the embryo was placed in W after his death,

(c) the man consented in writing (and did not withdraw the consent) –

   (i) to the use of his sperm after his death which brought about the creation of the embryo carried by W or (as the case may be) to the placing in W after his death of the embryo which was brought about using his sperm before his death, and

   (ii) to being treated for the purpose mentioned in subsection (3) as the father of any resulting child,

(d) W has elected in writing not later than the end of the period of 42 days from the day on which the child was born for the man to be treated for the purpose mentioned in subsection (3) as the father of the child, and

(e) no-one else is to be treated –

   (i) as the father of the child by virtue of section 35 or 36 or by virtue of section 38(2) or (3), or

   (ii) as a parent of the child by virtue of section 42 or 43 or by virtue of adoption, then the man is to be treated for the purpose mentioned in subsection (3) as the father of the child.

(2) Subsection (1) applies whether W was in the United Kingdom or elsewhere at the time of the placing in her of the embryo or of the sperm and eggs or of her artificial insemination.

(3) The purpose referred to in subsection (1) is the purpose of enabling the man's particulars to be entered as the particulars of the child's father in a relevant register of births.

(4) In the application of this section to Scotland, for any reference to a period of 42 days there is substituted a reference to a period of 21 days.'

In the case of *Warren v Care Fertility (Northampton) Ltd* [2014] EWHC 602 (Fam) the application before Hogg J was for a declaration that it was lawful for the sperm of Warren Brewer who died on 7 February 2012 to be stored for a period of up to 55 years, so that it could be used by the claimant Elizabeth Warren, his widow, for the purposes of conceiving a child or children. Mr Brewer was diagnosed with a brain tumour and before he commenced radiotherapy was referred to a clinic in Northampton so that samples of his sperm could be taken, frozen and stored to enable him to have children in the likely event he became infertile as a consequence of the radiotherapy. Mr Brewer consented in writing to his sperm being used to create embryos in vitro for his wife's treatment in the event of his death; he consented also to the embryos being stored.

In relation to the possible duration for the storage of embryos and gametes, the Human Fertilisation and Embryology (Statutory Storage Period for Embryos and Gametes) Regulations 2009 (SI 2009/2581) came into force on 1 October 2009. The maximum storage period shall be 55 years.

Mr Brewer did not give his written consent as required by regs 4(3)(a) or 7(3)(a) to the gametes being stored for a period in excess of 10 years for the provision of treatment services. Another issue under the regulations was that the appropriate medical opinion in relation to the requirements under regs 4(3)(b) or 7(3)(b) had been provided after his death and not whilst he was still alive.

The judge, as detailed within her judgment, found that the clinic had materially failed to fulfil its obligations to Mr Brewer. As a consequence he was deprived of relevant information and the opportunity to meet the requirements of regs 4(3) or 7(3). She said that the Authority had recognised this, and had sought by its guidance of 31 May 2012 to ensure that other providers and clinics did not fall into the same trap. The judge determined that the failure of the clinic produced a great and conspicuous unfairness to Mr Brewer and to Mrs Warren.

The claimant Mrs Warren sought to override the strict terms of the regulations relying upon s 3 of the Human Rights Act 1998 and Article 8 of the ECHR. Section 3 provides: '(1) So far as it is possible to do so primary legislation and subordinate legislation must be read and given effect in a way which is compatible with the Convention rights.' Article 8 provides that 'everyone has the right to respect for his/her private and family life'.

The judge stated that a strict interpretation of the regulations could produce a very restrictive outcome; she said that Parliament intended to enable the deceased man's sperm to be used by the named person, in this case his widow, provided it was the deceased's wish recorded in writing. She determined that the deceased's wish and intention was clearly known, be it all not recorded in accordance with the Regulations. The judge determined that she should interpret the statutory provisions in a purposive way and if possible interpret those provisions in the way which was compatible with Mrs Warren's right under Article 8 to decide to seek to become a parent by her deceased husband. Whilst recognising the need for there to be legal clarity and certainty, the Authority recognised the clear deficiencies of the clinic which had entrapped Mr Brewer, causing it to warn and advise clinics generally of the dangers of such deficiencies. The judge determined that it was right, proper and proportionate for her to make the declaration sought that it was lawful in the first instance for Mr Brewer's gametes to be stored for 10 years and then up to a maximum of 55 years.

13.3.6 Lesbian co-parenting

Section 42 of the 2008 Act encompasses women in civil partnership at the time of treatment.

Section 42 brings the provision for female civil partners into line with that which applies to married couples, which was not found in the 1990 Act. Where a female civil partner gives birth to a child conceived as a result of donor insemination (anywhere in the world), she is the mother of the child and her civil partner will automatically be the other parent, unless the other civil partner did not consent to the mother's treatment. The terminology is different, but otherwise the legal provisions are the same as for married couples.

Sections 43 and 44 of the 2008 Act make provision about same-sex female couples who are not civil partners. This is similar to the provision made about opposite-sex unmarried couples by ss 36 and 37. Where one of the women has a child as a result of donor insemination (DI) in a UK licensed clinic and the couple have in place, at the time of the transfer of the sperm or embryo which results in conception, current notices of consent to the other woman being treated as a parent, then she will be a legal parent. The same provisions about withdrawing consent and providing information to the other party will apply. Again, notice cannot be given by two persons who are within the prohibited degrees of relationship to each other. A notice under s 44 must be in writing and signed by the person giving their consent. The requirement for a signature is waived, however, if any of the parties involved are unable to sign because of illness, injury or physical disability.

The case of *Re E (Assisted Reproduction: Parent)* [2013] EWHC 1418 (Fam) before Cobb J grapples with the consequences of non-compliance with the requirements of the 2008 Act. The two women, AB and CD, were cohabiting in a same-sex relationship. They were not civil partners. They had decided they wished to create a family and approached a fertility clinic offering a complete range of infertility treatments and had a well-established donal sperm bank. CD became pregnant. As a result of the implementation of the new statutory provisions, AB and CD signed revised consent forms which purported to give their bilateral agreement to AB becoming a legal parent of any child born as a consequence of the treatment, in accordance with the new law. Twin boys were born. The two women registered the boys' birth, with CD as the 'mother' and AB being recorded as 'the parent'. AB played an integral role in the lives of the children until she left CD. AB applied for contact with the twins. CD opposed this application and sought a declaration pursuant to s 55A of the Family Law Act 1986 that AB was not the parent of the twins as a result of non-compliance with the requirements of the 2008 Act. Sections 43 and 44 of the 2008 Act were material, as well as the number of guidance documents and codes of practice issued by the Human Fertilisation and Embryology Authority, as well as the licence conditions for treatments offered by clinics.

In the 'Commencement Arrangements Guidance' it includes saying: 'if the consents are not in place before gamete or embryo transfer, the partner of the woman receiving treatment will not be legally recognised as the second parent of any child born as a result of the treatment'. The judge determined that the current consent forms were not signed or submitted to the clinic prior to treatment; to be effective to bestow parental status on AB, the forms would have had to be submitted before the treatment. There is much analysis in the judgment of the clinic's non-compliance with the conditions of its licence.

The judge determined that the consent forms were in any event completed and submitted in breach of the clinic's licence conditions in that there was no offer of counselling to the parties on that issue and the consent on the forms was not 'informed consent' as defined in the guidance. The judge made a declaration that AB was not the parent of the twins. He directed the court to notify the registrar general of his decision so that the births of the twins could be reregistered. He also directed that AB's application for leave to make a contact application be listed before him. AB had no biological connection with the twins, and had to come to terms with her lack of legal recognition as a parent to them following the judgment. She also faced opposition from her ex-partner to there being any contact between her and the twins.

During his judgment, the judge referred to the 'twin pillars' supporting Parliamentary regulation of this difficult field being intended to be: (a) the requirement for informed consent, capable of being withdrawn at any point prior to the transfer of the embryos to the woman receiving treatment; and (b)s the focus on child welfare required by s 13(5). He said that it was essential that the courts pay proper respect to the scheme laid down by Parliament, and supported by the Human

Fertilisation and Embryology Authority, for the regulation of assisted reproduction. As Hale LJ (as she then was) said in the case of *Centre for Reproductive Medicine v U* [2002] EWCA Civ 565 at paragraph 24:

'The whole scheme of the 1990 Act lays great emphasis upon consent. The new scientific techniques which have developed since the birth of the first IVF baby in 1978 open up the possibility of creating human life in ways and circumstances quite different from anything experienced before then. These possibilities bring with them huge practical and ethical difficulties. These have to be balanced against the strength and depth of the feelings of people who desperately long for the children which only these techniques can give them, as well as the natural desire of clinicians and scientists to use their skills to fulfil those wishes. Parliament has devised a legislative scheme and a statutory authority for regulating assisted reproduction in a way which tries to strike a fair balance between the various interests and concerns. Centres, the HFEA and the courts have to respect that scheme, however great their sympathy for the plight of particular individuals caught up in it.'

13.3.7   The role (if any) of the sperm donor in lesbian co-parenting

The case of *Re G, Re Z (Children) (Children: Sperm Donors: Leave to Apply for Children Act Orders)* [2013] EWHC 134 (Fam) before Baker J concerned linked cases in which two males had each donated sperm to a lesbian couple in a civil partnership. In each case the lesbian couple were known to them. In the first case, D and E were female civil partners, who conceived a child, G, by the sperm donor S who was known to them. S had a civil partner T. In the second case, X and Y were female civil partners, who conceived a child, Z, by the sperm donor T. The adults involved did not use a clinic authorised under the HEFA; there was no written agreement. The relationship between the parties involved deteriorated, leading the two males to issue proceedings, including S seeking leave to apply for contact with the child G, and T seeking leave to apply for contact with the child Z. There was a conflict of evidence in each case as to the role intended to be played by the males in the lives of the children.

It is clear, as indicated in the judgment, in any event that the effect of ss 42(1), 45(1) and 48(2) of the 2008 Act is that S and T were not to be treated in law as the parents of G and Z respectively for any purpose. The judge observed that the policy underpinning the above statutory provisions is to put lesbian couples in a civil partnership and their children in exactly the same legal position as other types of parents and children. As a result of the statutory provisions of the 2008 Act accordingly, S and T were not legal fathers of the children in question and could not bring an application for orders under s 8 of the Children

Act 1989 (CA 1989)without first obtaining the leave of the court. S and T each sought leave of the court to apply for relief under the CA 1989.

The respective cases were clearly contrasting. The case on behalf of the lesbian couples was that to grant leave to the applicant males to make an application for contact would have the effect of frustrating the legislative intention behind the 2008 statutory reforms. The case on behalf of the applicant males was that the potential importance of genetic parenthood was not automatically extinguished by the removal of the status of legal parenthood.

The judge accepted throughout that the 2008 Act denies the biological father the status of legal parent, but said that it does not prevent the lesbian couple, in whom legal parenthood is rested, from encouraging or enabling the biological father to become a psychological parent. The judge said at paragraph 118 of the judgment:

> 'By choosing friends, S and T, to provide sperm to enable them to conceive children, and by allowing them to have regular and frequent contact and to play some role (albeit disputed) in the lives of their families, D and E in one case, and X and Y in the other, were exercising their parental responsibility to facilitate some sort of relationship between their children and their biological fathers.'

The judge rejected the submission on behalf of the lesbian couples that granting leave to the applicant males would have the effect of frustrating the legislative intention behind the 2008 reforms. He accepted the submissions on behalf of the male applicants that the potential importance of genetic and psychological parenthood is not automatically extinguished by the removal of the status of legal parenthood, and that social and psychological relationships amounting to parenthood can and often do co-exist with legal parenthood. Applying the provisions of CA 1989, s 10(9), the judge granted leave to S to apply for a contact order with the child G, and granted leave to T to apply for a contact order with the child Z.

It is clear from this case that it was important that the genetic fathers S and T were not strangers to the respective children. More particularly, S and T were known to the respective mothers of the children. Such a situation as arose in this case is far removed from the circumstances where the sperm donor genetic father is unknown to both mothers and children.

13.3.8 Schedule 7 Part 2 to the Same Sex (Married Couples Act) 2013

'37 The Human Fertilisation and Embryology Act 2008 is amended as follows.

38(1) Section 35 (woman married at time of treatment) is amended in accordance with this paragraph.

(2) The title: after "married" insert "to a man".

(3) Subsection (1)(a): after "marriage" insert "with a man".

39 Section 40 (embryo transferred after death of husband etc who did not provide sperm), subsection (1)(b): after "marriage" insert "with a man".

40(1) Section 42 (woman in civil partnership at time of treatment) is amended in accordance with this paragraph.

(2) The title: after "partnership" insert "or marriage to a woman"

(3) Subsection (1) –
(a)   after "partnership" (in the first place) insert "or a marriage with another woman";
(b)   after "partnership" (in the second place) insert "or marriage".

41(1) Section 46 (embryo transferred after death of civil partner or intended female parent) is amended in accordance with this paragraph.

(2) The title: after "civil partner" insert "or wife".

(3) Subsection (1) –
(a)   paragraph (b), after "partnership" insert "or marriage with another woman";
(b)   paragraphs (c), (d) and (e), after "partnership" insert "or marriage";
(c)   the words after paragraph (f), after "partnership" insert "or marriage"'

13.4 SURROGACY: PARENTAL ORDERS

Section 54 of the 2008 Act in relation to parental orders is set out below in full.

'(1) On an application made by two people ("the applicants"), the court may make an order providing for a child to be treated in law as the child of the applicants if –

(a)   the child has been carried by a woman who is not one of the applicants, as a result of the placing in her of an embryo or sperm and eggs or her artificial insemination,

(b)   the gametes of at least one of the applicants were used to bring about the creation of the embryo, and

(c)   the conditions in subsections (2) to (8) are satisfied.

(2) The applicants must be –

(a)   husband and wife,

(b)   civil partners of each other, or

(c)   two persons who are living as partners in an enduring family relationship and are not within prohibited degrees of relationship in relation to each other.

(3) Except in a case falling within subsection (11), the applicants must apply for the order during the period of 6 months beginning with the day on which the child is born.

(4) At the time of the application and the making of the order –

(a)   the child's home must be with the applicants, and

(b)   either or both of the applicants must be domiciled in the United Kingdom or in the Channel Islands or the Isle of Man.

(5) At the time of the making of the order both the applicants must have attained the age of 18.

(6) The court must be satisfied that both –

(a)   the woman who carried the child, and

(b)   any other person who is a parent of the child but is not one of the applicants (including any man who is the father by virtue of section 35 or 36 or any woman who is a parent by virtue of section 42 or 43), have freely, and with full understanding of what is involved, agreed unconditionally to the making of the order.

(7) Subsection (6) does not require the agreement of a person who cannot be found or is incapable of giving agreement; and the agreement of the woman who carried the child is ineffective for the purpose of that subsection if given by her less than six weeks after the child's birth.

(8) The court must be satisfied that no money or other benefit (other than for expenses reasonably incurred) has been given or received by either of the applicants for or in consideration of –

(a)   the making of the order,

(b)   any agreement required by subsection (6),

(c)   the handing over of the child to the applicants, or

(d)   the making of arrangements with a view to the making of the order, unless authorised by the court.

(9) For the purposes of an application under this section –

(a) in relation to England and Wales, section 92(7) to (10) of, and Part 1 of Schedule 11 to, the Children Act 1989 (jurisdiction of courts) apply for the purposes of this section to determine the meaning of "the court" as they apply for the purposes of that Act and proceedings on the application are to be "family proceedings" for the purposes of that Act,

(b) in relation to Scotland, "the court" means the Court of Session or the sheriff court of the sheriffdom within which the child is, and

(c) in relation to Northern Ireland, "the court" means the High Court or any county court within whose division the child is.

(10) Subsection (1)(a) applies whether the woman was in the United Kingdom or elsewhere at the time of the placing in her of the embryo or the sperm and eggs or her artificial insemination.

(11) An application which –

(a) relates to a child born before the coming into force of this section, and

(b) is made by two persons who, throughout the period applicable under subsection (2) of section 30 of the 1990 Act, were not eligible to apply for an order under that section in relation to the child as husband and wife, may be made within the period of six months beginning with the day on which this section comes into force.'

Within the above terms of s 54 there are new provisions extending the categories of couples who can apply for a parental order where a child has been conceived using the gametes of at least one of the couple, and has been carried by a surrogate mother. Under the new provisions, civil partners are able to apply, as can unmarried opposite-sex couples or same-sex couples not in a civil partnership. The other provisions relating to parental orders remain the same as the existing provisions of the 1990 Act. A single person remains unable to apply for a parental order.

13.5 SCIENTIFIC TESTING: PATERNITY TESTING

13.5.1 Power of court to direct the use of scientific tests

The Family Law Reform Act 1969, s 20 provides:

'(1) In any civil proceedings in which the parentage of any person falls to be determined, the court may, either of its own motion or on an application by any party to the proceedings, give a direction –

(a) for the use of scientific tests to ascertain whether such tests show that a party to the proceedings is or is not the father or mother of that person; and

(b)   for the taking, within a period specified in the direction, of bodily samples from all or any of the following, namely, that person, any party who is alleged to be the father or mother of that person and any other party to the proceedings;

and the court may at any time revoke or vary a direction previously given by it under this subsection.

(1A) Tests required by a direction under this section may only be carried out by a body which has been accredited for the purposes of this section by –

(a)   the Lord Chancellor, or

(b)   a body appointed by him for the purpose.

(2) The individual carrying out scientific tests ("the tester") in pursuance of a direction under subsection (1) above shall make to the court a report in which he shall state –

(a)   the results of the tests;

(b)   whether any party to whom the report relates is or is not excluded by the results from being the father or mother of the person whose parentage is to be determined; and

(c)   in relation to any party who is not so excluded, the value, if any, of the results in determining whether that party is the father or mother of that person;

and the report shall be received by the court as evidence in the proceedings of the matters stated in it.

(2A) Where the proceedings in which the parentage of any person falls to be determined are proceedings on an application under section 55A or 56 of the Family Law Act 1986, any reference in subsection (1) or (2) of this section to any party to the proceedings shall include a reference to any person named in the application.

(3) A report under subsection (2) of this section shall be in the form prescribed by regulations made under section 22 of this Act.

(4) Where a report has been made to a court under subsection (2) of this section, any party may, with the leave of the court, or shall, if the court so directs, obtain from the tester a written statement explaining or amplifying any statement made in the report, and that statement shall be deemed for the purposes of this section (except subsection (3) thereof) to form part of the report made to the court.

(5) Where a direction is given under this section in any proceedings, a party to the proceedings, unless the court otherwise directs, shall not be entitled to call as a witness the tester, or any other person by whom anything necessary for the purpose of enabling those tests to be carried out was done, unless within fourteen days after receiving a copy of the report he serves notice on the other parties to the proceedings, or on such of them

as the court may direct, of his intention to call the tester or that other person; and where the tester or any such person is called as a witness the party who called him shall be entitled to cross-examine him.

(6) Where a direction is given under this section the party on whose application the direction is given shall pay the cost of taking and testing bodily samples for the purpose of giving effect to the direction (including any expenses reasonably incurred by any person in taking any steps required of him for the purpose), and of making a report to the court under this section, but the amount paid shall be treated as costs incurred by him in the proceedings.

13.5.2 Consents required for taking of bodily sample

The Family Law Reform Act 1969, s 21 provides:

'(1) Subject to the provisions of subsections (3) and (4) of this section, a bodily sample which is required to be taken from any person for the purpose of giving effect to a direction under section 20 of this Act shall not be taken from that person except with his consent.

(2) The consent of a minor who has attained the age of sixteen years to the taking from himself of a bodily sample shall be as effective as it would be if he were of full age; and where a minor has by virtue of this subsection given an effective consent to the taking of a bodily sample it shall not be necessary to obtain any consent for it from any other person.

(3) A bodily sample may be taken from a person under the age of sixteen years, not being such a person as is referred to in subsection (4) of this section,
(a)   if the person who has the care and control of him consents; or
(b)   where that person does not consent, if the court considers that it would be in his best interests for the sample to be taken.

(4) A bodily sample may be taken from a person who is suffering from mental disorder within the meaning of the Mental Health Act 1983 and is incapable of understanding the nature and purpose of scientific tests if the person who has the care and control of him consents and the medical practitioner in whose care he is has certified that the taking of a bodily sample from him will not be prejudicial to his proper care and treatment.

(5) The foregoing provisions of this section are without prejudice to the provisions of section 23 of this Act.'

13.5.3 Failure to comply with direction for taking scientific tests

The Family Law Reform Act 1969, s 23 provides:

'(1) Where a court gives a direction under section 20 of this Act and any person fails to take any step required of him for the purpose of giving effect to the direction, the court may draw such inferences, if any, from that fact as appear proper in the circumstances.

(2) Where in any proceedings in which the parentage of any person falls to be determined by the court hearing the proceedings there is a presumption of law that that person is legitimate, then if –
(a)   a direction is given under section 20 of this Act in those proceedings, and
(b)   any party who is claiming any relief in the proceedings and who for the purpose of obtaining that relief is entitled to rely on the presumption fails to take any step required of him for the purpose of giving effect to the direction,
the court may adjourn the hearing for such period as it thinks fit to enable that party to take that step, and if at the end of that period he has failed without reasonable cause to take it the court may, without prejudice to subsection (1) of this section, dismiss his claim for relief notwithstanding the absence of evidence to rebut the presumption.

(3) Where any person named in a direction under section 20 of this Act fails to consent to the taking of a bodily sample from himself or from any person named in the direction of whom he has the care and control, he shall be deemed for the purposes of this section to have failed to take a step required of him for the purpose of giving effect to the direction.'

It is clear under the inherent jurisdiction, as decided by the House of Lords in *S (An Infant, by her guardian ad litem the Official Solicitor to the Supreme Court) v S; W v Official Solicitor (acting as guardian ad litem for a male infant named PHW)* [1972] AC 24, and also under the Family Law Reform Act 1969, that an adult cannot be forced to provide a blood sample against his or her will.

However, s 23(1) of the Act provides that, where a court gives a direction under s 20 and any person fails to take any step required of him for the purposes of giving effect to the direction, the court may draw such inferences, if any, from that fact as appears proper in the circumstances.

Section 20(1) of the Act does not empower the court to order scientific tests, but merely permits it to make a direction for the use of blood tests to ascertain paternity (*Re H (A Minor)* [1997] Fam 89).

13.5.4 Jurisdiction of the court

Whereas the welfare of the child is the paramount consideration in deciding, for example, an application for parental responsibility and contact in an application under s 20 of the 1969 Act, the paramountcy test does not apply. The child's welfare is an important factor to be weighed alongside a number of other factors, including, for example, whether there is a refusal of a party to undergo blood testing and the likely outcome of the proceedings in which the issue arises. Nevertheless, the court should refuse to make a direction for the use of a blood test to ascertain paternity, if satisfied that it would be against the child's interests to order it (*Re H (A Minor)* [1997] Fam 89 at 103, 104).

In the case of *Re R (A Minor) (Blood Tests: Constraint)* [1998] Fam 66, an issue of paternity arose in respect of a child aged 22 months. The court was satisfied that it was in the child's best interests that her paternity should be determined, if at all possible, but the mother was not prepared to give her consent under s 21(3) of the Family Law Reform Act 1969 to blood samples being taken. The question then arose as to whether and how the blood tests could be effected. The court held that there was nothing in principle to prevent the court, under its inherent jurisdiction, from requiring a child under 16 to provide a blood sample, if satisfied that that was the right course. Nevertheless, on the facts, it was held to be possible to implement the terms of s 21(3) by making a direction under s 20 for the provision of a blood sample and ordering the delivery of the child for that specific purpose into the care and control of the Official Solicitor, granting him permission to consent on the child's behalf.

13.6 ABORTION

A child capable of being born alive is protected by the criminal law from intentional destruction and, by the Abortion Act 1967, from termination otherwise than as permitted by the Act.

The Infant Life (Preservation) Act 1929, by s 1, provides a criminal offence for the intentional destruction of a child, capable of being born alive, before it has an existence independent of its mother.

Under the Abortion Act 1967, s 1 (as amended by the Human Fertilisation and Embryology Act 1990) pregnancies up to 24 weeks may in certain defined circumstances, be terminated. Pregnancies after 24 weeks may be terminated where it is necessary to prevent grave injury to the mental or physical health of the pregnant woman. The Act gives precedence to the health of the mother over the unborn child.

13.6.1　New guidance

The new guidance for healthcare professionals on compliance with the Abortion Act entitled 'Guidance for doctors on compliance with the Abortion Act', published on 23 May 2014, clarifies;

- that abortion on the grounds of gender alone is not lawful;
- the expectation that two doctors, when certifying that an abortion meets the criteria set out in the Act, must consider the individual circumstances of the woman and be prepared to justify their decision;
- that it is good practice for at least one of the doctors to have seen the pregnant woman before reaching a decision about the termination;
- that pre-signing of statutory abortion certificates prior to consideration of a woman's circumstances is not compliant with the Act;
- that doctors have a legal duty to report all abortions to the Chief Medical Officer.

The above Guidance is reproduced at the end of this Chapter.

The position in law generally of the unborn child is examined in detail in Chapter 11 in relation to medical treatment as it pertains to children. Applications seeking to prevent abortions taking place are also considered in Chapter 8 of this book.

13.7　TATTOOING AND BODY PIERCING; OTHER FORMS OF BODY MODIFICATION

The use of legislation in this area of activity is primarily to ensure that infection control arrangements are adequate and effectively carried out wherever so called special treatments are carried out.

Special treatments are usually defined as treatments for persons requiring massage, manicure, acupuncture, tattooing, cosmetic piercing, chiropody, light, electric or other special treatment of a like kind or vapour, sauna or other bath.

The primary means of enforcing infection control arrangements is by use of the licensing or registration provisions. The licensing and registration provisions are largely concerned with setting requirements for good standards by requiring the maintenance of established hygiene controls in respect of premises, equipment, procedures and practices. However, there are additional controls contained in primary legislation that do contain provisions for the immediate prohibition of activities or persons or for the closure of premises where risk of infection can be demonstrated.

In the case of *R v Brown* [1994] 1 AC 212, the House of Lords ruled on appeal that consent cannot be a defence to what otherwise remains a criminal assault. However the law recognises that certain activities that give rise to harm are lawful. This includes surgery, tattooing, ordinary piercing and violent sport.

Consent is material in this area relating to tattooing, body piercing and other forms of body modification. The material and comments below will concentrate on the position of minors.

13.7.1   Tattooing

The Tattooing of Minors Act 1969 imposes a statutory minimum age of 18 years for permanent tattooing (except when carried out for medical reasons by a duly qualified medical practitioner or by a person working under their direction).

A tattoo practitioner or tattoo artist cannot tattoo anyone under the age of 18 years even if they gain parental permission. They have a defence if they can show that they had good reason to believe that the person was over 18 years of age. The consent of a client under 18 is not a defence.

The legislation is enforced by the Police, with heavy fines ensuing upon any conviction.

13.7.2   Body piercing

Body piercing is effected on the varying parts of the body, including the eyebrow, ear, nose, lip, navel, nipples and genitalia.

Cosmetic body piercing generally

Cosmetic piercing is, generally speaking, legal and regulated in the way described above.

However, there is no statutory minimum age for any form of body piercing to the skin.

The courts have held that the law permits children under the age of 16 to consent to cosmetic body piercing providing they are sufficiently mature to understand the nature of the request. This kind of assessment is clearly a subjective matter for the practitioner or body artist who will need to ensure that the child is provided with sufficient information to allow him or her to proceed in an informed way and without pressure. The child will need to fully understand the implications of the request for them to be able to make a sound decision.

If it can be established that the child has not reached sufficient maturity and did not receive sufficient information to be able to make a sound decision, then the practitioner or body artist would be vulnerable to an allegation of assault, which would be a matter for the police.

Ear and nose piercing

Ear piercing and nose piercing are considered by some as acceptable when carried out on a child, even sometimes below the age of five, provided that a parent or legal guardian gives consent and is present whilst the procedure is carried out.

Piercing of nipples and genitalia

Under the Sexual Offences Act 1956, girls and boys under the age of 13 cannot legally give consent to intimate sexual contact under any circumstances, so piercing of nipples and genitalia (for girls) or genitalia (for boys) are capable of being regarded as an offence under the Act.

Evidence that any such contact to those parts of the body by the practitioner or body artist was of a sexual nature or for sexual gratification would be required to constitute an indecent assault.

In the absence of such a sexual element, the practitioner or body artist may still be susceptible to an allegation of criminal assault, whether common assault or an offence under ss 20 and 47 of the Offences Against the Person Act 1861.

13.7.3 Acupuncture and electrolysis

When carried out properly these do not cause harm to the body, and leave no permanent markings. For this reason they are not likely to raise any concerns over common assault charges. Consent should still be obtained before treatment takes place, and in the case of a child should be obtained from the parents or legal guardian.

13.7.4   Extreme forms of body modification

Practices such as beading, branding, scarring, cutting, tongue splitting, amputation and any other extreme forms of bodied modification have no specific legislation to regulate them.

They may leave permanent marks and can result in disfigurement, and those carrying out such activities are likely to be at risk of being accused of assault.

It is to be reminded that consent cannot be a defence to what would otherwise be a criminal assault.

13.8   GENDER RECOGNITION ACT 2004

The purpose of the Gender Recognition Act 2004 is to provide transsexual people with legal recognition in their acquired gender. Legal recognition will follow from the issue of a full gender recognition certificate by a Gender Recognition Panel. Before issuing a certificate, the Panel must be satisfied that the applicant: has, or has had, gender dysphoria, has lived in the acquired gender throughout the preceding 2 years, and intends to continue to live in the acquired gender until death.

Where applicants have been recognised under the law of another country or territory as having changed gender, the Panel need only be satisfied that the country or territory in question has been approved by the Secretary of State.

In practical terms, legal recognition will have the effect that, for example, a male-to-female transsexual person will be legally recognised as a woman in English law. On the issue of a full gender recognition certificate, the person will be entitled to a new birth certificate reflecting the acquired gender (provided a UK birth register entry already exists for the person) and will be able to marry someone of the opposite gender to his or her acquired gender.

Under the previous law, transsexual people were not recognised in their acquired gender under the law of any part of the United Kingdom. Although transsexual people could obtain some official documents in their new name and gender, they could not obtain new birth certificates or enjoy any rights confined by law to people of the gender to which they feel they belong. For instance, they could not marry in their acquired gender. These issues were first considered by an Interdepartmental Working Group convened in 1999. The Government announced its intention to bring forward legislation in this area on 13 December

2002. A draft Bill was published on 11 July 2003, and underwent pre-legislative scrutiny by the Joint Committee on Human Rights.

On 11 July 2002, the ECtHR delivered its judgments in the case of *Goodwin v The United Kingdom and I v The United Kingdom* (2002) 35 EHRR 18. The Court found that the UK had breached the Convention rights of these two transsexual people, under Articles 8 (the right to respect for private life) and 12 (the right to marry). The UK Government had a positive obligation under international law to secure the Convention rights and freedoms and to rectify these ongoing breaches.

On 10 April 2003, the House of Lords gave judgment in the case of *Bellinger v Bellinger* [2003] 2 All ER 593. Mrs Bellinger, a male-to-female transsexual person, was seeking legal recognition of her 1981 marriage to a man. Their Lordships were sympathetic to Mrs Bellinger's plight but ruled that the marriage was void. They declared that s 11(c) of the Matrimonial Causes Act 1973 was incompatible with the Human Rights Act 1998. The result of this was that legislation was needed to enable transsexual people to marry in their new gender.

13.8.1   The Act

In the Act:

(a) ss 1 to 8, and Schs 1 and 2, establish a process for the issue of a gender recognition certificate, that is, for gaining recognition in the acquired gender. They create the Gender Recognition Panels and set out the requirements for making an application and the criteria by which the Panels will decide applications;

(b) ss 9 to 21, and Schs 3 to 6, set out the consequences of the issue of a certificate. The general principle is that the transsexual person will for all purposes be regarded as being of the acquired gender. These sections go on to describe particular consequences in terms of the issue of a new birth certificate, marriage, parenthood, benefits and pensions, discrimination, inheritance, sport, gender-specific offences and foreign gender change; and

(c) ss 22 to 29 contain supplementary provisions. For example, they include a prohibition on disclosure of information relating to a person's application for a certificate or the gender history of a successful applicant. They also limit applications, for the first six months after the Act comes into force, to those transsexual people who have been living in the acquired gender for at least 6 years. As these applicants will have been living in the acquired gender for so long, the criteria to be applied are also slightly different.

The December 2005 Guidance of the President of the Gender Recognition Panel as to the evidential requirements for applications under section 1(1)(a) of the Gender Recognition Act 2004 is reproduced at the end of this chapter.

13.9   FEMALE GENITAL MUTILATION ACT 2003

This statute states that certain procedures in respect of female genitals are illegal unless carried out for medical reasons.

Much has been written and commented upon as to the very serious concerns arising from how to contain, reduce and eliminate if possible, with the assistance of the criminal law to the extent necessary, the unacceptable practices in this regard.

The full terms of the 2003 Act are reproduced at the end of this chapter.

On 1 November 2013 the Royal Colleges of Obstetricians and Gynaecologists, Nursing and Midwives published a report entitled 'Tackling FGM in the UK – Intercollegiate Recommendations for Identifying, Recording and Reporting'.

On 25 June 2014 the House of Commons Home Affairs Committee published its report 'Female Genital Mutilation: The Case for a National Action plan Second Report of Session 2014–15'.

This report is comprehensive and to be commended for a detailed understanding of the issues arising on this subject. Following this report, it is likely that there will be changes in the law, with the terms of the 2003 Act being strengthened.

13.10   MALE CIRCUMCISION

At the end of this chapter the guidance for doctors on the law and ethics of male circumcision published by the British Medical Association is reproduced.

APPENDICES TO CHAPTER 13

GUIDANCE IN RELATION TO REQUIREMENTS OF THE ABORTION ACT 1967 FOR ALL THOSE RESPONSIBLE FOR COMMISSIONING, PROVIDING AND MANAGING SERVICE PROVISION

Prepared by
Sexual Health Policy Team
Richmond House
London
SW1A 2NS

Introduction

1. The Chief Medical Officer ("CMO") wrote to all Registered Medical Practitioners (RMPs) on 23 February 2012 and 22 November 2013 stressing the need for full compliance with the requirements of the Abortion Act 1967 ("the Abortion Act"). In the letter of 22 November, it was announced that the Department of Health would provide more detailed guidance to doctors in relation to the Abortion Act.

2. It is acknowledged that there have been advances in abortion care since the passage of the Abortion Act. Increasingly, abortions are provided through medical rather than surgical methods, at earlier gestations and there is generally multidisciplinary team ("MDT") involvement. However, apart from amendments made in 1990, the Abortion Act remains unchanged. It is essential that all those involved in commissioning and providing abortion care, including those managing services, should understand the legal requirements placed on RMPs to ensure that their practice is lawful.

3. Abortion is an area in which people can hold very strong views. All those involved in abortion care, particularly clinicians, can be faced with working in a sometimes difficult and challenging environment with a number of vulnerable clients. This guidance is intended to support all those involved in commissioning, providing and managing abortion services to provide a high quality, legal service that meets the needs of women.

Background

4. Following the decision by the CPS in August 2013 not to prosecute two doctors investigated for certifying abortions based on the gender of

the foetus, the CPS highlighted[1] the lack of guidance for doctors about abortion law. In particular, the statement made by the CPS in relation to those cases highlighted that "there is no guidance on how a doctor should go about assessing the risk to physical or mental health, no guidance on where the threshold of risk lies and no guidance on a proper process for recording the assessment carried out".

5. In response, the Department of Health agreed to produce guidance on these issues. The guidance does not, and indeed cannot, change the law in relation to abortion, which is governed by the criminal law and the Abortion Act and is ultimately a matter for Parliament and the courts to determine. **However, the intention is to provide support for doctors by setting out how the law is interpreted by the Department of Health.** More detailed guidance for health professionals on abortion is also available from the General Medical Council (GMC), British Medical Association (BMA), Royal College of Obstetricians and Gynaecologists (RCOG) and the Royal College of Nursing (RCN).

6. Although there is no legal requirement for at least one of the certifying doctors to have seen the pregnant woman before reaching a decision about a termination, the Department's view is that it is good practice for this to be the case. It is recognised however that, with technological advances, this may well mean that a doctor does not physically see the woman, e.g. there could be a discussion by phone or over a webcam.

This paragraph should also be read in conjunction with paragraphs 20 and 21 of this guidance.

Abortion legislation

7. The Offences Against the Person Act 1861 makes it a criminal offence to intentionally unlawfully procure a miscarriage, including for a woman to procure her own miscarriage. The Infant Life (Preservation) Act 1929 makes it an offence to intentionally kill a child, capable of being born alive, before it has a life independent of its mother. The Abortion Act creates exceptions to these offences in certain limited circumstances.

---

[1]   http://blog.cps.gov.uk/2013/10/statement-from-director-of-public-prosecutions-on-abortion-related-cases.html.

8. The Abortion Act makes abortion legal where the pregnancy is terminated by an RMP and, except in emergencies, where two RMPs are of the opinion formed in good faith that one of the lawful grounds specified in the Act are met.

Forming an opinion in good faith

9. If there is evidence that either certifying doctor has not formed their opinion in good faith then the doctor performing the termination is not protected by section 1(1) of the Abortion Act and has potentially committed a criminal offence by terminating the pregnancy. It is also possible that the doctor could be acting contrary to their professional duties.

10. Practices have come to light recently which call into question whether doctors have acted in accordance with their legal obligations under the Abortion Act. These practices include the signing of HSA1 forms by doctors before a woman has been referred, and doctors signing forms relying solely on decisions made about the woman in question by other doctors or members of the multi-disciplinary team without any other information.

Abortion certification

11. Form HSA1 must be completed, signed and dated by two RMPs **before** an abortion is performed[2]. The HSA1 form must be kept with the patient notes for 3 years from the date of termination[3]. The form must be completed by both RMPs certifying their opinion, formed in good faith that at least one and the same ground for abortion in section 1(1) of the Abortion Act exists[4]. The certification takes place in the light of their clinical opinion of the circumstances of the pregnant woman's individual case. The lawful grounds for abortion are set out in Annex A.

Assessing risk to physical or mental health, the threshold of risk and recording how the assessment is carried out

12. Whilst there is no statutory requirement for either doctor to have seen and/or examined the woman, it is the Department's interpretation of the law that both doctors should ensure that they have considered

---

[2] Regulation 3(2) Abortion Regulations 1991 S.I. 1991/499.
[3] Regulation 3(4) Abortion Regulations 1991 S.I. 1991/499.
[4] See the form in Part 1 to Schedule 1 and regulation 3(ii)(d) of the Abortion Regulations 1991.

sufficient information specific to the woman seeking a termination to be able to assess whether the woman satisfies one of the lawful grounds under the Abortion Act.

13. This assessment will include consideration of any risk to the woman's physical or mental health as one of the lawful grounds. The identification of where the threshold of risk to the physical or mental health of the woman lies is a matter for the clinical opinion for each of the doctors.

14. Although the burden of proof would be on a prosecutor to show that an opinion was not formed in good faith, DH recommend that RMPs should be prepared to justify how they considered information specific to the woman when forming their opinion, for example by recording in the patient record that they have assessed the relevant information and reached the conclusion based on this information. This is in line with guidance from the GMC[5],[6] (see Annex B).

15. It should be noted that ultimately, if challenged, the question as to whether an individual doctor formed an opinion in good faith would be for a court to decide based on the facts in the individual case.

What is pre-signing of HSA1 forms?

16. In February 2012, CQC inspectors identified a number of cases where signatures on HSA1 certificates predated the referral and assessment of women in a clinic. For example, one woman was referred to the clinic on 20 December and assessed on the 22 December. The certificate reflected that a doctor at the clinic had seen the woman and signed the form on 22 December. However, the signature of the second doctor, also a practitioner at the clinic, was dated 19 December. Therefore, on the information provided, the second doctor had certified the abortion before being assigned the case, and before having any opportunity to consider the clinical files or other specific information to the woman.

17. The pre-signing of HSA1 forms calls into question whether a doctor could turn his or her mind to a specific woman's circumstances and form a good faith opinion about which, if any, of the lawful grounds under the Abortion Act might apply (see Annex A). In subsequent investigations the CQC identified a further 14 services where there was clear evidence of pre-signing of HSA1 forms. Poor practice identified

---

[5]   Section 19, Good Medical Practice, General Medical Council (2013).
[6]   Section 71, Good Medical Practice, General Medical Council (2013).

included photocopying of signatures on forms. DH considers pre-signing of forms (without subsequent consideration of any information relating to the woman) to be incompatible with the requirements of the Abortion Act.

Signing HSA1 forms based on the decisions of another doctor

18. It has also come to light that, in some cases, the second RMP might simply sign an HSA1 based on the decision of the first RMP, relying solely on that doctor's judgment to provide a second signature without considering any information specific to the woman concerned.

19. An example of where this situation could arise would be where an "on-call" doctor is asked to sign an HSA1 form without access to the patient records to form their opinion in good faith with no other information specific to the woman being available. Junior doctors, in particular, may feel under pressure to comply with such a request.

20. The purpose of the requirement that **two** doctors certify the ground(s) for termination is to ensure that the law is being observed; this provides protection for the woman and for the doctors providing the termination[7]. One of the two certifying doctors may also be the doctor that terminates the pregnancy. The clear intention of the Act is for *each* doctor to consider the woman's circumstances in forming a good faith opinion. This is reflected in the recognition that the doctors may find that different grounds are met (although they must both find the same ground is met for the abortion to be lawful[8]). Treating certification by one or either doctor as a 'rubber stamp' exercise is therefore contrary to the spirit of the Act and calls into question whether that doctor is in fact providing an opinion that they have formed themselves in good faith rather than relying solely on a colleague's opinion, however trusted that colleague's judgement may be. DH considers the signing of forms without consideration of any information relating to the woman to be incompatible with the requirements of the Abortion Act.

The role of the MDT

21. It is acknowledged that the MDT, including nurses and counsellors (it is possible that the MDT would include a midwife where a congenital abnormality has been diagnosed antenatally) plays an important role in

---

[7] Scientific Developments Relating to the Abortion Act 1967, Twelfth Report of Session 2006-7, House of Commons, Science and Technology Committee.

[8] Regulation 3(ii)(d) Abortion (Amendment) (England) Regulations 2002 S.I. 2002/887.

supporting women seeking an abortion and in obtaining information from women[9]. RMPs can rely on information obtained by members of the MDT but it is DH's interpretation of the law that the RMPs should themselves review the information before reaching an opinion, for example by considering the paperwork or speaking to members of the team. The RMP must be satisfied that they can justify how they reached their decision in good faith if later challenged. The opinions required under the Act are clearly those of the RMP, not of any other member of an MDT, however experienced or trusted. DH does not think that the Act can be read to enable the opinion required to be that of another person entirely, or the opinion of a team as a whole. An RMP may, of course, take into account the opinions and views of colleagues in forming an opinion and it is often important to do so, but the opinion provided must be their own.

Faxing of HSA1 forms

22. If the first doctor signs and dates a HSA1, which is faxed to the second doctor who then signs and dates the faxed copy certificate then, although they will have technically signed and dated two separate certificates, in DH's view the doctors will have complied with the requirements as to certification set out in the Abortion Regulations 1991[10] ("the Abortion Regulations"). However, as set out above, it is still expected that both doctors should take positive steps to obtain information specific to the woman seeking a termination as part of reaching their decision as to whether there are grounds under the Abortion Act.

23. As the certificate will contain sensitive personal data, it must be processed (transmitted, stored, disposed of etc.) in accordance with the Data Protection Act 1998 (DPA). The DPA permits the "sensitive personal" data to be transmitted from one doctor to another if the patient explicitly consents, or the processing is necessary for medical purposes and is undertaken by a health professional or by someone who is subject to an equivalent duty of confidentiality[11]. Data Protection Principle 7 requires that: 'Appropriate technical and organisational measures shall be taken against unauthorised or unlawful processing of personal data and against accidental loss or destruction of, or damage to, personal data'[12].

---

[9]   Section 35, Good Medical Practice, General Medical Council (2013).
[10] Regulation 3(2) Abortion Regulations 1991 S.I. 1991/499.
[11] Paragraph 8, Schedule 3, Data Protection Act 1998.
[12] Paragraph 7, Schedule 1, Data Protection Act 1998.

24. There are some recent examples of fines being imposed by the Information Commissioners Office (ICO) where faxes containing sensitive personal data were sent to the wrong fax number. For example an NHS Trust in London was fined £90,000 for persistently committing this error. Abortion providers therefore need to consider whether fax is a sufficiently secure method of transmitting the forms. Providers' should consider the ICO's guidance about the use of faxes:

http://www.ico.gov.uk/for_organisations/data_protection/security_measures.aspx

Abortion on the ground of gender

25. Abortion on the grounds of gender alone is illegal. Gender is not itself a lawful ground under the Abortion Act (see Annex A for the lawful grounds under Section 1(1)). However, it is lawful to abort a fetus where two RMPs are of the opinion, formed in good faith, "that there is a substantial risk that if the child were born it would suffer from such physical or mental abnormalities as to be seriously handicapped", and some serious conditions are known to be gender-related.

Completion of Form HSA4

26. Section 2 of the Abortion Act requires all RMPS terminating a pregnancy to give notice to the Chief Medical Officer (CMO). **It is a criminal offence for RMPs not to notify the CMO of every termination they perform.** In England, the Abortion Regulations[13] require that Form HSA4 be submitted to the CMO within 14 days of the procedure. This notification is used by the Department of Health as an aid to checking that terminations are carried out within the law. Form HSA4 requires detailed information relating to the procedure, including the names and addresses of the doctors who certified there were lawful grounds under the Abortion Act, gestation, method used and place of termination. Every form is checked and monitored by DH officials authorised by the CMO. Data derived from the forms is used to publish annual statistics on abortion. It is crucial that all abortions performed are notified to the CMO, both as a matter of law and for there to be appropriate public and Parliamentary scrutiny and trust in the data that are published.

27. Forms can be submitted electronically or using the paper based system would strongly encourage the use of electronic reporting as this

---

[13] Regulation 3(2) Abortion Regulations 1991 S.I. 1991/499.

is a more secure system and reduces the risk of lost or misplaced forms or missing data. More information on electronic reporting can be found at:

http://media.dh.gov.uk/network/261/files/2012/05/F-Detailed-guidance-note-for-HSA4-Webform1.pdf

28. Currently, around 10% of paper HSA4 forms received are returned to RMPs because of missing, incomplete or invalid data. The main errors that occur are missing doctors' names on page one, missing gestation and missing ground information, both on page four. Incomplete forms will be returned to either the RMP terminating the pregnancy or to the place of termination. If an amended form is not returned within 6 weeks, reminders will be sent until the information is received. Incomplete forms are a financial burden: they generate additional work for those completing the forms and for those who process them on behalf of the CMO. The MDT may have a role in filling in the detail of the form but the RMP terminating the pregnancy is the person legally responsible for giving notice to the CMO. DH therefore recommends that RMPs always check the form before signing it and returning it to the CMO. Clinics and hospitals should have protocols and processes in place to ensure that HSA4 forms are being returned in a timely and accurate manner. Reporting an abortion for fetal abnormality to a fetal abnormality register does not negate the legal requirement for RMPs to also notify the CMO.

Role of the RMP in abortion procedures

29. For medical abortions, the Courts have determined that provided the RMP personally decides upon and initiates the process of medical induction and takes responsibility for it throughout the termination, the protection under the Act applies to both the RMP and any other person participating in the termination under his or her authority. The nurse or midwife would not be responsible for leading or directing the procedure or care, or taking the overall decisions, this is firmly the responsibility of the doctor. The Nursing and Midwifery Council's (NMC) Code will apply to all actions taken or decisions made by the nurse or midwife.

Place of termination

30. Unless performed in an emergency, the Abortion Act states that all abortions must take place in an NHS hospital or a place approved by the Secretary of State. Within the NHS, abortions have traditionally been carried out in gynaecology wards and day care units. Independent sector hospitals or clinics which are outside the NHS must obtain the

Secretary of State's approval and have agreed to comply with the Required Standard Operating Procedures set out in the Procedures for the Approval of Independent Sector Places for the Termination of Pregnancy.[14]

31. The Care Quality Commission (CQC) is responsible for implementing the regulatory framework set out in the Regulations made under the Health and Social Care Act 2008. The Department is currently updating The Health and Social Care Act 2008 (Regulated Activities) Regulations 2010, and in parallel with this, the CQC guidance about compliance with those regulations will also be updated. CQC is also making other changes to how they inspect and regulate health and social care services to ensure that those services provide people with safe, effective, compassionate and high-quality care[15]. It is the responsibility of registered providers and registered managers to comply with the registration requirements and keep up to date with guidance on compliance issued by the CQC.

Counselling

32. Guidance on the provision of non-judgemental counselling was included in the Government's Framework for Sexual Health Improvement published in March 2013. Patients should be able to expect impartial advice from the NHS and CCGs and NHS providers should be accountable for the services they recommend.

Annex A

Grounds for Abortion under Section 1 of the Abortion Act

Subject to the provisions of this section, a person shall not be guilty of an offence under the law relating to abortion when a pregnancy is terminated by a registered medical practitioner if two registered medical practitioners are of the opinion, formed in good faith that:

A. The continuance of the pregnancy would involve risk to the life of the pregnant woman greater than if the pregnancy were terminated (Abortion Act, 1967 as amended, section 1(1)(c))

B. The termination is necessary to prevent grave permanent injury to the physical or mental health of the pregnant woman (section 1(1)(b))

---

[14] Interim Procedures for the Approval on Independent Sector Places for the Termination of Pregnancy, DH, August 2012.

[15] http://www.cqc.org.uk/public/about-us/our-performance-and-plans/our-strategy-and-business-plan.

C. The pregnancy has not exceeded its twenty-fourth week and that the continuance of the pregnancy would involve risk, greater than if the pregnancy were terminated, of injury to the physical or mental health of the pregnant woman (section 1(1)(a))

D. The pregnancy has not exceeded its twenty-fourth week and that the continuance of the pregnancy would involve risk, greater than if the pregnancy were terminated, of injury to the physical or mental health of any existing children of the family of the pregnant woman (section 1(1)(a))

E. There is a substantial risk that if the child were born it would suffer from such physical or mental abnormalities as to be seriously handicapped (section 1(1)(d))

Or, in an emergency, certified by the operating practitioner as immediately necessary:

F. To save the life of the pregnant woman (section 1(4))

G. To prevent grave permanent injury to the physical or mental health of the pregnant woman (section 1(4))

In determining whether the continuance of a pregnancy would involve such risk of injury to health account may be taken of the pregnant woman's actual or reasonably foreseeable environment.

Annex B

Relevant Guidance from Good Medical Practice, General Medical Council (2013)

(1) Section 19: "Documents you make (including clinical records) to formally record your work must be clear, accurate and legible. You should make records at the same time as the events you are recording or as soon as possible afterwards."

(2) Section 35: "You must work collaboratively with colleagues, respect their skills and contributions"

(3) Section 71: "You must be honest and trustworthy when writing reports, and when completing or signing forms, reports and other documents. You must make sure that any documents you write or sign are not false or misleading.

　　a. You must take reasonable steps to check the information is correct.

　　b. You must not deliberately leave out relevant information."

PRESIDENT'S GUIDANCE NO. 1
EVIDENTIAL REQUIREMENTS FOR APPLICATIONS UNDER SECTION 1(1)(A) OF THE GENDER RECOGNITION ACT 2004

1. Section 2 of the Gender Recognition Act 2004 (the Act) says that the Panel must grant an application if it is satisfied that the applicant
   a. has or has had gender dysphoria,
   b. has lived in the acquired gender throughout the period of two years ending with the date on which the application is made,
   c. intends to live in that gender until death, and
   d. has complied with the evidential requirements set out in section 3 of the Act.

2. The evidential requirements in section 3 relate to the medical evidence which must be provided. For standard applications there must be two reports from registered medical practitioners, one of whom works in the field of gender dysphoria. Alternatively, the application may include one report from a registered medical practitioner and a second report from a chartered psychologist working in the field of gender dysphoria. The reports must give details of the diagnosis of gender dysphoria and details of any treatment carried out or planned with a view to modifying sexual characteristics.

3. It is the responsibility of the Panel to decide whether the applicant has satisfied all of the section 2 requirements by considering the evidence provided in support of each of the four requirements. In the case of section 2(a), the Panel must therefore examine the medical evidence provided in order to determine whether it is satisfied that the applicant has or has had the diagnosis of gender dysphoria. In order to do so the Panel requires more than a simple statement that such a diagnosis was made. The medical practitioner practising in the field who supplies the report should include details of the process followed and evidence considered over a period of time to make the diagnosis in the applicant's case. Nor is it sufficient to use the broad phrase, 'gender reassignment surgery' without indicating what surgery has been carried out. Nor should relevant treatments be omitted, such as hormone therapy. These requirements are particularly pertinent in assisting the Panel to be satisfied not only that the applicant has or has had gender dysphoria but also has lived in the acquired gender for at least 2 years and intends to live in that gender until death.

4. On the other hand, doctors need not set out every detail which has led them to make the diagnosis. What the Panel needs is sufficient

detail to satisfy itself that the diagnosis is soundly based and that the treatment received or planned is consistent with and supports that diagnosis.

5. It would be impossible to set out precisely what should be provided in all cases. Each will have its own individual facts and the detail which might be sufficient in one case may be inadequate in another. The Panels perform a judicial function. In the ultimate analysis it is for each Panel to determine precisely what is required. At the same time, doctors and applicants need to know in broad terms what is expected of them and what detail is likely to satisfy a Panel. The burden upon them of providing the evidence should not be such as to deter applicants from applying in the first place or to deter doctors from supporting them.

6. The detail required should normally be no greater than can be set out in the space provided in the medical report pro forma.
    Under paragraph 11 the Panel should see:
    a. the diagnosis,
    b. details of when and by whom the diagnosis was made,
    c. the principal evidence relied on in making the diagnosis,
    d. details of the non-surgical (eg hormonal) treatment to date (giving details of medications prescribed, with dates) and an indication of treatment planned, and
    e. date of referral for surgery, or, if no referral, the reasons for non-referral.

7. If the report is prepared by a registered medical practitioner or by a chartered psychologist who did not make the initial diagnosis of gender dysphoria it will be necessary for the person writing the report to confirm the diagnosis and indicate the basis upon which that confirmation is made.

8. Under paragraph 12 the Panel should see the details of the surgical procedures which have been carried out and their dates, together with any surgery planned. Please note that the mere assertion that gender reassignment surgery has been carried out will not be sufficient to satisfy the requirements. Reference should be made to each individual procedure.

9. It is not the role of the Panel to impose unnecessary or excessive evidential burdens on applicants. However the Act does place on Panels the responsibility of ensuring that the requirements of sections 2 and 3 are complied with before an application is granted. The Panel takes these responsibilities seriously. The purpose of this note is to provide guidance to those seeking a gender recognition certificate, and those advising them, on the minimum requirements

which Panels will expect to be met. It is hoped this will assist applicants in making their applications and acquiring their certificates.

HIS HONOUR JUDGE MICHAEL HARRIS
PRESIDENT OF THE GENDER RECOGNITION PANEL
December 2005

FEMALE GENITAL MUTILATION ACT 2003

1 Offence of female genital mutilation

(1) A person is guilty of an offence if he excises, infibulates or otherwise mutilates the whole or any part of a girl's labia majora, labia minora or clitoris.

(2) But no offence is committed by an approved person who performs—

(a) a surgical operation on a girl which is necessary for her physical or mental health, or

(b) a surgical operation on a girl who is in any stage of labour, or has just given birth, for purposes connected with the labour or birth.

(3) The following are approved persons—

(a) in relation to an operation falling within subsection (2)(a), a registered medical practitioner,

(b) in relation to an operation falling within subsection (2)(b), a registered medical practitioner, a registered midwife or a person undergoing a course of training with a view to becoming such a practitioner or midwife.

(4) There is also no offence committed by a person who—

(a) performs a surgical operation falling within subsection (2)(a) or (b) outside the United Kingdom, and

(b) in relation to such an operation exercises functions corresponding to those of an approved person.

(5) For the purpose of determining whether an operation is necessary for the mental health of a girl it is immaterial whether she or any other person believes that the operation is required as a matter of custom or ritual.

2 Offence of assisting a girl to mutilate her own genitalia

A person is guilty of an offence if he aids, abets, counsels or procures a girl to excise, infibulate or otherwise mutilate the whole or any part of her own labia majora, labia minora or clitoris.

3 Offence of assisting a non-UK person to mutilate overseas a girl's genitalia

(1) A person is guilty of an offence if he aids, abets, counsels or procures a person who is not a United Kingdom national or permanent United Kingdom resident to do a relevant act of female genital mutilation outside the United Kingdom.

(2) An act is a relevant act of female genital mutilation if—

    (a)   it is done in relation to a United Kingdom national or permanent United Kingdom resident, and

    (b)   it would, if done by such a person, constitute an offence under section 1.

(3) But no offence is committed if the relevant act of female genital mutilation—

    (a)   is a surgical operation falling within section 1(2)(a) or (b), and

    (b)   is performed by a person who, in relation to such an operation, is an approved person or exercises functions corresponding to those of an approved person.

4 Extension of sections 1 to 3 to extra-territorial acts

(1) Sections 1 to 3 extend to any act done outside the United Kingdom by a United Kingdom national or permanent United Kingdom resident.

(2) If an offence under this Act is committed outside the United Kingdom—

    (a)   proceedings may be taken, and

    (b)   the offence may for incidental purposes be treated as having been committed, in any place in England and Wales or Northern Ireland.

5 Penalties for offences

A person guilty of an offence under this Act is liable—

    (a)   on conviction on indictment, to imprisonment for a term not exceeding 14 years or a fine (or both),

    (b)   on summary conviction, to imprisonment for a term not exceeding six months or a fine not exceeding the statutory maximum (or both).

6 Definitions

(1) Girl includes woman.

(2) A United Kingdom national is an individual who is—

    (a)   a British citizen, a British overseas territories citizen, a British National (Overseas) or a British Overseas citizen,

    (b)   a person who under the British Nationality Act 1981 (c 61) is a British subject, or

    (c)   a British protected person within the meaning of that Act.

(3) A permanent United Kingdom resident is an individual who is settled in the United Kingdom (within the meaning of the Immigration Act 1971 (c 77)).

(4) This section has effect for the purposes of this Act.

7 Consequential provision

(1) The Prohibition of Female Circumcision Act 1985 (c 38) ceases to have effect.

(2) In paragraph 1(b) of the Schedule to the Visiting Forces Act 1952 (c 67) (offences against the person in respect of which a member of a visiting force may in certain circumstances not be tried by a United Kingdom court), for paragraph (xi) there is substituted—
"(xi) the Female Genital Mutilation Act 2003;".

8 Short title, commencement, extent and general saving

(1) This Act may be cited as the Female Genital Mutilation Act 2003.

(2) This Act comes into force on such day as the Secretary of State may by order made by statutory instrument appoint.

(3) An order under subsection (2) may include transitional or saving provisions.

(4) This Act does not extend to Scotland.

(5) Nothing in this Act affects any criminal liability arising apart from this Act.

THE LAW AND ETHICS OF MALE CIRCUMCISION: GUIDANCE FOR DOCTORS

© British Medical Association (June 2006)

Reproduced with kind permission of the British Medical Association

1 Aim of the guidelines

One of the BMA's roles is to issue guidance to doctors on ethical and medico-legal issues. Accordingly, this guidance addresses the queries medical practitioners raise with the BMA about both therapeutic and non-therapeutic[16] male circumcision. The two procedures raise different issues. It does not cover circumcision carried out by non-medical practitioners, but we note that there may be no requirement in law for these practitioners to have proven expertise. Nor does the guidance address female genital mutilation, that is sometimes referred to as female circumcision.[17]

Circumcision of male babies and children at the request of their parents is an increasingly controversial area and strongly opposing views about circumcision are found within society and within the BMA's membership. The medical evidence about its health impact is equivocal.

As with any aspect of medical practice, doctors must use their skills in a way that promotes their patients' interests. They must act within the boundaries of the law and their own conscience, and weigh the benefits and harms of circumcision for the particular child. This guidance outlines good practice and safeguards which the BMA believes doctors should follow in the circumcision of male babies and children.

The General Medical Council has also issued advice on circumcision[18], and advocates similar safeguards to those suggested here.

---

[16] By "therapeutic" we mean that the procedure is necessary to deal specifically with a medical problem (see section 3). By non-therapeutic we mean that the procedure is for any other purpose than medical benefit (see section 4).

[17] Female genital mutilation is a separate issue. The BMA's views on the issue and guidance for doctors are published in British Medical Association. *Female genital mutilation*. London: BMA, 2004. Available from http://www.bma.org.uk/ap.nsf/Content/FGM.

[18] General Medical Council. *Guidance for doctors who are asked to circumcise male children*. London: GMC, 1997.

2 Principles of good practice

- The welfare of child patients is paramount and doctors must act in the child's best interests.

- Children who are able to express views about circumcision should be involved in the decision-making process.

- Consent for circumcision is valid only where the people (or person) giving consent have the authority to do so and understand the implications and risks.

- Both parents[19] must give consent for non-therapeutic circumcision.

- Where people with parental responsibility for a child disagree about whether he should be circumcised, doctors should not circumcise the child without the leave of a court.

- As with all medical procedures, doctors must act in accordance with good clinical practice and provide adequate pain control and aftercare.

- Doctors must make accurate, contemporaneous notes of discussions, consent, the procedure and its aftercare.

3 Circumcision for medical purposes

Unnecessarily invasive procedures should not be used where alternative, less invasive techniques, are equally efficient and available. It is important that doctors keep up to date and ensure that any decisions to undertake an invasive procedure is based on the best available evidence. Therefore, to circumcise for therapeutic reasons where medical research has shown other techniques to be at least as effective and less invasive would be unethical and inappropriate.

---

[19] The term "parents" is used in these guidelines to indicate holders of parental responsibility. The law relating to parental responsibility changed on 1 December 2003. In relation to children born before this date both of a child's parents have parental responsibility if they were married at the time of the child's conception, or birth, or at some time after the child's birth. Neither parent loses parental responsibility if they divorce. If the parents have never married, only the mother automatically has parental responsibility. The father may acquire it by entering into a parental responsibility agreement with the mother, or through a parental responsibility order made by a court. From 1 December 2003 unmarried fathers in England and Wales who are registered on the child's birth certificate have automatic parental responsibility. Clearly where a child has only one parent with parental responsibility, that person is responsible for decision making, although his or her views may not be determinative. For further information on parental responsibility see BMA guidance: *Parental responsibility*. London: BMA, 2005. Available from: http://www.bma.org.uk/ap.nsf/Content/Parental.

Male circumcision in cases where there is a clear clinical need is not normally controversial. Nevertheless, normal anatomical and physiological characteristics of the infant foreskin have in the past been misinterpreted as being abnormal. The British Association of Paediatric Surgeons advises that there is rarely a clinical indication for circumcision.[20] Doctors should be aware of this and reassure parents accordingly.

If there is doubt about whether treatment is needed, or what is the most appropriate course of management, specialist advice should be sought. It is recommended that circumcision for medical purposes must only be performed by or under the supervision of doctors trained in children's surgery in premises suitable for surgical procedures.[21]

4 Non-therapeutic male circumcision

Male circumcision that is performed for any reason other than physical clinical need is termed non-therapeutic (or sometimes "ritual") circumcision. Some people ask for non-therapeutic circumcision for religious reasons, some to incorporate a child into a community, and some want their sons to be like their fathers. Circumcision is a defining feature of some faiths.

There is a spectrum of views within the BMA's membership about whether non-therapeutic male circumcision is a beneficial, neutral or harmful procedure or whether it is superfluous, and whether it should ever be done on a child who is not capable of deciding for himself. The medical harms or benefits have not been unequivocally proven but there are clear risks of harm if the procedure is done inexpertly. The Association has no policy on these issues. Indeed, it would be difficult to formulate a policy in the absence of unambiguously clear and consistent medical data on the implications of the intervention. As a general rule, however, the BMA believes that parents should be entitled to make choices about how best to promote their children's interests, and it is for society to decide what limits should be imposed on parental choices. What those limits currently are is discussed below, together with the legal and ethical considerations for doctors asked to perform non-therapeutic circumcision.

---

[20] British Association of Paediatric Surgeons, Royal College of Nursing, Royal College of Paediatrics and Child Health, Royal College of Surgeons of England and Royal College of Anaesthetists. *Statement on male circumcision*. London: Royal College of Surgeons of England, March 2001.

[21] Ibid.

4.1 The law

Male circumcision is not grounded in statute, however judicial review assumes that, provided both parents consent, non-therapeutic male circumcision is lawful:

> "Even when violence is intentionally afflicted and results in actual bodily harm, wounding or serious bodily harm the accused is entitled to be acquitted if the injury was a foreseeable incident of a lawful activity in which the person injured was participating. Surgery involves intentional violence resulting in actual or sometimes serious bodily harm but surgery is a lawful activity. Other activities carried on with consent by or on behalf of the injured person have been accepted as lawful notwithstanding that they involve actual bodily harm or may cause serious bodily harm. Ritual circumcision, tattooing, ear-piercing and violent sports including boxing are lawful activities".[22]

This comment was made in passing by a judge considering a case about the extent to which a person could consent to physical interference by another and was relied on by a judge in a subsequent case considering the religious circumcision of a 5-year-old boy whose parents disagreed.[23] In that case the judge concluded that "as an exercise of joint parental responsibility, male ritual circumcision is lawful". This approach was followed by the Court of Appeal in the case of *Re S*.[24] Following divorce a Muslim mother applied for permission for her 8 year old son to be circumcised. The son's father opposed and the opposition was held on the basis that the mother's application stemmed from the mother's need to portray herself as a practising Muslim rather than the son's best interests.[25]

Despite the common law assumption that, provided both parents consent, the procedure is lawful, the legality is not uncontroversial and has been challenged by some.[26] To end all doubt, in the mid-1990s the English Law Commission said that although in its view ritual

---

[22] *R v Brown* [1993] 2 All ER 75, HL, *per* Lord Templeman.

[23] *Re J (A Minor) (Prohibited Steps Order: Circumcision)*, sub nom *Re J (Child's Religious Upbringing and Circumcision)* and *Re J (Specific Issue Orders : Muslim Upbringing & Circumcision)* [2000] 1 FLR 571; [2000] 1 FCR 307; [2000] 52 BMLR 82.

[24] *Re S. (Children) (Specific issue: circumcision)* [2005] 1 FLR 236.

[25] Ibid.

[26] M Fox and M Thomson. *A covenant with the status quo? Male circumcision and the new BMA guidance to doctors.* London: JME 2005; 31; 463-469.

circumcision is lawful, law reform to "put the lawfulness of ritual male circumcision beyond any doubt" would be useful.[27] This, however, has not been forthcoming.

With the exception of *Re S*, these legal cases were heard before the implementation of the Human Rights Act which, in 2000, incorporated Articles of the European Convention on Human Rights[28] into UK law. Doctors must consider whether their decisions impact on a person's human rights and, if so, whether the interference can be justified. Rights that might be relevant to non-therapeutic circumcision include:

- Article 3: "No one shall be subjected to torture or to inhuman or degrading treatment or punishment".

- Article 5(1): "Everyone has the right to liberty and security of the person".

- Article 8: "Everyone has the right to respect for his private and family life" except for the "protection of health or morals, or for the protection of the rights and freedom of others".

- Article 9(1): "Everyone has the right to freedom of thought, conscience and religion".

- Article 9(2): "Freedom to manifest one's religion or beliefs shall be subject only to such limitations as are prescribed by law and are necessary in a democratic society in the interests of public safety, for the protection of public order, health or morals, or for the protection of the rights and freedoms of others".

Many aspects of good practice – including careful assessment of best interests, balancing conflicting rights and consulting with patients and their families – have taken on added importance as a result of the Human Rights Act, which makes them a required part of the decision making process. As yet, the full impact of the Act on medical decision making is not known, and the rights in the Act are used by commentators to both support and reject non-therapeutic circumcision. One reason why it is not clear where the balance of rights lies is that the medical evidence is equivocal. Some argue that circumcision is a relatively neutral procedure, that, competently performed, carries little risk but can confer important psychosocial benefits. Others argue that circumcision has, or can have, profound and long-lasting adverse effects on the person who has been circumcised. If it was shown that circumcision where there is no clinical need is prejudicial to a child's

---

[27] Law Commission. *Consent in the Criminal Law. Law Commission Consultation Paper No 139*. London: HMSO, 1995: 119, 128.

[28] Convention for the Protection of Human Rights and Fundamental Freedoms (4. ix. 1950; TS 71; Cmnd 8969). Human Rights Act 1988.

health and wellbeing, it is likely that a legal challenge on human rights grounds would be successful. Indeed, if damage to health were proven, there may be obligations on the state to proscribe it. The UN Convention on the Rights of the Child, which has been ratified by the UK, requires ratifying states to "take all effective and appropriate measures with a view to abolishing traditional practices prejudicial to the health of children".[29] At present, however, the medical evidence is inconclusive.

4.1.1 Summary: the law

Male circumcision is generally assumed to be lawful provided that:
- it is performed competently;
- it is believed to be in the child's best interests; and
- there is valid consent (see below).

The Human Rights Act may affect the way non-therapeutic circumcision is viewed by the courts. There has been no reported legal case involving circumcision since the Act came into force. If doctors are in any doubt about the legality of their actions, they should seek legal advice.

4.2 Consent and refusal

Consent for any procedure is valid only if the person or people giving consent understand the nature and implications of the procedure. To promote such an understanding of circumcision, parents and children should be provided with up-to-date written information about the risks. The BMA is concerned that they may not have easy access to up-to-date information, however, and has called on appropriate bodies such as the Royal College of Paediatrics and Child Health and the British Association of Paediatric Surgeons to produce an information leaflet.

4.2.1 Children's own consent

All children who are capable of expressing a view should be involved in decisions about whether they should be circumcised, and their wishes taken into account. The BMA cannot envisage a situation in which it is ethically acceptable to circumcise a competent, informed young person who consistently refuses the procedure. As with any form of medical treatment, doctors must balance the harms caused by violating a child's refusal with the harm caused by not circumcising. Often surgery for non-medical reasons is deferred until children have sufficient maturity

---

[29] United Nations Convention on the Rights of the Child (20. xi. 1989; TS 44; Cm 1976) Article 24(3).

and understanding to participate in the decision about what happens to their bodies, and those that are competent to decide are entitled in law to give consent for themselves. When assessing competence to decide, doctors should be aware that parents can exert great influence on their child's view of treatment. That is not to say that decisions made with advice from parents are necessarily in doubt, but that it is important that the decision is the child's own independent choice.

4.2.2 Parents' consent

Where children cannot decide for themselves, their parents usually choose for them. Although they usually coincide, the interests of the child and those of the parents are not always synonymous. There are, therefore, limits on parents' rights to choose and parents are not entitled to demand medical procedures contrary to their child's best interests (see section 4.3).

The BMA and GMC have long recommended that consent should be sought from both parents. Although parents who have parental responsibility are usually allowed to take decisions for their children alone, non-therapeutic circumcision has been described by the courts as an "important and irreversible" decision that should not be taken against the wishes of a parent.[30] It follows that where a child has two parents with parental responsibility, doctors considering circumcising a child must satisfy themselves that both have given valid consent. If a child presents with only one parent, the doctor must make every effort to contact the other parent in order to seek consent. If parents disagree about having their child circumcised, the parent seeking circumcision could seek a court order authorising the procedure which would make it lawful, although doctors are advised to consider carefully whether circumcising against the wishes of one parent would be in the child's best interests. Where a child has only one parent, obviously that person can decide.

In all cases, doctors should ask parents to confirm their consent in writing by signing a consent form.

4.2.3 Summary: consent and refusal
- Competent children may decide for themselves.
- The wishes that children express must be taken into account.

---

[30] *Re J (A Minor) (Prohibited Steps Order: Circumcision)*, sub nom *Re J (Child's Religious Upbringing and Circumcision)* and *Re J (Specific Issue Orders: Muslim Upbringing & Circumcision)* [2000] 1 FLR 571; [2000] 1 FCR 307; [2000] 52 BMLR 82. Op cit.

- If parents disagree, non-therapeutic circumcision must not be carried out without the leave of a court.
- Consent should be confirmed in writing.

4.3 Best interests

In the past, circumcision of boys has been considered to be either medically or socially beneficial or, at least, neutral. The general perception has been that no significant harm was caused to the child and therefore with appropriate consent it could be carried out. The medical benefits previously claimed, however, have not been convincingly proven, and it is now widely accepted, including by the BMA, that this surgical procedure has medical and psychological risks (see section 4.4). It is essential that doctors perform male circumcision only where this is demonstrably in the best interests of the child. The responsibility to demonstrate that non-therapeutic circumcision is in a particular child's best interests falls to his parents.

It is important that doctors consider the child's social and cultural circumstances. Where a child is living in a culture in which circumcision is required for all males, the increased acceptance into a family or society that circumcision can confer is considered to be a strong social or cultural benefit. Exclusion may cause harm by, for example, complicating the individual's search for identity and sense of belonging. Clearly, assessment of such intangible risks and benefits is complex. On a more practical level, some people also argue that it is necessary to consider the effects of a decision not to circumcise. If there is a risk that a child will be circumcised in unhygienic or otherwise unsafe conditions, doctors may consider it better that they carry out the procedure, or refer to another practitioner, rather than allow the child to be put at risk.

On the other hand, very similar arguments are also used to try and justify very harmful cultural procedures, such as female genital mutilation or ritual scarification. Furthermore, the harm of denying a person the opportunity to choose not to be circumcised must also be taken into account, together with the damage that can be done to the individual's relationship with his parents and the medical profession if he feels harmed by the procedure.

The BMA identifies the following as relevant to an assessment of best interests in relation to non-therapeutic circumcision:
- the patient's own ascertainable wishes, feelings and values;
- the patient's ability to understand what is proposed and weigh up the alternatives;

- the patient's potential to participate in the decision, if provided with additional support or explanations;
- the patient's physical and emotional needs;
- the risk of harm or suffering for the patient;
- the views of parents and family;
- the implications for the family of performing, and not-performing, the procedure;
- relevant information about the patient's religious or cultural background; and
- the prioritising of options which maximise the patient's future opportunities and choices.[31]

The BMA is generally very supportive of allowing parents to make choices on behalf of their children, and believes that neither society nor doctors should interfere unjustifiably in the relationship between parents and their children. It is clear from the list of factors that are relevant to a child's best interests, however, that parental preference alone is not sufficient justification for performing a surgical procedure on a child.

The courts have also identified some factors that are important in a decision about circumcision. J was a 5 year old boy who lived with his mother, a non-practising Christian. His father, a non-practising Muslim, wanted him to be circumcised. Asked to decide whether J should be circumcised, the court considered all the factors relevant to J's upbringing and concluded that J should not be circumcised because of three key facts:

- he was not, and was not likely to be, brought up in the Muslim religion;
- he was not likely to have such a degree of involvement with Muslims as to justify circumcising him for social reasons; and as a result of these factors,
- the "small but definite medical and psychological risks" of circumcision outweighed the benefits of the procedure.[32]

4.3.1 Summary: best interests

- Doctors must act in the best interests of the patient.

---

[31] Based on checklist in British Medical Association. *Consent, rights and choices in health care for children and young people*. London: BMJ Books, 2001: ch 1.

[32] *Re J (A Minor) (Prohibited Steps Order: Circumcision)*, sub nom *Re J (Child's Religious Upbringing and Circumcision)* and *Re J (Specific Issue Orders: Muslim Upbringing & Circumcision)* [2000] 1 FLR 571; [2000] 1 FCR 307; [2000] 52 BMLR 82. Op cit.

- Even where they do not decide for themselves, the views that children express are important in determining what is in their best interests.

- The BMA does not believe that parental preference alone constitutes sufficient grounds for performing a surgical procedure on a child unable to express his own view. Parental preference must be weighed in terms of the child's interests.

- The courts have confirmed that the child's lifestyle and likely upbringing are relevant factors to take into account. The particular situation of the case needs to be considered.

- Parents must explain and justify requests for circumcision, in terms of the child's interests.

4.4 Health issues

There is significant disagreement about whether circumcision is overall a beneficial, neutral or harmful procedure. At present, the medical literature on the health, including sexual health, implications of circumcision is contradictory, and often subject to claims of bias in research. Doctors performing circumcisions must ensure that those giving consent are aware of the issues, including the risks associated with any surgical procedure; pain, bleeding, surgical mishap and complications of anaesthesia. All appropriate steps must be taken to minimise these risks. It may be appropriate to screen patients for conditions that would substantially increase the risks of circumcision, for example haemophilia.

Doctors should ensure that any parents seeking circumcision for their son in the belief that it confers health benefits are fully informed of the lack of consensus amongst the profession over such benefits, and how great any potential benefits and harms are. The BMA considers that the evidence concerning health benefit from non-therapeutic circumcision is insufficient for this alone to be a justification for doing it.

4.5 Standards

Doctors unfamiliar with circumcision who are asked about it should seek advice about the physical risks from doctors experienced in conducting circumcisions. Religious and cultural organisations may be able to give advice and suggest practitioners who perform circumcisions. It may be necessary to refer a family to a paediatric surgeon, urologist or other doctor experienced in performing the operation for advice and care.

Poorly performed circumcisions have legal implications for the doctor responsible. An action could be brought against the doctor responsible on the child's behalf if the circumcision was carried out negligently. Alternatively, the child could issue such proceedings in his own name on reaching the age of 18 and the normal time limit for starting legal proceedings would run from that birthday. However, unless the lawfulness of circumcision itself is successfully challenged, action cannot currently be taken against a doctor simply because a man is unhappy about having been circumcised at all. A valid consent from a person authorised to give it on the patient's behalf is legally sufficient in such cases. It goes without saying that a health professional who is not currently registered must never give the impression of so being even though there is no legal requirement for non-therapeutic circumcision to be undertaken by a registered health professional.

The General Medical Council does not prohibit doctors from performing non-therapeutic circumcision, although it would take action if a doctor was performing such operations incompetently. The Council explicitly advises that doctors must "have the necessary skills and experience both to perform the operation and use appropriate measures, including anaesthesia, to minimise pain and discomfort".[33]

4.6 Facilities

Doctors must ensure that the premises in which they are carrying out circumcision are suitable for the purpose. In particular, if general anaesthesia is used, full resuscitation facilities must be available.

4.7 Charging patients

Although circumcision is not a service which is provided free of charge, some doctors and hospitals have been willing to provide circumcision without charge rather than risk the procedure being carried out in unhygienic conditions. In such cases doctors must still be able to justify any decision to circumcise a child based on the considerations above.

4.8 Conscientious objection

Some doctors may refuse to perform non-therapeutic circumcisions for reasons of conscience. Doctors are under no obligation to comply with a request to circumcise a child. If doctors are asked to circumcise a child

---

[33] General Medical Council. *Guidance for doctors who are asked to circumcise male children.* London: GMC, 1997. Op cit.

but have a conscientious objection, they should explain this to the child and his parents. Doctors may also explain the background to their conscientious objection if asked.

Clearly where patients or parents request a medical procedure, doctors have an obligation to refer on promptly if they themselves object to it (for example termination of pregnancy). Where the procedure is not therapeutic but a matter of patient or parental choice, there is arguably no ethical obligation to refer on. The family is, of course, free to see another doctor and some doctors may wish to suggest an alternative practitioner.

INDEX

References are to paragraph numbers.

Abortion
guidance   13.6.1
legality of   13.6
pregnancy in young persons
court powers   11.6.7
Abuse
children
medical examinations and
interviews   11.8.3
Acupuncture
consent to   13.7.3
Admissions to hospital
assessment and treatment of mental
disorders   10.2
mental illness
informal   10.5
Adults *see also* Adults lacking capacity;
adults with capacity
refusal of medical treatment
adjudging capacity   9.3, 9.3.1, 9.3.2
overriding refusal   9.4, 9.4.1, 9.4.2,
9.4.3, 9.4.4
presumption of capacity to
decide   9.1, 9.1.1
reasonable force, use of   9.5
Adults lacking capacity *see also* Adults;
Adults with capacity
'best interests of the patient' test 2.2,
3.3.1, 4.4
process   4.5
wishes and feelings   4.6
bone marrow transplants
incapacity to consent to
donation   13.2.3
consent to treatment   1.3, 1.3.2, 10.3,
10.3.1, 10.3.2
next of kin   1.4
Court of Protection procedure
commencement of proceedings   8.1.3
declarations   8.1.2
definitions under COP rules   8.1.1
interim applications   8.1.3
legal status of P   8.1.4
Official Solicitor   8.1.5
urgent applications   8.1.3
court procedure outwith MHA
1983   8.1.6

Adults lacking capacity —*continued*
deputies   10.3.2
appointment of   4.8
hearings in private   8.1.7
jurisdiction   8.1
lasting power of attorney   4.9, 10.3.1
mental illness
informality of decision-making 10.4
organ donation
code of practice   13.2.2
refusal of medical treatment   9.2
sterilisation
case law   13.1.4, 13.1.5
practice and procedure   13.1.6
prior sanction by court   13.1.1
special features of procedure   13.1.2
treatment against clinical
judgment   3.3.2
Adults with capacity *see also* Adults;
Adults lacking capacity
'best interests of the patient' test 2.1
consent to treatment   1.3, 1.3.1
treatment against clinical
judgment   3.3.2
Advance decisions to refuse treatment
generally   12.3
introduction   12.1
jurisdiction   12.5
life-sustaining treatment   12.4
presumption of capacity to
decide   9.1.1
statutory provisions   12.2
Advanced care plans
children   6.8
Allocation of resources
choice of medication   3.4
Amputation
ability to consent to   13.7.4
refusal of consent to treatment   9.4.4
Anorexia
refusal of consent to treatment   9.4.4
Artificial feeding
'best interests of the patient' test 2.6
Artificial ventilation, withdrawal of
children   6.6, 6.7
Assisted reproduction
parenthood, establishing   13.3.4
death of sperm donor   13.3.5
lesbian co-parenting   13.3.6, 13.3.7

Assisted reproduction—*continued*
  parenthood, establishing—*continued*
    same sex marriages   13.3.8
Assisted suicide
  right to die   7.3
Attorneys
  life-sustaining treatment   5.6
Autonomy, right to
  right to die   7.1

Beading
  ability to consent to   13.7.4
'Best interests of the patient' test
  adults lacking capacity   2.2, 3.3.1
  adults with capacity   2.1
  children   2.3, 3.3.1
    overriding child's refusal   11.6.5
    overriding parental refusal   3.1, 11.3,
                                       11.3.2
  considerations   4.4
  deputies, powers of   4.8
  end of life care   2.6
  lasting power of attorney   4.9
  life-sustaining treatment   5.8.3, 5.8.4
  Mental Capacity Act 2005   2.7, 4.4,
                                       4.5, 4.6
  process for   4.5
  prolongation of life   2.5
  sanctity of life   2.4
  weight attached to factors   4.5
  wishes and feelings of person lacking
    capacity   4.6
Blood donation
  children's rights   11.4.3
Blood transfusions
  'best interests of the patient' test
    overriding parental refusal   11.3.2
  refusal of consent to treatment   9.4.4
Body modification
  ability to consent to   13.7.4
Body piercings
  consent to   13.7, 13.7.2
Bone marrow transplants
  'best interests of the patient' test
    overriding parental refusal   11.3.2
  incapacity to consent to
    donation   13.2.3
Brain damage, irreversible
  children
    life-sustaining treatment   6.5
Branding
  ability to consent to   13.7.4

Caesarean sections
  consent to treatment
    mental illness   10.1.3
  refusal of consent to treatment   9.4.4
Capacity
  adults lacking
    consent to treatment   1.3, 1.3.2, 1.4,
                                10.3, 10.3.1, 10.3.2

Capacity—*continued*
  adults with
    consent to treatment   1.3, 1.3.1
  assumption of   4.1
  children
    refusal of consent to
      treatment   11.6.3
  statutory test for incapacity   4.2, 4.3
Capacity to consent
  common law test   10.1.1
Cardio-pulmonary resuscitation (CPR)
  do not activate CPR
    consultation with family   5.8.1
    consultation with patient   5.8.2
  end of life care   5.8.1
  GMC guidance   5.8.1
Care
  objective of   3.2
Care plans, advanced
  children   6.8
Changed circumstances
  refusal of consent to treatment   9.4.3
Chemotherapy
  'best interests of the patient' test
    overriding parental refusal   11.3.2
Child
  meaning   11.1
Children
  'best interests of the patient' test   2.3,
                                       2.4, 3.3.1
    prolongation of life   2.5
  bone marrow transplants
    incapacity to consent to
      donation   13.2.3
  consent to treatment   1.3, 1.3.3
    child's rights   11.4, 11.4.1, 11.4.2,
                                       11.4.3
  end of life care
    life-sustaining treatment   6.1, 6.2,
                          6.3, 6.4, 6.5, 6.6, 6.7, 6.8, 6.9
  family proceedings
    practice and procedure   8.2.2
  hearings in private   8.2.7
  incapacity to consent to treatment
    court powers to authorise
      abortion   11.6.7
  interviews with   11.8
    abuse allegations   11.8.3
  jurisdiction   8.2
    expert evidence   8.2.3
    guardians, appointment of   8.2.5
    medical examinations   8.2.3, 8.2.4
    parents lacking capacity,
      representation of   8.2.6
    twofold jurisdiction   8.2.1
  medical examinations   11.8
    abuse allegations   11.8.3
    during family proceedings   11.8.2
    jurisdiction   8.2.3
    legal status   8.2.4
    prior to or absence of legal
      proceedings   11.8.1

Children—*continued*

organ donation

  code of practice   13.2.2

overriding refusal   11.3, 11.3.1, 11.3.2

parental consent to treatment   11.2

  disagreement between parents   11.2.4

  emergencies   11.2.2

  general requirement   11.2.1

paternity testing   13.5.2

prolongation of life   2.5

refusal of consent to treatment

  child's rights   11.5, 11.5.1

  court powers to overrule   11.6.1,

     11.6.2, 11.6.3, 11.6.4, 11.6.5,

     11.6.6

  parental consent   11.5.2

sterilisation

  case law   13.1.3

  practice and procedure   13.1.6

  prior sanction by court   13.1.1

  special features of procedure   13.1.2

treatment against clinical

  judgment   3.3.2

unborn children

  legal status   11.7, 11.7.1, 11.7.2,

     11.7.3

Clinical judgment

treatment against   3.3.2

Community treatment orders

mental disorders   10.2

Conjoined twins

doctrine of double effect   6.9

Consent

bodily samples

  paternity testing   13.5.2

code of practice under Human

  Tissue Act 2004   13.2.1

Consent to treatment

adults lacking capacity   1.3, 1.3.2,

     10.3, 10.3.1, 10.3.2

  next of kin   1.4

adults with capacity   1.3, 1.3.1

children   1.3, 1.3.3

common law test of capacity   10.1.1

deputies   10.3.2

GMC guidance   3.3, 3.3.1

lasting powers of attorney   10.3.1

meaning   1.1, 10.2.2

mental illness   10.1.2

  caesarean sections   10.1.3

purpose   1.2

Court of Protection

commencement of proceedings   8.1.3

declarations   8.1.2

definitions   8.1.1

hearings in private   8.1.7

interim applications   8.1.3

legal status of P   8.1.4

Official Solicitor   8.1.5

transfer of proceedings   8.3

transparency   8.1.7

urgent applications   8.1.3

Courts

doctors, interface with   3.1

Cutting

ability to consent to   13.7.4

Deprivation of liberty

challenging   10.6.2

distinction from restriction of

  liberty   10.6.1

life-saving measures   10.6.3

restriction of rights

  introduction   10.6

Deputies

adults lacking capacity   1.4, 10.3.2

appointment   4.8

life-sustaining treatment   5.6

refusal of medical treatment

  presumption of capacity to

    decide   9.1.1

Detention of children

refusal of medical treatment

  court powers   11.6.6

Dialysis

refusal of consent to treatment   9.4.4

Do not activate CPR

consultation with family   5.8.1

consultation with patient   5.8.2

Doctors

allocation of resources   3.4

choice of medication   3.4

courts, interface with   3.1

duty of   3.3

standard of care   3.3.1

treatment against clinical

  judgment   3.3.2

  children   6.4

Downs syndrome

'best interests of the patient' test

  overriding parental refusal   11.3.2

Electrolysis

consent to   13.7.3

Embryos

consent to use or storage of   13.3.2

  withdrawal of   13.3.3

meaning of   13.3.1

parenthood of   13.3.4

  death of sperm donor   13.3.5

  lesbian co-parenting   13.3.6, 13.3.7

  same sex marriages   13.3.8

Emergency situations

children

  life-sustaining treatment   6.3

  parental consent to treatment   11.2.2

End of life care *see also* Terminally ill

persons

adults

  code of practice   5.2

  guidance   5.3

  statutory provisions   5.1

'best interests of the patient' test   2.6

End of life care —*continued*
 cardio-pulmonary resuscitation
  (CPR) 5.8.1
  consultation with patient 5.8.2
 children
  advanced care plans 6.8
  conjoined twins 6.9
  due process 6.3
  emergency situations 6.3
  framework 6.1
  irreversible brain damage 6.5
  palliative care 6.6, 6.7
  parental consent 6.2
  treatment against clinical
   judgment 6.4
 desire to bring about death 5.5
Euthanasia
 right to die 7.4
 terminally ill persons 2.4

Family proceedings
 practice and procedure
  children 8.2.2
  transparency 8.1.7, 8.2.7
Fear of needles
 refusal of consent to treatment 9.4.4
Feeding *see* Artificial feeding; Force
 feeding
Female Mutilation Act 2003 13.9
Force feeding
 hunger strikes 2.4
 refusal of consent to treatment 9.4.4

Gametes
 consent to use or storage of 13.3.2,
    13.3.3
  withdrawal of 13.3.3
 meaning of 13.3.1
Gender Recognition Act 2004
 introduction 13.8
 key provisions 13.8.1
Guardians
 appointment 8.2.5

Hearings in private
 adults 8.1.7
 children 8.2.7
**Human Fertilisation and Embryology
 Act 1990**
 assisted reproduction
  parenthood 13.3.4, 13.3.5, 13.3.6,
     13.3.7, 13.3.8
 embryos
  consent to use or storage of 13.3.2,
    13.3.3
  meaning of 13.3.1
Human Tissue Act 2004
 codes of practice
  bone marrow transplants 13.2.3
  consent 13.2.1
  organ donation 13.2.2

Human Tissue Act 2004—*continued*
 key provisions 13.2
Hunger strikes
 force feeding 2.4
 refusal of consent to treatment 9.4.4

Inability to make decision
 meaning 4.2
Incapacity *see also* Capacity
 statutory test 4.2, 4.3
Induced delivery
 refusal of consent to treatment 9.4.4
Informal admissions to hospital
 mental illness 10.5
Interim applications
 Court of Protection 8.1.3
Interviews with children 11.8
 abuse allegations 11.8.3

Jehovah's witnesses
 'best interests of the patient' test
  overriding parental refusal 11.3.2
Jurisdiction
 adults lacking capacity 8.1
 children 8.2
  expert evidence 8.2.3
  family proceedings 8.2.2
  guardians, appointment of 8.2.5
  medical examinations 8.2.3, 8.2.4
  parents lacking capacity,
   representation of 8.2.6
  twofold jurisdiction 8.2.1

Lasting power of attorney
 adults lacking capacity 1.4, 10.3.1
 refusal of medical treatment
  presumption of capacity to
   decide 9.1.1
 use of 4.9
Lesbian co-parenting
 parenthood, establishing 13.3.6
  sperm donor's role 13.3.7
Life support
 discontinuance of 3.3
Life-sustaining treatment
 advance decisions to refuse
  treatment 12.4
 attorneys 5.6
 'best interests of the patient' test 2.6
 children
  advanced care plans 6.8
  conjoined twins 6.9
  due process 6.3
  emergency situations 6.3
  framework 6.1
  irreversible brain damage 6.5
  parental consent 6.2
  refusal of treatment 11.6.4
  reinstating artificial ventilation 6.7
  treatment against clinical
   judgment 6.4

Life-sustaining treatment—*continued*
children—*continued*
    withdrawal of artificial
        ventilation   6.6
  deputies   5.6
  desire to bring about death   5.5
  end of life care
    adults   5.1, 5.2, 5.3, 5.4, 5.5, 5.6,
                5.7, 5.8
    advanced care plans   6.8
    children   6.1, 6.2, 6.3, 6.4, 6.5, 6.6,
                6.7, 6.8, 6.9
    code of practice   5.2
    conjoined twins   6.9
    due process   6.3
    emergency situations   6.3
    framework   6.1
    guidance   5.3
    irreversible brain damage   6.5
    parental consent   6.2
    reinstating artificial ventilation   6.7
    statutory provisions   5.1
    treatment against clinical
        judgment   6.4
    withdrawal of artificial
        ventilation   6.6, 6.7
  non-PVS cases
    'best interests of the patient'
        test   5.8.3, 5.8.4
    cardio-pulmonary resuscitation
        (CPR)   5.8.1, 5.8.2
    do not activate CPR   5.8.1, 5.8.2
    introduction   5.8
  PVS cases
    meaning of PVS   5.7.1
  PVS cases 5.7
    case law   5.7.2
    clinical feature absent   5.7.5
    family opposition to
        withdrawal   5.7.4
    sanctity of life   5.7.3
  treatment whilst decision sought in
    court   4.7
  withholding treatment
    court declarations   5.4
Litigation friend
  Official Solicitor   8.1.5
  parents lacking capacity   8.2.6
Liver transplants
  overriding parental refusal   11.3.2
Living wills
  adults lacking capacity   1.4

Male circumcision   13.10
Medical examinations
  children   11.8
    abuse allegations   11.8.3
    family proceedings   11.8.1
    jurisdiction   8.2.3
    legal status   8.2.4
    prior to or absence of legal
        proceedings   11.8.1

Medical Innovation Bill
  text   3.4
Medical practitioners *see also* Doctors
  negligence
    liability for   4.7
  physical restraint of persons   4.7
  statutory protection from liability   4.7
Medical treatment *see also* Consent to
  treatment
  allocation of resources   3.4
  choice of medication   3.4
  clinical judgment, against   3.3.2
  meaning   3.2, 10.2.1
  objective of   3.2
  standard of care   3.3.1
Medication, choice of
  allocation of resources   3.4
Mental Capacity Act 2005
  'best interests of the patient' test   2.7,
                4.4
    process   4.5
    wishes and feelings of person
        lacking capacity   4.6
  deprivation of liberty
    challenging   10.6.2
    distinction between restriction and
        deprivation   10.6.1
    introduction   10.6
    life-saving measures   10.6.3
  deputies, appointment of   4.8
  general principles   4.1
  interface with Mental Health Act
    1983   10.7
  lasting power of attorney   4.9
  medical practitioners
    statutory protection from
        liability   4.7
  test for incapacity   4.2, 4.3
Mental disorders
  meaning   10.2
Mental Health Act 1983
  consent to treatment, meaning
    of   10.2.2
  informal admissions to hospital   10.5
  interface with Mental Capacity Act
    2005   10.7
  key provisions   10.2
  medical treatment, meaning of   10.2.1
Mental illness
  caesarean sections   10.1.3
  consent to treatment   10.1.2
  informal admissions to hospital   10.5
  informality of decision-making   10.4
  self-determination   10.1
Mercy killing
  right to die   7.4
MMR vaccine
  overriding parental refusal   11.3.2

Necessity, doctrine of
  conjoined twins   6.9
  statutory provisions replacing   4.7

Needle phobia
refusal of consent to treatment   9.4.4
Negligence
medical practitioners
no protection from liability   4.7
Next of kin
adults lacking capacity
consent to treatment   1.4
Non-competence
refusal of consent to treatment   9.4.1

Official Solicitor
role of   8.1.5
Organ donation
children's rights   11.4.3
code of practice
Human Tissue Act 2004   13.2.2

Palliative care
children
withdrawal of artificial
ventilation   6.6, 6.7
Parental responsibility
meaning   11.2.3
Parental rights
consent to treatment   1.3.3, 11.2
disagreement between parents   11.2.4
emergencies   11.2.2
general requirement   11.2.1
refusal of treatment
overriding refusal   11.3, 11.3.1,
11.3.2
treatment without consent   1.3.3
'best interests of the patient'   2.3
life-sustaining treatment   6.2
prolongation of life   2.5
Parenthood
assisted reproduction   13.3.4
death of sperm donor   13.3.5
lesbian co-parenting   13.3.6, 13.3.7
same sex marriages   13.3.8
surrogacy   13.4
Parents lacking capacity
representation of   8.2.6
Paternity testing
consent to taking samples   13.5.2
court powers to order   13.5.1
failure to comply with direction   13.5.3
jurisdiction   13.5.4
Permanent vegetative state
interface between MHA 1983 and
MCA 2005   10.7
life-sustaining treatment   5.7
case law   5.7.2
clinical feature absent   5.7.5
family opposition to
withdrawal   5.7.4
sanctity of life   5.7.3
meaning of   5.7.1
Physical restraint
protection from liability   4.7

Piercings
consent to   13.7, 13.7.2
Power of attorney
adults lacking capacity   10.3.1
use of   4.9
Presumption of capacity
refusal of medical treatment   9.1, 9.1.1
Principle of sanctity of life *see* Sanctity
of life, principle of
Principle of self-determination *see*
Self-determination, principle of
Prisoners *see also* Deprivation of
liberty
hunger strikes
force feeding   2.4
Privacy
court proceedings
adults   8.1.7
children   8.2.7
Prolongation of life
'best interests of the patient' test   2.5
children
advanced care plans   6.8
conjoined twins   6.9
due process   6.3
emergency situations   6.3
framework   6.1
irreversible brain damage   6.5
parental consent   6.2
reinstating artificial ventilation   6.7
treatment against clinical
judgment   6.4
withdrawal of artificial
ventilation   6.6, 6.7
desire to bring about death   5.5
end of life care
code of practice   5.2
guidance   5.3
statutory provisions   5.1
life-sustaining treatment
withdrawal   5.7.3
objective of medical treatment   3.2
withholding treatment
court declarations   5.4
PVS *see* Permanent vegetative state

Radiotherapy
'best interests of the patient' test
overriding parental refusal   11.3.2
Reasonable force
refusal of medical treatment
adults   9.5
children   11.6.6
Restraint, physical
protection from liability   4.7
Restriction of liberty
distinction from deprivation of
liberty   10.6.1
Right to die
assisted suicide   7.3
human rights   7.1

Right to die—*continued*
mercy killings 7.4
suicide 7.2
voluntary euthanasia 7.4
Right to life
adults 5.1, 5.2, 5.3, 5.4, 5.5, 5.6, 5.7, 5.8
children
conjoined twins 6.9
end of life care 6.1, 6.2, 6.3, 6.4, 6.5, 6.6, 6.7, 6.8, 6.9
end of life care
adults 5.1, 5.2, 5.3, 5.4, 5.5, 5.6, 5.7, 5.8
children 6.1, 6.2, 6.3, 6.4, 6.5, 6.6, 6.7, 6.8, 6.9
life-sustaining treatment
attorneys 5.6
'best interests of the patient' test 5.8.3, 5.8.4
cardio-pulmonary resuscitation (CPR) 5.8.1
deputies 5.6
desire to bring about death 5.5
do not activate CPR 5.8.1, 5.8.2
non-PVS cases 5.8, 5.8.1, 5.8.2
PVS cases 5.7, 5.7.1, 5.7.2, 5.7.3, 5.7.4, 5.7.5
withholding treatment
court declarations 5.4
Right to private and family life
right to die 7.1
sterilisation 13.1.5

Same sex marriages
parenthood 13.3.8
Sanctity of life, principle of
'best interests of the patient' test 2.4
life-sustaining treatment, withdrawal of 5.7.3
Scarring
ability to consent to 13.7.4
Secretary of State
directions to health authorities 3.2
duty to provide services 3.2
Self-determination, principle of
adults with capacity 1.3.1, 2.1
mental illness 10.1
right to die 7.1
Sexual abuse
children
medical examinations and interviews 11.8.3
Sperm donors
death of before use or transplantation of embryo 13.3.5
lesbian co-parenting 13.3.7
Sterilisation
adults lacking capacity
case law 13.1.4, 13.1.5

Sterilisation—*continued*
adults lacking capacity—*continued*
practice and procedure 13.1.6
prior sanction by court 13.1.1
special features of procedure 13.1.2
children
case law 13.1.3
practice and procedure 13.1.6
prior sanction by court 13.1.1
special features of procedure 13.1.2
Suicide
right to die 7.2
assisted suicide 7.3
Surrogacy
parental orders 13.4

Tattooing
consent to 13.7, 13.7.1
Terminally ill persons *see also* End of life care
euthanasia 2.4
treatment without consent 2.4
Tongue splitting
ability to consent to 13.7.4
Transfer of proceedings
Court of Protection 8.3
Transparency
hearings in private
adults 8.1.7
children 8.2.7

Unborn children
legal status
application by father to prevent abortion 11.7.1
applications towards child 11.7.2
mother's refusal of medical treatment 11.7.3
Undue influence
refusal of consent to treatment 9.4.2
Urgent applications
Court of Protection 8.1.3

Ventilation, artificial
withdrawal of
children 6.6, 6.7
Voluntary euthanasia
right to die 7.4
Vulnerable adults
court procedure outwith MHA 1983 8.1.6

Withdrawing artificial ventilation
children
palliative care 6.6, 6.7
Withdrawing treatment
children
advanced care plans 6.8
due process 6.3
framework 6.1

Withdrawing treatment—*continued*
  children—*continued*
    irreversible brain damage   6.5
    treatment against clinical
      judgment   6.4
Withholding treatment
  children
    advanced care plans   6.8
    due process   6.3

Withholding treatment—*continued*
  children—*continued*
    framework   6.1
    irreversible brain damage   6.5
    parental consent   6.2
    treatment against clinical
      judgment   6.4
  court declarations   5.4